The Basic
George B. Dantzig

The Basic
George B. Dantzig

Edited by Richard W. Cottle

Stanford Business Books
An Imprint of Stanford University Press
Stanford, California
2003

Stanford University Press
Stanford, California

Library of Congress Cataloging-in-Publication Data

Dantzig, George Bernard
    [Essays, Selections, 2003]
    The basic George B. Dantzig / edited by Richard W. Cottle.
        p. cm.
    Includes bibliographical references and index.
    ISBN 0-8047-4834-9 (acid-free paper)
        1. Programming (Mathematics) 2. Mathematical optimization.
        3. Mathematical statistics. 4. Dantzig, George Bernard, 1914–
    I. Cottle, Richard. II. Title.

    QA402.5.D26 2003
    519–dc21   2003057275

Typeset by Richard W. Cottle in 10/12 Computer Modern Roman
using a LaTeX macro package
Frontispiece photo of George Dantzig by Edward Souza / Stanford News
Service

Original Printing 2003

Last figure below indicates year of this printing:
12   11   10   09   08   07   06   05   04   03

Contents

Preface

Among those familiar with linear programming, George B. Dantzig is well known as its father. Eighteen years ago, on the occasion of his seventieth birthday, I had the pleasure of editing a two-volume set of essays written in his honor.[1] In its preface I wrote, "to say that George Dantzig is the father of linear programming is to underestimate his paternal accomplishments. Enlarging the list of 'offspring' to include all of mathematical programming comes closer to the truth." I believe the sample of his work assembled here illustrates that assertion.

This volume is an anthology of twenty-four publications authored or co-authored by George B. Dantzig. Of these, twenty-two are journal articles, one is an abstract, and one is a section from his book *Linear Programming and Extensions*. Each of these items is presented here as a separate chapter, even though their lengths differ markedly.

It is fair to ask how these publications were chosen. After embarking on this project, I visited Professor Dantzig and, with his lengthy publication list in hand, requested his input on the question. This is not the sort of thing about which one (especially an author) makes snap judgments. I left the list with him and promised to return after he had had time to reflect on the matter. When I did so and looked at how the list had been marked, it was clear that he did not intend to influence the selection process very much. Too many publications had "made the cut." The decision needed to satisfy other constraints. For a start, it was necessary to represent most of the areas in which he has worked. A second criterion was impact, as measured by the frequency of citation in the literature. Finally, I used my own preferences, keeping in mind the desired overall length of the book. Readers familiar with Dantzig's work will notice the omission of representatives of projects that occupied his attention for years. These include the Mathematical Programming Language (MPL), the monograph *Compact City* (San Francisco: Freeman, 1973) written jointly with Thomas L. Saaty, and a work in progress of the science-fiction type. Still, I am pleased to say that the choices I made have George Dantzig's approval.

Another question needed to be answered as well. This concerned the physical appearance of the material to be used. Using photocopies of

---

[1] *Mathematical Programming Essays in Honor of George B. Dantzig, Parts I & II*, Amsterdam: North-Holland, 1985.

the original publications—as some advocated—would have saved labor and would have enhanced their look of authenticity. This alternative was wisely ruled out by the publisher. Instead, the papers have been composed afresh, but with a deliberate effort made to mimic the house styles used in the originals. This explains the diversity of typesetting practice to be found in this volume. Even so, there is one element of constancy: all equation numbers are set on the left-hand side of the line.

The chapters of this book are grouped according to subject into nine different parts, none of them containing fewer than two publications. Each part opens with a brief introduction. In writing these, I have attempted (where possible) to identify the publications used in the included chapters, to set the stage for their appearance, and to put them into historical and intellectual context with reference to past, lateral, and future connections. I also wanted these "openers" to be relatively free of jargon and even freer of mathematical notation—a decidedly challenging task.

On the assumption that the introductions to the parts serve their intended purpose, I shall refrain from previewing them here and running the risk of reducing their effectiveness. Instead, I wish to comment on some *other* things included in this volume, namely, the three components of the back matter: a set of editor's notes, a list of publications, and an index.

The editor's notes cover each of the twenty-four chapters. These are much like footnotes except for the fact that they are assembled (by chapter) in one place and are marked alphabetically rather than numerically. This is done to differentiate these editorial remarks from the standard author's footnotes that appear in many of these publications. The footnotes are set with numerals, as they were in the originals.

The editor's notes are followed by a section called "Publications of George B. Dantzig," about which a few words are in order. Running to almost fourteen full pages, this is a relatively complete compilation of George Dantzig's published writings. In dealing with this, I have chosen to favor the inclusion of bibliographical details corresponding to publications in scholarly journals, books, conference proceedings and the like over technical reports and internal memoranda. Although this selection principle might diminish the value of this list to those concerned with issues of priority, the user can take comfort in knowing that the details of what is included have been checked with great care.

The more than six decades of George Dantzig's amazing professional life can be divided into five main stages: post-master's-degree employment as a junior statistician at the Bureau of Labor Statistics (1937–1939); doctoral study and analytical defense work at U. S. Army Air Force Headquarters at the Pentagon (1939–1952); mathematical research at the RAND Corporation (1952–1960); professorship at the University of California, Berkeley (1960–1966); and, finally, professorship at Stanford University (1966–).

Upon assuming his post at Berkeley, Dantzig established the Operations Research Center.[2] At Stanford, with the modest assistance of several colleagues, he founded and directed the Systems Optimization Laboratory. It became a leading center for research on optimization and the development of software for the numerical solution of such problems. This development reflects Dantzig's conviction, as expressed in the opening line of the preface of his classic work *Linear Programming and Extensions*, that "the final test of a theory is its capacity to solve the problems which originated it."

Dantzig's discovery of the Simplex Algorithm dates to the late 1940s, at which time his title was Mathematical Advisor at the Pentagon. This discovery led to contacts with leading researchers in the world of mathematics, logistics, and economics. As the richness of linear programming and the concommitant need for fundamental research became evident, Dantzig moved from the Pentagon to the Mathematics Department of the RAND Corporation, which at the time was closely linked to the Air Force. There he joined a vibrant group of mathematicians and economists, many of whom were intensely interested in game theory and linear programming, along with other topics in optimization and its applications. Among these individuals were (alphabetically) Richard E. Bellman, Melvin Dresher, Lester R. Ford, Jr., D. Ray Fulkerson, Murray Geisler, Oliver Gross, T. E. (Ted) Harris, Selmer Johnson, Alan Manne, Harry Markowitz, Lloyd Shapley, and Philip Wolfe. John D. Williams, head of the Mathematics Department, was especially admired for enlightened administrative skills that fostered the energy and high productivity of his team. The outstanding regulars were augmented by a steady stream of visitors and consultants, making RAND an exciting hotbed of activity in this field of research. Indeed, the output of George Dantzig alone attests to RAND's vitality as a source of fruitful ideas.

In moving from RAND to the academic world—first Berkeley and then Stanford—Dantzig sought the opportunity to stimulate another generation of scholars, primarily doctoral students. This he did in grand style. Over a period of approximately thirty years, he advised scores of students across a broad range of mathematical programming specialties. Many of these graduates are highly acclaimed leaders in their respective areas of expertise. Dantzig's record as a mentor stands out as one to be emulated.

---

[2]Located initially on the grounds of the university's Richmond Field Station in the city of Richmond, a community not far from Berkeley, the OR Center was as forlorn-looking a structure as one could ever imagine. Once a house, the wood-frame building was enclosed by a chain-link fence topped with barbed wire, a remnant of its former use by the Atomic Energy Commission. In the neighboring lot, a site belonging to a chemical works, there lay mountains of sulphur, exposed to the open air. In these dismal surroundings, Dantzig and a few other faculty managed to inspire a large number of graduate students, initiating them to the world of research. In its own humble way, this house devoid of visual delights or comfortable furnishings was the birthplace of many influential works on operations research, particularly linear programming and extensions.

It should be no surprise that George Bernard Dantzig has received many honors and awards. He was elected to the National Academy of Sciences in 1971 and to the National Academy of Engineering in 1985. In 1975 he became a Fellow of the National Academy of Arts and Sciences and received the National Medal of Science from President Gerald Ford and the John von Neumann Theory Prize from the Operations Research Society of America (ORSA) and the Institute for Management Sciences (TIMS), now merged as INFORMS. He has received many other prestigious awards and a long string of honorary doctorates from universities the world over. The impact of his highly original thinking is difficult to gauge in economic, mathematical, or social terms, but by any measure it is astounding. What makes the record all the more impressive is the gentle manner in which he deals with people at all levels, especially students. His kindly way— on top of a giant scientific reputation—intensifies the admiration he has earned from those who know him. If ever a person gave meaning to the characterization *sui generis*, it is George B. Dantzig.

Lest there be any misunderstanding of—or failure to catch the intended humor in—the title of this book, I would like to quote what *Webster's New Collegiate Dictionary* has to say about the word "basic."

^{1}**basic**\\'bā-sik, -zik*adj*(1842) **1** : of, or pertaining to, or forming the base or essence : FUNDAMENTAL **2** : constituting or serving as the basis or starting point

The humor (if that is not too strong a word for it) stems from the fact that the Simplex Algorithm of linear programming, for which George B. Dantzig is rightly famous, uses what are called "basic solutions" of a system of linear equations. Read on, and see what I mean.

Acknowledgments

This anthology would not have been possible without the cheerful cooperation of many friends and colleagues, whose advice I gratefully acknowlege. These include George Dantzig, Kenneth Arrow, Alan Hoffman, Phil Wolfe, Harold Kuhn, Curtis Eaves, Gerd Infanger, John Stone, Mukund Thapa, Dick Van Slyke, Roger Wets, Ashish Goel, and Tim Keely.

My staff contacts at the Stanford University Press have been extraordinarily helpful throughout the entire process. Here I am referring to the late (and missed) Ken Macleod, Kate Wahl, Alan Harvey, and, most of all, Anna Eberhard Friedlander. Anna's devotion to the task and prompt attention to my e-mail queries were remarkable. No less remarkable has been my wife Sue's good-natured acceptance of my immersion in this project. All these people have my sincere thanks.

Thanks are due—and gladly extended—to the authors of the articles included in this volume who gave their permission to reprint them. Finally, it is a pleasure to acknowledge the permissions granted by the copyright holders of these articles. They are listed by chapter number as they appear in the volume.

1. GEORGE B. DANTZIG, On the nonexistence of tests of "Students" hypothesis having power functions independent of σ, *Annals of Mathematical Statistics* 11 (1940) 186–192. Copyright © 1940. Reprinted by permission of the Institute of Mathematical Statistics.

2. GEORGE B. DANTZIG and ABRAHAM WALD, On the fundamental lemma of Neyman and Pearson, *Annals of Mathematical Statistics* 22 (1951) 87–93. Copyright © 1951. Reprinted by permission of the Institute of Mathematical Statistics.

3. GEORGE B. DANTZIG, Programming in a linear structure, *Econometrica* 17 (1949) 73–74. Copyright © 1949 by the Econometric Society.

4. GEORGE B. DANTZIG, Maximization of a linear function of variables subject to linear inequalities, in T.C. KOOPMANS, ed., *Activity Analysis of Production and Allocation*, New York: John Wiley & Sons, 1951, Chapter XXI, pp. 339–347. Copyright © 1951 by the Yale University Press.

5. GEORGE B. DANTZIG, ALEX ORDEN, and PHILIP WOLFE, The generalized simplex method for minimizing a linear form under linear inequality constraints, *Pacific Journal of Mathematics* 5 (1955) 183–195. Copyright © 1955 by the RAND Corporation. Permission to reprint also approved by the *Pacific Journal of Mathematics*.

6. GEORGE B. DANTZIG, Upper bounds, secondary constraints, and block triangularity in linear programming, *Econometrica* 23 (1955) 174–183. Copyright © 1955 by the Econometric Society.

7. GEORGE B. DANTZIG and PHILIP WOLFE, Decomposition principle for linear programs, *Operations Research* 8 (1960) 101–111. Copyright © 1960. Reprinted by permission, the Institute for Operations Research and the Management Sciences (INFORMS), 901 Elkridge Landing Road, Suite 400, Linthicum, Maryland 21090-2909 USA.

8. G. B. DANTZIG and R. M. VAN SLYKE, Generalized upper bounding techniques, *Journal of Computer and System Sciences* 1 (1967) 213–226. Copyright © 1967. Reprinted with permission from Elsevier Science.

9. G.B. DANTZIG and D.R. FULKERSON, Minimizing the number of tankers to meet a fixed schedule, *Naval Research Logistics Quarterly* 1 (1954) 217–222. Copyright © 1954. Reprinted with permission of John Wiley & Sons, Inc.

10. G.B. DANTZIG, S. JOHNSON and W. WHITE, A linear programming approach to the chemical equilibrium problem, *Management Science* 5 (1958) 38–43. Copyright ©1958. Reprinted by permission, the Institute for Operations Research and the Management Sciences (INFORMS), 901 Elkridge Landing Road, Suite 400, Linthicum, Maryland 21090-2909 USA.

11. G.B. DANTZIG, P.H. MCALLISTER, and J.C. STONE, Formulating an objective for an economy, *Mathematical Programming, Series B* 42 (1988), 11–32. Copyright © 1988. Reprinted with permission of the Mathematical Programming Society.

12. GEORGE B. DANTZIG, Linear programming under uncertainty, *Management Science* 1 (1955) 197–206. Copyright © 1955. Reprinted by permission, the Institute for Operations Research and the Management Sciences (INFORMS), 901 Elkridge Landing Road, Suite 400, Linthicum, Maryland 21090-2909 USA.

13. GEORGE B. DANTZIG and A. MADANSKY, On the solution of two-stage linear programs under uncertainty, in J. NEYMAN, ed., *Proceedings of the Fourth Berkeley Symposium on Mathematical Statistics and Probability, Volume I, Theory of Statistics*, Berkeley: University of California Press, 1961, pp. 165–176. Copyright © 1961. Reprinted

by the permission of the Regents of the University of California.

14. GEORGE B. DANTZIG and PETER W. GLYNN, Parallel processors for planning under uncertainty, *Annals of Operations Research* 22 (1990) 1–21. Copyright © 1990. Reprinted by permission of Kluwer Academic / Plenum Publishers.

15. GEORGE B. DANTZIG and GERD INFANGER, Multi-stage stochastic linear programs for portfolio optimization, *Annals of Operations Research* 45 (1993) 59–76. Copyright © 1993. Reprinted by permission of Kluwer Academic / Plenum Publishers.

16. G. DANTZIG, R. FULKERSON, and S. JOHNSON, Solution of a large-scale traveling-salesman problem, *Journal of the Operations Research Society of America* 2 (1954) 393–410. Copyright © 1954. Reprinted by permission, the Institute for Operations Research and the Management Sciences (INFORMS), 901 Elkridge Landing Road, Suite 400, Linthicum, Maryland 21090-2909 USA.

17. GEORGE B. DANTZIG and D.R. FULKERSON, On the max-flow min-cut theorem of networks, in H.W. KUHN and A.W. TUCKER, eds., *Linear Inequalities and Related Systems*, Annals of Mathematics Studies No. 38, Princeton: Princeton University Press, 1956, pp. 215–221. Copyright © 1956, renewed 1984 by Princeton University Press. Reprinted by permission of Princeton University Press.

18. GEORGE B. DANTZIG, On the shortest route through a network, *Management Science* 6 (1960) 187-190. Copyright © 1960. Reprinted by permission, the Institute for Operations Research and the Management Sciences (INFORMS), 901 Elkridge Landing Road, Suite 400, Linthicum, Maryland 21090-2909 USA.

19. GEORGE B. DANTZIG, On the significance of solving linear programming problems with some integer variables, *Econometrica* 28 (1960) 30–44. Copyright © 1960. Reprinted by permission of the Econometric Society.

20. GEORGE B. DANTZIG and B. CURTIS EAVES, Fourier-Motzkin elimination and its dual, *Journal of Combinatorial Theory, Series A* 14 (1973) 288–297. Copyright © 1973. Reprinted with permission from Elsevier Science.

21. GEORGE B. DANTZIG, Quadratic programming, Section 24-4 of *Linear Programming and Extensions*, Princeton: Princeton University Press, 1963, pp. 490–497. Reprinted by permission of the RAND Corporation.

22. GEORGE B. DANTZIG, JON FOLKMAN, and NORMAN SHAPIRO, On the continuity of the minimum set of a continuous function, *Mathematical Analysis and Applications* 17 (1967), 519-548. Copyright ©

1967. Reprinted with permission from Elsevier Science.

23. RICHARD W. COTTLE and GEORGE B. DANTZIG, Complementary pivot theory of mathematical programming, *Linear Algebra and its Applications* 1 (1968) 103–125. Copyright © 1968. Reprinted with permission from Elsevier Science.

24. RICHARD W. COTTLE and GEORGE B. DANTZIG, A generalization of the linear complementarity problem, *Journal of Combinatorial Theory* 8 (1970) 79–90. Copyright © 1970. Reprinted with permission from Elsevier Science.

The Basic
George B. Dantzig

Part I: Mathematical Statistics

The two papers grouped here represent part of the George B. Dantzig legend. Although the story has been told many times,[1] it bears being repeated here because the papers give the reader a sense of what was involved.

In 1937, after completing the requirements for the M.A. in mathematics at the University of Michigan, George Dantzig became a Junior Statistician at the Bureau of Labor Statistics. In conjunction with the project to which he was assigned, he was asked to review a paper by the famous statistician Jerzy Neyman, who was then at University College, London, and would later move to the University of California, Berkeley. Strongly stimulated by the paper, Dantzig wrote to Neyman expressing his desire to write a doctoral dissertation under his supervision. This ambition was realized; in 1939, he became a doctoral student in mathematics, Neyman's department.

At Berkeley, Dantzig took just two courses in theoretical statistics, both taught by Neyman. One day, as Dantzig tells the story, he arrived late to one of Neyman's lectures. Upon entering the classroom he saw two problems written on the blackboard. (In those days, and for a long time thereafter, it was customary for instructors to communicate homework assignments that way.) Dantzig copied the problems down and set to work on them. The problems seemed harder than usual, but he persisted. A few days later, Dantzig asked Neyman if he wanted the solutions turned in. Neyman (probably a bit distracted at the moment) said something like "yes, throw them on my desk." The desk being messy, Dantzig feared that what he had written would be lost forever. Weeks passed. Then, one Sunday morning, Neyman appeared at Dantzig's door in a state of excitement and with papers in hand. He explained that what Dantzig assumed to be homework problems were in fact unsolved problems. Neyman had written an introduction to one of them and asked Dantzig to read it over so that the paper could be submitted for publication. That paper (Chapter 1 of this volume) was published in 1940.

And what of the solution to the other unsolved problem? At one point Neyman told Dantzig that he would accept the solutions to these two unsolved problems as a doctoral dissertation. By June of 1941, this matter was settled, but there remained other requirements, such as a disserta-

---

[1] It is related quite effectively in the book *More Mathematical People* by Donald J. Albers, Gerald L. Alexanderson, and Constance Reid (Harcourt Brace Jovanovich, Boston, 1990).

tion defense and a minor thesis. Then along came World War II. George Dantzig interrupted his doctoral studies and returned to Washington to work for the U.S. Army Air Force Headquarters at the Pentagon. In 1946, Dantzig returned to Berkeley and completed his Ph.D. requirements. The solution of the second problem remained unpublished. Dantzig was too busy with other professional pursuits. He returned to the Pentagon and worked there until 1952, at which time he joined the RAND Corporation in Santa Monica, California. He might never have published the second paper if it were not that in 1950 Abraham Wald wrote to him, saying that he had had a paper accepted for publication but that it had been pointed out to him that his main result was the same as in one part of Dantzig's Ph.D. thesis. What to do? Dantzig replied that, since Wald's paper was already in galley proof, the best solution would be to add his name as an author. That is what happened. "On the Fundamental Lemma of Neyman and Pearson," was published in 1950 as a joint paper by George Dantzig and Abraham Wald.[2] This paper is included here as Chapter 2.

It is interesting to compare Dantzig's Ph.D. thesis with these two journal articles. First of all, the thesis is composed of two distinct parts. There is no interlocking text other than the Acknowledgment, which says

> The two subjects found in this dissertation were inspired by the Lectures of Professor J. Neyman. They represented two "unsolved" problems in the Foundations of Mathematical Statistics. Appreciation is expressed to Professor George Polya for his valuable suggestions.

The first of the two parts in Dantzig's thesis is, in effect, the one that became the joint paper with Wald (Chapter 2), although its title is "Complete Form of the Neyman-Pearson Fundamental Lemma." Under the historical circumstances, it is not surprising that the two documents differ in content and style. Again, considering the history involved, it is not surprising that the second part of Dantzig's thesis is almost identical to the article published in 1940 (Chapter 1). More than five years separated the publication of the paper and the submission of the thesis. In 1945, Charles Stein had published an article[3] following up on Danztig's publication. "Stein ..." as Dantzig put it in a footnote "to counteract the negative result of this paper, shows that by taking two samples, the size of the second sample depending on the size of the first, the desired test can be constructed."

---

[2]Later that year, Wald and his wife perished in an airplane crash in India.

[3]C. Stein, "A two sample test for a linear hypothesis whose power function is independent of the variance," *Annals of Mathematical Statistics* 16 (1945) 243–258.

Chapter 1

ON THE NONEXISTENCE OF TESTS OF "STUDENT'S" HYPOTHESIS HAVING POWER FUNCTIONS INDEPENDENT OF σ

By George B. Dantzig

1. Introduction. Consider a system of n random variables x_1, x_2, $\cdots$, x_n where each is known to be normally distributed about the same but unknown mean, ξ, and the same, but also unknown standard deviation σ. The assumption, H_0, that ξ has some specified value, ξ_0, e.g. $\xi_0 = 0$, while nothing is assumed about σ, is known as the "Student" Hypothesis. Two aspects of the hypothesis H_0 have been already studied extensively. If the alternatives with respect to which it is desired to test H_0 assume specifically that $\xi > \xi_0$, (or $\xi < \xi_0$),[a] then we have the so-called asymmetric case of "Student's Hypothesis" and it is known, [1], that there exists a uniformly most powerful test of H_0. This consists in the rule, originally suggested by "Student," of rejecting H_0 whenever

$$(1) \qquad T = \frac{\bar{x} - \xi_0}{S}\sqrt{n-1} > t_\alpha$$

where $\bar{x}$ and S denote the mean and the standard deviation of the observed x_i's and t_α is taken, for example, from Fisher's Tables [2] with his $P = 2\alpha$. In other words, t_α is such that

$$(2) \qquad P\{t > t_\alpha | H_0\} = \alpha,$$

where α is the chosen level of significance. In accordance with the definition of the uniformly most powerful test, whenever any other rule, R offered to test the hypothesis H_0 has the same probability α of H_0 being rejected when it is true, the power of this alternative test cannot exceed that of "Student's" test. In other words, if it happens that the true value of ξ is not equal to ξ_0 but is greater, then the probability of this circumstance being detected by "Student's" test is at least equal to that corresponding to rule R.

If the set of alternative hypotheses is not limited to those specifying the value of ξ either greater or smaller than ξ_0, but includes both those categories, then it is known, [1], that there is no uniformly most powerful test of the hypothesis, H_0. However, in this case there exists a slightly different test, also based on "Student's" criterion t, possessing the remarkable property of being unbiased of type B_1, [3]. The test, in common use for a long time, consists in rejecting H_0 when

$$(3) \qquad\qquad\qquad |t| > t_\alpha,$$

with t_α being taken again from Fisher's tables, this time corresponding to his $P = \alpha$, where α is the chosen level of significance.

In order to describe the optimum property of this test we must use the concept of the power function of a test, [3]. Denote by $\beta(\xi, \sigma)$ the probability of the hypothesis H_0 being rejected when ξ and σ are the true mean and the true standard error of the observable x_i's. The function $\beta(\xi, \sigma)$ is just what is called the power function of the test. If we substitute $\xi = \xi_0$, then we shall have $\beta(\xi_0, \sigma) = \alpha$ irrespective of the value of σ. Now the optimum property of "Student's" test mentioned above consists in that (1) its power function has a minimum at $\xi = \xi_0$, and this is true whatever be the value of σ, (2) whatever be any other test of the same hypothesis which has the same level of significance σ and has property (1), its power function $\beta'(\xi, \sigma)$ cannot exceed that of "Student's" test.

These two properties, demonstrating the excellence of the criterion suggested by "Student," fully justify the general confidence in the test as described above, or in its extended form where it is applied to two or more samples. However, it is known that "Student's" test in both its forms, $t > t_\alpha$, and $|t| > t_\alpha$, has one very undesirable property which causes great difficulties in various problems of rational planning of experiments.

One of the most important questions to have in mind when planning an experiment is: What is the probability that the experiment and the subsequent statistical test will detect a difference or effect when it actually exists? If we perform an experiment and then apply some statistical analysis to test "Student's" hypothesis that $\xi = \xi_0$, we do hope that, if the actual value of ξ is different from ξ_0, the test will discover this circumstance. But apart from mere hope, it is desirable to take precautions so that when the *difference*, $\xi - \xi_0 = \Delta$, has some appreciable value, the chance of the hypothesis H_0 being rejected will be reasonably large. This may be done by calculating the value of the power function $\beta(\xi, \sigma)$ corresponding to the value $\xi = \xi_0 + \Delta$. And here we come to the unfortunate property of "Student's" test.

Although the form of the power function of "Student's" test is known and tabled [4], [5], [6], [7], there are occasionally considerable difficulties in applying these tables, because it appears that the values n and Δ are not all its arguments, for it also depends on σ. Consequently in order to have an idea of the probability that the test will detect the falsehood of the hypothesis H_0 that $\xi = \xi_0$ when actually $\xi = \xi_0 + \Delta$, we need not only the knowledge of n but also a likely value of σ. The latter is known accurately only in exceptional cases and then in those cases one would apply a test which is different from "Student's" test. Usually we have only a vague notion of the magnitude of σ and accordingly the tables of $\beta(\xi, \sigma)$ may be used to obtain a rough idea as to whether the arrangement of the experiment planned is satisfactory or not. Frequently we have no idea of what may be the values of σ.

To Dr. P. L. Hsu is due the idea of looking for tests, the power of which is independent of the parameters unspecified by the hypothesis tested. In an unpublished paper, he proved among other things that the λ test of the general *linear hypothesis* is the most powerful of all those, the power function of which depends on the same argument as that of the λ test and not on other parameters. The above circumstances suggest the following problem: to see whether it is possible to devise a test of "Student's" hypothesis such that its power function would be independent of σ. If such a test could be devised and proved to be reasonably powerful then the tables of its power function could be used for the purpose of planning experiments.

The purpose of the present paper is to show that no such test exists and, consequently, this negative result implies in still another way that it is impossible to improve on the test originally suggested by "Student."

2. Statement of the Problem. The problem of finding a test whose power function is independent of σ is equivalent to finding a critical region w such that the value of the power function

$$(4) \qquad \beta(\xi, \sigma) = P\{E \in w \,|\, \xi, \sigma\}$$

for any fixed ξ is independent of the value of σ, where E denotes the sample point $(x_1, x_2, \cdots, x_n)$. We shall show specifically that if this is the case, then the power function is also independent of ξ; so that the test will reject the hypothesis tested with the same frequency independently of whether it be correct or wrong.

3. THEOREM. *If there exists a region w such that, whatever be the value of σ,*

$$(5) \qquad \left(\frac{1}{\sqrt{2\pi}\,\sigma}\right)^n \int \cdots \int_w e^{-\frac{1}{2\sigma^2}\sum_{i=1}^{n}(x_i - \xi_0)^2}\, dx_1\, dx_2 \cdots dx_n \equiv \alpha$$

$$(6) \qquad \left(\frac{1}{\sqrt{2\pi}\,\sigma}\right)^n \int \cdots \int_w e^{-\frac{1}{2\sigma^2}\sum_{i=1}^{n}(x_i - \xi_1)^2}\, dx_1\, dx_2 \cdots dx_n \equiv \beta,$$

where $\xi_0 \neq \xi_1$, α, β are constants, then

(7) $$\alpha = \beta.$$

A region w is called *similar* [1] to the whole sample space, W, of size α, with respect to a set of elementary probability laws $p(E \,|\, \theta)$ given in terms of a parameter θ, if $P\{E \in w \,|\, \theta\} = \alpha$, whatever be the value of θ. Essentially, then, the region, w, above is a similar region with respect to two different sets of elementary laws each being given parametrically in terms of the parameter σ. Denote by w_r the portion of the surface of the hypersphere, $\sum_{i=1}^{n} (x_i - \xi_0)^2 = r^2$, which is common to w, and let the total surface be denoted W_r. Neyman and Pearson have shown [1], that a necessary and sufficient condition that w be a similar region, in the above sense, is that, whatever be r, the probability that the sample point E will fall on the subsurface w_r, when it is known that the sample point lies on the surface W_r is α, i.e.

(8) $$P\{E \in w_r \,|\, (E \in W_r)(\xi = \xi_0)\} = \alpha$$

for all r.

In a similar matter let w_ρ denote the portion of the surface of the hypersphere $\sum_{i=1}^{n} (x_i - \xi_1)^2 = \rho^2$, common to w, and let the total surface be denoted by W_ρ. Since w is similar to the set of probability laws indicated in (6), we have also

(9) $$P\{E \in w_\rho \,|\, (E \in W_\rho)(\xi = \xi_1)\} = \beta$$

for all ρ.

Since on the surface W_r, the elementary probability law,

(10) $$\left(\frac{1}{\sqrt{2\pi}\,\sigma}\right)^n e^{-\frac{1}{2\sigma^2}\sum_{i=1}^{n} (x_i-\xi_0)^2} = \left(\frac{1}{\sqrt{2\pi}\,\sigma}\right)^n e^{-\frac{r^2}{2\sigma^2}},$$

is constant, we see that an equivalent statement of (8) is that the *hyper-area of w_r is a constant proportion*, α, *of the total hyper-area W_r*. Similarly, from (9), we have that the *hyper-area of w_ρ is a constant proportion*, β, *of the total area of the hypersurface W_r, whatever be the values of r and ρ*.

Consider the transformation which expresses $x_1, x_2, \cdots, x_n$ in terms of generalized polar coordinates with pole at the point $(\xi_0, \xi_0, \cdots, \xi_0)$, i.e.

(11)
$$
\begin{aligned}
x_1 &- \xi_0 = r\cos\theta_2 \cos\theta_3 \cdots \cos\theta_{n-2}\cos\theta_{n-1}\cos\theta_n \\
x_2 &- \xi_0 = r\cos\theta_2 \cos\theta_3 \cdots \cos\theta_{n-2}\cos\theta_{n-1}\sin\theta_n \\
x_2 &- \xi_0 = r\cos\theta_2 \cos\theta_3 \cdots \cos\theta_{n-2}\sin\theta_{n-1} \\
&\cdots\cdots\cdots\cdots\cdots\cdots\cdots\cdots\cdots \\
&\cdots\cdots\cdots\cdots\cdots\cdots\cdots\cdots\cdots \\
x_{n-1} &- \xi_0 = r\cos\theta_2 \sin\theta_2 \\
x_n &- \xi_0 = r\sin\theta_2
\end{aligned}
$$

Let Δ be the Jacobian of the transformation:

$$(12) \qquad |\Delta| = r^{n-1} \left| \prod_{i=2}^{n} cos^{i}\theta_{n+2-i} \right| = r^{n-1}T(\theta_i).$$

Consider also a transformation which expresses $(x_1, x_2, \cdots, x_n)$ in terms of polar coordinates, the point $(\xi_1, \xi_1, \cdots, \xi_1)$ being pole. It may be obtained by replacing in (11), ξ_0 by ξ_1, r by ρ, and θ_i by $\bar{\theta}_i$. The Jacobian of this transformation is given by $|\bar{\Delta}| = \rho^{n-1}T(\bar{\theta}_i)$.

We are now able to express the hyper-area of W_r:

$$(13) \qquad \iint_{W_r} |\Delta| d\theta_2 d\theta_3 \cdots d\theta_n = r^{n-1} \iint_{W_r} T(\theta_i) d\theta_2 d\theta_3 \cdots d\theta_n$$
$$= Kr^{n-1},$$

where the integral $K > 0$ is a constant independent of r. Similarly the hyper-area of W_ρ is $K\rho^{n-1}$, where K is the same as in (13). According to (8) and (9) we have, now

$$(14) \qquad \iint_{W_r} |\Delta| d\theta_2 d\theta_3 \cdots d\theta_n = \alpha \cdot K \cdot r^{n-1}$$

$$(15) \qquad \iint_{W_\rho} |\bar{\Delta}| d\bar{\theta}_2 d\bar{\theta}_3 \cdots d\bar{\theta}_n = \beta \cdot K \cdot \rho^{n-1}$$

Let us consider the distances between the three points: $(x_1, x_2, \cdots, x_n)$, $(\xi_0, \xi_0, \cdots, \xi_0)$, and $(\xi_1, \xi_1, \cdots, \xi_1)$. The distances of the first point to the second point and to the third point we have already denoted by r and ρ. Let the distance between the last two be L; then, since the sum of two sides is at least equal to the third side of a triangle, we have [b]

$$(16) \qquad r \leq \rho + L, \qquad \rho \leq r + L, \quad \text{where} \quad L = \sqrt{n}\,|\xi_0 - \xi_1|.$$

Let $\varphi(t) \geq 0$ be an *arbitrary* monotonic nonincreasing function of t, such that the product $t^{n-1}\varphi(t)$ is integrable from 0 to $+\infty$. Since $\varphi(t)$ is a decreasing function it follows from (16) that

$$(17) \qquad \varphi(r) \geq \varphi(\rho + L) \quad \text{and} \quad \varphi(\rho) \geq \varphi(r + L).$$

Consider the integral I:

$$(18) \qquad I = \iint_w \varphi(r) dx_1 dx_2 \cdots dx_n.$$

We shall express it in terms of the variables $r, \theta_2, \cdots, \theta_n$ and also in terms of $\rho, \bar{\theta}_2, \cdots, \bar{\theta}_n$ and compare the results. Thus

$$
\begin{aligned}
I &= \iint_w |\Delta|\,\varphi(r)\,dr\,d\theta_2 \cdots d\theta_n \\[1em]
(19) \qquad &= \int_0^\infty \varphi(r)\,dr \iint_{w_r} |\Delta|\,d\theta_2 \cdots d\theta_n \\[1em]
&= \alpha \cdot K \cdot \int_0^\infty r^{n-1}\varphi(r)\,dr.
\end{aligned}
$$

Also we have by (16)

$$
\begin{aligned}
I &= \iint_w |\bar{\Delta}|\,\varphi(r)\,dr\,d\bar{\theta}_2 \cdots d\bar{\theta}_n \\[1em]
(20) \qquad &\geq \iint_w |\bar{\Delta}|\,\varphi(\rho + L)\,d\rho\,d\bar{\theta}_2 \cdots d\bar{\theta}_n \\[1em]
&\geq \int_0^\infty \varphi(\rho + L)\,d\rho \iint_{w_\rho} |\bar{\Delta}|\,d\bar{\theta}_2 \cdots d\bar{\theta}_n
\end{aligned}
$$

and consequently

$$
(21) \qquad I \geq \beta \cdot K \int_0^\infty \rho^{n-1}\varphi(\rho + L)\,d\rho.
$$

Since $K > 0$, we have from (19) and (21)

$$
(22) \qquad \alpha/\beta \geq \int_0^\infty t^{n-1}\varphi(t + L)\,dt \Big/ \int_0^\infty t^{n-1}\varphi(t)\,dt.
$$

By interchanging ρ and r in (18), (19), (20), and (21) we have also

$$
(23) \qquad \beta/\alpha \geq \int_0^\infty t^{n-1}\varphi(t + L)\,dt \Big/ \int_0^\infty t^{n-1}\varphi(t)\,dt.
$$

Let us set in (22) and (23), $\varphi(t) = e^{-pt}$ and $\varphi(t + L) = e^{-pL}e^{-pt}$ where $p > 0$ is arbitrary. Then

$$
(24) \qquad \alpha/\beta \geq e^{-pL} \quad \text{and} \quad \beta/\alpha \geq e^{-pL}.
$$

Since (24) holds for all $p > 0$, let p approach zero. Then $\mathrm{Lim}\, e^{-pL} = 1$, and the above inequalities can hold only if

$$
(25) \qquad\qquad\qquad \alpha = \beta, \qquad\qquad\qquad \text{Q.E.D.}
$$

It is of interest to note that there do not exist regions such that the power function is independent of both ξ and σ. For example, let S_n be the standard deviation of the observed values $(x_1, x_2, \cdots, x_n)$ and S_{n-1} be the standard deviation of the values $(x_1, x_2, \cdots, x_{n-1})$, then the region given by all points $(x_1, x_2, \cdots, x_n)$ which satisfy the inequality $(S_{n-1}/S_n) \geq C$ is such a region, i.e.

$$(26) \qquad P\{(S_{n-1}/S_n) \geq C \,|\, \xi, \sigma\}$$

is constant, whatever be the values of ξ and σ. Such regions are, however, unsuitable for testing "Student's" hypothesis $\xi = \xi_0$, because they will reject this hypothesis when it is wrong and when it is correct with equal frequency.

The author is indebted to Professor J. Neyman for assistance in preparing the present paper.

REFERENCES

[1] J. NEYMAN AND E. S. PEARSON, "On the problem of the most efficient tests of statistical hypotheses," *Phil. Trans. Roy. Soc. London*, Vol. 231(1933), pp. 289-337.

[2] R. A. FISHER, *Statistical method for research workers*. Oliver & Boyd, 7th edition, London, 1938.

[3] J. NEYMAN, "Sur la vérification des hypothèses statistiques composées," *Bull. Soc. Math. de France*, T. 63(1935), pp. 246-266.

[4] S. KOLODZIEJCZYK, "Sur l'erreur de la deuxième catégorie dans le problème de 'Student,'" *Comptes Rendus.* T. 197(1933), p. 814.

[5] J. NEYMAN with co-operation of K. IWASZKIEWICZ AND S. KOLODZIEJCZYK, "Statistical problems in agricultural experimentation," *Suppl. Jour. Roy. Stat. Soc.*, Vol. II(1935), pp. 107-80.

[6] J. NEYMAN AND B. TOKARSKA, "Errors of the second kind in testing 'Student's' hypothesis," *Jour. Am. Stat. Ass.*, Vol. 31(1936), pp. 318-26.

[7] P. C. TANG, "The power function of the analysis of variance tests with tables and illustrations of their use," *Stat. Res. Memoirs*, Vol.II(1938), pp. 126-57.

UNIVERSITY OF CALIFORNIA
BERKELEY, CALIFORNIA

Chapter 2

ON THE FUNDAMENTAL LEMMA OF NEYMAN AND PEARSON[1]

BY GEORGE B. DANTZIG AND ABRAHAM WALD[2]

Department of the Air Force and Columbia University

1. Summary and introduction. The following lemma proved by Neyman and Pearson [1] is basic in the theory of testing statistical hypotheses:

LEMMA. *Let* $f_1(x), \cdots, f_{m+1}(x)$ *be* $m+1$ *Borel measurable functions defined over a finite dimensional Euclidean space* R *such that* $\int_R |f_i(x)| dx < \infty$ $(i = 1, \cdots, m + 1)$. *Let furthermore,* $c_1, \cdots, c_m$ *be* m *given constants and* $\mathcal{S}$ *the class of all Borel measurable subsets* S *of* R *for which*

$$(1.1) \qquad \int_S f_i(x)\, dx = c_i \qquad\qquad (i = 1, \cdots, m).$$

Let, finally, $\mathcal{S}_0$ *be the subclass of* $\mathcal{S}$ *consisting of all members* S_0 *of* $\mathcal{S}$ *for which*

$$(1.2) \qquad \int_{S_0} f_{m+1}(x)\, dx \geq \int_S f_{m+1}(x)\, dx \quad \text{for all } S \text{ in } \mathcal{S}.$$

If S *is a member of* $\mathcal{S}$ *and if there exist* m *constants* $k_1, \cdots, k_m$ *such that*

$$(1.3) \qquad f_{m+1}(x) \geq k_1 f_1(x) + \cdots + k_m f_m(x) \qquad \text{when } x \in S,$$

$$(1.4) \qquad f_{m+1}(x) \leq k_1 f_1(x) + \cdots + k_m f_m(x) \qquad \text{when } x \notin S,$$

then S *is a member of* $\mathcal{S}_0$.

The above lemma gives merely a sufficient condition for a member S of $\mathcal{S}$ to be also a member of $\mathcal{S}_0$. Two important questions were left open by Neyman and Pearson: (1) the question of existence, that is, the question

[1]The main results of this paper were obtained by the authors independently of each other using entirely different methods.

[2]Research under contract with the Office of Naval Research.

whether S_0 is non-empty whenever S is non-empty; (2) the question of necessity of their sufficient condition (apart from the obvious weakening that (1.3) and (1.4) may be violated on a set of measure zero).

The purpose of the present note is to answer the above two questions. It will be shown in Section 2 that S_0 is not empty whenever S is not empty. In Section 3, a necessary and sufficient condition is given for a member of S to be also a member of S_0. This necessary and sufficient condition coincides with the Neyman-Pearson sufficient condition under a mild restriction.

2. Proof that S_0 is not empty whenever S is not empty. Each function $f_i(x)$ determines a finite measure μ_i given by the equation

$$(2.1) \qquad \mu_i(S) = \int_S f_i(x)\, dx \qquad\qquad (i = 1, 2, \cdots, m+1).$$

Let μ be the vector measure with the components $\mu_1, \cdots, \mu_{m+1}$; i.e., for any measurable set S the value of $\mu(S)$ is the vector $(\mu_1(S), \cdots, \mu_{m+1}(S))$. Thus, for each S the value of $\mu(S)$ can be represented by a point in the $m+1$-dimensional Euclidean space E. A point $g = (g_1, , \cdots g_{m+1})$ of E is said to belong to the range of the vector measure μ if and only if there exists a measurable subset S of R such that $\mu(S) = g$.

It was proved by Lyapunov [2] (see also [4]) that the range M of μ is a bounded, closed and convex subset of E. Let L be the line in E which is parallel to the $(m+1)$-th axis and goes through the point $(c_1, c_2, \cdots, c_m, 0)$. Suppose that S is not empty. Then the intersection M^* of L with M is not empty. Because of Lyapunov's theorem, M^* is a finite closed interval (which may reduce to a single point). There exists a subset S of R such that $\mu(S)$ is equal to the upper end point of M^*. Clearly, S is a member of S_0.

3. Necessary and sufficient condition that a member of S be also a member of S_0. Let $\nu(S)$ be the vector measure with the components $\mu_1(S), \cdots \mu_m(S)$. According to the aforementioned theorem of Lyapunov, the range N of ν is a bounded, closed and convex subset of the m-dimensional Euclidean space.

By the dimension of a convex subset Q of a finite dimensional Euclidean space we shall mean the dimension of the smallest dimensional hyperplane that contains Q. A point q of a convex set Q is said to be an interior point of Q if there exists a sphere V with center at q and positive radius such that $V \cap \Pi \subset Q$, where Π is the smallest dimensional hyperplane containing Q. Any point q that is not an interior point of Q will be called a boundary point. We shall now prove the following theorem.

THEOREM 3.1. *If $(c_1, \cdots, c_m)$ is an interior point of N, then a necessary and sufficient condition for a member S of S to be a member of S_0 is that there exist m constants $k_1, \cdots, k_m$ such that (1.3) and (1.4) hold for all x except perhaps on a set of measure zero.*

PROOF. The Neyman-Pearson lemma cited in Section 1 states that our condition is sufficient. Thus, we merely have to prove the necessity of our condition. Assume that $(c_1, \cdots, c_m)$ is an interior point of N. Let c^* be the largest value for which $(c_1, \cdots, c_m, c^*) \in M$, and c^{**} the smallest value for which $(c_1, \cdots, c_m, c^{**}) \in M$.

We shall first consider the case when $c^* = c^{**}$. Let $(\bar{c}_1, \cdots, \bar{c}_m)$ be any other interior point of N. We shall show that there exists exactly one real value $\bar{c}$ such that $(\bar{c}_1, \cdots, \bar{c}_m, \bar{c}) \in M$. For suppose there are two different values $\bar{c}^*$ and $\bar{c}^{**}$ such that both $(\bar{c}_1, \cdots, \bar{c}_m, \bar{c}^*)$ and $(\bar{c}_1, \cdots, \bar{c}_m, \bar{c}^{**})$ are in M. Since $(c_1, \cdots, c_m)$ and $(\bar{c}_1, \cdots, \bar{c}_m)$ are interior points of N, there exists a point $(c'_1, \cdots, c'_m)$ such that $(c_1, \cdots, c_m)$ lies in the interior of the segment determined by $(c'_1, \cdots, c'_m)$, and $(\bar{c}_1, \cdots, \bar{c}_m)$. There exists a real value c' such that $(c'_1, \cdots, c'_m, c') \in M$. Consider the convex set T determined by the 3 points $(\bar{c}_1, \cdots, \bar{c}_m, \bar{c}^*)$, $(\bar{c}_1, \cdots, \bar{c}_m, \bar{c}^{**})$ and $(c'_1, \cdots, c'_m, c')$. Obviously, $T \subset M$. But T contains points $(c_1, \cdots, c_m, h)$ and $(c_1, \cdots, c_m, h')$ with $h \neq h'$, contrary to our assumption that $c^* = c^{**}$. Thus, for any interior point $(\bar{c}_1, \cdots, \bar{c}_m)$ of N there exists exactly one real value $\bar{c}$ such that $(\bar{c}_1, \cdots, \bar{c}_m, \bar{c}) \in M$. Since M is closed and convex, this remains true also when $(\bar{c}_1, \cdots, \bar{c}_m)$ is a boundary point of N. Thus, there exists a single valued function $\varphi(g_1, \cdots, g_m)$ such that $g_{m+1} = \varphi(g_1, \cdots, g_m)$ holds for all points $g = (g_1, \cdots g_m, g_{m+1})$ in M. Since M is convex, φ must be linear; i.e., $\varphi(g_1, \cdots, g_m) = \sum_{i=1}^{m} k_i g_i + k_0$. Since the origin is obviously contained in M, we have $k_0 = 0$. Thus, we have $g_{m+1} = \sum_{i=1}^{m} k_i g_i$ for all points g in M. But then $f_{m+1}(x) = \sum_{i=1}^{m} k_i f_i(x)$ must hold for all x, except perhaps on a set of measure zero. Thus, for any subset S of R, the inequalities (1.3) and (1.4) are fulfilled for all x, except perhaps on a set of measure zero. This completes the proof of our theorem in the case when $c^* = c^{**}$.

We shall now consider the case when $c^{**} < c^*$. Let c be any value between c^{**} and c^*; i.e., $c^{**} < c < c^*$. We shall show that $(c_1, \cdots, c_m, c)$ is an interior point of M. For this purpose, consider a finite set of points $c^i = (c^i_1, \cdots, c^i_m)$ in N $(i = 1, \cdots, n)$ such that $c^1, \cdots, c^n$ are linearly independent, the simplex determined by $c^1, \cdots, c^n$ has the same dimension as N and contains the point $(c_1, \cdots, c_m)$ in its interior. Such points c^i in N obviously exist. There exist real values h_i $(i = 1, \cdots, n)$ such that $(c^i_1, \cdots, c^i_m, h_i) \in M$ $(i = 1, \cdots, n)$. Let T be the smallest convex set containing the points $(c^i_1, \cdots, c^i_m, h_i)$ $(i = 1, \cdots, n)$, $(c_1, \cdots, c_m, c^*)$ and $(c_1, \cdots, c_m, c^{**})$. Clearly the dimension of T is the same as that of M and $(c_1, \cdots, c_m, c)$ is an interior point of T. The point $(c_1, \cdots, c_m, c^*)$ is obviously a boundary point of M. Let $g = (g_1, \cdots, g_{m+1})$ be the generic designation of a point in the $m + 1$-dimensional Euclidean space E. Since $(c_1, \cdots, c_m, c^*)$ is a boundary point of M, there exists an m-dimensional hyperplane Π through $(c_1, \cdots, c_m, c^*)$ such that Π contains only boundary points of M and M lies entirely on one side of Π.[3] Let the equation of Π be given by

$$(3.1) \qquad k_{m+1}g_{m+1} - \sum_{i=1}^{m} k_i g_i = k_{m+1}c^* - \sum_{i=1}^{m} k_i c_i.$$

Since Π contains only boundary points of M, and since $(c_1, \cdots, c_m, c)$ is not a boundary point when $c^{**} < c < c^*$, the hyperplane Π cannot be parallel to the $(m+1)$-th coordinate axis; i.e., $k_{m+1} \neq 0$. We can assume without loss of generality that $k_{m+1} = 1$. Since M lies entirely on one side of Π, and since for $(g_1, \cdots, g_m, g_{m+1}) = (c_1, \cdots, c_m, c^{**})$ the left hand member of (3.1) is smaller than the right hand member, we must have

$$(3.2) \qquad g_{m+1} - \sum_{i=1}^{m} k_i g_i \leq c^* - \sum_{i=1}^{m} k_i c_i$$

for all $g \in M$. Let S be a subset of R such that

$$(3.3) \qquad (\mu_1(S), \cdots, \mu_m(S), \mu_{m+1}(S)) = (c_1, \cdots, c_m, c^*).$$

It can easily be seen that (3.2) and (3.3) can be fulfilled simultaneously only if S satisfies the conditions (1.3) and (1.4) for all x, except perhaps on a set of measure zero. This completes the proof of our theorem.

It remains to investigate the case when $(c_1, \cdots, c_m)$ is a boundary point of N. For this purpose, we shall introduce some definitions and prove some lemmas.

Let $\xi = (\xi_1, \cdots, \xi_m)$ be an m-dimensional vector with real valued components at least one of which is not zero. We shall say that ξ is maximal relative to the point $c = (c_1, \cdots, c_m)$ if

$$(3.4) \qquad \sum_{i=1}^{m} \xi_i g_i \leq \sum_{i=1}^{m} \xi_i c_i$$

for all points $(g_1, \cdots, g_m)$ in N.

We shall say that a set $\{\xi^i\}$ $(i = 1, \cdots, r; r > 1)$ of vectors is maximal relative to the point $c = (c_1, \cdots, c_m)$ if the set $\{\xi^i\}$ $(i = 1, \cdots, r-1)$ is maximal relative to c, not all components of ξ^r are zero and

$$(3.5) \qquad \sum_{j=1}^{m} \xi_j^r g_j \leq \sum_{j=1}^{m} \xi_j^r c_j$$

holds for all points $(g_1, \cdots, g_m)$ of N for which

$$(3.6) \qquad \sum_{j=1}^{m} \xi_j^i g_j = \sum_{j=1}^{m} \xi_j^i c_j \qquad (i = 1, \cdots, r-1).$$

---

[3]This follows from well-known results on convex bodies. See, for example, [3], p. 6.

A set of vectors $\{\xi^i\}$ $(i = 1, \cdots, r)$ is said to be a complete maximal set relative to $c = (c_1, \cdots, c_m)$ if $\{\xi^i\}$ $(i = 1, \cdots, r)$ is maximal relative to c and no vector ξ^{r+1} exists such that ξ^{r+1} is linearly independent of the sequence $(\xi^1, \cdots, \xi^r)$ and $(\xi^1, \cdots, \xi^r, \xi^{r+1})$ is maximal relative to c.

LEMMA 3.1. *If $c = (c_1, \cdots, c_m)$ is a boundary point of N, then there exists a positive integer r and a set $\{\xi^1, \cdots, \xi^r\}$ of vectors that is a complete maximal set relative to c.*

PROOF. Since c is a boundary point of N, there exists an $(m-1)$-dimensional hyperplane Π through c such that N lies entirely on one side of Π.[a] Let the equation of Π be given by

$$\sum_{i=1}^m \xi_i g_i = \sum_{i=1}^m \xi_i c_i.$$

Since N lies entirely on one side of Π, either $\sum_{i=1}^m \xi_i g_i \geq \sum_{i=1}^m \xi_i c_i$ for all points $(g_1, \cdots, g_m)$ in N, or $\sum_{i=1}^m \xi_i g_i \leq \sum_{i=1}^m \xi_i c_i$ for all $(g_1, \cdots, g_m)$ in N. We put $\xi^1 = -\xi$ if $\sum_{i=1}^m \xi_i g_i \geq \sum_{i=1}^m \xi_i c_i$ for all points $(g_1, \cdots, g_m)$ in N. Otherwise, we put $\xi^1 = \xi$. Clearly, ξ^1 is maximal relative to c. If ξ^1 is not a complete maximal set relative to c, there exists a vector ξ^2 such that ξ^2 is linearly independent of ξ^1 and (ξ^1, ξ^2) is maximal relative to c. If (ξ^1, ξ^2) is not a complete maximal set, we can find a vector ξ^3 such that ξ^3 is linearly independent of (ξ^1, ξ^2) and (ξ^1, ξ^2, ξ^3) is a maximal set relative to c, and so on. Continuing this procedure, we shall arrive at a set $(\xi^1, \cdots, \xi^r)$ $(r \leq m)$ that is a complete maximal set relative to c. This completes the proof of Lemma 3.1.

LEMMA 3.2. *If $(\xi^1, \cdots, \xi^r)$ is a maximal set of vectors relative to $c = (c_1, \cdots, c_m)$ and if $\nu(S) = c$, then the following two conditions are fulfilled for all x (except perhaps on a set of measure zero).*

a) *If x is a point in R for which $\sum_{j=1}^m \xi_j^i f_j(x) = 0$ for $i = 1, 2, \cdots, u-1$ and $\sum_{j=1}^m \xi_j^u f_j(x) > 0$, then $x \in S$.*

b) *If x is a point in R for which $\sum_{j=1}^m \xi_j^i f_j(x) = 0$ for $i = 1, 2, \cdots, u-1$ and $\sum_{j=1}^m \xi_j^u f_j(x) < 0$ $(u = 1, 2, \cdots, r)$, then $x \notin S$.*

PROOF. Assume that $(\xi^1, \cdots, \xi^r)$ is maximal relative to c. Then ξ^1 is maximal relative to c. This implies that for all x (except for a set of measure zero) the following condition holds: $x \in S$ when $\sum_{j=1}^m \xi_j^1 f_j(x) > 0$ and $x \notin S$ when $\sum_{j=1}^m \xi_j^1 f_j(x) < 0$. Thus, conditions (a) and (b) of our lemma must be fulfilled for $u = 1$. We shall now show that if (a) and (b) hold for $u = 1, \cdots, v$, then (a) and (b) must hold also for $u = v + 1$. For this purpose, consider the set R' of all points x for which $\sum_{j=1}^m \xi_j^i f_j(x) = 0$ for $i = 1, \cdots, v$. If R is replaced by R', the ξ^{v+1} is maximal relative to $c' = (c_1', \cdots, c_m')$ where $c_i' = \int_{R'} f_i(x)dx$ and $S' = S \cap R'$. Hence, for any x in R' (except perhaps on a set of measure zero) the following condition holds: $x \in S$ when $\sum_{j=1}^m \xi_j^{v+1} f_j(x) > 0$ and $x \notin S$ when $\sum_{j=1}^m \xi_j^{v+1} f_j(x) < 0$.

But this implies that (a) and (b) hold for $u = v + 1$. This completes the proof of our lemma.

LEMMA 3.3. *Let $(\xi^1, \cdots, \xi^r)$ be a complete maximal set of vectors relative to $c = (c_1, \cdots, c_m)$, and let T be the set of all points $g = (g_1, \cdots, g_m)$ of N for which $\sum_{j=1}^m \xi_j^i g_i = \sum_{j=1}^m \xi_j^i c_i$ for $i = 1, 2, \cdots, r$. Then T is a bounded, closed and convex set and c is an interior point of T.*

PROOF. Clearly, T is a bounded, closed and convex set. Suppose that c is a boundary point of T. Then there exists a hyperplane Π of dimension $m - 1$ such that Π goes through c, Π contains only boundary points of T and T lies entirely on one side of Π.[b] Let the equation of Π be given by

$$\sum_{j=1}^m \xi_j g_i = \sum_{j=1}^m \xi_j c_j$$

where ξ is independent of $\xi^1, \cdots, \xi^r$. Since T lies on one side of Π, we have either $\sum_{j=1}^m \xi_j g_i \geq \sum_{j=1}^m \xi_j c_j$ for all $g = (g_1, \cdots, g_m)$ in T, or $\sum_{j=1}^m \xi_j g_i \leq \sum_{j=1}^m \xi_j c_j$ for all g in T. Let $\xi_j^{r+1} = \xi_j$ $(j = 1, \cdots, m)$ in the latter case, and $\xi_j^{r+1} = -\xi_j$ in the former case. Then $\sum_{j=1}^m \xi_j^{r+1} g_i \leq \sum_{j=1}^m \xi_j^{r+1} c_i$ for all g in T. But then $(\xi^1, \cdots, \xi^r, \xi^{r+1})$ is a maximal set relative to c, contrary to our assumption that $(\xi^1, \cdots, \xi^r)$ is a complete maximal set. Thus, c must be an interior point of T and our lemma is proved.

THEOREM 3.2. *If $c = (c_1, \cdots, c_m)$ is a boundary point of N and if $(\xi^1, \cdots, \xi^r)$ is a complete maximal set of vectors relative to c, then a necessary and sufficient condition for a member S of $\mathcal{S}$ to be a member of $\mathcal{S}_0$ is that there exist m constants $k_1, \cdots, k_m$ such that for all x in R' (except perhaps on a set of measure zero) the inequalities (1.3) and (1.4) hold, where R' is the set of all points x for which*

$$\sum_{j=1}^m \xi_j^i f_j(x) = 0 \quad for \quad i = 1, 2, \cdots, r.$$

PROOF. Suppose that $c = (c_1, \cdots, c_m)$ is a boundary point of N and that $(\xi^1, \cdots, \xi^r)$ is a complete maximal set of vectors relative to c. Let R^* be the set of all points x for which the following two conditions hold: (1) $\sum_{j=1}^m \xi_j^i f_j(x) \neq 0$ for at least one value i; (2) $\sum_{j=1}^m \xi_j^i f_j(x) > 0$ where i is the smallest integer for which $\sum_{j=1}^m \xi_j^i f_j(x) \neq 0$. For any member S of $\mathcal{S}$ let S^* denote the intersection of S with $R - R'$. It follows from Lemma 3.2 that $R^* - R^* \cap S^*$ and $S^* - R^* \cap S^*$ are sets of measure zero. Thus

(3.7) $\int_{S^*} f_i(x)\, dx = \int_{R^*} f_i(x)\, dx$ $(i = 1, \cdots, m + 1)$

for all $S \in \mathcal{S}$. Let

(3.8) $f_i^*(x) = f_i(x)$ for $x \in R'$ $(i = 1, \cdots, m + 1)$

and

(3.9) $f_i^*(x) = 0$ for $x \in R - R'$ $(i = 1, \cdots, m + 1)$

Let, furthermore,

(3.10) $c_i^* = c_i - \int_{R^*} f_i(x)\, dx$ $(i = 1, \cdots, m).$

Let μ^*, ν^*, M^*, N^*, S^* and S_0^* have the same meaning with reference to the functions $f_1^*(x), \cdots, f_{m+1}^*(x)$ and the point $c^* = (c_1^*, \cdots, c_m^*)$ as μ, ν, M, N, S and S_0 have with reference to the functions $f_1(x), \cdots, f_{m+1}(x)$ and the point $c = (c_1, \cdots, c_m)$.

It follows from Lemma 3.2 that for any subset S of R for which $\nu(S)$ is a point of the set T defined in Lemma 3.3 we have

$$\int_S f_i(x)\, dx = \int_S f_i^*(x)\, dx + \int_{R^*} f_i(x)\, dx \qquad (i = 1, \cdots, m + 1).$$

Since the range of $\nu^*(S)$ is equal to N^* even when S is restricted to subsets S for which $\nu(S) \in T$, the set N^* is obtained from the set T by a translation. The same translation brings the point $c = (c_1, \cdots, c_m)$ into $c^* = (c_1^*, \cdots, c_m^*)$. It then follows from Lemma 3.3 that c^* is an interior point of N^*. Application of Theorem 3.1 gives the following necessary and sufficient condition for a member S of S^* to be a member of S_0^*: There exist m constants $k_1, \cdots, k_m$ such that for all x (except perhaps on a set of measure zero)[c]

(3.11) $f_{m+1}^*(x) \geq k_1 f_1^*(x) + \cdots + k_m f_m^*(x)$ when $x \in S$

and

(3.12) $f_{m+1}^*(x) \leq k_1 f_1^*(x) + \cdots + k_m f_m^*(x)$ when $x \notin S.$

It follows from (3.8) and (3.9) that (3.11) and (3.12) are equivalent to

(3.13) $f_{m+1}(x) \geq k_1 f_1(x) + \cdots + k_m f_m(x)$ when $x \in S \cap R'$

and

(3.14) $f_{m+1}(x) \leq k_1 f_1(x) + \cdots + k_m f_m(x)$ when $x \in (R - S) \cap R'.$

Theorem 3.2 follows from this and the fact that every member S of S is a member of S^* and that a member of S of S is a member of S_0^* if and only if S is a member of S_0.

It may be of interest to note that if the set R' is of measure zero, the members of S can differ from each other only by sets of measure zero; i.e., S consists essentially of one element. This is an immediate consequence of Lemma 3.2.

REFERENCES

[1] J. NEYMAN AND E. S. PEARSON, "Contributions to the theory of testing statistical hypotheses," *Stat. Res. Memoirs*, Vol. 1 (1936). pp. 1–37.

[2] A. LYAPUNOV, "Sur les fonctions-vecteurs complètement additives," *Izvestiya Akad. Nauk SSSR, Ser. Mat.*, Vol. 4 (1940), pp. 465–78.

[3] T. BONNESEN AND W. FENCHEL, *Theorie der Konvexen Körper*, Chelsea Publishing Company, New York, 1948.

[4] P. R. HALMOS, "The range of a vector measure," *Bull. Am. Math. Soc.*, Vol. 54 (1948), pp. 416–421.

Part II: The Simplex Method of Linear Programming

From the 7th to the 10th of September 1948, the Econometric Society convened (jointly with the American Mathematical Society, the Mathematical Association of America, and the Institute of Mathematical Statistics) at the University of Wisconsin in Madison. A report of the Econometric Society's sessions appeared the following year in its journal *Econometrica*. As summarized there, the 9th of September was devoted to a symposium on the theory of games. There were two sessions in the morning (one a "Survey on the Theory of Games" given by John von Neumann, the other a talk on "Economics and the Theory of Games" by Oskar Morgenstern); the afternoon featured a panel discussion with talks by G. B. Dantzig, M. A. Girshick, I. Kaplansky, S. Karlin, J. C. C. McKinsey, O. Morgenstern, E. W. Paxson, L. S. Shapley, and J. W. Tukey. The session was chaired by J. von Neumann, who invited H. Hotelling to provide some supplementary comments.

An abstract of Dantzig's talk, called "Programming in a Linear Structure," was printed in the aforementioned *Econometrica* report. For historical and other reasons, it is included in this collection as Chapter 3. It is believed to be Dantzig's first announcement of the problem class we now call "linear programming" (a name later proposed to Dantzig, by T. C. Koopmans) in the scholarly literature. Dantzig's investigation of this subject began at the Pentagon, and it was there, in the summer of 1947, that he discovered his world-famous Simplex Method.

The abstract is brief, yet remarkable for its visionary scope. In it one finds the verbal statement of the linear programming problem with its emphasis on constrained optimization, a mention of dynamic systems, an allusion to connections with the theory of games, a reference to computational procedures for use on "large scale digital computers," and the suggestion that the solutions of such problems could actually be implemented (not merely discussed). The themes announced in this abstract would occupy Dantzig, and scores of others for decades.

The "Conference on Activity Analysis of Production and Allocation" held at the University of Chicago June 20–24, 1949, ranks as perhaps the most influential gathering of its kind in the history of mathematical programming. The proceedings volume *Activity Analysis of Production and Allocation*, edited by Tjalling C. Koopmans and published in 1951, further enhanced the impact of the meeting. That book opens with a high-level paper by Marshall K. Wood and George B. Dantzig, in which the authors explain that

> programming, or program planning, may be defined as the con-
> struction of a schedule of actions by means of which the econ-
> omy, organization, or other complex of activities may move
> away from one defined state to another, or from one a defined
> state toward some specifically defined objective. Such a sched-
> ule implies, and should explicitly prescribe, the resources and
> the goods and services utilized, consumed, or produced in the
> accomplishment of the programmed activities.

(This notion of programming differs from computer programming, a term not generally in use at that time.) Although the idea of including an *objective* in the analysis today seems commonplace, it was, at the time "programming in a linear structure" was introduced, a novel idea.

This Wood-Dantzig, paper (and a companion paper by Dantzig, alone) had already appeared in 1949 (*Econometrica* v. 17). One of the other three papers by Dantzig, in the aforementioned proceedings volume is presented here as Chapter 4. Among Dantzig's publications, this paper can be regarded as the earliest in which the details of the Simplex Method are presented using the apparatus of linear algebra. It is here that we encounter (potentially very large) systems of linear equations in nonnegative variables and learn to appreciate the great importance of their basic feasible solutions.

In this pioneering work, Dantzig, showed that not only can one include an objective function in the model, but one can actually do something about finding an optimal solution of the constraints if, indeed, such a solution exists. The implementation of this discovery transformed program planning from the mere discussion of alternate solutions of the constraints to the art of actually computing *optimal* solutions.

Two crucial theoretical issues in Dantzig's Simplex Method are (1) obtaining a basic feasible solution with which to start the computation, and (2) ensuring that the algorithm terminates in a finite number of steps — either with an optimal solution or else with an indication that no optimal solution exists. The paper on which Chapter 4 is based addresses both issues. But in dealing with the second, Dantzig, imposes a rather strong "nondegeneracy" assumption: the linear independence of every set of m columns drawn from the coefficient matrix of the system of m linear equations *augmented by* the right-hand side column. This assumption has two important implications. The first is that every set of m columns from the coefficient matrix of the left-hand side is a basis (though not necessarily a feasible basis). The second is that the right-hand side vector cannot be expressed as a linear combination of fewer than m columns of the coefficient matrix. Although this assumption allowed Dantzig, to establish finite termination, it is not very satisfactory because it is unrealistic and, worse yet, not really the sort of thing one could check in practice when solving a large problem.

That *something* is needed to take care of degeneracy was demonstrated independently by Alan J. Hoffman and Philip Wolfe. They showed that when the Simplex Algorithm is applied to a degenerate problem (now defined as one in which the right-hand side column can be expressed as a *nonnegative* linear combination of fewer than m columns of the coefficient matrix) it is possible to generate a sequence of feasible bases that returns to a member of the sequence, thereby forming a "cycle." Within this cycle, there is no change in the objective function value. So, to put the matter bluntly, Dantzig's nondegeneracy assumption was too crude, but the consequences of doing without a device for handling degeneracy (at least theoretically) were equally unsatisfactory. Dantzig, was aware of the desirability of weakening his nondegeneracy assumption. In footnote 2 of that paper (Chapter 4), he sketched a technique for accomplishing just that.

The need for a suitable degeneracy resolution technique provided the motivation for the paper of Chapter 5 by Dantzig, Orden, and Wolfe. At the time of that collaboration, it was known that degeneracy could be resolved by perturbing the constants on the right-hand side of the system equations. A technique of this sort had been reported in 1952 by Abraham Charnes. The team of Dantzig, Orden, and Wolfe addressed the problem by recasting the linear programming problem as a "generalized matrix problem." In effect, the scalar variables and the constants on the right-hand of the system were replaced by vectors. Significantly, the original nonnegativity condition on the variables was generalized to *lexicographic nonnegativity* of the vectors. In particular, a lexicographically nonnegative vector is one that is either the zero vector, or else is a nonzero vector whose first nonzero component is positive. The success of this approach depends on choosing the generalized right-hand side matrix in such a way that its rows are linearly independent. Doing so is not at all difficult, but in practice it can impose an unwelcome computational burden. The paper by Dantzig, Orden, and Wolfe sparked interest in truly efficient degeneracy resolution techniques. Such a technique was published years later by Wolfe.

Chapter 3

PROGRAMMING IN A LINEAR STRUCTURE

GEORGE B. DANTZIG

Mathematical Advisor, United States Air Forces, Comptroller

W. Leontief, Schlesinger, Wald, von Neumann, and T. C. Koopmans have studied economic models of the type considered here. This paper differs essentially from those of the above authors in that it is concerned with the basic problem of programming in a rapidly changing "economy."

The basic assumptions of the model lead to a fundamental set of linear equations expressing the conditions which must be satisfied by the various levels of activity, X_i, in the dynamic system. These variables are subject to the further restriction $X_i \geq 0$. The determination of the "best" choice of X_i is made to depend on the maximization (or minimization) of [a] linear form in X_i. A typical example would be the minimization of the total budget over several time periods. The problem is equivalent to the maximization of a linear form whose variables are subject to linear inequalities. It is also closely related to the problem of determining a Min-Max of a bilinear form. It is proposed that computational techniques such as those developed by J. von Neumann and by the author be used in connection with large scale digital computers to implement the solution of programming problems.

Chapter 4

MAXIMIZATION OF A LINEAR FUNCTION OF VARIABLES SUBJECT TO LINEAR INEQUALITIES[1]

By George B. Dantzig

The general problem indicated in the title is easily transformed, by any one of several methods, to one which maximizes a linear form of nonnegative variables subject to a system of linear equalities. For example, consider the linear inequality $ax + by + c > 0$. The linear inequality[a] can be replaced by a linear inequality in nonnegative variables by writing, instead, $a(x_1 - x_2) + b(y_1 - y_2) + c - z = 0$, where $x_1 \geq 0$, $x_2 \geq 0$, $y_1 \geq 0$, $y_2 \geq 0$, $z \geq 0$. The basic problem throughout this chapter will be considered in the following form:

PROBLEM: *Find the values of* $\lambda_1, \lambda_2, \cdots, \lambda_n$ *which maximize the linear form*

$$(1) \qquad \lambda_1 c_1 + \lambda_2 c_2 + \cdots + \lambda_n c_n$$

subject to the conditions that

$$(2) \qquad \lambda_j \geq 0 \qquad\qquad (j = 1, 2, \cdots, n)$$

and

$$
(3) \qquad
\begin{aligned}
\lambda_1 a_{11} + \lambda_2 a_{12} + \cdots + \lambda_n a_{1n} &= b_1 \\
\lambda_1 a_{21} + \lambda_2 a_{22} + \cdots + \lambda_n a_{2n} &= b_2 \\
\cdots \cdots \cdots \cdots \cdots \cdots \cdots \\
\lambda_1 a_{m1} + \lambda_2 a_{m2} + \cdots + \lambda_n a_{mn} &= b_m,
\end{aligned}
$$

where a_{ij}, b_i, c_j *are constants* $(i = 1, 2, \cdots, m; j = 1, 2, \cdots, n)$.

---

[1]The author wishes to acknowledge that his work on this subject stemmed from discussions in the spring of 1947 with Marshall K. Wood, in connection with Air Force programming methods. The general nature of the "simplex" approach (as the method discussed here is known) was stimulated by discussions with Leonid Hurwicz.

The author is indebted to T. C. Koopmans, whose constructive observations regarding properties of the simplex led directly to a proof of the method in the early fall of 1947. Emil D. Schell assisted in the preparation of various versions of this chapter. Jack Ladermann has written a set of detailed working instructions and has tested this and other proposed techniques on several examples.

Each column of coefficients in (3) may be viewed as representing the coordinates of a point in Euclidean R_m space.[b] Let P_j denote the jth column of coefficients and P_0 the constants on the right-hand side, i.e., by definition,

$$(4) \qquad [P_1, P_2, \cdots, P_n; P_0] = \begin{bmatrix} a_{11} & a_{12} & \cdots & a_{1n} & b_1 \\ a_{21} & a_{22} & \cdots & a_{2n} & b_2 \\ \cdots & \cdots & \cdots & \cdots & \cdots \\ a_{m1} & a_{m2} & \cdots & a_{mn} & b_m \end{bmatrix}.$$

The basic problem is to determine nonnegative $\lambda_j \geq 0$ such that

$$(5) \qquad \lambda_1 P_1 + \lambda_2 P_2 + \cdots + \lambda_n P_n = P_0,$$

$$(6) \qquad \lambda_1 c_1 + \lambda_2 c_2 + \cdots + \lambda_n c_n = z = \max.^{\text{c}}$$

A set of λ_j which satisfy (5) without necessarily yielding the maximum in (6) will be termed a *feasible* solution; one which maximizes (6) will be called a *maximum feasible* solution. The purpose of this chapter is to discuss the so-called "simplex" technique, which consists in constructing first a feasible, and then a maximum feasible solution. In many applications, of course, feasible solutions are easily obtained by inspection. For this reason, and because an arbitrary feasible solution can be obtained in a manner analogous to the construction of a maximum feasible solution, we shall consider first the construction of a maximum feasible solution from a given feasible solution.[2]

ASSUMPTION (nondegeneracy): *Every subset of m points from the set $(P_0; P_1, P_2, \cdots, P_n)$ is linearly independent.*[d]

The theorems given in Sections 1 and 2 below come about naturally in the construction of a feasible and a maximum feasible solution to (5) and (6). They may be used to prove the following important propositions (actually, the proofs of Theorems A and B do not require the nondegeneracy assumption):

---

[2]The nondegeneracy assumption has been made to simplify the development that follows. There are obvious ways in which this assumption could be weakened. For example, the m equations implied in (5) may not all be linearly independent, in which case $k < m$ independent equations could be chosen and the remainder dropped. When this is done it may still be true that P_0 is linearly dependent on less than k of the P_i. One way to avoid this type of "degeneracy" is to alter slightly the values of the components of P_0. This method is extensively employed in the transportation problem [XXIII]. Recently a workable numerical procedure has been developed for the general case as well. The procedure augments the original set of points, P_j, by a set of unit vectors V_i where the c_i for maximizing form (1) associated with the points V_i are assumed "small." By choosing either V_i or $-V_i$, a feasible solution can be obtained by inspection rather than through the method of Section 2 of this paper. This cuts the computations in half. Moreover, the rank of the system is automatically m, i.e., $k = m$, so that by this approach all problems connected with degeneracy are solved.

THEOREM A: *If one feasible solution exists, then there exists a feasible solution (called a basic feasible solution) with, at most, m points P_i with positive weights λ_i and $n - m$, or more, points P_i with $\lambda_i = 0$.*

THEOREM B: *If the values of z for the class of feasible solutions have a finite upper bound, then a maximum feasible solution exists which is a basic feasible solution.*

1. CONSTRUCTION OF A MAXIMUM FEASIBLE SOLUTION

Assume as given a feasible solution consisting of exactly m points, P_i, with nonzero weights; that is,

$$(7) \qquad \lambda_1 P_1 + \lambda_2 P_2 + \cdots + \lambda_m P_m = P_0 \qquad \lambda_i > 0,$$

$$(8) \qquad \lambda_1 c_1 + \lambda_2 c_2 + \cdots + \lambda_m c_m = z_0$$

In establishing the condition for and the construction of a maximum feasible solution, it will be necessary first to express all points, P_j, in terms of a *basis* consisting of m points which form the above feasible solution; that is,

$$(9) \qquad x_{1j} P_1 + x_{2j} P_2 + \cdots + x_{mj} P_m = P_j \qquad (j = 1, 2, \cdots, n).$$

We now define z_j by

$$(10) \qquad x_{1j} c_1 + x_{2j} c_2 + \cdots + x_{mj} c_m = z_j \qquad (j = 1, 2, \cdots, n).$$

THEOREM 1: *If, for any j, the condition*

$$(11) \qquad c_j > z_j$$

holds, then a set of feasible solutions can be constructed such that

$$(12) \qquad z > z_0$$

for any member of the set, where the upper bound of z is either finite or infinite.

CASE I: *If finite, a feasible solution consisting of exactly m points with positive weights can be constructed.*

CASE II: *If infinite, a feasible solution consisting of exactly $m+1$ points with positive weights can be constructed such that the upper bound of $z = +\infty$.*

PROOF: Multiplying (9) by θ and subtracting from (7), and similarly multiplying (10) by θ and subtracting from (8), we get

$$(13) \quad (\lambda_1 - \theta x_{1j}) P_1 + (\lambda_2 - \theta x_{2j}) P_2 + \cdots + (\lambda_m - \theta x_{mj}) P_m + \theta P_j = P_0,$$

$$(14) \quad (\lambda_1 - \theta x_{1j}) c_1 + (\lambda_2 - \theta x_{2j}) c_2 + \cdots + (\lambda_m - \theta x_{mj}) c_m + \theta c_j$$
$$= z_0 + \theta(c_j - z_j),$$

where the term θc_j has been added to both sides of (14).

Since $\lambda_i > 0$ for all i in (13), it is clear that there is, for $\theta \geq 0$, either a finite range of values $\theta_0 > \theta \geq 0$ or an infinite range of values such that the coefficients of P_i remain positive. It is clear from (14) that the z of this set of feasible solutions is a strictly monotonically increasing function of θ,

$$(15) \qquad z = z_0 + \theta(c_j - z_j) > z_0, \qquad \theta > 0,$$

since $c_j > z_j$ by hypothesis (11), thus establishing (12).

CASE I: If $x_{ij} > 0$ for at least one $i = 1, 2, \cdots, m$ in (13) or (9), the largest value of θ for which all coefficients in (13) remain nonnegative is given by

$$(16) \qquad \theta_0 = \min_i (\lambda_i/x_{ij}), \qquad x_{ij} > 0.$$

If $i = i_0$ yields θ_0 in (15), it is clear that the coefficient corresponding to i_0 in (13) and (14) will vanish, hence *a feasible solution, given by $\theta = \theta_0$, has been constructed with exactly m positive weights; moreover, $z > z_0$.* It will be noted that this new set of m points consists of the new point, P_j, and $(m-1)$ of the m points previously used. This, then, is a desired solution for Case I of Theorem 1.

The new set of m points may be used as a *new basis*, and again, as in (9) and (10), all points may be expressed in terms of the new basis and the values of c_j compared with the newly computed z_j's. If any $c_j > z_j$, the value of z can be increased. If at least one $x_{ij} > 0$, another new basis can be formed. We shall assume that the process is iterated until it is not possible to form a new basis. This must occur in a *finite* number of steps because, of course, there are at most $\binom{n}{m}$ bases and none of these bases can recur, for in that case their z-values would also recur, whereas the process gives strictly increasing values of z. Thus it is clear that the iteration must eventually terminate, either because at some stage

$$(17) \qquad x_{ij} \leq 0 \quad \text{for all} \quad i = 1, 2, \cdots, m$$

and some fixed j, or because

$$(18) \qquad c_j \leq z_j \quad \text{for all} \quad j = 1, 2, \cdots, n.$$

CASE II: If (17) holds (i.e., for all i, $x_{ij} \leq 0$), then it is clear that θ has no finite upper bound and that a class of feasible solutions has been constructed consisting of $m+1$ points with nonzero weights such that the upper bound of z is $+\infty$.

In all problems in which there is a finite upper bound to z, the iterative process must necessarily lead to condition (18). We shall prove, however, that the feasible solution associated with the final basis, which has the property $c_j \leq z_j$ for all $j = 1, 2, \cdots, m$ is also a maximum feasible solution (Theorem 2). Hence, *in all problems in which there is no finite upper bound to z, the iterative process must necessarily lead to condition* (17); moreover, by rewriting (9) as

$$(19) \qquad P_j + (-x_{1j})P_1 + (-x_{2j})P_2 + \cdots + (-x_{mj})P_m = 0, \qquad x_{ij} \leq 0,$$

for the fixed j of (17), we have shown that *a nonnegative linear combination of $(m+1)$ points vanishes if the upper bound of z is $+\infty$.* In many practical problems physical conditions will dictate the impossibility of (19).

As a practical computing matter the iterative procedure of shifting from one basis to the next is not as laborious as would first appear because the basis, except for the deletion of one point and the insertion of a new point, is the same as before. In fact, a shift of a basis involves less than mn multiplications and an equal number of additions. It has been observed *empirically* that the number of shifts of basis can be greatly reduced not by arbitrarily selecting any point, P_j, satisfying $c_j > z_j$, but by selecting the one which gives the greatest immediate increase[e] in z; from (15) the criterion for choice of j is such that

$$(20) \qquad\qquad \theta_0(c_j - z_j) = \max_j,$$

where θ_0 is given by (16) and is a function of j. A criterion that involves considerably less computation and apparently yields just as satisfactory results is to choose j such that

$$(21) \qquad\qquad (c_j - z_j) = \max_j.$$

By the use of either (20) or (21) approximately m changes in basis are encountered in practice, so that about $m^2 n$ multiplications are involved in getting a maximum feasible solution from a feasible solution. There exist further refinements of computations by which $2m^2 + n$ computations are required per shift in basis if criterion (21) is used, or roughly $2m^3 + mn$ in all. However, to obtain a feasible solution will also require about $2m^3 + mn$ multiplications if one such solution is not readily available, and the selection of an original basis will require m^3 more—hence the method involves about $5m^3 + 2mn$ multiplications.[3]

THEOREM 2: *If, for all $j = 1, 2, \cdots,, n$, the condition $c_j \leq z_j$ holds, then* (7) *and* (8) *constitute a maximum feasible solution.*

PROOF: Let

$$(22) \qquad\qquad \mu_1 P_1 + \mu_2 P_2 + \cdots + \mu_n P_n = P_0, \qquad \mu_j \geq 0,$$

---

[3]See footnote 2.

(23) $\mu_1 c_1 + \mu_2 c_2 + \cdots + \mu_n c_n = z^*,$

constitute any other feasible solution. We shall show that $z_0 \geq z^*$.

By hypothesis, $c_j \leq z_j$, so that by replacing c_j by z_j in (23) yields

(24) $\mu_1 z_1 + \mu_2 z_2 + \cdots + \mu_n z_n \geq z^*.$

Substituting the value of P_j given in (9) into (22) and the value of z_j given by (10) into (24), we obtain

(25) $\left(\sum_{j=1}^{n} \mu_j x_{1j} \right) P_1 + \left(\sum_{j=1}^{n} \mu_j x_{2j} \right) P_2 + \cdots + \left(\sum_{j=1}^{n} \mu_j x_{mj} \right) P_m = P_0,$

(26) $\left(\sum_{j=1}^{n} \mu_j x_{1j} \right) c_1 + \left(\sum_{j=1}^{n} \mu_j x_{2j} \right) c_2 + \cdots + \left(\sum_{j=1}^{n} \mu_j x_{mj} \right) c_m \geq z^*.$

According to our assumption of nondegeneracy, the corresponding coefficients of P_i in (7) and (25) must be equal; hence (26) becomes

(27) $\lambda_1 c_1 + \lambda_2 c_2 + \cdots + \lambda_n c_n \geq z^*;$

or, by (8),

(28) $z_0 \geq z^*.$

In order that another maximum feasible solution exist it is necessary that $c_j = z_j$ for some P_j (not in the final basis). It will be noted, however, that in this case the extended matrix

(29) $\begin{bmatrix} P_1 & P_2 & \cdots & P_n \\ c_1 & c_2 & \cdots & c_n \end{bmatrix}$

[see (4) above] has at least one set of $m + 1$ columns which are linearly dependent. *Thus a sufficient condition that the maximum feasible solution constructed from the given feasible solution be unique is that every set of $(m + 1)$ points, defined by columns in (29), be linearly independent.*

2. CONSTRUCTION OF A FEASIBLE SOLUTION[4]

We begin by selecting an arbitrary basis of $(m - 1)$ points, P_j, and P_0. Denote this set by $(P_0; P_1, \cdots, P_{m-1})$. Any P_j can be expressed in terms of this basis by[f]

(30) $y_{0j} P_0 + y_{1j} P_1 + \cdots + y_{(m-1)j} P_{m-1} = P_j$ $(j = 1, 2, \cdots, m).$

---

[4]See footnote 2.

THEOREM 3: *A sufficient condition that there exist no feasible solution is that $y_{0j} \leq 0$ for all j.*

PROOF: Assume on the contrary that there exists a feasible solution

$$(31) \qquad \lambda_1 P_1 + \lambda_2 P_2 + \cdots + \lambda_n P_n = P_0, \qquad \lambda_j \geq 0.$$

Substitute the expressions for P_j given by (30) into (31):

$$(32) \quad P_0 \left(\sum_1^n \lambda_j y_{0j} - 1 \right) + P_1 \left(\sum_1^n \lambda_j y_{1j} \right) + \cdots$$

$$+ P_{m-1} \left(\sum_1^n \lambda_j y_{(m-1)j} \right) = 0.$$

In view of the assumed independence of $(P_0; P_1, \cdots, P_{m-1})$ it is clear that each coefficient in (32) must vanish; in particular,

$$(33) \qquad \sum_1^n \lambda_j y_{0j} - 1 = 0.$$

this is impossible if simultaneously $\lambda_j \geq 0$ and $y_{0j} \leq 0$ for all j.

To construct a feasible solution we first define a fixed reference point, G, given by

$$(34) \qquad G = w_1 P_1 + w_2 P_2 + \cdots + w_{m-1} P_{m-1} - \rho_0 P_0,$$

where $w_i > 0$ $(i = 1, \cdots, m-1)$ and $\rho_0 > 0$ are arbitrarily chosen. For convenience we rewrite (34) in the form

$$(35) \qquad G + \rho_0 P_0 = w_1 P_1 + w_2 P_2 + \cdots + w_{m-1} P_{m-1}.$$

In the development that follows, ρ_0 will play a role analogous to z_0.

By Theorem 3, if there exists a feasible solution, there exists at least one j (which we shall consider fixed) such that

$$(36) \qquad y_{0j} > 0.$$

Multiplying (30) by θ and subtracting from (35), we obtain

$$(37) \quad G + (\rho_0 + \theta y_{0j}) P_0$$

$$= \theta P_j + (w_1 - \theta y_{1j}) P_1 + \cdots + (w_{m-1} - \theta y_{(m-1)j}) P_{m-1}.$$

For a range of $\theta_0 > \theta > 0$ we can construct, in a manner analogous to (13) and (14), a set of points of the form $G + \rho P_0$, each given by a positive linear combination of points P_j. Since ρ will play a role analogous to z, we are interested in the highest value of ρ for which this is possible. It will be noted that

$$(38) \qquad \rho = \rho_0 + \theta y_{0j} > \rho_0$$

since $y_{0j} > 0$ has been assumed.

If, in the representation of P_j in (30), all $y_{ij} \leq 0$ $(i = 1, \cdots, m-1)$, the coefficients of P_j will be positive and $\rho \to +\infty$ as $\theta \to +\infty$. At the same time it will be seen, by solving (30) for P_0,

$$(39) \qquad P_0 = (1/y_{0j})P_j + (-y_{1j}/y_{0j})P_1 + \cdots + (-y_{(m-1)j}/y_{0j})P_{m-1},$$

that a feasible solution has been obtained (i.e., P_0 has been expressed as a positive linear combination of $P_1, P_2, \cdots, P_{m-1}$ and P_j). If at least one $y_{ij} > 0$ $(i = 1, \cdots, m-1)$, the largest value of θ is given by

$$(40) \qquad \theta_0 = \min_i(w_i/y_{ij}), \qquad y_{ij} > 0.$$

Setting $\theta = \theta_0$, the coefficient of at least one point, P_i, will vanish and a new point,

$$G + \rho_1 P_0,$$

will be formed from (34) which is expressed as a positive linear combination of just $m - 1$ points, P_i, where

$$(41) \qquad \rho_1 = \rho_0 + \theta_0 y_{0j} > \rho_0.$$

Expressing all points P_j in terms of the new basis, the process may be repeated, each time obtaining a higher value of ρ (or an infinite value, i.e., a feasible solution). The process must terminate in a finite number of steps. For, otherwise, since there is only a finite number of bases, the same combination of $(m - 1)$ points P_i would appear a second time; that is,

$$(42) \qquad G + \rho' P_0 = w_1' P_1 + w_2' P_2 + \cdots + w_{m-1}' P_{m-1},$$

$$(43) \qquad G + \rho'' P_0 = w_1'' P_1 + w_2'' P_2 + \cdots + w_{m-1}'' P_{m-1},$$

where $\rho'' > \rho'$. Subtracting (42) from (43), we obtain a nonvanishing expression giving P_0 in terms of $(m - 1)$ points P_i, contradicting the non-degeneracy assumption.

There are, however, only two conditions which will terminate the process; i.e., after a finite number of iterations either

$$(44) \qquad y_{0j} \leq 0 \quad \text{for all} \quad j = 1, \cdots, n,$$

in which case, by Theorem 3, no feasible solution exists; or, for some fixed j,

$$(45) \qquad\qquad y_{ij} \le 0 \quad \text{for all} \quad i = 1, \cdots, m,$$

in which case, by solving (30) for P_0, as was done in (40), we obtain the desired feasible solution.

The term "simplex" technique arose in a geometric version of this development which assumes that one of the m equations (3) is of the form

$$(46) \qquad\qquad \lambda_1 + \lambda_2 + \cdots + \lambda_n = 1.$$

A point, P_j, is defined by the remaining coordinates in a column including c_j from (1) as an additional "z"-coordinate. We may interpret (1) and (3) as defining the center of gravity of a system of points with weights λ_j. The problem consists, then, in finding weights λ_j so that the center of gravity lies on a line L defined by $m - 1$ of the relationships $x_1 = b_1, x_2 = b_2, \cdots, x_m = b_m$, such that the z-coordinate is maximum. A basis $P_1, P_2, \cdots, P_m$ may be considered one of the faces of a simplex formed by $P_1, P_2, \cdots, P_m$ and P_j. The z-coordinate of P_j is c_j; the z-coordinate of the projection parallel to the z-axis of the point P_j on the plane of the face formed by the basis is z_j. Because $c_j > z_j$ by (11), all points in the simplex lie "above" the plane of this face. The line L cuts the base in an interior point whose z-value is z_0, hence it must intersect another face of the simplex in a "higher" point (i.e., a point whose z-value is greater than z_0).

Chapter 5

THE GENERALIZED SIMPLEX METHOD FOR MINIMIZING A LINEAR FORM UNDER LINEAR INEQUALITY RESTRAINTS

George B. Dantzig, Alex Orden, Philip Wolfe

1. Background and summary. The determination of "optimum" solutions of systems of linear inequalities is assuming increasing importance as a tool for mathematical analysis of certain problems in economics, logistics, and the theory of games [1; 5]. The solution of *large systems* is becoming more feasible with the advent of high-speed digital computers; however, as in the related problem of inversion of large matrices, there are difficulties which remain to be resolved connected with rank. This paper develops a theory for avoiding assumptions regarding rank of underlying matrices which has import in applications where little or nothing is known about the rank of the linear inequality system under consideration.

The simplex procedure is a finite iterative method which deals with problems involving linear inequalities in a manner closely analogous to the solutions of linear equations or matrix inversion by Gaussian elimination. Like the latter it is useful in proving fundamental theorems on linear algebraic systems. For example, one form of the fundamental duality theorem associated with linear inequalities is easily shown as a direct consequence of solving the main problem. Other forms can be obtained by trivial manipulations (for a fuller discussion of these interrelations, see [13]); in particular, the duality theorem [8; 10; 11; 12] leads directly to the Minmax theorem for zero-sum two-person games [1d] and to a computational method (pointed out informally by Herman Rubin and demonstrated by Robert Dorfman [1a]) which simultaneously yields strategies for both players and the value of the game.

The term "simplex" evolved from an early geometrical version in which (like in game theory) the variables were nonnegative and summed to unity. In that formulation a class of "solutions" was considered which lay in a simplex.

The generalized method given here was outlined earlier by the first of the authors (Dantzig) in a short footnote [1b] and then discussed somewhat more fully at the Symposium of Linear Inequalities in 1951. Its purpose, as we have already indicated, is to remove the restrictive assumptions regarding the rank of the matrix of coefficients and constant elements without which the condition called "degeneracy" can occur.

Under degeneracy it is possible for the value of the solution to remain unchanged from one iteration to the next under the original simplex method. This causes the proof that no basis can repeat to break down. In fact, for certain examples Alan Hoffman [14] and one of the authors (Wolfe) have shown that it was possible to repeat the basis and thus cycle forever with the value of the solution remaining unchanged and greater than the desired minimum. On the other hand, it is interesting to note that while most problems that arise from practical sources (in the authors' experience) have been degenerate, none have ever cycled [9].

The essential scheme for avoiding the assumptions on rank is to replace the original problem by a "perturbation" that satisfies these conditions. That such perturbations exist is, of course, intuitively evident; but the question remained to show how to make the perturbations in a simple way. For the special case of the transportation problem a simple method of producing a perturbation is found in [1c]. The second of the authors (Orden) has considered several types of perturbations for the general case. A. Charnes has extensively investigated this approach and his writing represents probably the best available published material in this regard [2;3;4].

It was noticed early in the development of these methods that the limit concept in which a set of perturbations[a] tends in the limit to one of the solutions of the original problem was not essential to the proof. Accordingly, the third author (Wolfe) considered a purely algebraic approach which imbeds the original problem as a component of a *generalized matrix problem* and replaces the original nonnegative real variables by lexicographically ordered vectors. Because this approach gives a simple presentation of the theory, we adopt it here.

2. The generalized simplex method. As is well known, a system of linear inequalities by trivial substitution and augmentation of the variables can be replaced by an equivalent *system of linear equations in nonnegative variables*; hence, with no loss of generality, we shall consider the basic problem in the latter form throughout this paper. One may easily associate with such a system another system in which the constant terms are placed by ℓ-component constant row vectors and the real variables are replaced by real ℓ-component variable row vectors. In the original system the real variables are nonnegative; in the generalized system we shall mean by a vector variable $\bar{x} > 0$ in the *lexicographic sense* that is has some nonzero components, the first of which is positive, and by $\bar{x} > \bar{y}$ that $\bar{x} - \bar{y} > 0$. It is easy to see that the first components of the vector variables of the generalized system satisfy a linear system in nonnegative variables in which the constant terms are the first components of the constant vectors.

Let $P = [P_0, P_1, \cdots, P_n]$ be a given matrix whose jth column, P_j, is a vector of $m + 1$ components. Let M be a fixed matrix of rank $m + 1$ consisting of $m+1$ ℓ-component row vectors. The generalized matrix problem is concerned with finding a matrix $\tilde{X}$ satisfying

$$(1) \qquad P\tilde{X} = \sum_{0}^{n} P_j \bar{x}_j = M,$$

where $\bar{x}_j$ (the jth row of $\tilde{X}$) is a row vector of ℓ-components satisfying the conditions, in the lexicographic sense,

$$(2) \qquad \bar{x}_j \geq 0 \qquad\qquad\qquad (j = 1, 2, \cdots, n),$$

$$(3) \qquad \bar{x}_0 = \text{max},$$

where the relationship between max $\bar{x}_0$ and the minimization of a linear form will be developed in § 3.

Any set X of "variables" $(\bar{x}_0; \bar{x}_1, \bar{x}_2, \cdots, \bar{x}_n)$ satisfying (1) and (2) in the foregoing lexicographic sense will be referred to as a "feasible solution" (or more simply as a "solution")—a term derived from practical applications in which such a solution represents a situation which is physically realizable but not necessarily optimal. The first variable, $\bar{x}_0$, which will be called the "value" of the solution, is to be maximized; it is not constrained like the others to be nonnegative. In certain applications (as in §3) it may happen that some of the other variables also are not restricted to be nonnegative. This leads to a slight variation in the method (see the discussion following Theorem 5).

Among the class of feasible solutions, the simplex method is particularly concerned with those called "basic." These have the properties, which we mention in passing, (a) that whenever any solution exists a basic solution also exists (Theorem 8), and (b) that when whenever a maximizing solution exists and is unique it is [a] basic solution, and whenever a maximizing solution is not unique there is a basic solution that has the same maximizing value (Theorem 6). A basic solution is one in which only $m + 1$ variables (including $\bar{x}_0$) are considered in (1), the remaining being set equal to zero; that is, it is of the form

$$(4) \qquad BV = P_0 \bar{v}_0 + \sum_{i=1}^{m} P_{j_i} \bar{v}_i = M \qquad\qquad (\bar{v}_i \geq 0, \ j_i \neq 0),$$

where $B = [P_0, P_{j_1}, \cdots, P_{j_m}]$ is an $(m+1)$-rowed *square matrix* and V is a matrix of $m + 1$ rows and ℓ columns whose ith row is $\bar{v}_i$ $(i = 0, 1, \cdots, m)$.

It is clear from (4) that since M is of rank $m+1$ so are B and V. From this it readily follows that the $m+1$ columns of B constitute a *basis* in the space of vectors P_j, and the solution V is uniquely determined. Moreover, since the rank of V is $m+1$, none of the $m+1$ rows of V can vanish; that is, it is not possible that $\bar{v}_i = 0$. *Thus in a basic solution all variables associated with the vectors in the basis (except possibly $\bar{v}_0$) are positive; all others are zero.* The condition in (4) can now be strengthened to strict inequality

$$(5) \qquad\qquad \bar{v}_i > 0 \qquad\qquad\qquad\qquad (i = 1, 2, \cdots, m).$$

Let β_i denote the ith *row* of B inverse:

$$(6) \qquad B^{-1} = [P_0,\ P_{j_1},\ P_{j_2},\ \cdots,\ P_{j_m}]^{-1} = [\beta_0',\ \beta_1',\ \cdots,\ \beta_m']'$$

where primed letters stand for transpose.

THEOREM 1. *A necessary and sufficient condition that a basic solution be a maximizing solution is*

$$(7) \qquad\qquad \beta_0 P_j \geq 0 \qquad\qquad\qquad\qquad (j = 1, 2, \cdots, n).$$

THEOREM 2. *If a basic solution is optimal, then any other solution (basic or not) with the property that $\bar{x}_j = 0$ whenever $(\beta_0 P_j) > 0$ is also optimal; any solution with $\bar{x}_j > 0$ for some $(\beta_0 P_j) > 0$ is not optimal.*

Proofs. Let $\tilde{X}$ represent *any* solution of (1), and V a basic solution with basis B; then multiplying both (1) and (4) through by β_0 and equating, one obtains, after noting from (6) that $\beta_0 P_0 = 1$ and $\beta_0 P_{j_i} = 0$,

$$(8) \qquad\qquad \bar{x}_0 + \sum_1^n (\beta_0 P_j)\bar{x}_j = \bar{v}_0;$$

whence, assuming $\beta_0 P_j \geq 0$, one obtains $\bar{x}_0 \leq \bar{v}_0$ (which establishes the sufficiency of Theorem 1); moreover the condition $\bar{x}_j = 0$ whenever $\beta_0 P_j > 0$ $(j \neq 0)$ implies the summation term of (8) vanishes and $\bar{x}_0 = \bar{v}_0$; whereas denial of this condition implies the summation term is positive if Theorem 1 is true (establishing Theorem 2).

In order to establish the necessity of (7) for Theorem 1, let Y_s be a column vector which expresses a vector P_s as a linear combination of the vectors in the basis:

$$(9) \qquad P_s = B(B^{-1}P_s) = BY_s = \sum_{i=0}^m P_{j_i} y_{is} \qquad\qquad (P_0 = P_{j_0}),$$

where it is evident from (6) that, by definition,

$$(10) \qquad\qquad y_{is} = \beta_i P_s \qquad\qquad\qquad\qquad (i = 0, 1, \cdots, m).$$

Consider a *class of solutions* which may be formed from (4) and (9), of the form

$$(11) \qquad B[V - Y_s\bar{\theta}] + P_s\bar{\theta} = M,$$

or more explicitly

$$(12) \qquad P_0[\bar{v}_0 - y_{0s}\bar{\theta}] + \sum_{i=1}^{m} P_{j_i}[\bar{v}_i + y_{is}\bar{\theta}] + P_s\bar{\theta} = M.$$

It is clear that, since $\bar{v}_i > 0$ for $i \geq 1$ has been established earlier [see (5)], a class of solutions with $\bar{\theta} > 0$ (that is, with $\bar{\theta}$ *strictly positive*) always exists such that the variables associated with P_s and P_{j_i} in (12) are nonnegative, hence admissible as a solution of (1). If $y_{0s} < 0$, then the values of these solutions are

$$(13) \qquad \bar{v} - y_{0s}\bar{\theta} > \bar{v}_0 \qquad\qquad (y_{0s} < 0, \ \bar{\theta} > 0).$$

For a given increase in $\bar{\theta}$ the greatest increase in the value of the solution (that is, *direction of steepest ascent*) is obtained by choosing $s = j$ such that

$$(14) \qquad \beta_0 P_s = \min_j(\beta_0 P_j) < 0.$$

This establishes Theorem 3 (below) which is clearly only a restatement of the necessity condition (7) of Theorem 1.

THEOREM 3. *There exists a class of solutions with values $\bar{x}_0 > \bar{v}_0$, if, for some $j = s$,*

$$(15) \qquad y_{0s} = \beta_0 P_s < 0.$$

THEOREM 4. *There exists a class of solutions with no upper bound for values $\bar{x}_0$ if, for some s, $y_{0s} < 0$ and $y_{is} \leq 0$ for all i.*

THEOREM 5. *There exists a new basic solution with value $\bar{x}_0 > \bar{v}_0$, (obtained by introducing P_s into the basis and dropping a unique P_{j_r}), if, for some s, $y_{0s} < 0$, and, for some i, $y_{is} > 0$.*

Proofs. From (12), if $y_{is} \leq 0$ for all i, then $\bar{\theta}$ can be arbitrarily large (that is, its first component can tend to $+\infty$) and the coefficients of P_{j_i} will remain nonnegative. The value of these solutions (13) will also be arbitrarily large provided that $y_{0s} < 0$ (establishing Theorem 4). In the event that some $y_{is} > 0$, the maximum value of $\bar{\theta}$ becomes

$$(16) \qquad \max \bar{\theta} = (1/y_{rs})\bar{v}_r = \min_{y_{is}>0} (1/y_{is})\bar{v}_i > 0 \qquad (y_{rs} > 0, \ i \neq 0),$$

where the minimum of the vectors (taken in the lexicographic sense) occurs for a *unique* $i = r$ (since the rank of V is $m + 1$, no two rows of V can be proportional, whereas the assumption of nonuniqueness in (16) would imply two rows of V to be so—a contradiction). Setting $\bar{\theta} = \max \bar{\theta}$ in (12) yields a new basic solution since the coefficient of P_{j_i} vanishes. Thus a new basis has been formed consisting of $[P_0, P_{j_1}, \cdots, P_s, \cdots, P_{j_m}]$, where P_{j_r} is omitted and P_s is put in instead (Theorem 5).

The next section considers an application of the generalized simplex procedure in which the restriction $\bar{x}_j \geq 0$ is not imposed on all variables $(j = 1, 2, \cdots, n)$. This leads to a slight modification of the procedure: first, for all j for which $\bar{x}_j \geq 0$ is not required, both P_j and $-P_j$ should be considered as columns of P; secondly, if P_{j_i} is in the basis and the restriction $\bar{v}_i > 0$ is not required, then this term cannot impose a bound on $\bar{\theta}$; hence the corresponding i should be omitted from (16) in forming the minimum.

Starting with any basis $B = B^{(k)}$, one can determine a new basis $B^{(k+1)}$ by first determining the vector P_s to introduce into the basis by (14). If there exists no $\beta_0 P_s < 0$, then, by Theorem 1, the solution is optimal and $B^{(k)}$ is the *final basis*. If a P_s exists, then one forms $y_{is} = (\beta_i P_s)$ and determines the vector P_{j_r} to drop from the basis by (16) provided that there are $y_{is} > 0$. If there exist no $y_{is} > 0$, then, by Theorem 4, a class of solutions is obtained from (12) with no upper bound for $\bar{v}_0$ for arbitrary $\bar{\theta} > 0$. If P_{j_r} can be determined, then a new basis $B^{(k+1)}$ is formed dropping P_{j_r} and replacing it by P_s; by (13), the value, $\bar{v}_0$, of this solution is strictly greater for $B^{(k+1)}$ than for $B^{(k)}$ since $\bar{\theta} > 0$ is chosen by (16). Thus one may proceed iteratively starting with the assumed initial basis and forming $k = 0, 1, 2, \cdots$ until the process stops because (a) an optimal solution has been obtained, or (b) a class of solutions with no finite upper bound has been obtained.

The number of different bases is finite, not exceeding the number of combinations of n things taken m at a time; associated with each basis B is a unique basic solution $V = B^{-1}M$—hence the number of distinct basic solutions is finite; finally, no basis can be repeated by the iterative procedure because contrariwise this would imply a repetition of the value $\bar{v}_0$, whereas by (13) *the values for successive basic solutions are strictly monotonically increasing*—hence the number of iterations is finite.

The $(k + 1)$st iterate is closely related to the kth by simple transformations that constitute the computational algorithm [6;7] based on the method: thus for $i = 0, 1, \cdots, m$ $(i \neq r)$,

(17.0) $\bar{v}_i^{k+1} = \bar{v}_i^k + \eta_i \bar{v}_r^k$; $\bar{v}_i^{k+1} = \eta_r \bar{v}_r^k$

(17.1) $\beta_i^{k+1} = \beta_i^k + \eta_i \beta_r^k$; $\beta_r^{k+1} = \eta_r \beta_r^k$, where the *superscripts* $k+1$ and k are introduced here to distinguish the successive solutions and bases, and where η_i are constants,

(18) $\eta_i = -y_{is}/y_{rs} = -(\beta_i P_s)/(\beta_r P_s),$ $(i \neq r)$

$\eta_r = 1/y_{rs} = 1/(\beta_r P_s).$

Relation (17.0) is a consequence of (12) and (16); it is easy to verify that the matrix whose rows are defined by (17.1) satisfies the proper orthogonality properties for the inverse when multiplied on the right by the $(k+1)$st basis $[P_0, P_{j_1}, \cdots, P_s, \cdots, P_{j_m}]$. As a consequence of the iterative procedure we have established two theorems:

THEOREM 6. *If solutions exist and their values have a finite upper bound, then a maximizing solution exists which is a basic solution with the properties*

(19) $BV = \displaystyle\sum_{i=0}^{m} P_{j_i}\bar{b}_i = M$ $(P_{j_0} = P_0, \, \bar{v}_i > 0, \, i = 1, \cdots, m),$

$\beta_0 P_0 = 1, \; \beta_0 P_{j_i} = 0, \; \beta_0 P_j \geq 0$ $(j = 1, 2, \cdots, n),$

$\bar{v}_0 = \beta_0 M = \max \bar{x}_0,$

where β_0 is the 1st *row of B^{-1}.*

THEOREM 7. *If solutions exist and their values have no finite upper bound, then a basis B and a vector P_s exist with the properties*

(20) $BV = \displaystyle\sum_{i=0}^{m} P_{j_i}\bar{v}_i = M$ $(P_{j_0} = P_0, \bar{v}_i > 0, \, i = 1, \cdots, m),$

$\beta_0 P_s < 0, \; \beta_i P_s \leq 0,$

$\displaystyle\sum P_{j_i}[\bar{v}_i - (\beta_i P_s)\bar{\theta}] + P_s\bar{\theta} = M,$

where the latter, with $\bar{\theta} \geq 0$ arbitrary, forms a class of solutions with unbounded values (β_i is the $(i+1)$st row of B^{-1}).

Closely related to the methods of the next section, a constructive proof[b] will now be given to:

THEOREM 8. *If any solution exists, then a basic solution exists.*

For this purpose adjust M and P so that the first nonzero component of each row of M

$$(20.1) \quad \sum_{j=0}^{n} \begin{bmatrix} P_j \\ 0 \end{bmatrix} \bar{x}'_j + \sum_{i=1}^{m} \begin{bmatrix} U_i \\ 1 \end{bmatrix} \bar{x}'_{n+i} + \begin{bmatrix} \cdot \\ 1 \end{bmatrix} \bar{x}'_{n+m+i} = \begin{bmatrix} M & \cdot \\ \cdot & 1 \end{bmatrix}$$

$$(\bar{x}'_j \geq 0; \; j = 1, \cdots, n+m),$$

where $\bar{x}'_j$ has one more component than $\bar{x}_j$, and $\cdot$ represents the null vector. Noting that neither $\bar{x}'_0$ nor $\bar{x}'_{n+m+1}$ is required to be positive, one sees that an obvious basic solution is obtained using the variables $[\bar{x}'_0, \bar{x}'_{n+1}, \cdots, \bar{x}'_{n+m+1}]$. It will be noted that the hypothesis of the theorem permits construction of a solution for which

$$\bar{x}'_{n+i} = 0 \qquad\qquad (i = 1, 2, \cdots, m).$$

Indeed, for $j \leq n$ $\bar{x}'_j = (\bar{x}_j, 0) > 0$. However, it will be noted also that

$$\sum \bar{x}'_{n+i} = [\cdot \; 1]$$

so that

$$\max \bar{x}_{n+i} = [\cdot \; 1].$$

Accordingly, one may start with the basic solution for the augmented system, keeping the vectors corresponding to x'_0 and x'_{n+m+1} always in the basis[1], and use the simplex algorithm to maximize x'_{n+m+1}. Since at the maximum,

$$\bar{x}'_{n+i} = 0 \qquad\qquad (i \neq m + 1),$$

the corresponding vectors are not in the basis any longer [see (5)]. By dropping the last component of this basic solution and by dropping x'_{n+m+1}, one is left with a basic solution to the original system.

3. Minimizing a linear form. The application of the generalized simplex method to the problem of minimizing a linear form subject to linear inequality constraints consists in bordering the matrix of coefficients and constant terms of the given system by appropriate vectors. This can be done in many ways—the one selected is one which identifies the inverse of the basis as the additional components in a generalized matrix problem so that computationally no additional labor is required when the inverse is known.

The fundamental problem which we wish now to solve is to find a set $x = (x_0, x_1, \cdots, x_n)$ of real numbers satisfying the equations

$$(21) \quad x_0 + \sum_{1}^{n} a_{0j}x_j = 0, \quad \sum_{1}^{n} a_{kj}x_j = b_k \quad (b_k \geq 0; \; k = 2, 3, \cdots, m)$$

---

[1]To accomplish this omit $i = 0$ and $i = m + 1$ in (16).

such that

(22) $x_j \geq 0$

(23) $x_0 = \max,$

where without loss of generality one may assume $b_k \geq 0$. It will be noted that the subscript $k = 1$ has been omitted from (21). After some experimentation it has been found convenient[2] to augment the equations of (21) by a redundant equation formed by taking the negative sum of equations $k = 2, \cdots, m$. Thus

(24) $\displaystyle\sum_1^n a_{1j}x_j = b_1$ $\left(a_{1j} = -\displaystyle\sum_{k=2}^m a_{kj}, \; b_1 = -\displaystyle\sum_2^m b_k \right).$

Consider the generalized problem of finding a set of vector "variables" (in the sense of §2) $(\bar{x}_0, \bar{x}_1, \cdots, \bar{x}_n)$, and auxiliary variables $(\bar{x}_{n+1}, \bar{x}_{n+2}, \cdots, \bar{x}_{n+m})$ satisfying the matrix equations

(25) $\displaystyle\bar{x}_0 + \sum_1^n a_{0j}\bar{x}_j = (0, 1, 0, \cdots, 0),$

$$\bar{x}_{n+k} + \sum_1^n a_{kj}\bar{x}_j = (b_k, 0, 0, \cdots, 1, \cdots, 0)$$

$$(b_1 \leq 0; \; b_k \geq 0, \; k = 2, \cdots, m),$$

where the constant vectors have $\ell = m + 2$ components with unity in position $k + 2$, $\bar{x}_0$ and $\bar{x}_{n+1}$ are unrestricted as to sign and, for all other j,

(26) $\bar{x}_j \geq 0$ $(j = 1, \cdots, n, \; n + 2, \cdots, n + m).$

Adding equations $k = 1, \cdots, m$ in (25) and noting the definitions of a_{1j} and b_1 given in (24), one obtains

(27) $\displaystyle\sum_1^m \bar{x}_{n+k} = (0, 0, 1, 1, \cdots, 1).$

There is a close relationship between the solutions of (25) and those of (21) when $\bar{x}_{n+1} \geq 0$, for then the first components of $\bar{x}_j$, for $j = 0, \cdots, n$, satisfy (21). Indeed, by (27), if all $\bar{x}_{n+k} \geq 0$, the first component of all $\bar{x}_{n+k}$ must *vanish*; but the first component of the vector equations (25)

---

[2]Based on a recent suggestion of W. Orchard-Hays.

reduces to (21) when the terms involving x_{n+k} are dropped. This proves the sufficiency of Theorem 9 (below).

THEOREM 9. *A necessary and sufficient condition for a solution of* (21) *to exist is for a solution of* (25) *to exist with* $x_{n+1} \geq 0$.

THEOREM 10. *Maximizing solutions* (*or a class of solutions with unbounded values*) *of* (21) *are obtained from the* 1st *components of* $(\bar{x}_0, \cdots, \bar{x}_n)$ *of the corresponding type solution of* (25) *with* $\bar{x}_{n+1} \geq 0$.

Proofs. To prove necessity in Theorem 9, assume $(x_0, \cdots, x_n)$ satisfies (21); then the set

$$(28) \qquad \begin{aligned} \bar{x}_0 &= (x_0, 1, 0, \cdots, 0), \\ \bar{x}_j &= (x_j, 0, 0, \cdots, 0) \qquad\qquad (1 \leq j \leq n), \\ \bar{x}_{n+k} &= (0, 0, \cdots, 1, \cdots, 0) \geq 0 \qquad (1 \leq k \leq m) \end{aligned}$$

(where unity occurs in position $k + 2$) satisfies (25). Because of the possibility of forming solutions of the type (28) from solutions of (21), it is easy to show that 1st components of maximizing solutions of (25) must be maximizing solutions of (28) (Theorem 10).

It will be noted that (25) satisfies the requirements for the generalized simplex process: first the right side considered as a matrix is of the form

$$M = [Q, U_0, U_1, \cdots, U_m],$$

where U_k is a unit column vector with unity in component $k + 1$, and is of *rank* $m + 1$ (the number of equations); second, an *initial basic solution* is available. Indeed, set $\bar{x}_0, \bar{x}_{n+1}, \bar{x}_{n+2}, \cdots, \bar{x}_{n+m}$ equal to the corresponding constant vectors in (25) where $\bar{x}_{n+k} \geq 0$ for $k = 2, \cdots, m$ because $b_k \geq 0$.

In applying the generalized simplex procedure, however, *both* $\bar{x}_0$ *and* $\bar{x}_{n+1}$ *are not restricted to be nonnegative*. Since $\bar{x}_{n+k} \geq 0$ for $k = 2, \cdots, m$, it follows that the values of the solutions $\bar{x}_{n+1}$, of (27) have the right side of (27) as an upper bound.

To obtain a maximizing solution of (25), the *first phase* is to apply the generalized simplex procedure to maximize the variable $\bar{x}_{n+1}$ (with no restriction on $\bar{x}_0$). Since $\bar{x}_{n+1}$ has a finite upper bound, a basic solution will be produced after a finite number of changes of basis in which $\bar{x}_{n+1} \geq 0$. If during the first phase. $\bar{x}_{n+1}$ reaches a maximum less than zero, then, of course, by Theorem 9 there is *no solution* of (21) and the process terminates. If, in the iterative process, $\bar{x}_{n+1}$ becomes positive (even though not maximum), the *first phase*, which is the search for a solution of (21), is completed and the *second phase*, which is the search for an optimal solution, begins. Using the final basis of the first phase in the second phase, one seems that $\bar{x}_0$ is maximized under the additional constraint $\bar{x}_{n+1} \geq 0$.

Since the basic set of variables is taken in the initial order $(\bar{x}_0, \bar{x}_{n+1}, \cdots, \bar{x}_{n+m})$, and in the *first phase* the variable $\bar{x}_{n+1}$ is maximized, the *second row of the basis*, β_1, is used to "select" the candidate P_s to introduce into the basis in order to increase $\bar{x}_{n+1}$ [see (14)]; hence s is determined such that

(29) $$\beta_1 P_s = \min_j, (\beta_1 P_j) < 0.$$

However, in the *second phase*, since the variable to be maximized is $\bar{x}_0$ and the order of the basic set of variables is $(\bar{x}_0, \bar{x}_{n+1}, \cdots)$, then the *first row of the inverse of the basis*, β_0, is used; that is, one reverts back to (14). Application of the generalized simplex procedure in the second phase yields, after a finite number of changes in basis, either a solution with max $\bar{x}_0$ or a class of solutions of the form (12) with no upper bound for $\bar{x}_0$. By Theorem 10 the first components of $\bar{x}_0, \bar{x}_1, \cdots, \bar{x}_n$ form the corresponding solutions of the real variable problem.

The computational convenience of this setup is apparent. In the first place (as noted earlier), the right side of (21) considered as a matrix is of the form

$$M = [Q, U_0, U_1, \cdots, U_m],$$

where U_k is a unit column vector with unity in component $k+1$. In this case, by (4), the basic solution satisfies

$$V = B^{-1}M = [B^{-1}Q; B^{-1}],$$

This means (in this case) that of the $\ell = m+2$ components of the vector $\bar{v}_i$ *the last $m+1$ components of the vector variables $\bar{v}_i$* are artificial in the sense that they belong to the perturbation and not to the original problem and it is desirable to obtain them with as little effort as possible. In the event that M has the foregoing special form, no additional computational effort is required when the inverse of the basis is known. Moreover, the columns of (25) corresponding to the $m+1$ variables $(\bar{x}_0, \bar{x}_{m+1}, \cdots, \bar{x}_{n+m})$ for the *initial identity basis* $(U_0, U_1, \cdots, U_m)$, so that the inverse of the initial basis is readily available as the identity matrix to initiate the first iteration.

REFERENCES

1. *Activity analysis of production and allocation*, T.C. Koopmans, Editor, John Wiley and Sons, New York, 1951.

(a) R. Dorfman, *Application of the simplex method to a game theory problem*, Chapter XXII.

(b) G. Dantzig, *Maximization of a linear function of variables subject to linear inequalities*, Chapter XXI.

   (c) G. Dantzig, *Application of the simplex method to a transportation problem,* Chapter XXIII.

   (d) D. Gale, H. Kuhn, and A. Tucker, *Linear programming and the theory of games,* Chapter XIX.

2. A. Charnes, *Optimality and degeneracy in linear programming, Econometrica* April 1952, pages 160–170.

3. A. Charnes, W.W. Cooper, and A. Henderson, *An introduction to linear programming,* John Wiley and Sons, New York, 1953.

4. A. Charnes and C.E. Lemke, *Computational problems of linear programming,* Proceeding of the Association of Computation Machinery, Pittsburgh, 1952, pages 97-98.

5. *Contributions to Theory of Games,* H. Kuhn and A.W. Tucker, Editors, Princeton University Press; Vol. I, 1950; Vol. II 1953.

6. G. Dantzig, *Computational Algorithm of the Revised Simplex Method,* RAND P-394-1, October 1953.

7. G. Dantzig and W. Orchard-Hays, *The product form for the inverse in the simplex method,* RAND P-394-1, October 1953; also RAND P-460, November 1953.[c]

8. G. Dantzig and A. Orden, *A duality theorem based on the simplex method,* Symposium on Linear Inequalities, USAF-Hq., SCOOP Publication No. 10, dated 1 April 1952, pages 51–55.

9. A. Hoffman, M. Mannos, D. Sokolowsky, and N. Wiegmann, *Computational experience in solving linear programs,* Journal of the Society for Industrial and Applied Mathematics, Vol. 1, No. 1, September 1953, pages 17–33.

10. T.S. Motzkin, *Two consequence of the transposition theorem of linear inequalities,* Econometrica, Vol. 19, No. 2, April 1951, pages 184–185.

11. _____ *Beiträge zur Theorie der linearen Ungleichungen,* Dissertation, Basel, 1933; Azriel, Jerusalem, 1936.

12. J. von Neumann, *Discussion of a maximization problem,* Institute for Advanced Study, 1947 Manuscript.[d]

13. A. Orden, *Solution of systems of linear inequalities on a digital computer,* Proceedings of the Association of Computing Machinery, Pittsburgh, 1952, pages 91–95.

14. A.J. Hoffman, *Cycling in the simplex algorithm,* National Bureau of Standards Report, No. 2974, December 16, 1953.

RAND CORPORATION

BURROUGHS CORPORATION

PRINCETON UNIVERSITY

Part III: Large-Scale Linear Programming

From the abstract "Programming in a Linear Structure" (Chapter 3), it is evident that Dantzig immediately recognized the practical importance of being able to solve large-scale linear programming problems. Of course, his first utterances of this thought were made with reference to problems that would not qualify as large-scale problems today, but relative to the computing power of the time they certainly were. As in many fields that require computation to solve difficult problems, Dantzig was at the forefront of the effort within mathematical programming, and especially linear programming, to develop mathematical methods to cope with large-scale problems. The aim was always to solve larger problems more efficiently. The papers assembled in this part represent a portion of Dantzig's work in this important area.

The reader may ask: why should a linear programming problem be large? There are several factors that can contribute to its size. The constraints of a linear programming problem can be thought of as a system of many linear equations in many, many more variables; at least some—and typically all—of the variables are required to be nonnegative. In a model in which the constraints represent material balance conditions, each equation corresponds to some kind of "item." It could express the consumption of a resource or, alternatively, the production of a commodity in final demand. Constraints can also express relationships such as the conservation of flows. The variables represent levels of "activities" that either consume resources or produce output (or both). Because of the complexity of some processes, this description alone can lead to what some would regard as a large system of equations. When factors such as space (geographical distribution of items and activities) and time (or dynamics) are taken into consideration in the modeling, a simple (static) problem formulation can become dramatically larger than it was at first.

Fortunately, it is common for the constraints of large-scale problems to exhibit structure that can be exploited computationally, thereby serving the twin goals of solving ever large problems and doing so more efficiently than in the past. The three papers in Part III exemplify this research direction.

In the early paper "Upper Bounds, Secondary Constraints, and Block Triangularity in Linear Programming," Dantzig mentions progress in solving transportation problems by taking account of the properties of the linear system as evidence that it would be prudent to undertake research "to facilitate ready solution of larger systems." This article is probably the first of this kind in linear programming. Published in 1955, the paper gives what Dantzig calls "short cuts" for solving "an important class of problems whose matrices may be generally described as 'block triangular.'"

To appreciate the meaning of the term block triangular (matrix), one starts with the notion of a matrix, which is just a rectangular array (some would say "table") of numbers. A square matrix is one with many rows as columns. The entries along the line from the upper left to the lower right of a square matrix are said to lie on its diagonal. A square matrix is lower triangular (upper triangular) if all the entries above (below) the diagonal are zero. A block matrix is a rectangular (not necessarily square) array of matrices (rather than a rectangular array of numbers). The meaning of "block triangular matrix" should now be clear. In the paper of Chapter 6, Dantzig demonstrates how to take advantage of the structure of such problems. In some cases, this takes no more than a slight modification of the Simplex Algorithm. For others, the modifications are a bit more complicated, but a key feature of block triangularity unifies the treatment.

From the standpoint of publication date, the classic paper "Decomposition Principle for Linear Programs" by George Dantzig and Philip Wolfe is the earlier (1960) of two papers on this subject by these authors, the other being "The Decomposition Algorithm for Linear Programming," published (1961) in a different journal.[1]

In general, a decomposition technique attempts to break a large problem into smaller problems that can be solved "easily" and whose solutions can be coordinated so as to provide a solution to the overall problem. The Dantzig-Wolfe paper (presented as Chapter 7) is of precisely this type. It makes strong use of a matrix property called block angular structure that arises in many models, particularly in ones that represent a large central organization having somewhat independent suborganizations (with their own corresponding constraints) that are linked to the central organization by coupling constraints. The algorithm also makes use of a structural property of a polyhedron, namely that every such set is the sum of a polytope and a cone.

Matrix structure also plays an essential role in "Generalized Upper Bounding Techniques" by Dantzig and Van Slyke. In this case, one can think of the coefficient matrix as being block angular, as in the type of model treated by the Dantzig-Wolfe decomposition approach. In this case,

---

[1]There is a story behind what would seem to be a "duplication of effort" in this instance. Through an administrative error, the wrong version of the paper was submitted for publication. The submitting of the second paper, which is different (some believe, better), was a recourse action.

however, the subproblems all have a very simple structure in their own right.

Indeed, the system of equations through which the problem constraints of this type of model are specified consists of M coupling equations followed by L other equations with the property that every problem variable appears in at most one of these L equations and if it appears there, then the coefficient of that variable is positive. All L of the corresponding right-hand side constants are also positive. After some scaling of the equations and variables, one obtains an equivalent system of equations, in which all the nonzero parameters in the last L equations are $+1$. When the equations and the variables are arranged so that the $+1$s in one of these last L equations are grouped together, and the $+1$s of any subsequent row are in columns farther to the right, one obtains a kind of block angular matrix with L very special one-rowed blocks. Because this particular block structure comes up in many large-scale models relating to a broad range of applications (e.g., distribution, production scheduling, and optimal control), it is of interest to have an efficient general algorithm for solving instances of this problem class.

The Simplex Algorithm confines its attention to basic solutions; it searches for an optimal basis. In this paper, Dantzig and Van Slyke work out a way to construct what are called "compact" working bases of order M rather than $M + L$ as would normally be done in this case. This, of course, is especially advantageous when M is much smaller than L.

Chapter 6

UPPER BOUNDS, SECONDARY CONSTRAINTS, AND BLOCK
TRIANGULARITY IN LINEAR PROGRAMMING

By George B. Dantzig

Short-cut computational methods are developed for solving systems whose matrices may be generally described as block triangular.

With the growing awareness of the potentialities of the linear programming approach to both dynamic and static problems in industry, of the economy, and of the military, the main obstacle toward full application is the inability of current computational methods to cope with the magnitude of the technological matrices for even the simplest situations. However, in certain cases, such as the now classical Hitchcock-Koopmans transportation model, it has been possible to solve the linear inequality system in spite of size because of simple properties of the system [1c]. This suggests that considerable research be undertaken to exploit certain special matrix structures in order to facilitate ready solution of larger systems.

Indeed, recent computational experience has made it clear that standard techniques such as the simplex algorithm, which have been used to solve successfully general systems involving one hundred equations (in any reasonable number of nonnegative unknowns), are too tedious and lengthy to be practical for extensions much beyond this figure.[a] Our purpose here will be to develop short-cut computational methods for solving an important class of systems whose matrices may be generally described as "block triangular." Consider a system of equations

(1)
$$x_0 + \sum_{j=1}^{n} a_{0j}x_j = 0, \quad x_j \geq 0 \qquad (j = 1, 2, \cdots, n),$$
$$\sum_{j=1}^{n} a_{ij}x_j = b_i \qquad (i = 1, 2, \cdots, m),$$

where it is desired to obtain values of x_j such that *the form $\sum a_{0j}x_j$ is to be minimized* (or, what is the same thing, to *maximize the variable x_0*).

1. VARIABLES WITH UPPER BOUNDS

The size of the matrix associated with such a linear programming problem may become uncomfortably large when, in addition to (1), many (or all) variables of the initial set have upper bounds. Thus, if each variable satisfies $0 \leq x_j \leq \alpha_j$, it is customary to add an additional variable, say x'_j, and a new equation

$$(2) \qquad x_j + x'_j = \alpha_j \qquad\qquad (x_j \geq 0, \, x'_j \geq 0)$$

to take care of each such restriction. To illustrate, by way of example, a linear programming problem of the transportation type involving m destinations and n origins has a matrix involving $m+n$ rows and $m \cdot n$ variables x_{ij} associated with $m \cdot n$ possible routes joining origins with destinations. Suppose now there is a *capacity limitation* r_{ij} on a route so that in addition to the original system of equations and linear inequalities, $0 \leq x_{ij}$, one must impose $m \cdot n$ additional restraints

$$x_{ij} + x'_{ij} = r_{ij} \qquad\qquad (x_{ij} \geq 0, \, x'_{ij} \geq 0).$$

It is clear now the original system has been expanded to $(mn + m + n)$ rows and $2m \cdot n$ variables. Not only has the system become enormously enlarged but it is not clear what has happened to that wonderful triangularity property for transportation type models of a basis which permits ease of hand computation. We shall refer to the *original system* plus these upper bound restrictions as the *enlarged system*. The purpose of this section is to show that the upper-bound restraints, which is a special case of block triangularity (see Section 2), may be provided for by applying the simplex algorithm [1b], [3], [8a], to the *original system* with due care that the range of values of a variable appearing in a basic solution stays within its upper and lower bounds.[1] In this paper it will be assumed that the reader is familiar with this method. By way of review, a basic solution to (1) is defined as a solution in which $n - m$ variables x_j are set equal to zero and the remainder $x_0, x_{j_1}, \cdots, x_{j_m}$ satisfy (1) such that $x_{j_i} \geq 0$ and

---

[1] A problem of Optimum Scheduling of Projects on Punch Card Equipment considered by Clifford Shaw of RAND was characterized by many variables with fixed upper bounds. (These represented the maximum number of hours that could be assigned to a project in a work period.) The method described here was developed to provide a short-cut computing routine and was first reported by Clifford Shaw and the author before the joint RAND-U.C.L.A Seminar on Industrial Scheduling in the winter of 1952.

For other applications of the method described above see A. Charnes and C. Lemke [4].

Quite often in linear programming problems it is possible to obtain a starting basis for an enlarged system from a basis of a smaller system. A typical case occurs when a feasible basis for the enlarged system exists which differs from a feasible basis for the original system by having additional rows and corresponding *unit vector columns*. An example of this technique for bounded variables is found in Charnes [2].

the submatrix $B = [P_0, P_{j_1}, \cdots, P_{j_m}]$ formed from the columns P_{j_i} of coefficients of these variables is nonsingular. In each iteration of the simplex algorithm a new basic solution is formed in which one of the basic variables x_{j_r} is replaced by a non-basic variable x_s and one of [the] columns P_{j_r} of the "basis" B is replaced by P_s.

We shall assume that one starts out with a basic solution to the original system which does not violate conditions (2). It is possible of course that such a solution may not exist or may be difficult to determine. However, if we begin with phase I of the simplex process where the problem is to determine a basic feasible solution, we will be in the position of having a basic feasible solution to a related problem which satisfies the relations $x_j \leq \alpha_j$.

The regular simplex rules for shifting from one basic solution of the original system (1) to the next apply *unless* the value of a variable in the basic set changes from $x_j \leq \alpha_j$ to a new value $x_j + \theta y_j > \alpha_j$ or $x_s = \theta > \alpha_s$. Then it is necessary to reduce the permissible range of θ so that $x_j + \theta y_j \leq \alpha_j$ and $x_s = \theta \leq \alpha_s$ in order to preserve feasibility in system (2). Let $\theta = \theta_0$ be the largest value for which all relations $0 \leq x_j \leq \alpha_j$ are satisfied and suppose for this critical value, θ_0, one of the variables x_t in the basic set $x_{j_1}, x_{j_2}, \cdots, x_{j_m}$ (or the variable x_s being introduced into the basic set) attains its upper bound α_t.

Consider now a new (equivalent) linear programming problem, obtained from the original problem by replacing x_t by $\alpha_t - x_t'$. Letting P_j denote the column of coefficients associated with x_j, the effect is to replace

(a) the constant vector Q by $Q - \alpha_t P_t$;

(b) the vector P_t by $-P_t$;

(c) the variable x_t by x_t';

(d) column P_t in the basis by P_s unless $t = s$ (in which case basis vectors are unchanged); and

(e) to substitute the new basic variables x_j^* according to

$$
\begin{aligned}
x_{j_i}^* &= x_{j_i} - \theta_0 y_{j_i}, && (j_i \neq t) \\
x_s^* &= \theta_0, && (s \neq t)
\end{aligned}
$$

(3)

where $\theta = \theta_0$ is the critical value of θ. The basic solution of the equivalent programming problem has improved value for the minimizing form (excluding the possibility of degeneracy).

We are now in a position to iterate using the regular simplex algorithm or the modified one as appropriate. It may be of passing interest to note that the row vector β ("pricing vector") used to determine which vector P_j to introduce into a basis B in subsequent iterations is unaffected whether one (or several columns) of the columns P_{j_i} of the basis are replaced by $-P_{j_i}$ since β is defined so that $\beta B = \beta[P_0, P_{j_1}, P_{j_2}, \cdots, P_{j_m}] = [1, 0, \cdots, 0]$. The vector to be introduced into the basis is determined by Min $\beta P_j < 0$ or, if x_j has been replaced by x_j' and P_j' is not in the basis, by Min $\beta(-P_j) < 0$.

This says that *a variable x_j at its upper bound may be decreased from its upper bound with improvement in the value of the solution providing the negative of the usual simplex criterion is satisfied.*[b]

There is a close relation between the simplex algorithm for the original problem (as modified above for variables with upper bounds) and the one which would be obtained if one were to apply directly the regular simplex procedure to the enlarged problem. The procedure just described was first obtained by noting that when the simplex procedure is applied to the enlarged problem certain computational simplifications could be obtained because the vector associated with x_j' is a unit vector.

2. BLOCK TRIANGULARITY (GENERAL CASE)

By "block" triangular[2] we mean that if one partitions the matrix of coefficients of the technology matrix into submatrices, the submatrices (or blocks) considered as elements form a *triangular system,*

$$(4) \qquad \begin{bmatrix} A_{11} & & & \\ A_{21} & A_{22} & & \\ & & \ddots & \\ A_{T1} & A_{T2} & \cdots & A_{TT} \end{bmatrix}.$$

For example, von Neumann, [9], in considering a constantly expanding economy, developed a linear dynamic model whose matrix of coefficients may be written in the form (5)

$$(5) \qquad \begin{bmatrix} A & & & & \\ -B & A & & & \\ & -B & A & & \\ & & -B & \ddots & \\ & & & \ddots & \ddots \\ & & & & -B & A \end{bmatrix},$$

where A is the submatrix of coefficients of activities initiated in period t, and B is the submatrix of *output* coefficients of these activities in the following period. When activities extend over many time periods, it is not difficult to show that they can be subdivided into a set of interlocked subactivities over time, whose input occurs at time t and output occurs at time $t + 1$. Moreover, it is not necessary that the input-output blocks A, B be identical from one time period to the next. Because of the general

---

[2] A term suggested by Walter Jacobs.

applicability of such a model, the author in an earlier paper suggests that it is worthwhile to give special attention to the solution of linear programming problems where the matrices are of this form, [1a]. In this paper, however, we shall consider the partitioned form (4) as standard; primarily because, cast in this form, most models will involve fewer equations and variables and because the essential feature of block triangularity is preserved.

Now the main obstacle toward the full application of standard linear programming techniques to dynamic systems is the magnitude of the matrix even for the simplest situations. For example, a trivial 15-activity—7-item static model, when set up as a 12-period dynamic model, would become a 180-activity by 84-item system, which is considered a large problem for application of the standard simplex method. A fancy model involving, say, 200 activities and 100 items for a static case would become a 2000×1000 matrix if recast as a 10-period model. It is clear that dynamic models must be treated with special tools if any progress is to be made toward solutions of these systems.

From a computational point of view, there are a number of observed characteristics of the dynamic models which are often true for static models as well. These are:

(1) The matrix (or its transpose) can be arranged in triangular form (4).

(2) Most submatrices A_{ij} are either zero matrices or composed of elements most of which are zero.[c]

(3) A basis for the simplex method is often block triangular with its diagonal submatrices square and nonsingular (referred to as a "square block triangular" basis).

(4) For dynamic models similar type activities are likely to persist in the basis for several periods.

To illustrate, consider a dynamic version of the Leontief model in which (a) alternative activities are permitted (a simple case would be where steel can be obtained from direct production or storage); (b) inputs to an activity for production in the tth time period may occur in the same or earlier time periods. It can be shown in this model that (a) a basic solution will have exactly m activities in each time period (where m = number of time dependent equations), (b) each shift in basis will bring in a substitute activity in the same time period, and (c) optimization can be carried out as a sequence of one-period optimization problems; i.e., the optimum choice of activities (but not their amounts) can be determined for the first time period (independent of the later periods); this permits a determination for the second time period (independent of the later periods), etc. [8c].

When flow models are replaced with more complex models which include initial inventories, capacities, and the building of new capacities, the ideal structure of a basis (see third characteristic above) no longer holds. However, tests (carried on since 1950) on a number of cases indicate that bases while often *not square block triangular in the sense above, could be made so by changing relatively few columns in the basis* (e.g., one or two activities in small models). This characteristic of *near-square block* triangularity of the basis, i.e., with nonsingular square submatrices down the diagonal, is, of course, computationally convenient and this paper will be concerned with ways to exploit it.

There appears, however, to be a strong alternative possibility which may be built around bases whose nonzero elements either cluster above or below the main diagonal. An example of this approach is found in the Production Smoothing Problem proposed by Jacobs [6]. Selmer Johnson and the author have been able to show that the basis in that problem either does not extend beyond the main diagonal or if it does, it does so by not more than one column. This will be the subject of another paper.[d] *These considerations point up the need for further research on the structure of a basis whose columns are drawn from a block triangular matrix.*[3]

The remainder of this section will be concerned with a technique which should reduce materially the size of the computation job when the given model satisfies the first three empirical properties. Extensions can be introduced to take advantage of property (4) also, but these are beyond the scope of the present paper.

Let the system (4) be the form of the matrix of coefficients. Let A_{tt} be a matrix with n_t columns and m_t rows ($t = 0, 1, \cdots, T$). Column vectors P_j which have elements in common with A_{tt}, as well as their corresponding variables, will be considered as "belonging to" the tth period. Similarly, the m_t equations which have coefficients in common with A_{tt} are considered as belonging to the tth period.

We wish to apply the simplex algorithm and will do so for each iteration through the use of an *artificial basis* $\bar{B}$ and a *true basis* B. The artificial basis will be square block triangular. As many columns as possible of $\bar{B}$ will be made the same as B.[4]

---

[3]Recently H. Markowitz of RAND has pointed out that inverses for bases composed largely of zero elements (randomly distributed or in blocks) may be avoided. Instead, he conjectures, the direct solution of the associated system of equations for each iteration (as is done in the transportation model, [1c]) can be done at a fraction of the usual computational effort for a general system of this size. He is currently developing an electronic computer code to test this method out on large systems.

[4]The use of true and artificial bases has many important applications. Some of these will be considered in subsequent papers. In general the purpose of the artificial basis is to have a basis in a desirable form for computations; the purpose of the *side conditions* is to transform the computations based on an artificial basis to their correct value in terms of the true basis. Application of such a device calls for some judgment, since it is clear that if the number of side conditions becomes too large, the method will have no advantage over a standard solution.

For our purposes it is not strictly necessary that these artificial vectors be part of the original set of vectors P_j; they could (if convenient) be any vectors (such as the artificial unit vectors found in the regular simplex process).

It is assumed that expressions are known which express any column P_α of $\bar{B}$ as a linear combination of the columns P_{j_i} of B.

(6) $$P_\alpha = \sum_{i=0}^m \eta_{i\alpha} P_{j_i} \qquad (P_{j_0} \equiv P_0),$$

so that we may write

(7) $$\bar{B} = B \cdot \eta$$

where η is a matrix whose αth column has coefficients $\eta_{i\alpha}$. If $\bar{B}$ has many columns in common with B, it is clear that η will be composed largely of unit vectors so that the *essential part* of η consists of those columns which give the representations in terms of P_{j_i} of those vectors P_{α_i} in $\bar{B}$ and *not* in B (called artificial vectors) in terms of P_{j_i}.

In the standard application of the revised simplex algorithm [8a], it is customary to maintain the inverse of the basis (or the inverse in product form [5]) in order to solve readily the system of equations

(8) $$\beta B = [1, 0, \cdots, 0], \text{ and}$$

(9) $$BY = P_s$$

where β is the *price vector*[5] and Y is the representation of the vector entering the next basis in terms of the vectors of the preceding basis. This we replace by

(10) $$\beta \bar{B} = [1, 0, \cdots, 0]\eta, \text{ and}$$

(11) $$\bar{B}\bar{Y} = P_s; \qquad Y = \eta \cdot \bar{Y}.$$

In order to solve readily systems involving $\bar{B}$ as matrix, it is only necessary to maintain the inverses of the smaller nonsingular diagonal matrices of $\bar{B}$ (or their inverses in product form) which we denote by $\bar{B}_{00}, \bar{B}_{11}, \cdots$. For example, in solving (11) the inverse of $\bar{B}_{00}$, when multiplied by the first m_0 components of the right-hand row vector will give the first m_0 components of $\bar{Y}$. Because of triangularity, these values can be substituted into equations associated with the second time period and the next m_1 components of $\bar{Y}$ obtained through application of the inverse of $\bar{B}_{11}$, etc.

Except for elements associated with the inverses of the diagonal blocks (either in direct or product form), it will be noted that all other operations involve scalar products with parts of columns of $\bar{B}$ in their original form. These often are entirely null or composed largely of zero elements. This

---

[5]This definition of β applies only to phase II of the simplex procedure; for phase I, replace the right-hand side by $[0, 1, 0, \cdots, 0]$ (see [8a]), where it is assumed that the first column of the basis is P_0 corresponding to the variable x_0 in [1]. In phase I, however, the second column corresponds to the dummy variable x_{m+1} whose value is being maximized.

advantage is to be contrasted with the case where the entire artificial basis $\bar{B}^{-1}$ (or B^{-1}) is maintained.

Each change in true basis replaces a vector P_{j_r} by P_s. The representation of P_{j_r} in terms of the vectors of the next basis is given by

$$(12) \qquad\qquad P_{j_r} = \sum_{i \neq r} \eta_{ij_r} P_{j_i} + \eta_{rj_r} P_s$$

where η_{ij_r} is given in terms of the components of y_i of Y by

$$(13) \qquad\qquad \eta_{ij_r} = -y_i/y_r, \qquad \eta_{rj_r} = 1/y_r \qquad\qquad (i \neq r).$$

By substituting the expression for P_{j_r} in (6), vectors P_α can be re-expressed in terms of the next basis. This constitutes the *transformation of* η from one cycle to the next. If P_{j_r} is in $\bar{B}$ also, then in the next cycle P_{j_r} will be an artificial vector, and expression (12) forms part of the essential part of η for the next cycle. If P_{j_r} is not in $\bar{B}$, its expression (12) in terms of the true basis is no longer of any interest and may be thrown away. In the former case the size of η (where by "size" is meant the number of essential columns) has increased. In the latter it has remained the same. On the other hand if P_s was artificial in $\bar{B}$ in the previous cycle and introduced into B in the next, then the size of η would decrease.

We next consider the possibility of modifying the definition of $\bar{B}$ in order to decrease the number of essential columns in η. This is important because unless the size of η can be kept relatively low, the transformations of η are the same as the transformations on the columns of B^{-1} in the standard simplex algorithm and no advantage would accrue by using this approach. Let P_β be a column of B, not in $\bar{B}$, belonging to period t, and suppose there are artificial vectors also belonging to this period. We form the representation of the *partitioned part* of P_β belonging to period t in terms of the columns of $\bar{B}_{tt}$, thus

$$(14) \qquad\qquad P_\beta^{(t)} = \bar{B}_{tt} \bar{Y}^{(t)}$$

where those components of a vector associated with period t are denoted by a *superscript* (t). Consider now those components of $\bar{Y}^{(t)}$, corresponding to artificial column vectors P_α. If any of these components are *nonzero*, then it is clear that P_β can replace the corresponding P_α in $\bar{B}$ and thus reduce the size of the essential part of η; moreover, $\bar{Y}^{(t)}$ may be used as in the regular simplex routine to obtain the corrected inverse of $\bar{B}_{tt}^{-1}$ (in direct or product form).

It will be noted that, because of block triangularity of the original matrix, the first step in the representation of P_s in terms of columns of B by (11) gives the representation of $P_s^{(t)}$ in terms of the columns of $\bar{B}_{tt}$ (where P_s belongs to period t). This, however, is the relation required by (14) and may be used to determine if P_s can replace an artificial vector in $\bar{B}$. Hence, in this case it is not necessary to make a separate calculation to determine whether P_β can replace P_α in $\bar{B}$. Moreover, by saving the relations that express $P_s^{(t)}$ in terms of the columns of $\bar{B}_{tt}$ (and transforming them, should the columns of $\bar{B}_{tt}$ change) it is possible to have all relations (14) readily available. There are, of course, as many such relations as there are essential columns in η; however, the work involved in maintaining these relations is a fraction of that required for η.

3. SECONDARY CONSTRAINTS

Here, as in the special case of variables with upper bounds, we suppose in addition to (1) that the variables must satisfy a "secondary" system of constraints of the form

$$(15) \qquad \sum_{j=1}^{n} a_{kj} x_j + x_{n+k} = b_k \qquad (k = 1, 2, \cdots, m'; \; x_{n+k} \geq 0).$$

Mathematically, these latter restrictions differ in no way from the former, but from the physical point of view it is anticipated that only a small subset of the restrictions (15) will be *active* in an optimal solution. By a constraint being "active" is meant that its "slack" variable $x_{n+k} = 0$.

To illustrate: In a gasoline blending problem there may be a number of equations controlling the performance characteristics of a blend, for example its viscosity, specific gravity, etc. It is expected that only one or two of these characteristics are limiting in a given run. A second related example would be *capacity restraints* on various processes within the refinery, for example, the capacity of a thermal cracking unit, the storage capacity of tanks, etc. Again it may be expected that *some* of these restraints will be active, but *not many* will be active for any particular problem on any particular iteration of the simplex process.

To take advantage of the expected small number of active secondary constraints, we shall make use (as in Section 2) of a *true basis* and of an *artificial square block triangular basis* in executing the simplex algorithm.

For this problem the artificial basis will have a special form; its columns will consist of vectors $P_0, P_{\beta_1}, P_{\beta_2}, \cdots, P_{\beta_m}; P_{n+1}, P_{n+2}, \cdots, P_{n+m'}$ where $1 \leq \beta_i \leq n$. The vectors P_{n+i} are obviously unit vectors. $\bar{B}$ may be partitioned into the form

$$(16) \qquad \bar{B} = \begin{bmatrix} \bar{B}^{(1)} & \\ \bar{B}^{(2)} & I_{m'} \end{bmatrix},$$

where $\bar{B}^{(1)}$ are the components associated with system (1), $\bar{B}^{(2)}$ with system (15), and $I_{m'}$ is an $m' \times m'$ identity matrix. Since (16) is in "square block" triangular form, it is clear that *it is only necessary to know the inverse of the smaller $m \times m$ submatrix $\bar{B}^{(1)}$ (or its equivalent) to determine Y or β through η.*

Let the true basis consist of vectors P_0, P_{j_1}, $\cdots$, $P_{j+m'}$. It will be supposed that many of the vectors of the artificial basis are the same as those in the true one. However, some of the unit vectors in the artificial basis may not be found in the true basis. In this case, the side conditions (6) are simply the representations of these artificial unit vectors in terms of the vectors of the true basis. With these observations one may now proceed to apply the algorithm of Section 2 to the special case of secondary constraints.

The method of additional restraints has been found to be a powerful tool in solving many large-scale systems, for example the recent successful solution of a 49-city traveling salesman problem. Indeed, in some problems it is easier to find a point p where a function assumes a minimum for a region R^* than for a smaller required region R in R^*. If, by good luck, the minimum value of the function is assumed at a point p of R^* which is also a point of R, then it is obvious that this point is also the required optimum solution for R.

To illustrate, suppose an optimum solution is obtained for (1) without regard to whether the slack variables x_{n+i} defined by the secondary constraint conditions (15) are nonnegative or not. If by luck all $x_{n+i} \geq 0$ then the solution is an optimal solution for (1) and (15) combined. Consider now a situation where only a few of the secondary constraints are expected to be active, i.e., where the solution may be expected to have some but only a few negative values. In this case it appears reasonable to take this optimum solution of (1) as a good starting point from which to begin a corrective procedure to clean up the negative values of the variables in order to obtain an optimum solution for (1) and (15) combined. This approach can be formalized as follows:

(a) Find an optimum basic solution $(x_0, x_{j_1}, x_{j_2}, \cdots, x_{j_m})$ to the smaller system (1) without regard to (15). (The fact that the smaller system is being solved first can be an important computational advantage in practice over method which work always with the entire system.)

(b) Determine the values of the slack variables by substitution in (15) and regard $[P_0, P_{j_1}, \cdots, P_{j_m}; P_{n+1}, \cdots, P_{n+m}]$ as a starting basis for the combined system (1) and (15). If $x_{n+i} \geq 0$ for the solution associated with this basis, then this is an optimal solution for the combined system and this terminates the algorithm. If not, it is clear that the "price vector" β for this basis satisfies $\beta P_j \geq 0$ for $j = 1, 2, \cdots n, n+1, , \cdots, n+m'$. Indeed, β clearly has zero components for those corresponding to equations of system (15) while those corresponding to system (1) are the same as the optimal β for the smaller system.

(c) This basis can be used to initiate the *dual simplex algorithm* of Lemke, as this method requires that all $\beta P_j \geq 0$. See [7], [8b]. Computationally, the latter procedure resembles the simplex algorithm in that it shifts from one basis to the next and differs only in the selection criteria for determining the column to drop and to introduce into the next basis. It does not require that x_{j_i} remain nonnegative from one iteration to the next.

(d) Although the initial basis B is block triangular, the subsequent basis will not be. However, by introducing an artificial basis as given in (16) as well as side conditions in order to express the artificial unit vectors in terms of the vectors of the true basis, the computational advantages discussed in Section 2 of the near block triangularity of B can also be realized.

Finally, it should be remarked that if it is known in advance that a certain variable x in a general linear programming problem must be a basic variable in the optimum solution, this variable can be eliminated from all but one of the equations and from the objective function. Thus resulting smaller system can then be optimized and the values of this solution substituted in the remaining equation (which is treated like a secondary constraint equation) to determine the value [of] x. To illustrate, in a dynamic economic model it is highly likely that the stock production activities will be operating in all time periods. In a recent example H. M. Wagner[6] has shown that it is convenient to eliminate the corresponding variables from all but one equation each and to optimize the remaining system. In a few examples tested by this approach it turned out to be a trivial matter to make proper adjustments in order to correct the negative stock production activities even without recourse to the dual simplex algorithm recommended earlier.

The RAND Corporation

REFERENCES

[1] *Activity Analysis of Production and Allocation*, T. C. Koopmans, Editor, John Wiley and Sons, 1951.

    (a) DANTZIG, GEORGE B., "Programming of Interdependent Activities," Chapter II, p. 31.

    (b) _____, "Maximization of Linear Function of Variables Subject to Linear Inequalities," Chapter XXI, p. 339.

    (c) _____, "Application of the Simplex Method to a Transportation Problem," Chapter XXIII, p. 359.

[2] CHARNES, A., "Optimality and Degeneracy in Linear Programming," *Econometrica*, April 1952, p. 160–70.

[3] CHARNES, A., W. W. COOPER, AND A. HENDERSON, *An Introduction to Linear Programming*; New York, John Wiley and Sons, Inc., 1953; London, Chapman and Hall, Ltd.

---

[6]Unpublished.

[4] CHARNES, A., AND C. E. LEMKE, "Computational Theory of Linear Programming: I. The 'Bounded Variables' Problem," *O.N.R. Research Memorandum No. 10,* Carnegie Institute of Technology, January 7, 1954.

[5] DANTZIG, G. B., WM. ORCHARD-HAYS, "The Product Form for the Inverse in the Simplex Method," *Mathematical Tables and Other Aids to Computation,* VIII, No. 46, April, 1954.

[6] HOFFMAN, A., AND W. JACOBS, "Smooth Patterns of Production," *National Bureau of Standards Report* (no date).[e]

[7] LEMKE, CARLTON E., "The Dual Method of Solving Linear Programming Problem," *Naval Research Logistics Quarterly,* Vol. I, No. 1, March, 1954, p. 36.

[8] Notes on Linear Programming, The RAND Corporation, Santa Monica, California.

  (a) DANTZIG, G. B., A. ORDEN, AND P. WOLFE, *The Generalized Simplex Method for Minimizing a Linear Form under Linear Restraints,* The RAND Corporation, Research Memorandum RM-1264, 5 April 1954.

  (b) DANTZIG, G. B., *The Dual Simplex Algorithm,* The RAND Corporation, RM-1270, 3 July 1954.

  (c) _____, *Optimal Solution of a Dynamic Leontief Model with Substitution,* Research Memorandum RM-1281, 15 June 1954.

[9] VON NEUMANN, J. "A Model of General Economic Equilibrium," *The Review of Economic Studies,* 1945–46 Vol. XIII (1). *Ergebnisse eines mathematischen Kolloquiums* 8 (1937) 73-83.

Chapter 7

DECOMPOSITION PRINCIPLE FOR LINEAR PROGRAMS[1]

George B. Dantzig and Philip Wolfe

The Rand Corporation, Santa Monica, California

A technique is presented for the decomposition of a linear program that permits the problem to be solved by alternate solutions of linear sub-programs representing its several parts and a coordinating program that is obtained from the parts by linear transformations. The coordinating program generates at each cycle new objective forms for each part, and each part generates in turn (from its optimal basic feasible solutions) new activities (columns) for the interconnecting program. Viewed as an instance of a 'generalized programming problem' whose columns are drawn freely from given convex sets, such a problem can be studied by an appropriate generalization of the duality theorem for linear programming, which permits a sharp distinction to be made between those constraints that pertain only to a part of the problem and those that connect its parts. This leads to a generalization of the Simplex Algorithm, for which the decomposition procedure becomes a special case. Besides holding promise for the efficient computation of large-scale systems, the principle yields a certain rationale for the 'decentralized decision process' in the theory of the firm. Formally the prices generated by the coordinating program cause the manager of each part to look for a 'pure' sub-program analogue of pure strategy in game theory, which he proposes to the coordinator as best he can do. The coordinator finds the optimum 'mix' of pure sub-programs (using new proposals and earlier ones) consistent with over-all demands and supply, and thereby generates new prices that again generates new proposals by each of the parts, etc. The iterative process is finite.

---

[1] The material of this paper appeared originally under the same title as Rand Corporation P-1544, November 10, 1958, and was presented at the Rand Symposium on Mathematical Programming in March 1959. It was also presented before the American Mathematical Society, January 20, 1959, in Philadelphia, Pennsylvania (see *Am. Math. Society Notices,* Abstract No. 553–559, Vol. 5, No. 7, Issue No. 35, December, 1958, p. 811).

A vector P interconnecting two parts of a program is viewed as obtained by linear transformations from linear sub-programs L and L' (more generally as drawn from convexes[a]) defining the parts. P is represented as a convex combination of a finite set of possible P from each part and equated to a similar representation for the other—the selected vectors correspond to extreme points and certain homogeneous solutions of the sub-programs. Starting with some admissible m-component vector $P = P^0$, the total vectors (points) used in the two representations can be reduced to $m + 2$. This forms a basis whose Lagrange (simplex) multipliers π relative to a form being extremized are used to test optimality or for generating a better interconnecting vector. This is done by solving two independent linear programs for points in L and L' that minimize two linear forms dependent on π.

The entire procedure may be simulated as a *decentralized decision* process. Each independent part initially offers a possible bill of goods (a vector of outputs while supporting inputs including outside costs) to a central coordinating agency. As a set these are mutually feasible with each other and the given resources and demands from outside the system. The coordinator works out a system of 'prices' for paying for each component of the vector plus a special subsidy for each part that just balances the cost. A bonus or some other form of award is then offered the manager of each part if he can offer, based on these prices, a new feasible program for his part with lower cost *without regard to whether it is feasible for any other part.* The coordinator, however, combines these new offers with the set of earlier offers so as to preserve mutual feasibility and consistency with exogenous demand and supply and to minimize cost. Using the improved over-all solution he generates a revised set of prices, subsidies, and new offers. *The essential idea is that old offers are never forgotten by the central agency* (unless using "current" prices they are unprofitable); the former are mixed with the new offers to form new prices.

Computationally if P is an m-component vector and L is defined by k equations in n nonnegative variables and L' by k' equations in n' nonnegative variables, then each major simplex cycle consists in solving two $k \times n$ and $k' \times n'$ auxiliary linear programs after $m(m + n + n')$ multiplications to set up π and adjust the solution. The iterative procedure is finite. The principle is applied to decompose typical structures into several parts.[b]

Credit is due to Ford and Fulkerson for their proposal for solving multicommodity network problems as it served to inspire the present development.[2]

---

[2]L.R. Ford, Jr., and D.R. Fulkerson, "A Suggested Computation for Maximal Multicommodity Network Flow." *Management Sci.* 5, 97 (1958).

THE GENERAL PRINCIPLE

Suppose we have a linear program expressed in vector notation in the form

$$(1) \qquad P_0 x_0 + P_1 x_1 + \cdots + P_n x_n = Q$$

where P_j, Q are given vectors and the problem is to choose $\text{Max}\, x_0$ and $x_j \geq 0$ for $j = 1, 2, \cdots, n$. Ordinarily the objective form of a linear-programming problem is written as

$$(2) \qquad c_1 x_1 + c_2 x_2 + \cdots + c_n x_n = z(\text{Min}),$$

which may be rewritten

$$(3) \qquad x_0 + c_1 x_1 + \cdots + c_n x_n = 0,$$

where x_0 is to be maximized. In this case P_0 is a unit vector.[c]

Let us now consider the general problem of solving the linear-programming problem of finding vectors $X \geq 0$, $Y \geq 0$ and $\text{Max}\, x_0$ satisfying

$$(4) \qquad P_0 x_0 + \bar{A}_1 X + \bar{A}_2 Y = \bar{b}$$

subject to linear programs L and L' defined by

$$(5) \qquad \begin{aligned} L: & \quad A_1 X = b_1, & (X \geq 0) \\ L': & \quad A_2 Y = b_2, & (Y \geq 0) \end{aligned}$$

where A_i, $\bar{A}_i$ are matrices, P_0, $\bar{b}$, b_i are vectors and $\bar{b}$ has m components.[3] We shall show later how multistage models such as dynamic models with discrete time periods, angular systems, multistage and block-triangular models can be readily decomposed into several parts each exhibiting the above structure.

Let us define the vectors S and T corresponding to X and Y by the linear transformations

$$(6) \qquad S = \bar{A}_1 X \quad \text{for arbitrary} \quad X \geq 0 \quad \text{and} \quad A_1 X = b_1;$$

$$(7) \qquad T = \bar{A}_2 Y \quad \text{for arbitrary} \quad Y \geq 0 \quad \text{and} \quad A_2 X = b_2.$$

Starting Assumption I: Let us suppose first that a starting feasible solution is at hand: $X = X_0$, $Y = Y_0$, $x_0 = x_0^0$; that is to say one which satisfies all the constraints (4) and (5) except x_0 is not maximal. Such a

---

[3]We assume for convenience that $b_1 \neq 0$, $b_2 \neq 0$. If $b_i = 0$ the restriction requiring convex combinations of solutions of L and L' in the development that follows [second equation of (9) or (12)].

solution could have been generated for example, by the Phase I procedure of linear programming using artificial variables. If so the methods we are about to discuss would be applied to Phase I first.

Let $S_0 = \bar{A}_1 X_0$ and $T_0 = \bar{A}_2 Y_0$ so that

$$(8) \qquad P_0 x_0^0 + S_0 + T_0 = \bar{b}.$$

Starting Assumption II: We shall suppose further that S_0 has been represented with weights $\lambda_i = \bar{\lambda}_i$ in the form

$$(9) \qquad \begin{aligned} S_0 &= S_1 \bar{\lambda}_1 + S_2 \bar{\lambda}_2 + \cdots + S_k \bar{\lambda}_k, & (\bar{\lambda}_i \geq 0) \\ 1 &= \delta_1 \bar{\lambda}_1 + \delta_2 \bar{\lambda}_2 + \cdots + \delta_k \bar{\lambda}_k, \end{aligned}$$

where each

$$(10) \qquad S_i = \bar{A}_1 X_i, \qquad\qquad (X_i \geq 0)$$

where X_i is either an extreme point or homogeneous solution [see (11)] of L and δ_i is defined by [d]

$$(11) \qquad \left. \begin{matrix} \delta_i = 1 \\ \delta_i = 0 \end{matrix} \right\} \text{ if } X_i \geq 0 \text{ is } \left\{ \begin{matrix} \text{extreme point} \\ \text{homogeneous} \end{matrix} \right\} \text{ solution of } \left\{ \begin{matrix} A_1 X_i = b_1 \\ A_1 X_i = 0 \end{matrix} \right\}.$$

Similarly T_0 has been represented with weights $\mu_i = \bar{\mu}_i$ in the form

$$(12) \qquad \begin{aligned} T_0 &= T_1 \bar{\mu}_1 + T_2 \bar{\mu}_2 + \cdots + T_l \bar{\mu}_l, & (\bar{\mu}_i \geq 0) \\ 1 &= \delta_1' \bar{\mu}_1 + \delta_2' \bar{\mu}_2 + \cdots + \delta_l' \bar{\mu}_l, \end{aligned}$$

where T_i corresponds to some solution Y_i of L'.

$$(13) \qquad T_i = \bar{A}_2 Y_i, \qquad\qquad (Y_i \geq 0)$$

such that

$$(14) \qquad \left. \begin{matrix} \delta_i' = 1 \\ \delta_i' = 0 \end{matrix} \right\} \text{ if } Y_i \geq 0 \text{ is } \left\{ \begin{matrix} \text{extreme point} \\ \text{homogeneous} \end{matrix} \right\} \text{ solution of } \left\{ \begin{matrix} A_2 Y_i = b_2 \\ A_2 Y_i = 0 \end{matrix} \right\}.$$

We now consider in place of (4) the obviously equivalent "*interconnecting linear program*" of determining weights $\lambda_i \geq 0$, $\mu_i \geq 0$, and Max x_0 satisfying

$$(15) \quad P_0 x_0 + S \lambda_0 + S_1 \lambda_1 + \cdots + S_k \lambda_k + T \mu_0 + T_1 \mu_1 + \cdots + T_l \mu_l = \bar{b},$$

$$(16) \qquad\qquad\qquad\qquad\qquad \delta \lambda_0 + \delta_1 \lambda_1 + \cdots + \delta_k \lambda_k = 1,$$

$$(17) \qquad\qquad\qquad\qquad\qquad \delta' \mu_0 + \delta_1' \mu_1 + \cdots + \delta_l' \mu_l = 1,$$

where S, T correspond to *arbitrary* extreme points ($\delta, \delta' = 1$) or homogeneous solutions ($\delta, \delta' = 0$) of (5). A particular feasible solution can be obtained by setting $\lambda = \mu = 0$ and $\lambda_i = \bar{\lambda}_i$, $\mu_j = \bar{\mu}_j$.

Starting Assumption III: Finally we suppose that the columns T_i, S_i, P_0 with added components for equations (16) and (17) form a basis B, i.e., a $(m+2) \times (m+2)$ nonsingular matrix as in (18). Let the simplex multipliers associated with the rows of B be $(\pi; -s, -t)$ where $-s$, $-t$ are multipliers for the last two rows:

$$(18) \qquad B = \begin{Vmatrix} P_0; & S_1 & \cdots & S_k; & T_1 & \cdots & T_l \\ 0 & \delta_1 & \cdots & \delta_k & 0 & \cdots & 0 \\ 0 & 0 & \cdots & 0 & \delta'_1 & \cdots & \delta'_l \end{Vmatrix}; \quad \begin{Vmatrix} \pi \\ -s \\ -t \end{Vmatrix}.$$

Since we are maximizing x_0 the simplex multipliers by definition satisfy

$$(19) \qquad \pi P_0 = 1, \qquad \pi S_i - \delta_i s = 0, \qquad \pi T_i - \delta'_i t = 0.$$

To test optimality of the proposed solution we now form the row vectors

$$(20) \qquad \pi \bar{A}_1 = \gamma_1, \qquad \pi \bar{A}_2 = \gamma_2.$$

THEOREM 1: *The solution* (X_0, Y_0, x_0^0) *is maximal if for all* $X \geq 0$, $Y \geq 0$, z_1, z_2 *satisfying*

$$(21) \qquad A_1 X = b_1, \qquad \gamma_1 X = z_1, \qquad (X \geq 0)$$
$$(22) \qquad A_2 Y = b_2, \qquad \gamma_2 Y = z_2, \qquad (Y \geq 0)$$

it is true that

$$(23) \qquad \mathrm{Min}\ z_1 = s, \qquad \mathrm{Min}\ z_2 = t.$$

Proof. Multiplication of (9) and (12) on the left by π yields, by (19) and (20),

$$(24) \qquad s = \gamma_1 X_0; \qquad t = \gamma_2 Y_0.$$

On the other hand multiplication of (4) on the left side by π yields, by (20), (21), and (22),

$$(25) \qquad x_0 + \gamma_1 X + \gamma_2 Y = \pi \bar{b},$$

or

$$(26) \qquad x_0 + z_1 + z_2 = \pi \bar{b}.$$

In particular for $Y = X_0$, $Y = Y_0$, $x_0 = x_0^0$ by (24):

$$(27) \qquad x_0^0 + s + t = \pi \bar{b}.$$

Subtracting (26) from (27),

$$(28) \qquad x_0^0 - x_0 = (z_1 + z_2) - (s + t).$$

The right-hand side is always nonnegative by (23); hence $x_0^0 \geq x_0$ so that the solution is maximal.

If the solution (X_0, Y_0, x_0^0) fails to satisfy the test for optimality (23), say Min $z_1 < s$, then there exists *either* an *extreme point solution* $X = X^*$ to (21) such that

$$(29) \qquad\qquad \text{Min } z = \gamma_1 X^* < s,$$

or there exists a *homogeneous solution* X^* satisfying

$$(30) \qquad\qquad A_1 X^* = 0 \quad \text{and} \quad \gamma_1 X^* < 0.$$

The latter possibility warrants some discussion. It may happen that the convex $A_1 X = b_1$, $X \geq 0$ is *unbounded* and that there is no lower bound for z_1. In this case *using the simplex method* a homogeneous solution, $A_1 X = 0$, $X \geq 0$, will be obtained with the above property. It is not difficult to show that the set of possible homogeneous solutions generated in this manner, excluding multiples, is finite.[e]

If we now define

$$(31) \qquad\qquad \bar{A}_1 X^* = S^*,$$

and $\delta^* = 1, 0$ depending on whether X^* is an extreme or homogeneous solution and substitute $S = S^*$, $\delta = \delta^*$, the interconnecting program has one more variable than the number of equations. The basic solution $\lambda = 0$, $\lambda_i = \bar{\lambda}_i$, $\mu_i = \bar{\mu}_i$ does not satisfy the test for optimality when the simplex multipliers $(\pi, -s, -t)$ are multiplied scalarly by the column of coefficients of λ_0; indeed by (31), then (20), (29), and (30), this yields

$$(32) \qquad \pi S^* - \delta^* s = \pi A_1 X^* - \delta^* s = \gamma_1 X^* - \delta^* s < 0.$$

Hence, assuming nondegeneracy by perturbing $\bar{b}$ if necessary, an improved solution can be obtained by introducing S^* from the auxiliary program into the basis of the interconnecting problem and dropping some other S_i or T_i. Multipliers with respect to the new basis can then be determined by (19); these will generate new values γ_1 and γ_2 by (20) and new definitions for z_1 and z_2; finally the two auxiliary linear programs (21) and (22) must be resolved to determine new points where z_1 and z_2 are minimized. The algorithm is finite because of the finiteness of the set of possible bases derived from extreme points and homogeneous solutions generated by the simplex method when applied to the auxiliary problems, and because no basis of the interconnecting program can repeat itself since x_0 is monotonically increasing (when Q is perturbed to avoid degeneracy).

If a record has been maintained of the solution vectors X_i and Y_i to the auxiliary problems, corresponding the vectors S_i and T_i in the final basis, then an optimal solution $\hat{X}$ and $\hat{Y}$ can be obtained by means of the relations

$$(33) \qquad \hat{X} = \sum \lambda_i X_i, \qquad \hat{Y} = \sum \mu_i Y_i.$$

From iteration to iteration it is not necessary, however, to maintain a record of the solutions X_i and Y_i to the auxiliary problems, but only a record of the S_i, T_i in the current basis and whether or not they correspond to extreme or homogeneous solutions. When an optimum has been achieved, the final selection of S_i and λ_i and T_i and μ_i are used to compute

$$(34) \qquad \hat{S} = \sum \lambda_i S_i, \qquad \hat{T} = \sum \mu_i T_i,$$

and to determine an optimum solution $X = \hat{X}$ and $Y = \hat{Y}$ by solving the auxiliary problems

$$(35) \qquad \begin{aligned} A_1 X &= b_1, \quad A_2 Y = b_2 \\ A_1 X &= \hat{S}, \quad A_2 Y = \hat{T} \quad (X \geq 0, \, Y \geq 0) \end{aligned}$$

where any feasible solution is an optimum solution. This is greatly simplified by observing that the choices of components of X and Y, which are basic and nonbasic, are further restricted to the set which minimize z_1 and z_2, respectively.

A GENERALIZED PROGRAMMING PROBLEM

Consider a generalized linear-programming problem in which for each P_j for $j \neq 0$ may be freely chosen to be any $P_j \in C_j$ where C_j is a convex set defined by linear inequalities. By a simple extension, Q and P_0 could also be replaced by any Q and P_0 in convex sets; however, for our purposes these are held constant. We shall assume that C_j is a convex polyhedron so that a general P_j can be represented by a convex combination of a finite set of extreme points of C_j and a nonnegative linear combination of homogeneous solutions (in case C_j is unbounded). Two easy theorems are:

THEOREM 2: *A solution (x_{j^*}, P_{j^*}) for $j = 0, 1, 2, \cdots, n$, is optimal if there exists a π such that $\pi P_0 = 1$, $\pi P_j \geq 0$ for all $P_j \in C_j$ and $\pi P_{j^*} = 0$ for all $x_{j^*} > 0$ $(j \neq 0)$.*

THEOREM 3: *Only a finite number of iterations of the simplex algorithm is required if each basic feasible solution is improved by introducing into the basis either an extreme point $P_{j^*} \in C_{j^*}$ chosen so that*

$$(36) \qquad \pi P_{j^*} = \mathrm{Min}_{P_{j^*} \in C_{j^*}} \, \pi P_j < 0, \qquad (j = 1, 2, \cdots, n)$$

where π are the simplex multipliers of the basis or any homogeneous solution P_{j^*} from the finite set such that $\pi P_{j^*} < 0$.

The reader will recognize that our Theorem 1 is a special case of Theorem 2. Also that we followed the procedure implicit in Theorem 3 except we introduced vectors into the basis of the interconnecting problem *other than* extreme points and homogeneous rays of the convex (for the extreme points and homogeneous solutions of the auxiliary problems need not transform into similar solutions of C and C' under the mappings $\bar{A}_1 X$ and $\bar{A}_2 Y$).

DECOMPOSING SPECIAL SYSTEMS

Angular Systems

This will be a direct application to an important class of linear programs. It will serve as a review of the decomposition principle given earlier in which no new concepts will be introduced. Consider for convenience a special case of an "angular system with three block-diagonal terms"

$$(37) \quad \begin{aligned} A_1 X_1 &\qquad\qquad\qquad\qquad = b_1, \\ + A_2 X_2 &\qquad\qquad\quad = b_2, \\ + A_3 X_3 &= b_3, \\ + \bar{A}_1 X_1 + \bar{A}_2 X_2 + \bar{A}_3 X_3 + P_0 x_0 &= \bar{b}, \end{aligned} \qquad (X_i \geq 0)$$

where A_i is an $m_i \times n_i$ matrix, X_i is a column vector of n_i components and b_i, b column vectors with m_i and m components.

We consider the linear programming problem in the general form

$$(38) \qquad P_1 + P_2 + P_3 + P_0 x_0 = \bar{b},$$

where P_i is defined by the linear transformation

$$(39) \qquad \bar{A}_i X_i = P_i,$$

and X_i satisfies the sub-program L_i:

$$(40) \qquad A X_i = b_i \qquad (X_i \geq 0)$$

It will be convenient to assume each L_i is bounded; adjustments for the unbounded case can be made by forming nonnegative linear combinations instead of convex combinations for points corresponding to homogeneous solutions.

We shall require however, that each P_i be represented as a convex combination (positive weights that sum to unity) of points P_{ti} of [the form] $P_{ti} = \bar{A} X_{ti}$ where $X_t = X_{ti} \geq 0$ are extreme points of L_i.

Let us consider in place of (38), the linear-programming problem of finding $\lambda_i \geq 0$, $\lambda_{ij} \geq 0$, Max x_0 satisfying

$$(41) \quad \begin{aligned} \sum_{k=1}^{k=k_1} P_{1k} \lambda_{1k} + P_1 \lambda_1 + \sum_{k=1}^{k=k_2} P_{2k} \lambda_{2k} + P_2 \lambda_2 \\ + \sum_{k=1}^{k=k_3} P_{3k} \lambda_{3k} + P_3 \lambda_3 + P_0 x_0 = \bar{b}, \end{aligned}$$

$$\sum \lambda_{1k} + \lambda_1 = 1, \qquad \sum \lambda_{2k} + \lambda_2 = 1, \qquad \sum \lambda_{3k} + \lambda_3 = 1.$$

These two problems are equivalent because the convexity of L_t implies that a convex combination of vectors P_{ti} and P_t corresponds to a feasible X in L_t. Suppose at some stage of the simplex process several points $P_{t1}, P_{t2}, \cdots, P_{tk_t}$ have been introduced into the basis so that a feasible solution $\lambda_{ik} \geq 0$ can be obtained by setting $\lambda_1 = \lambda_2 = \lambda_3 = 0$ subject to $\sum \lambda_{ik} = 1$ for $i = 1, 2, 3$.

We are now interested in testing whether or not the basic solution maximizes x_0. To find a better solution we determine the simplex multipliers associated with the basis

$$(42) \quad B = \begin{Vmatrix} P_{11} \ P_{12} \cdots \ P_{1k_1}; & P_{21} \ P_{22} \cdots \ P_{2k_2}; & P_{31} \ P_{32} \cdots \ P_{3k_3} & P_0 \\ 1 \quad 1 \ \cdots \ 1 & & & \\ & 1 \quad 1 \ \cdots \ 1 & & \\ & & 1 \quad 1 \ \cdots \ 1 & \end{Vmatrix}$$

by the relations

$$(43) \quad \pi P_0 = 1, \quad \pi P_{ij} + p_j = 0, \quad (j = 1, 2, \cdots, k_i; \ i = 1, 2, 3)$$

where $\pi = \|\bar{\pi}; p_1, p_2, p_3\|$ and p_1, p_2, p_3 are the multipliers associated with the last three equations. To test optimality or to find a better vector to introduce into the basis, we solve for each t the auxiliary problems

$$(44) \quad \begin{aligned} A_t X_t &= b_t, & (X_t \geq 0) \\ (\pi \bar{A}_t) X_t + p_t &= z_t \text{ (Min)} \end{aligned}$$

where $\pi \bar{A}_t$ is a constant row vector. If Min $z_i \geq 0$ for all t, the solution is optimal. If not, $P_t = P_t^*$ is introduced into the basis corresponding to that t such that $X_t = X_t^*$ yields

$$(45) \quad \text{Min}_t \ \text{Min}_{X_t} \ z_t.$$

To summarize, the linear programming problem consists of iterative cycling between two parts:

PART I: Determine new multipliers by a simple change of basis for the set of $m + 3$ equations (40) and (41).

PART II: Solve several auxiliary $m_j \times n_j$ linear programs (44), for testing optimality of the solution and the introduction of new vectors $\bar{A}_t X_t^*$ into the basis of Part I by (45).

Multi-Stage Systems

Consider a system with structure

$$(46) \quad \begin{aligned} A_1 X_1 & & & = e_1 \\ + \bar{A}_1 X_1 + A_2 X_2 & & & = e_2 \\ + \bar{A}_2 X_2 + A_3 X_3 & & = e_3 & \quad (X_j \geq 0) \\ + \bar{A}_3 X_3 + A_4 X_4 &= e_4 \\ c_4 X_4 &= z_4 \text{(Min)}, \end{aligned}$$

where X_t are vectors, A_t matrices, e_t and c_4 vectors.

We replace this formally by

$$(47) \qquad \begin{aligned} + P_3 + A_4 X_4 &= e_4, \\ c_4 X_4 &= z_4 (\text{Min}), \end{aligned} \qquad (X_4 \geq 0)$$

where $P_3 = \bar{A}_3 X_3$ is any vector corresponding to (X_1, X_2, X_3) satisfying the first three relations of (46) and $X_j \geq 0$. We shall require again however, that P_3 be represented by a convex combination with weights $\lambda_{3i} = \bar{\lambda}_{31} P_{3i}$ of C_3 derived from extreme points. (This assumes boundedness; if not appropriate changes discussed earlier should be made for homogeneous solutions.)

$$(48) \qquad \sum \bar{\lambda}_{3i} = 1. \qquad (\bar{\lambda} \geq 0)$$

The interconnecting "stage 4" linear program is to determine λ_3, λ_{3i}, X_i and Min z_4 satisfying

$$(49) \qquad \begin{aligned} \sum \lambda_{3i} P_{3i} + \lambda_3 P_3 + A_4 X_4 &= e_4 \\ \sum \lambda_{3i} \quad + \lambda_3 \qquad\qquad &= 1 \qquad (\lambda_{3i} \geq 0, \ \lambda_3 \geq 0, \ X_4 \geq 0) \\ c_4 X_4 &= z_4 (\text{Min}). \end{aligned}$$

We assume a basic solution is at hand using columns P_{3i} and columns from A_4. Let $\pi = (\bar{\pi}, p_i)$ be the simplex multipliers associated with the basis where p_i is the multiplier associated with the last equation. The solution is optimal if

$$(50) \qquad \pi P_3 + p_4 \geq 0,$$

for all P_3 in C_3. To ascertain this we consider the subproblem to find $X_j \geq 0$, Min z_3 satisfying

$$(51) \qquad \begin{aligned} A_1 X_1 \qquad\qquad\qquad\qquad &= e_1 \\ \bar{A}_1 X_1 + A_2 X_2 \qquad\qquad &= e_2 \\ \bar{A}_2 X_2 + A_3 X_3 \qquad &= e_3 \\ c_3 X_3 + p_4 &= z_3 (\text{Min}), \end{aligned}$$

where

$$(52) \qquad c_3 = \pi \bar{A}_3.$$

If Min $z_3 \geq 0$ the solution is optimal. With respect to this sub-problem, in an analogous manner we set up a "stage 3" linear-programming problem

$$(53) \qquad \begin{aligned} \sum \lambda_{2i} P_{2i} + \lambda_2 P_2 + A_3 X_3 \qquad &= e_3, \\ \sum \lambda_{2i} \quad + \lambda_2 \qquad\qquad &= 1, \\ c_3 X_3 + p_4 &= z_3 (\text{Min}). \end{aligned}$$

This in turn induces a "stage 2" and a "stage 1" linear-programming problem.

This nested set of programming problems is not as ideal as may appear at first because there could be a great deal of jockeying up and down the various stages seeking improved solutions. One procedure could be

1. Optimize *stage 4* over the columns P_{3i} and A_i with $\lambda_3 = 0$ and use simplex multipliers (π_4, ρ_4) to determine c_3.

2. Use c_3 to optimize *stage 3* over the columns P_{2i} with $\lambda_2 = 0$ and use simplex multipliers (π_3, P_3) to determine c_2.

3. Use c_2 to optimize *stage 2* over the columns P_{1i} with $\lambda_1 = 0$ and use simplex multipliers (π_2, p_2) to determine c_1.

4. Use c_1 to optimize *stage 1* over the columns of A_1 to determine $X_1 = X_1^*$.

5. Substitute $P_1 = \bar{A}_1 X_1^*$ into *stage 2* and continue optimization of *stage 2* allowing λ_1 to vary to determine $X_2 = X_2^*$.

6. Substitute $P_2 = \bar{A}_2 X_2^*$ into *stage 3* and continue optimization of *stage 3* allowing λ_2 to vary to determine $X_3 = X_3^*$.

7. Substitute $P_3 = \bar{A}_3 X_3^*$ into *stage 4* and continue optimization of *stage 4* allowing λ_3 to vary to determine $X_4 = X_4^*$.

8. *Recycle*, treating each P_i generated as above as a new P_{ij}. All P_{ij} are preserved for use in step **9.**

9. When no new P_{ij} are generated, the fourth stage is optimized, any feasible solution to the third stage is optimal subject to $\bar{A}_3 X_3 = \sum \lambda_{3i}^* P_{3i}$ where $\lambda_{3i} = \lambda_{3i}^*$, $\lambda_3 = 0$ are optimal fourth-stage weights. This in turn permits optimal solution of the second stage via the best third-stage weights, etc.

Block-Triangular Systems

The treatment of the block-triangular case is similar to the multistage case just considered.

Chapter 8

Generalized Upper Bounding Techniques[1]

G. B. Dantzig[2] and R. M. Van Slyke[3]

Operations Research Center, University of California, Berkeley, California 94720

Abstract

A variant of the revised simplex method is given for solving linear programs with $M + L$ equations, L of which have the property that each variable has at most one nonzero coefficient in them. Special cases include transportation problems, programs with upper bounded variables, assignment and weighted distribution problems. The algorithm described uses a working basis of M rows for pivoting, pricing, and inversion which for large L can result in a substantial reduction of computation. This working basis is only $M \times M$ and is a further reduction of the size found in an earlier version.[a]

I. Introduction and Notation

The application of linear programming to large systems inevitably leads to programs with special structure. One such structure arising frequently in distribution, production scheduling and optimal control problems is a linear program in which each variable has at most one nonzero coefficient in the last L equations which is nonnegative, and the last L constant terms are positive.[b] This is the problem we study here. See also [1]. In Section IV we indicate the necessary modifications to handle negative coefficients in the last L equations. By normalizing the variables and multiplying the

---

[1] This research has been partially supported by the Office of Naval Research under Contract Nonr-222(83) with the University of California. Reproduction in whole or in part is permitted for any purpose of the United States Government.

[2] Present address: Stanford University (Operations Research House), Stanford, California.

[3] Also with the Department of Electrical Engineering, University of California, Berkeley.

equations by constants, we can assume without loss of generality that all nonzero coefficients and constants in the last L equations are 1's [See Eq. (1)].

The lth *set of variables or columns*, S_l, will refer (depending on context) to those variables or columns corresponding to the columns of coefficients in (1) with 1 as the $M + l$th component. S_0, *the* 0th *set*, is the set corresponding to columns with zeros for the $M+1$st through $M + L$th coefficients.

We assume that the system (1) is of full rank and denote by $[\mathbf{A}^{j_1}, \ldots, \mathbf{A}^{j_{M+L}}]$, a basis for the system. We always assume $\mathbf{A}^{j_1} = \mathbf{A}^0$, the coefficient of variable to be optimized. Bold-face type is used to differentiate coefficient vectors with all $M + L$ components from the reduced vectors of the first M coefficients, which are in lightface type. Individual components A_i^j of these two different types of vectors will not be bold-faced since they differ only in the *number* of their components.

THEOREM 1. *At least one variable from each set S_l is basic, $l = 0, \ldots, L$.*

Proof. Since our system is assumed to be full rank, if $[\mathbf{A}^{j_1}, \ldots, \mathbf{A}^{j_{M+L}}]$ is a basis any $M + L$ vector $\mathbf{b}$ can be expressed as a linear combination of the columns of basis. In particular, if the $M + l$th, $l = 1, \ldots, L$, component of $\mathbf{b}$ is nonzero at least one of the basic columns must have a nonzero element in this component and, therefore, belong to S_l. $A^0 = A^{j_1} \in S_0$.

THEOREM 2. *The number of sets containing two or more basic variables is at most $M - 1$.*

Proof. Of the $M + L$ basic variables, $L + 1$ of them are in different sets by Theorem 1. This leaves at most $M - 1$ basic variables to compose sets with more than one basic variable.

The sets containing two or more basic variables plus the set S_0 are called *essential* sets. An essential set for one basis may become an unessential one in the next.

In the next section we outline the method; in the following we formalize it as an algorithm. In the last section we indicate some extensions and, finally, in the Appendix the method is carried out on an example.

II. THE METHOD

Given a feasible basis[4] $\{\mathbf{A}^{j_1}, \ldots, \mathbf{A}^{j_{M+L}}\}$, we assume we have selected for each S_l, $l = 1, \ldots, L$ one basic variable x_{k_l} to be the *key variable*. A^{k_l} is said to be the *key column*. S_0 has no key column. We then consider the system obtained by subtracting the key columns from every other column in their respective sets [in (2) we assume for simplicity that the key variable was the first one in each set]. In this modified system

---

[4]Obtaining a first feasible solution is accomplished using this method with a Phase I setup as in the usual simplex method.

(1)

$$A_1^0 x_0 + A_1^1 x_1 + \cdots + A_1^{n_0} x_{n_0} + A_1^{n_0+1} x_{n_0+1} + \cdots + A_1^{n_1} x_{n_1} + A_1^{n_1+1} x_{n_1+1} + \cdots + A_1^{n_2} x_{n_2} + \cdots + A_1^{n_L-1+1} x_{n_L-1+1} + \cdots + A_1^N x_N = b_1$$

$$A_2^0 x_0 + A_2^1 x_1 + \cdots + A_2^{n_0} x_{n_0} + A_2^{n_0+1} x_{n_0+1} + \cdots + A_2^{n_1} x_{n_1} + A_2^{n_1+1} x_{n_1+1} + \cdots + A_2^{n_2} x_{n_2} + \cdots + A_2^{n_L-1+1} x_{n_L-1+1} + \cdots + A_2^N x_N = b_2$$

$$\cdots$$

$$A_M^0 x_0 + A_M^1 x_1 + \cdots + A_M^{n_0} x_{n_0} + A_M^{n_0+1} x_{n_0+1} + \cdots + A_M^{n_1} x_{n_1} + A_M^{n_1+1} x_{n_1+1} + \cdots + A_M^{n_2} x_{n_2} + \cdots + A_M^{n_L-1+1} x_{n_L-1+1} + \cdots + A_M^N x_N = b_M$$

$$x_{n_0+1} + \cdots + x_{n_1} = 1$$

$$x_{n_1+1} + \cdots + x_{n_2} = 1$$

$$\cdots$$

$$x_{n_L-1+1} + \cdots + x_N = 1$$

(2)

$$A^0 y_0 + \cdots + A^{n_0} y_{n_0} + A^{n_0+1} y_{n_0+1} + (A^{n_0+2} - A^{n_0+1})y_{n_0+2} + \cdots + (A^{n_1} - A^{n_0+1})y_{n_1} + \cdots + A^{n_L-1+1} y_{n_L-1+1} + \cdots + (A^{n_L} - A^{n_L-1+1})y_{n_L} = 1$$

$$1 \cdot y_{n_0+1} \quad 0 \text{ --------- } = 1$$

$$1 \cdot y_{n_L-1+1} \quad 0 \text{ --------- } = 1$$

$$\vdots$$

$$1 \cdot y_{n_L-1+1} = 1$$

where

$$y_j = x_j, \qquad\qquad j = 0, \ldots, n_0,$$

$$y_{n_i+1} = \sum_{j=n_i+2}^{n_{i+1}} x_j, \qquad i = 0, \ldots, L-1,$$

$$y_{n_i+j} = x_{n_i+j}, \qquad\qquad i = 0, \ldots, L-1; \; j = 2, \ldots, n_{i+1},$$

the value of the key variables corresponding to any feasible solution must clearly be one. We treat these variables as we would variables at upper bound in an upper bounded variables algorithm for the revised simplex method and subtract their coefficients from the right-hand side. We then introduce the following notation: if $A^j \in S_l$ we let

$$D^{k_l} = A^{k_l},$$

(3)
$$D^j = A^j - A^{k_l}, \quad j \neq k_l,$$

$$d = b - \sum_{i=1}^{L} D^{k_i} = b - \sum A^{k_i}.$$

We then can consider D^j for $j = k_l$ (key) to be absent from the system. The *working basis*, B, is given by $B = \{D^j \mid A^j \text{ is basic and not key}\}$. Since there are exactly L key columns it is clear that B has M columns. We assume $B^1 = A^0$ corresponding to the coefficient of the variable to be optimized. We define the *derived system* to be

(4)
$$\sum y_j D^j = d,$$

and it is easy to prove

THEOREM 3. *B is a basis for* (4).

Proof. Suppose $\sum \lambda_j B^j = 0$. Since B^j differs from $\mathbf{B}^j$ [the same column considered in the system depicted in (2)] by only 0 components $\sum \lambda_j \mathbf{B}^j = 0$. But this implies that the $\mathbf{B}^j$ plus the key columns are linearly dependent since the $\mathbf{B}^j$ by themselves are linearly dependent. On the other hand, this set is obtained from a (nonsingular) basis by subtraction of columns from within the set which does not reduce the rank, yielding a contradiction.

By Theorem 2 there exist at most $M - 1$ sets with more than one basic variable. These sets and S_0 are the only sets which contain members of B and will be referred to as the *essential* sets.

Thus, with each feasible basis for the original system (1), we have associated a set of L key variables and a basis for the derived system. We now show that we can carry out the steps of the simplex method using just the inverse B^{-1} of B, the reduced basis, and the corresponding basic solution of the derived system (4).

The first step is to obtain a set of prices for (1). Let us denote by $\pi = (\pi_1, \ldots, \pi_M)$ the prices on the first M equations and $\mu = (\mu_1, \ldots, \mu_L)$ the prices on the last L. These prices are determined uniquely by the condition that

$$(\pi, \mu)\mathbf{A}^0 = (\pi, \mu)\mathbf{A}^{j_1} = 1,$$

$$(\pi, \mu)\mathbf{A}^{j_i} = 0, \qquad i = 2, \ldots, M + L.$$

Let $\hat{\pi} = (B^{-1})_1$, the first row of the inverse of the working basis B. It has the property that

$$\hat{\pi}B^1 = \hat{\pi}A^0 = 1,$$

$$\hat{\pi}B^j = 0, \qquad j = 2, \ldots, M;$$

i.e., $\hat{\pi}$ is a set of prices for (4). To extend $\hat{\pi}$ to a set of prices for (2) is trivial, we simply set

(5) $$\hat{\mu}_l = -\hat{\pi}A^{k_l}, \qquad l = 1, \ldots, L.$$

Now for basic columns A^{j_i},

$$(\hat{\pi}, \hat{\mu})\mathbf{A}^{j_i} = (\hat{\pi}, \hat{\mu})\mathbf{A}^{k_l} = 0 \quad \text{if} \quad A^{j_i} \quad \text{is key}$$

or if A^{j_i} is not key,

$$(\hat{\pi}, \hat{\mu})\mathbf{A}^{j_i} = (\hat{\pi}, \hat{\mu})(\mathbf{B}^i + \mathbf{A}^k) \quad \text{for some } k$$

$$= (\hat{\pi}, \hat{\mu})\mathbf{B}^i + (\hat{\pi}, \hat{\mu})\mathbf{A}^k$$

$$= 0 + 0.$$

Thus $(\hat{\pi}, \hat{\mu})$ is a set of prices for the original system (1).

Using these prices we can "price out" the columns of (1) to find the next column to enter the basis. Using the usual simplex criterion, the incoming column A^s would be chosen by

$$\Delta_s = (\pi, \mu)\mathbf{A}^s = \min_j (\pi, \mu)\mathbf{A}^j = \min_j \Delta_j$$

where

$$\Delta_j = \sum \pi_i A_i^j + \mu_i \quad \text{for} \quad A^j \in S_l.$$

Suppose A^s S_σ. If $\Delta_s \geq 0$, we have an optimal basic feasible solution and we're done; otherwise, we bring $\mathbf{A}^s$ into the basis. To do this^c, we must express $\mathbf{A}^s$ and $\mathbf{b}$ in terms of the current basis *for* (1). If we let

$$\bar{D}^s = B^{-1}D^s = B^{-1}(A^s - A^{k_\sigma}),$$

then

$$(6) \qquad (A^s - A^{k_\sigma}) = \sum_{i=1}^{M} \bar{D}_i^s B^i = \sum \bar{D}_i^s (A^{\eta_i} - A^{\nu_i}),$$

where η_i indicates the column number in (2) corresponding to the ith column of the working basis and ν_i denotes the column number of the corresponding key variable.

We denote the representation of $\mathbf{A}^s$ in terms of the current basis by $\bar{A}_i^s$; that is,

$$\mathbf{A}^s = \sum_{i=1}^{M+L} \bar{A}_i^s \mathbf{A}^{j_i}.$$

From (6) we see

$$(7) \qquad \bar{A}_i^s = \begin{cases} 1 - \sum_{\nu_t = k_\sigma} \bar{D}_t^s & \text{if } A^{j_i} = A^{k_\sigma}, \text{ is key in } S_\sigma \\[2mm] \bar{D}_t^s & \text{if } A^{j_i} = A^{\eta_t} \quad \text{for some } t, \\[2mm] -\sum_{\nu_t = j_i} \bar{D}_t^s & \text{if } A^{j_i} = A^{k_l} \text{ is key in } S_l \ (l \neq \sigma). \end{cases}$$

The current values for the variables in the basis $\bar{b}_i$ are given either by updating the values of the previous iteration in the usual way or recomputed in a similar way in a similar way to $\bar{A}_j^s$ above. That is, let

$$\bar{d} = (\bar{d}_1, \ldots, \bar{d}_M)^T \quad \text{be given by}$$

$$(8) \qquad \bar{d} = B^{-1} \left(b - \sum A^{k_l} \right) = B^{-1} d;$$

then

$$\left(b - \sum A^{k_l} \right) = \sum \bar{d}_i B^i = \sum \bar{d}_i (A^{\eta_i} - A^{\nu_i})$$

and, as in (7), the $\bar{b}_i$ are given by

$$(9) \qquad \bar{b}_i = \begin{cases} 1 - \sum_{\nu_t = j_i} \bar{d}_i & \text{if } A^{j_i} \text{ is key} \\[2mm] \bar{d}_i & \text{if } A^{j_i} = A^{\eta_t} \quad \text{for some } t \end{cases}$$

Finding the variable to leave the basis is accomplished in exactly the same way as in the ordinary simplex method. Let

$$(10) \qquad \theta \triangleq \frac{\bar{b}_r}{\bar{A}_r^s} \triangleq \min_{\bar{A}_i^s > 0} \frac{\bar{b}_i}{\bar{A}_i^s}, \qquad i = 2, \ldots, M + L,$$

where we require that $\bar{A}_i^s > 0$. Let us assume $A^{j_r} \in S_\rho$. Three cases can occur in the updating process [d]:

(a) If S_σ is not essential and $A^{j_r} \in S_\sigma$; i.e., the outgoing variable is the key variable in S_σ then B remains unchanged, and A^s simply replaces A^{j_r} as the key variable in S_σ. This requires the updating of $\bar{d}$ which is accomplished as follows[5]:

$$\bar{d} := B^{-1}\left(b - \sum_{l \neq \sigma} A^{k_l} - A^{k_\sigma} + A^{j_r} - A^s\right)$$

$$(11) \qquad = B^{-1}\left(b - \sum_{l \neq \sigma} A^{k_l} - A^{k_\sigma}\right) - B^{-1}(A^s - A^{j_r})$$

$$= \bar{d} - B^{-1}(A^s - A^{j_r})$$
$$= \bar{d} - \bar{D}^s.$$

Observing that $A^{j_r} = A^{k_\sigma}$, we see that this is easy to compute since we already have $\bar{d}$ and the second term was generated in determining the $\bar{A}_i^s$.

(b) If A^{j_r} is not a key variable, then we update B^{-1} simply by pivoting on the column $\bar{D}^s$ on the row which $A^{j_r} - A^{k_\rho}$ occupies in the working basis. In symbols $B^{-1} := PB^{-1}$ where P is the matrix which performs the pivot. $\bar{d}$ is updated by applying this pivot to the old $\bar{d}$.

(c) If $A^{j_r} \in S_\rho$ is a key variable in an essential set, we must first change the key variable in S_ρ. To change the inverse of the working basis B, we consider all columns of B of the form $A^j - A^{j_r}$; there must be at least one such since after A^s enters the basis S_ρ must contain a basic variable. To get the new working basis $\bar{B}$ from the old one B we wish to multiply the column (in B) $A^k - A^{j_r}$ by -1 to obtain $A^{j_r} - A^k$ and we wish to subtract $A^k - A^{j_r}$ from every other column of the form $A^j - A^{j_r}$ for $j \neq k$ to obtain $A^j - A^k$. That is (see footnote 2),

$$B := BT \quad \text{where} \quad T \quad \text{is of the form}$$

---

[5]The symbol ":=" does not indicate equality, but rather that the expression on the right replaces (or updates) the variable on the left.

$$(12) \quad T = \begin{bmatrix} 1 & & & & & & & & & & & \\ & \ddots & & & & & & & & & & \\ & & 1 & & & & & & & & & \\ & & & 1 & & & & & & & & \\ & & & & \ddots & & & & & & & \\ & & & & & 1 & & & & & & \\ 0 & \cdots & 0 & -1 & \cdots & -1 & -1 & -1 & \cdots & -1 & 0 & \cdots & 0 \\ & & & & & & 1 & & & & & \\ & & & & & & & \ddots & & & & \\ & & & & & & & & 1 & & & \\ & & & & & & & & & 1 & & \\ & & & & & & & & & & \ddots & \\ & & & & & & & & & & & 1 \end{bmatrix}$$

The -1's occur in the columns corresponding to $A^j \in S_\rho$, and the row corresponds to the new key variable A^k.

$$B^{-1} := T^{-1} B^{-1}$$

and it is easily verified that $T^{-1} = T$, since applying the process twice replaces A^{jr} as the key variable. The values for $\bar{d}$ are updated by applying T^{-1}. Now with the new key variable in S_ρ, we simply apply the process outlined in (b).

With our updated B, y, and key variables, we are now ready to make another iteration.[e] If the inverse of the working-basis is expressed in product form we have

$$B^{-1} = \prod_{}^{t} T^t$$

where each T^t is either of the form (12) or (13) below, the latter resulting from a pivot on the rth element of the column $(\alpha_1, \ldots, \alpha_m)^T$,

$$(13) \qquad P = \begin{bmatrix} 1 & & & -\alpha_1/\alpha_r & & & \\ & \ddots & & \vdots & & & \\ & & 1 & -\alpha_{r-1}/\alpha_r & & & \\ & & & 1/\alpha_r & & & \\ & & & -\alpha_{r+1}/\alpha_r & 1 & & \\ & & & \vdots & & \ddots & \\ & & & -\alpha_m/\alpha_r & & & 1 \end{bmatrix}.$$

As Orchard-Hays has remarked to one of the authors, we can, if we wish, express each transformation of the form (12) as a sequence of transformations of the form (13). Suppose we wish to express a matrix T in terms of transformations of the form (13), where -1's appear in columns $h_0, h_1, \ldots, h_i$, and suppose that the -1 in column h_0 lies on the diagonal: in other words, all the -1's are in the h_0th row. Let $P(r, s)$ denote the pivot matrix (13) with $\alpha_j = 0$ $j \neq r$, or s, $\alpha_r = 1$ and $\alpha_s = -1$. When multiplying on the left, this matrix has the effect of subtracting the rth row from the sth row. Finally, let $P(r, r)$ be the matrix will all plus ones on the diagonal except in the rth diagonal element which is -1. Every other element is zero. When multiplying on the *right*, this has the effect of multiplying the rth column by -1. It is then easy to see that

$$T = P(h_0, h_k)P(h_0, h_{k-1}) \cdots P(h_0, h_1)P(h_0, h_1).$$

III. DESCRIPTION OF ALGORITHM

Referring to Fig. 1, the algorithm takes place in the following steps:

(1) We assume we enter the algorithm with the inverse B^{-1} of the working basis, the value $\bar{d}$ of the appropriate basic solution of the derived system (4) and the set of key variables. To get this initial solution, the usual phase I procedure can be carried out in the obvious way.

(2) Let $\pi_i = (B^{-1})_1^i$ for $i = 1, \ldots, M$ and for each set S_l ($l \neq 0$),

$$\text{let } \mu_i = -\sum_{i=1}^{M} \pi_i A_i^{k_l}, \quad \text{where} \quad A^{k_l} \text{ is the key column in } S_l$$

$$\text{Let } \Delta_j = \sum_{i=1}^{j} + \mu_l \text{ for } A^j \in S_l$$

$$\text{Let } \Delta_s = \min \Delta_j \quad \text{and suppose } A^s \in S_\sigma.$$

If $\Delta_s \geq 0$, we go to Step (3); otherwise, skip to (4).

(3) Terminate; we have an optimal solution.

(4) Find $\bar{D}^s = B^{-1}(A^2 - A^{k_\sigma})$, $\bar{\mathbf{A}}^s$ [by means of Eq. (7)], and $\bar{b}$ [by means of Eq. (9)]. Use the usual simplex decision rule [Eq. (10)] to find the variable to be dropped, A^{j_r}, and suppose $A^{j_r} \in S_\sigma$. If A^{j_r} is key, go to step (5); if not S_ρ is essential, go to (6); if $\rho = \sigma$, go to step (7).

(5) We pivot with respect to $\bar{D}^s$ in the row corresponding to D^{j_r} in B^{-1} and update $\bar{d}$ by applying the pivot transformation to it. We then return to step (1) for another iteration.

(6) Make some basic column, say A^k, $k \neq j_r$ in set S_ρ key instead of A^{j_r}. Update B^{-1} by applying a column transformation of the form (12) and update B^{-1} by $B^{-1} := T^{-1}B^{-1}$. $\bar{d}$ is updated by $\bar{d} := T^{-1}\bar{d}$. We then can go to step (5).

(7) Make A^s key instead of A^{j_r} and update $\bar{d}$ by $\bar{d} := \bar{d} - \bar{D}^s$. Return to step (1).

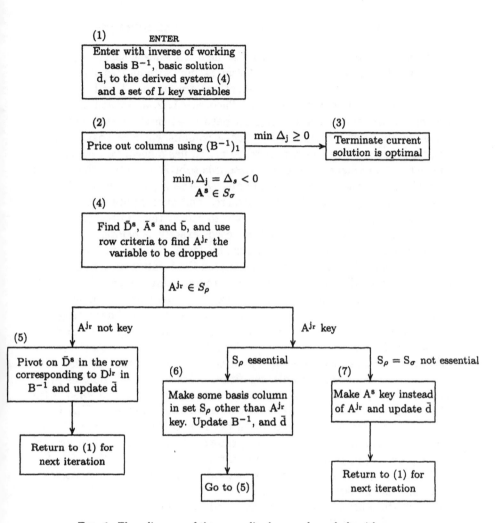

FIG. 1. Flow diagram of the generalized upper-bound algorithm.

IV. EXTENSIONS AND COMPUTATIONAL REMARKS

When negative coefficients appear in the last L equations, the algorithm is changed in a quite obvious way. We can assume without loss of generality that the coefficients in the last L equations are $+1$ or -1 and the last L right-hand side components are $+1$. Theorems 1, 2, and 3 still hold, and we can require that each key column have a $+1$ in the last L equations since clearly each set must have such a column which is basic. In the pricing process, if the column A^j to be priced has a negative coefficient in the last L components, the appropriate μ is subtracted rather than added to πA^j. To form the difference columns D^j, the key column, is added to columns with a -1 rather than subtracted and appropriate modifications in equations (7) and (9) must be made to reflect this. Other than these slight modifications, the algorithm proceeds exactly as before.

The algorithm has been implemented by James Bigelow in collaboration with Mike Kasatkin of the Crown Zellarbach Corporation on the IBM 7094 computer by modifying the M-3 linear programming system. The implementation was particularly easy because it required only a slight modification of features usually present in current large-scale linear programming codes. In particular, the separable-programming logic was modified to handle the partition of the variables into sets and the system used to indicate the state of a variable was a slight generalization of that used in the upper-bounded variable algorithm. This code will handle problems with $M \leq 100$, $L \leq 5,000$, and $N \leq 30,000$. A test problem with $N = 2,813$, $L = 780$, and $M = 39$ was solved in 15 minutes. The iterations were carried out at a rate of 50 per minute. Solution time is to be contrasted with an estimated running time of 150 using an efficient general linear programming code, a decrease in running time by a factor of 10.[f]

A further generalization of this method to the case of block staircase structure in the last L equations has been carried out by Kaul [2]. Similar approaches have also been investigated by Bennett [3], Rosen [4], and Charnes and Lemke [5].[6]

Example. Consider the following example with $M = 3$. We seek to maximize x_0.

---

[6]We are indebted to the referee for this last reference.

S_0	S_1			S_2	S_3	S_4		S_5		
A^0	A^1	A^2	A^3	A^4	A^5	A^6	A^7	A^8	A^9	b
1	0	2	0	3	4	5	1	-1	-12	15
1	1	-1	0	2	1	4	2	-3	6	7
0	0	0	1	0	0	0	0	0	0	0
	1	1	1							1
				1						1
					1					1
						1	1			1
								1	1	1

$$\bar b^T = (3 \quad \tfrac{1}{2} \quad \tfrac{1}{2} \quad 0 \quad 1 \quad 1 \quad 1 \quad \quad 1 \quad)$$

$$\quad x \qquad\qquad x \quad x \quad x \qquad\quad x$$

The initial basis is $A^0 A^1 A^2 A^3 A^4 A^5 A^6 A^8$ and $A^1 A^4 A^5 A^6 A^8$ are key. The working basis is $B = \{A^0, A^2 - A^1, A^3 - A^1\}$ is

$$B = \begin{bmatrix} 1 & 2 & 0 \\ 1 & -2 & -1 \\ 0 & 0 & 1 \end{bmatrix},$$

which has an inverse

$$B^{-1} = \begin{bmatrix} \tfrac{1}{2} & \tfrac{1}{2} & \tfrac{1}{2} \\ \tfrac{1}{4} & -\tfrac{1}{4} & -\tfrac{1}{4} \\ 0 & 0 & 1 \end{bmatrix}.$$

With the aid of (5) we find the prices $[\pi, \mu] = [\tfrac{1}{2}, \tfrac{1}{2}, \tfrac{1}{2}; -\tfrac{1}{2}, -\tfrac{5}{2}, -\tfrac{5}{2}, -\tfrac{9}{2}, 2]$. We then price out and find $A^7 \in S_4$ wins.

$$\bar A^7 - \bar A^6 = B^{-1}[A^7 - A^6] = B^{-1} = \begin{bmatrix} \tfrac{1}{2} & \tfrac{1}{2} & \tfrac{1}{2} \\ \tfrac{1}{4} & -\tfrac{1}{4} & -\tfrac{1}{4} \\ 0 & 0 & 1 \end{bmatrix} \begin{bmatrix} -4 \\ -2 \\ 0 \end{bmatrix}$$

$$= \begin{bmatrix} -3 \\ -\tfrac{1}{2} \\ 0 \end{bmatrix};$$

i.e., $A^7 - A^6 = -3A^0 - \tfrac{1}{2}(A^2 - A^1)$ or $A^7 = -3A^0 + \tfrac{1}{2}A^1 - \tfrac{1}{2}A^2 + A^6$ giving a representation of $\bar A^7$ in terms of the full basis;

$$\bar A^7 = (-3, \tfrac{1}{2}, -\tfrac{1}{2}, 0, 0, 0, 1, 0)^T.$$

We obtain the values of the variables by considering

$$B^{-1}\left[b - \sum A^{k_i}\right] = B^{-1}\begin{bmatrix} 4 \\ 2 \\ 0 \end{bmatrix} = \begin{bmatrix} 3 \\ \frac{1}{2} \\ 0 \end{bmatrix}.$$

This means

$$\mathbf{b} - \sum \mathbf{A}^{k_i} = 3\mathbf{A}^0 + \tfrac{1}{2}\mathbf{A}^1 + \tfrac{1}{2}\mathbf{A}^2$$

or

$$\mathbf{b} = 3\mathbf{A}^0 + \tfrac{1}{2}\mathbf{A}^1 + \tfrac{1}{2}\mathbf{A}^2 + \mathbf{A}^4 + \mathbf{A}^5 + \mathbf{A}^6 + \mathbf{A}^8;$$

hence

$$\mathbf{b} = [3, \tfrac{1}{2}, \tfrac{1}{2}, 0, 1, 1, 1, 1]^T.$$

We now determine the variable going out of the basis by

$$\theta = \min_{A_i^7 > 0} \frac{\bar{b}_i}{\bar{A}_i^7} \triangleq \frac{\bar{b}_r}{\bar{A}_r^7} = 1$$

and r could be 2 or 7. Taking it to be 7, we see that since the set S_4 is inessential and $\theta = 1$ we just replace A^6 by A^7 as a key variable and B remains unchanged. The new multipliers are

$$[\bar{\pi}, \bar{\mu}] = [\tfrac{1}{2}, \tfrac{1}{2}, \tfrac{1}{2}; -\tfrac{1}{2}, -\tfrac{5}{2}, -\tfrac{5}{2}, -\tfrac{3}{2}, 2]$$

and this time $\mathbf{A}^9 \in S_5$ prices out optimally.

$$B^{-1}[A^9 - A^8] = \begin{bmatrix} \frac{1}{2} & \frac{1}{2} & \frac{1}{2} \\ \frac{1}{4} & -\frac{1}{4} & -\frac{1}{4} \\ 0 & 0 & 1 \end{bmatrix} \begin{bmatrix} -11 \\ 9 \\ 0 \end{bmatrix}$$

$$= \begin{bmatrix} -1 \\ -5 \\ 0 \end{bmatrix},$$

that is, $\mathbf{A}^9 = -\mathbf{A}^0 + 5\mathbf{A}^1 - 5\mathbf{A}^2 + \mathbf{A}^8$ and $\bar{\mathbf{A}}^9 = [-1, 5, -5, 0, 0, 0, 0, 1]$.

$$B^{-1}\left[b - \sum A^{k_l}\right] = \begin{bmatrix} \frac{1}{2} & \frac{1}{2} & \frac{1}{2} \\ \frac{1}{4} & -\frac{1}{4} & -\frac{1}{4} \\ 0 & 0 & 1 \end{bmatrix} \begin{bmatrix} 8 \\ 4 \\ 0 \end{bmatrix}$$

$$= \begin{bmatrix} 6 \\ 1 \\ 0 \end{bmatrix},$$

$$b = 6A^0 + A^2 - A^1 + A^1 + A^4 + A^5 + A^7 + A^8$$

$$= 6A^0 + A^2 + A^4 + a^5 + A^7 + A^8,$$

$$\mathbf{b} = [6, 0, 1, 0, 1, 1, 1, 1]^T,$$

$$\theta = \min_{\bar{A}_i^9 > 0} \frac{\bar{b}_i}{\bar{A}_i^9} = \frac{\bar{\bar{b}}}{\bar{A}_2^9} = \frac{0}{5}; \ r = 2, \ j_r = 1$$

therefore, we want to drop A^1, which, however, is key. So first we must replace A^1 by A^2 as a key variable. To do this we take our current working basis

$$B = \{A^0 - 0, A^2 - A^1, A^3 - A^1\}$$

and postmultiply it by

$$T = \begin{bmatrix} 1 & 0 & 0 \\ 0 & -1 & -1 \\ 0 & 0 & 1 \end{bmatrix},$$

which has the effect of subtracting the second column from the third and reversing the sign of the second column.

$$B' = BT = [A^0 - 0, A^1 - A^2, A^3 - A^2],$$
$$(B')^{-1} = T^{-1}B^{-1},$$

where

$$T^{-1} = \begin{bmatrix} 1 & 0 & 0 \\ 0 & -1 & -1 \\ 0 & 0 & 1 \end{bmatrix}.$$

Hence

$$(B')^{-1} = \begin{bmatrix} 1 & 0 & 0 \\ 0 & -1 & -1 \\ 0 & 0 & 1 \end{bmatrix} \begin{bmatrix} \frac{1}{2} & \frac{1}{2} & \frac{1}{2} \\ \frac{1}{4} & -\frac{1}{4} & -\frac{1}{4} \\ 0 & 0 & 1 \end{bmatrix}$$

$$= \begin{bmatrix} \frac{1}{2} & \frac{1}{2} & \frac{1}{2} \\ -\frac{1}{4} & \frac{1}{4} & -\frac{3}{4} \\ 0 & 0 & 1 \end{bmatrix}.$$

We then pivot in the vector column

$$(B')^{-1}(A^9 - A^8) = \begin{bmatrix} \frac{1}{2} & \frac{1}{2} & \frac{1}{2} \\ -\frac{1}{4} & \frac{1}{4} & -\frac{3}{4} \\ 0 & 0 & 1 \end{bmatrix} \begin{bmatrix} -11 \\ 9 \\ 0 \end{bmatrix}$$

$$= \begin{bmatrix} -1 \\ 5 \\ 0 \end{bmatrix}$$

on the second component.
   This gives us a new inverse basis

$$B^{-1} = PB'^{-1}$$

$$= \begin{bmatrix} 1 & \frac{1}{5} \\ 0 & \frac{1}{5} & 0 \\ 0 & 0 & 1 \end{bmatrix} \begin{bmatrix} \frac{1}{2} & \frac{1}{2} & \frac{1}{2} \\ -\frac{1}{4} & \frac{1}{4} & -\frac{3}{4} \\ 0 & 0 & 1 \end{bmatrix}$$

$$= \begin{bmatrix} \frac{9}{20} & \frac{11}{20} & \frac{7}{20} \\ \frac{1}{20} & \frac{1}{20} & -\frac{3}{20} \\ 0 & 0 & 1 \end{bmatrix}.$$

The new prices are

$$\left[\frac{9}{20}, \frac{11}{20}, \frac{7}{20}; -\frac{7}{20}, -\frac{49}{20}, -\frac{47}{20}, -\frac{31}{20}, \frac{42}{20} \right],$$

and upon pricing out we find that all columns price out nonnegatively and the optimal solution is given by

$$\bar{\bar{B}}^{-1}\left[b - \sum A^{k_l}\right] = \begin{bmatrix} \frac{9}{20} & \frac{11}{20} & \frac{7}{20} \\ \frac{1}{20} & \frac{1}{20} & -\frac{3}{20} \\ 0 & 0 & 1 \end{bmatrix} \begin{bmatrix} 6 \\ 6 \\ 0 \end{bmatrix}$$

$$= \begin{bmatrix} 6 \\ 0 \\ 0 \end{bmatrix}$$

and

$$b - A^2 - A^4 - A^5 - A^7 - A^8 = 6A^0$$

or

$$\bar{\bar{b}} = [6, 1, 0, 1, 1, 1, 1, 0],$$

the values of the basic variables. Another way to compute $\bar{\bar{b}}$ is, of course, by

$$\bar{\bar{b}} = \bar{b} - \theta \bar{A}^0,$$

the usual formula for updating the values of the basic variables in the simplex method.

REFERENCES

[1] G. B. DANTZIG AND R. M. VAN SLYKE. A generalized upper-bounded technique for linear programming, "Proceedings of the IBM Scientific Computing Symposium on Combinatorial Problems" IBM, White Plains, New York, 1966, pp. 249–261.

[2] R. N. KAUL. "An Extension of Generalized Upper Bounded Techniques for Linear Programming." [(ORC 65-27), Operations Research Center, University of California, Berkeley, 1965].

[3] J. BENNETT. "An Approach to Some Structured Linear Programming Problems," Basser Computing Department, School of Physics, University of Sydney, Australia, 1963.

[4] J. B. ROSEN. Primal partition programming for block diagonal matrices. *Numerische Mathematik* 6, 250–260 (1964).

[5] A. CHARNES AND C. LEMKE. "Multi-copy Generalized Networks and Multi-page Programs" (R.P.I. Math Rep. No. 41, Rensselaer Polytechnic Institute; Troy, New York, 1960).

Part IV: Special Applications and Economic Modeling

Among linear programming problems, the (Hitchcock-Koopmans) transportation problem is exemplary for several reasons. For a start, it is easily stated and understood, hence a useful (albeit misleading) illustration of what linear programming is about. It has applications that go well beyond the traditional setting of shipping goods from production plants (sources) to warehouses (destinations). The transportation problem has special structure that makes it rather easy to solve. Furthermore, due to a property of the constraint matrix (known as total unimodularity), the transportation problem has the virtue that all problems with integral right-hand side data (supplies and demands) yield basic solutions that are also integral. The latter characteristic of the transportation problem is very significant when an integer solution is required, because no extra measures are needed to achieve it. These features qualities motivate the conversion of challenging combinatorial optimization problems into transportation (or transportation-like) problems whenever possible.

The article "Minimizing the Number of Tankers to Meet a Fixed Schedule," by Dantzig and Fulkerson, is of that sort. As announced in its title, the paper addresses a scheduling problem with practical applications (in this case naval logistics). Here, the scheduling problem is cleverly reformulated into a large transportation-type problem. The authors show that when certain conditions derived from the data hold, there are corresponding variables that must equal zero; this reduces the size of the problem to be solved and does not invalidate the guarantee of integrality. The reformulated problem could then be solved by the Simplex Algorithm.

The next item in this part relates to a problem in chemical physics, that of finding the equilibrium composition of a complex gaseous mixture. In addition to this paper, "A Linear Programming Approach to the Chemical Equilibrium Problem," which appeared in *Management Science*, Dantzig and his co-authors Selmer Johnson and Wayne White published a "companion paper" in the *Journal of Chemical Physics*. That one was aimed at a rather different audience. The main point of the *Management Science* publication was to draw attention to the use of linear programming—and, of course, the Simplex Algorithm—to solving linearly constrained convex, separable nonlinear programs.

Finding the equilibrium composition is cast as one of minimizing the total free energy subject to linear mass balance equations in nonnegative variables. Apart from its convexity, a salient feature of the objective function is its separability. By performing a piecewise linear approximation of this function, the authors obtain a linear programming problem. This increases the number of constraints and—depending on the desired degree of accuracy—can greatly increase the number of variables. Nonetheless, the conversion of the problem to solving a linear program was achieved. The technique of approximating a separable convex program by a linear program was an important part of the computational arsenal of the day.

One of George Dantzig's scholarly passions was the building of a macroeconomic model called PILOT. Initiated about 1975, the PILOT project brought together his keen interest in large-scale linear programming with national interest in technological innovation and its relationship to energy policy. This activity lasted for nearly 15 years. The PILOT model provided a "concrete" test problem for many computational proposals in the linear programming world and a laboratory for the development of many doctoral students.

But the PILOT project was more than just the study of large-scale linear programming. In building a macroeconomic model, those working on PILOT had economic issues to deal with. The third paper of this part, "Formulating an Objective for an Economy," by Dantzig, McAllister, and Stone is a sample of this line of research.

The authors' viewpoint is that there should exist an aggregate objective function for an economy (in particular, the U.S. economy) so that economic growth is a response to the maximization of this function which "measures in some sense the discounted 'standard of living' of the population over time." Having such a model would permit the use of mathematical programming software to obtain an optimal solution and along with it Lagrange multipliers (on the constraints) which would be interpreted as prices. Ideally, solving the optimality conditions of the mathematical program would provide an economic equilibrium.

Yet the existence of an appropriate objective function can be called into question because of the nonintegrability of the conditions that need to be satisfied to obtain an economic equilibrium. By making a number of assumptions about the utility functions of individuals, the authors manage to obtain a utility function for the economy and hence a mathematical program whose optimality conditions are equivalent to an economic equilibrium problem.

Chapter 9

MINIMIZING THE NUMBER OF TANKERS
TO MEET A FIXED SCHEDULE

G. B. Dantzig

and

D. R. Fulkerson

The Rand Corporation

It is shown that the problem of determining the minimum number of tankers required to meet a fixed schedule of transportation of Navy fuel oil can be made into a linear programming problem of the transportation type. The simplex algorithm is then applied to solve a particular scheduling problem.

1. INTRODUCTION

C. Tompkins (see [3]) has given a discrete idealization of a scheduling problem which arose in the routing of Navy fuel oil tankers. A combinatorial problem of this kind has been discussed by J. Robinson and J. Walsh [2], together with a proposed method of computation. The algorithm they outline, however, fails to narrow the number of possibilities sufficiently to make it a feasible combinatorial method for most problems.

In this note we show how the tanker scheduling problem can be made into a linear programming problem of transportation type, albeit large. The size of the system is mitigated somewhat by the following facts: (1) most of the variables are constrained to be zero, (2) the minimizing form is particularly simple, and (3) even a large transportation type problem having no special features can be solved by hand using the simplex algorithm [1].

2. THE PROBLEM

A rectangular array of spaces is furnished, one row for each pickup point and one column for each discharge point. In each space (i, j), $i = 1, 2, \ldots, m$; $j = 1, 2, \ldots, n$ is a sequence of numbers t_{ij}^k, $k = 1, 2, \ldots$ representing the times [a] at which a tanker is to load fully at pickup point i to deliver to destination j. For example, in the array [b]

	1	2	3
1	$1, 4, 7, 10, 13$	$9, 15$	$6, 12$
2	$3, 6, 9, 12$	$7, 10, 13, 15$	$5, 10, 15$

the sequence $3, 6, 9, 12$ in box $(2,1)$ means that at these times a tanker is to begin loading at pickup point 2 for delivery to discharge point 1. Multiple loads to go from i to j can be taken care of by repetitions in the sequence t_{ij}^k. We make the further assumption, not made in [3], that the total number of entries in the table $t = (t_{ij}^k)$ is finite.

In addition, two arrays of positive numbers a_{ij} and b_{ij} are given, where a_{ij} represents the loading-traveling time from i to j, and b_{ij} represents the unloading time from j to i.

The problem is to rearrange the numbers t_{ij}^k into s sequences such that

(2.1) each sequence is monotone increasing;

(2.2) if $t_{i_1 j_1}^{k_1} < t_{i_2 j_2}^{k_2}$ are consecutive numbers in any one of the s sequences, then

$$t_{i_2 j_2}^{k_2} - t_{i_1 j_1}^{k_1} \geq a_{i_1 j_1} + b_{i_2 j_1};$$

(2.3) s is minimal.

In other words, each sequence is a schedule for one tanker, the objective is to meet the fixed schedule given by table t with a minimum number of tankers.

If, in the example, we take

$$a_{ij} = b_{ij} = \frac{\begin{array}{|c|c|c|} \hline 2 & 3 & 2 \\ \hline 1 & 2 & 1 \\ \hline \end{array}}{},$$

then a feasible schedule using seven tankers would be represented by the rearrangement

(1)	$t_{11}^1 = 1$, $t_{23}^1 = 5$, $t_{22}^1 = 7$, $t_{11}^5 = 13$
(2)	$t_{21}^1 = 3$, $t_{21}^2 = 6$, $t_{21}^3 = 9$, $t_{21}^4 = 12$, $t_{12}^2 = 15$
(3)	$t_{11}^2 = 4$, $t_{12}^1 = 9$, $t_{22}^4 = 15$
(4)	$t_{13}^1 = 6$, $t_{22}^2 = 10$, $t_{23}^3 = 15$
(5)	$t_{11}^3 = 7$, $t_{23}^2 = 10$, $t_{22}^3 = 13$
(6)	$t_{13}^2 = 12$
(7)	$t_{11}^4 = 10$

3. REFORMULATION AS A PROGRAMMING PROBLEM

For convenience in exposition, we suppose that the numbers t_{ij}^k, a_{ij}, b_{ij} are positive integers. It will be clear that this is not essential to the method of solution.

First construct the tables of sequences $T = (t_{ij}^k + a_{ij})$. Thus, T_{ij}^k are the times when tankers loaded at i will arrive at j. Define

$$n_{\alpha i} = \text{number of times } t_{ij}^k = \alpha \text{ occurs in row } i \text{ of } t;$$

$$N_{\beta j} = \text{number of times } T_{ij}^k = \beta \text{ occurs in column } j \text{ of } T;$$

i.e., $n_{\alpha i}$ is the number of tankers loading at i at time α and $N_{\beta j}$ is the number arriving at j at time β. Thus, $n_{\alpha i}$ is defined for $\alpha = 1, 2, \ldots, \max t_{ij}^k$ and $N_{\beta j}$ is defined for $\beta = 1, 2, \ldots, \max T_{ij}^k$.

For any schedule, denote the number of reassignments from discharge point j at time β to loading point i at time α by $x_{\alpha i \beta j}$. More precisely, $x_{\alpha i \beta j}$ is the number of occurrences in a schedule of consecutive pairs $(t_{i'j}^k, t_{ij'}^\ell)$ with $T_{i'j}^k = \beta$, $t_{ij'}^\ell = \alpha$. Then for all possible schedules, the inequalities

$$(3.1) \qquad \begin{aligned} \sum_{\alpha, i} x_{\alpha i \beta j} &\leq N_{\beta j} \\[2mm] \sum_{\beta, j} x_{\alpha i \beta j} &\leq n_{\alpha i} \end{aligned}$$

$$(3.2) \qquad x_{\alpha i \beta j} \geq 0$$

are satisfied. In addition, it follows from (2.1) and (2.2) that

$$(3.3) \qquad b_{ij} > \alpha - \beta \text{ implies } x_{\alpha i \beta j} = 0.$$

The system (3.1) can be made into a system of equalities which is formally of transportation type by introducing non-negative slack variables $x_{\alpha i}$, $y_{\beta j}$ and $z = \sum_{\alpha, i} \sum_{\beta, j} x_{\alpha i \beta j}$. Then (3.1) can be rewritten as

$$(3.4) \qquad \begin{aligned} \sum_{\alpha, i} x_{\alpha i \beta j} + y_{\beta j} &= N_{\beta j}, & y_{\beta j} &\geq 0 \\[2mm] \sum_{\beta, j} x_{\alpha i \beta j} + x_{\alpha i} &= n_{\alpha i}, & x_{\alpha i} &\geq 0 \\[2mm] \sum_{\alpha, i} x_{\alpha i} + z &= \sum_{\alpha, i} n_{\alpha i}, & z &\geq 0 \\[2mm] \sum_{\beta, j} y_{\beta j} + z &= \sum_{\beta, j} N_{\beta j}. \end{aligned}$$

and hence each schedule leads to an integral solution of (3.2) and (3.4) which satisfies (3.3).

Conversely, given any integral solution of (3.2), (3.3), and (3.4), a schedule can be constructed from it as follows: Each $x_{\alpha i}$ will be the number of tankers which start their individual schedules at time α from loading point i; i.e., there will be $x_{\alpha i}$ sequences in the rearrangement which have $t_{ij}^k = \alpha$ as first member. Delete one such $t_{i_0 j_j}^{k_0} = \alpha_0$ from t; let $\beta_0 = T_{i_0 j_0}^{k_0} = \alpha_0 + a_{i_0 j_0}$. Since $N_{\beta_0 j_0} > 0$, at least one of the variables $x_{\alpha i \beta_0 j_0}$, $y_{\beta_0 j_0}$ has a positive value. Select one such.

Case 1. $x_{\alpha_1 i_1 \beta_0 j_0} > 0$ was selected. Then there is a $t_{i_1 j_1}^{k_1} = \alpha_1$, since $n_{\alpha_1 i_1} > 0$. Assign α_1 as second member of the sequence. Observe that by (3.3), $\alpha_1 - \beta_0 \geq b_{i_1 j_0}$, hence

$$t_{i_1 j_1}^{k_1} - t_{i_0 j_0}^{k_0} = \alpha_1 - \beta_0 + a_{i_0 j_0} \geq a_{i_0 j_0} + b_{i_1 j_0}$$

and (2.2) is satisfied. Strike out α_1 from t and reduce $x_{\alpha_1 i_1 \beta_0 j_0}$, $N_{\beta_0 j_0}$, $n_{\alpha_1 i_1}$ by unity.

Case 2. $y_{\beta_0 j_0} > 0$ was selected. In this case the sequence ends with α_0. Reduce $y_{\beta_0 j_0}$, $N_{\beta_0 j_0}$ by unity.

If Case 1 obtained, let $\beta_1 = T_{i_1 j_1}^{k_1} = \alpha_1 + a_{i_1 j_1}$, and examine the values of the variables $x_{\alpha i \beta_1 j_1}$, $y_{\beta_1 j_1}$. Again one of these must be positive. Apply either Case 1 or Case 2 with α_1 playing the role of α_0. Repetition of the procedure outlined must eventually end with the selection of some $y_{\beta_k j_k} > 0$ (since by (3.3), $\alpha \leq \beta$ implies $x_{\alpha i \beta j} = 0$), thus completing one of the sequences. The others can be gotten in the same way.

Notice that while many schedules can be constructed from an integral solution of (3.2), (3.3), and (3.4), the only physical difference between two such is that there may be more than one tanker available at the same time at the same pickup point or discharge point, in which case they may be interchanged without affecting the total number of tankers.

Thus, the tanker scheduling problem can be viewed as one of minimizing $\sum_{\alpha,i} x_{\alpha i}$, the number of sequences in a rearrangement (or what is the same thing, maximizing the variable z), over the set of integral solutions[1] of (3.2) and (3.4) in which the variables designated by (3.3) are fixed at zero. But it is well known [1] that the maximum of a linear form defined over all solutions of (3.2) and (3.4) is always assumed at some integral solution, and it is easy to see that this fact is not altered by imposing additional constraints of the form $x_{\alpha i \beta j} = 0$. Hence the scheduling problem can be solved by the simplex algorithm, since the nature of the algorithm is such as to obtain a required integral solution.[c] Moreover, the algorithm is

---

[1] Such whole-number solutions always exist, e.g., take all $x_{\alpha i \beta j} = 0$. This corresponds to the worst possible schedule of assigning a different tanker for each trip.

extremely simple to apply when the problem is of the transportation type, as is this one.

It is obvious that linear programming can be used to optimize schedules with respect to other costs. For example, it would be simply a matter of changing the minimizing form, holding z fixed, to find a schedule for a given number of tankers which has the least sailing time.

4. A NUMERICAL EXAMPLE

We continue with the example of Section 2. First form the table of arrival times

$$T = \begin{array}{c|c|c|c} & 1 & 2 & 3 \\ \hline 1 & 3, 6, 9, 12, 15 & 12, 18 & 8,\ 14 \\ \hline 2 & 4, 7, 10, 13 & 9, 12, 15, 17 & 6, 11, 16 \end{array}$$

Using this table and the one of loading times, compute all $n_{\alpha i}$ and $N_{\beta j}$. After discarding those rows and columns having $n_{\alpha i}$ or $N_{\beta j}$ zero, one is left with the transportation problem whose constraints are indicated schematically in Fig. 1. Crossed out cells mean that the corresponding variable is constrained to be zero by (3.3). The solution shown in Fig. 1 corresponds

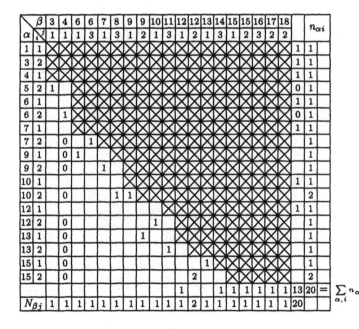

Fig. 1.

to the schedule using seven tankers given in Section 2. This is a degenerate solution to the programming problem and so it is necessary in applying the simplex algorithm to pick out other basic variables having zero values. One way of doing this is shown in Fig. 1 by the placement of the 0's.

An optimal solution, reached after a few iterations, is shown in Fig. 2. It corresponds to the following six-tanker schedule:

(1)	$t_{11}^1 = 1,\ t_{23}^1 = 5,\ t_{22}^1 = 7,\ t_{11}^5 = 13$
(2)	$t_{21}^1 = 3,\ t_{21}^2 = 6,\ t_{21}^3 = 9,\ t_{13}^2 = 12$
(3)	$t_{11}^2 = 4,\ t_{12}^1 = 9,\ t_{22}^4 = 15$
(4)	$t_{13}^1 = 6,\ t_{22}^2 = 10,\ t_{23}^3 = 15$
(5)	$t_{11}^3 = 7,\ t_{23}^2 = 10,\ t_{21}^4 = 12,\ t_{12}^2 = 15$
(6)	$t_{11}^4 = 10,\ t_{22}^3 = 13$

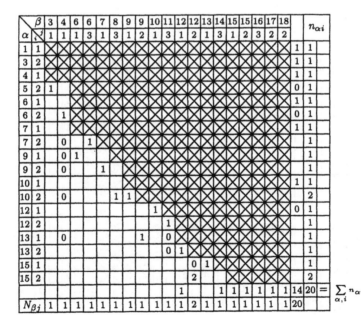

Fig. 2.

REFERENCES

[1] G. Dantzig, "Application of the Simplex Method to a Transportation Problem," *Activity Analysis of Production and Allocation,* Cowles Commission Monograph No. 13, 1951.

[2] J. Robinson and J. Walsh, *Routing of Empties for Fixed-Schedule Transportation,* The RAND Corporation, Memorandum M-406, June 12, 1950.

[3] C. Tompkins, *Discrete Problems and Computers,* INA-53-5, November 17, 1952, pp. 14-16.

Chapter 10

A LINEAR PROGRAMMING APPROACH TO THE CHEMICAL EQUILIBRIUM PROBLEM

GEORGE DANTZIG, SELMER JOHNSON AND WAYNE WHITE

The RAND Corporation, Santa Monica, California

The well known chemical equilibrium problem is expressed in the form of minimizing the free energy of a mixture in order to compute the chemical composition at equilibrium.

By piecewise linear approximations to the free energy function, the problem becomes a linear program which can be solved by a standard code on a computing machine. Successive approximations give any degree of accuracy.

1. Introduction

The extension of linear programming methods into the non-linear area is recognized as one of the outstanding areas of research today. One way to treat a general convex objective function is to locally linearize it by taking partial derivatives. However the authors believe that researchers in the linear programming field are interested in ideas that convert a "near" separable convex function into a completely separable case where more efficient methods can then take over [1], [2].

Although the particular problem resolved has a non-management application, it should also be of interest to a rather large audience scheduling for the Petroleum Industry. These are for the most part chemical engineers who are familiar with the application to the Chemical Equilibrium Problem and who can take advantage of the solution for their respective companies. They will find the companion paper [3] discusses more of the chemical background to the problem and gives an alternative procedure. The present paper stresses the mathematical development of the linear programming approach to this problem.[a]

The determination of the chemical composition of a complex mixture under chemical equilibrium conditions is a classic problem. There have been many computing techniques proposed and the constant appearance of new ones attests that none are entirely satisfactory. In our second paper

[3], entitled "Chemical Equilibrium in Complex Mixtures," the formulation of two methods discovered in the course of our researches were reviewed, one of which is a steepest descent based on a quadratic fit to the free energy function to be minimized, and the other which reduces it to a linear programming problem. The purpose of this paper is to give a complete account of the latter. Our purpose is to show that there is an elegant way to transform the free energy function into a *convex separable function* which permits convenient piecewise linear approximation and consequent solution by linear programming. Any desired degree of accuracy can be reached by successively improving the approximation.

2. The Problem

We consider an equilibrium mixture containing m different atom types. While in theory these will combine into all chemically possible molecular species, in practice only standard types are considered, including the monotonic types, which are known to occur in measurable amounts.

Let b_i = the number of atomic weights of species i present in the mixture.

x_j = the number of moles of molecular species j present in the mixture where

(1) $$x_j \geq 0, \qquad j = 1, 2, \cdots n.$$

$\bar{x}$ = the total number of moles of gas in the mixture, i.e.,

(2) $$\bar{x} = \sum x_j.$$

a_{ij} = the number of atoms of species i in a molecule of species j.

Then the mass balance equations are

(3) $$\sum_{j=1}^{n} a_{ij} x_j = b_i \text{ for } i = 1, 2, \cdots, m.$$

The determination of the equilibrium composition of a gaseous mixture is equivalent to the determination of the values of the mole numbers x_j that obey constraints (3) and minimize the total free energy of the mixture given by

(4) $$\begin{aligned} F(x_1, \cdots, x_n) &= \sum_{j=1}^{n} c_j x_j + \sum_{j=1}^{n} x_j \ln(x_j/\bar{x}) \\ &= \sum_{j=1}^{n} c_j x_j + \bar{x} \sum_{j=1}^{n} (x_j/\bar{x}) \ln(x_j/\bar{x}) \end{aligned}$$

which can be shown to be a convex function.[1] The values c_j are the modified Gibbs free energy function $F°/RT$ of the atomic species at a given temperature plus the natural logarithm of the pressure in atmospheres.

Our problem is to minimize (4) subject to the linear equality and inequality constraints (1), (2), (3).

In order to apply linear programming, we make a piecewise linear approximation to each of the terms $(x_j/\bar{x})\ln(x_j/\bar{x}_j)$ that appear in (4). If we set $\alpha = x_j/\bar{x}$ and $\beta = \alpha \ln \alpha$ then we shall replace each such curve by a broken line function $\beta = \beta(\alpha)$ such as shown in Fig. 1.[b]

The k points where the two curves agree are denoted by (α_i, β_i) where $i = 1, 2, \cdots, k$.

Let us imagine that the values of $\bar{x}$ and x_1 are fixed for the moment and that the values of $x_{11} \geq 0$, $x_{12} \geq 0, \cdots, x_{1k} \geq 0$ are chosen so as to satisfy

$$(5) \qquad \bar{x} = x_{11} + x_{12} + \cdots + x_{1k}$$

$$(6) \qquad x_1 = \alpha_1 x_{11} + \alpha_2 x_{12} + \cdots + \alpha_k x_{1k}$$

and to minimize z_1 where

$$(7) \qquad z_1 = \beta_1 x_{11} + \beta_2 x_{12} + \cdots + \beta_k x_{1k}.$$

We shall now prove that $\beta = \beta(\alpha)$ is convex, and that

$$(8) \qquad \text{Min } z_1 = \bar{x}\beta(x_1/\bar{x}) \doteq x_1 \ln(x_1/\bar{x}).$$

Proof: It is clear that $\beta = \beta(\alpha)$ will be convex if $\beta = \alpha \ln \alpha$ is convex and this follows by noting that

$$(9) \qquad \frac{d\beta}{d\alpha} = 1 + \ln \alpha$$

is monotonically increasing. Next let us substitute

$$(10) \qquad x_{11} = \lambda_1 \bar{x}, \quad x_{12} = \lambda_2 \bar{x}, \quad \cdots, x_{1k} = \lambda_k \bar{x};$$

then (5), (6), and (7) may be rewritten

$$(11) \qquad 1 = \lambda_1 + \lambda_2 + \cdots + \lambda_k$$

$$(12) \qquad (x_1/\bar{x}) = \alpha_1 \lambda_1 + \alpha_2 \lambda_2 + \cdots + \alpha_k \lambda_k$$

$$(13) \qquad (z_1/\bar{x}) = \beta_1 \lambda_1 + \beta_2 \lambda_2 + \cdots + \beta_k \lambda_k$$

---

[1] [3] contains a direct proof; alternatively the fact that the chemical equilibrium problem can be reduced to a linear programming problem to any degree of accuracy also proves convexity.

and the problem is equivalent to finding $\lambda_1 \geq 0$, $\lambda_2 \geq 0, \cdots, \lambda_k \geq 0$ satisfying (11), (12) for fixed x_1 and $\bar{x}$ minimizing $(z_1/\bar{x})$. If we interpret $\lambda_i \geq 0$ as the weights assigned to the points (α_i, β_i), then $\sum_1^k \alpha_i \lambda_i$ and $\sum_1^k \beta_i \lambda_i$ are coordinates of the *center of gravity* of the points. Hence we are seeking weights to assign to the points such that the abscissa of the center of gravity is $(x_1/\bar{x})$, see (12), and the ordinate $(z_1/\bar{x})$, see (13), is as small as possible. Obviously this smallest value, for any convex curve $\beta = \beta(\alpha)$ is $\beta(x_1/\bar{x})$, and this value is obtained for a broken line function by assigning $\lambda_i = 0$ to all points except the two points on either side of $(x_1/\bar{x})$ and weighting up those two points appropriately.

To solve the chemical equilibrium problem by linear programming, consider the problem of finding $x_j \geq 0$, $x_{jl} \geq 0$ and minimum z satisfying

$$
(14)
\begin{array}{l}
a_{11}x_1 + \cdots + a_{1n}x_n = b_1 \\
a_{21}x_1 + \cdots + a_{2n}x_n = b_2 \\
\quad\vdots \qquad\qquad\qquad\qquad \vdots \\
a_{m1}x_1 + \cdots + a_{mn}x_n = b_m \\
\hline
x_1 + \cdots + x_n - \bar{x} + \sum_{l=1}^{k} x_{1l} = 0 \\
\qquad\qquad\qquad\; -\bar{x} + \sum_{l=1}^{k} x_{2l} = 0 \\
\qquad\qquad \vdots \qquad\qquad \ddots \qquad\qquad \vdots \\
\qquad\qquad\qquad\; -\bar{x} + \sum_{l=1}^{k} x_{ml} = 0 \\
\hline
-x_1 \qquad\qquad + \sum_{l=1}^{k} \alpha_l x_{1l} = 0 \\
\qquad -x_2 \qquad\qquad + \sum_{l=1}^{k} \alpha_l x_{2l} = 0 \\
\qquad\quad \ddots \qquad\qquad \ddots \qquad\qquad \vdots \\
\qquad\qquad -x_n \qquad + \sum_{l=1}^{k} \alpha_l x_{nl} = 0 \\
\hline
c_1 x_1 + \cdots + c_n x_n + \sum_{l=1}^{k} \beta_l x_{1l} + \sum_{l=1}^{k} \beta_l x_{2l} + \cdots + \sum_{l=1}^{k} \beta_l x_{nl} = z
\end{array}
$$

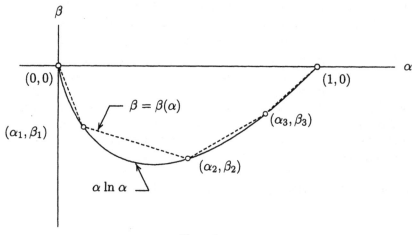

It will now be easy to see that the values $x_j = x_j^0$, that form part of the optimal solution to (14), give the optimal solution to (1), (2), (3), if (4) is replaced by the approximation

$$(15) \qquad F \doteq \bar{F} = \sum_{j=1}^n c_j x_j + \sum_{j=1}^n \bar{x} \beta(x_j/\bar{x}).$$

Proof: Consider an optimal solution to (14) and let the values of $x_j = x_j^0$. For these fixed values of x_j, it is clear from the structure of (14) that the optimal choice of values $x_{11}, x_{12}, \cdots, x_{1k}$ for example must satisfy (5) and (6) and minimize z_1 [as] given by (7). Moreover by (8) the value of $z_1 = \bar{x}^0 \beta(x_j^0/\bar{x}^0)$ and

$$\text{Min } z = \sum_{j=1}^n c_j x_j^0 + \sum_{j=1}^n \bar{x}^0 \beta(x_j^0/\bar{x}^0) = \bar{F}^0$$

Conversely, consider an optimal solution to (1), (2), (3), (15) with values $x_j = x_j^*$; we can always find values $x_{jl} = x_{jl}^* \geq 0$ such that

$$\bar{x}_j^* = \sum_{l=1}^k x_{jl}^*$$

$$x_j^* = \sum_{l=1}^k \alpha_l x_{jl}^*$$

$$\beta(x_j^*/\bar{x}_j^*) = \sum_{l=1}^k \beta_l \bar{x}_{jl}^*.$$

As we saw in the discussion following (13), these x_j^*, x_{jl}^* are a solution to (14) whose value $z = z^*$ is the same as the value Min $\bar{F}$ obtained by substituting $x_j = x_j^*$ in (15); hence Min $\bar{F} = z^*$. From the relations Min $\bar{F} = z^* \geq$ Min z and Min $\bar{F} \leq \bar{F}^0 =$ Min z follows Min $\bar{F} =$ Min z and our proof is complete.

This approach has several advantages over previous methods.

(1) It uses a standardized code of the simplex method of linear programming.

(2) Only one curve $\alpha \ln \alpha$, for $0 \leq \alpha \leq 1$, has to be approximated and this can be done as accurately as desired since the number of equations is not increased.

(3) There is no necessity of deciding in advance which are the so called major components and which are the minor ones as in the usual case for other methods.

The evaluation of $\alpha_j \ln \alpha_j$ can be included in the coding so that the successive approximations could be carried out automatically to any degree of accuracy.

In order not to tax the memory of the computing machine and also to reduce the number of computations of $\beta_l = \alpha_l \ln \alpha_l$, the following system of "screening" should be added to the code.

First compute $\beta_l = \alpha_l \ln \alpha_l$ at $\alpha_l = 0$, .5, 1 with grid size .5. Then after the first linear program approximation[c] has been solved, for each term $(x_j/\bar{x}) \ln(x_j/\bar{x})$, halve the grid size and compute only those new values which are adjacent to the current value of $\alpha = x_j/\bar{x}$. Thus on the second piecewise approximation, if some $x_j = 0$, compute $\beta_l = \alpha_l \ln \alpha_l = .25$, discarding the value at $\alpha_l = 1$; if $x_j/\bar{x} = .5$, compute $\alpha_l \ln \alpha_l$ at .25 and .75 and discard the values at 0 and 1. If $x_j/\bar{x}$ is a weighted average of two grid points 0 and .5, then include a grid value of α_l at .25 and discard the value at 1, etc. In this way for each new piecewise approximation we have at most three values of α_l and $\alpha_l \ln \alpha_l$ for each $j = 1, 2, \cdots, n$ such that the range of α_j values is halved each time. It has been observed empirically that successive values of $x_j/\bar{x}$ have stayed within the ranges set up for all previous cycles, i.e., the accuracy has doubled with each successive approximation.

After a sufficient number of cycles have been carried out, any x_j which is still at zero level in the approximate solution could be adjusted to a trace level by standard methods used to get the order of magnitude of such components when the non-trace level components have been determined very closely.

When there are a large number of problems to be run, it is recommended that the simplex code be modified to generate *internally* in the machine the columns associated with the variables x_{jl}. If this is done it is probably best to determine the best choice of α_l, β_l *analytically* for each j rather than by the above grid technique. The present RAND code is being modified along these lines.

There is also another improvement possible which takes further advantage of the structure by partitioning the basis into two parts—the first part associated with the first m rows and the other associated with the remaining rows. This results in an essential $m \times m$ subbasis whose inverse is needed—the remainder of the computation is then carried out implicitly.[d]

Bibliography

[1] CHARNES, A., AND LEMKE, C. E., "Minimization of Non-Linear Separable Convex Functions," *Naval Research Logistics Quarterly* vol. 1:4, pp. 301–312 (1954).

[2] DANTZIG, G. B., "Recent Advances in Linear Programming," *Management Science* January 1956, pp. 131–143.

[3] WHITE, W. B., JOHNSON, S. M., AND DANTZIG, G. B., "Chemical Equilibrium in Complex Mixtures," *Journal of Chemical Physics*, pp. 751–755, May 1958, vol. 28, no. 5.

Chapter 11

FORMULATING AN OBJECTIVE FOR AN ECONOMY

George B. DANTZIG, Patrick H. McALLISTER, and John C. STONE

Department of Operations Research, Stanford University, Stanford, CA 94305 USA

This paper is dedicated to the memory of E. M. L. Beale. Not a small part of Martin Beale's success in developing and solving large-scale mathematical programs is attributed to the care he took in properly formulating his models.

Our presentation concerns our efforts to also properly formulate a model. Our model is an economic model used for technology assessment. In order for it to be useful, it is important that the dual variables represent as realistically as possible real world prices. This required us to formulate the model as a time-staged economic equilibrium model. Our main result is a proof that an equilibrium formulation using expected aggregate demand can under certain conditions be replaced by one in which the economy is driven by an aggregate utility or objective function, one that promotes economic growth subject to physical flow constraints. We show that such an objective function always exists except for populations consisting of significantly large classes of people whose consumption patterns differ radically one from another. Assuming that the latter is not the case, this equivalent formulation means that mathematical programming software can be applied to efficiently solve the model. This paper summarizes an extensive paper entitled Deriving a Utility Function for the U.S. Economy [3]. The main theorems are stated without proof.

Key words: Economic equilibrium model, mathematical programming, model of economy, operations research, utility function, demand function.

Introduction

At Stanford, we have been developing since 1975 a macroeconomic model, called PILOT, to assess the impact of old and proposed new technologies on the growth of the U.S. economy, and how the state of the economy and economic policy may affect the pace at which innovation and modernization proceeds. We will give no technical details about the model, except to say

The authors wish to thank Kenneth Arrow, Gerard Debreu, Robert Dorfman, Dale Jorgenson, and Lawrence J. Lau for their helpful comments.

Research of this report was partially supported by the National Science Foundation Grants DMS-8420623, SES-8518662 and ECS-8617905; U.S. Department of Energy Grant DE-F03-87ER25028; Office of Naval Research Contract N0004-85-K-0343, Electric Power Research Institute Contract RP 5006-01, and the Center for Economic Policy Research at Stanford University.

that the physical constraints simply state that (a) final consumption in each period cannot exceed the amount produced, and (b) the amount produced cannot exceed industrial capacity built in current or earlier periods [3]. We will be concerned in this paper with what additional conditions are needed to realistically represent the forces that drive the economy over time.

One approach might be to postulate that the economy grows so as to maximize an aggregate *objective function* that measures in some sense the discounted "standard of living" of the population over time. Under this formulation, we would have a mathematical program for which software exists that can successfully solve very large-scale models [8]. This optimization problem, however, may be replaced by the set of Kuhn-Tucker conditions that must hold at a maximizing solution. Interpreting the Lagrange multipliers or dual variables as "prices" these state that certain relations must hold between prices and aggregate final consumption, and between prices and the choice of production and investment activities by producers/investors. In addition complementary-slackness conditions must also hold between primal and dual variables.

Economists often reverse this process. They do not postulate an objective function but instead formulate the model as a set of physical constraints, a set of behavioral constraints about how consumers respond to prices, called a *demand function*, a set of behavioral constraints about how producers/investors respond to prices, called a *supply function*, and a set of complementary-slackness conditions that must hold when an equilibrium between prices and quantities is achieved. Such a formulation is called an *economic equilibrium model*. This model, while structurally quite analogous to the mathematical-programming formulation, is mathematically more general. Indeed there is a famous result of Kenneth Arrow known as the *Impossibility Theorem*[a] that states that *in general* there may not exist an objective function which, when maximized subject to the physical constraints, implies the equilibrium [1, 4, 10]. A basic reference on aggregate consumer behavior is [6].

We initially formulated the PILOT model as a mathematical program because (1) software exists that could solve a problem with 2,000 physical constraints, 4,500 bounded variables, and 70,000 nonzero technical coefficients; and because (2) with a time separable objective function it is evident why the economy would grow if it has the potential for growth. The weakness of this initial approach is that the objective we concocted for measuring the standard of living implied behavioral reactions on the part of the producer/investor and of the final consumer to dual variables, interpreted as prices, that were inconsistent with their true behavior in the real world. It is very important that dual variables be interpreted as prices if our model is to have any validity.

This has caused us recently to reformulate PILOT as an economic equilibrium model. This approach presented us with two major difficulties: (1) no software existed that can efficiently solve truly large-scale equilibrium systems, and (2) it is not easy to see why reasonable economic growth should take place although we found in experimental trials it did so nicely. The latter property is very important because our goal is to predict the likely rate of introduction of new technology.

The path we chose to resolve these difficulties was to start with the utility functions of individual consumers and to develop from scratch the functional form of the expected aggregate demand function to see if there might be something special about its form that Arrow's Impossibility Theorem would not apply.[b] If so, it would imply that an aggregated utility function for the economy does exist. Hopefully its functional form would also make it self evident why growth in [the] economy would take place.

Our innovation lies in making the distribution of utility functions of individuals at any income level independent of the income level. We did this by placing a representative set of individual consumers utility functions in an imaginary "population urn" and randomly drawing them out (with replacement) and assigning them to the individuals at each income level. This leads to the notion of *expected* demand. We find under mild restrictions on the distribution of the preference parameters (such as the population is not too highly polarized as to their consumption tastes) that an expected aggregate objective function exists. When this happens, we say that the expected aggregate demand function is *integrable*.[c]

We begin by first presenting in a little more detail the general formulation of dynamic equilibrium and optimization versions of the model. We then set aside the formulation and focus on the functional form of the individual consumer demand functions, then on the form of the expected consumer demand function at a given income level, and then show that, if the range of the income distribution is not too broad, the function form of the expected per capita demand function can be derived independent of the exact form of the income distribution. We next present conditions that guarantee that the expected per capita demand function is integrable. Finally we return to finish the formulation of the time-staged model and show how the integrability within a time period enables us to formulate a mathematical programming problem which is equivalent to the equilibrium problem.

References denoted by [·] will be found at the end of the paper.

Formulation of the a multi-period model

The reader is referred to Table 1 which depicts a two-period economy model formulated with an objective. The problem is to maximize an aggregate utility function subject to primal physical flow constraints. The optimality conditions are expressed by the dual constraints[d] and the Kuhn-

Tucker complementary slackness conditions, [7]. The two-period equilibrium model has exactly the same structure except the objective statement is omitted and $\partial U_t / \partial X_t$ is replaced by a function $F_t(X_t)$, called an *inverse demand function*, which may or may not be more general depending on whether or not it is expressible as $\partial U_t / \partial X_t$ for some function $U_t(X_t)$.

The mathematical formulation of the multi-period equilibrium model is along the classical lines of an Arrow and Debreu [1, 4] or Scarf [9] model, with no surprises except perhaps for the interpretation of the profitability constraints of investors as rate-of-return formulae for selecting among different investment possibilities. A typical production/investment activity j in period t has a column consisting of three sets of fixed coefficients $[B_t(j), -A_t(j), -D_t(j)]'$ per unit level of activity where

Table 1
Two-period economy model

Objective Function	$U_1(X_1) + \delta U_2(X_2) = \max$

Primal

		Corresp. Dual Var.
$B_1 Y_1$	$\leq k_1$	$\sigma_1 \geq 0$
$-A_1 Y_1 + X_1$	≤ 0	$\pi_1 \geq 0$
$-D_1 Y_1 \qquad +B_2 Y_2$	$\leq k_2$	$\sigma_2 \geq 0$
$-A_2 Y_2 + X_2 \leq 0$		$\pi_2 \geq 0$

Dual

		Corresp. Primal Var.
$-B_1' \sigma_1 + A_1' \pi_1 + D_1' \sigma_2$	≤ 0	$Y_1 \geq 0$
$-\pi_1 \qquad + \partial U_1 / \partial X_1$	≤ 0	$X_1 \geq 0$
$-B_2' \sigma_2 + A_2' \pi_2$	≤ 0	$Y_2 \geq 0$
$-\pi_2 \qquad + \delta \partial U_2 / \partial X_2 \leq 0$		$X_2 \geq 0$

Complementary Slackness Conditions

$$\hat{\sigma}_t' \sigma_t = 0, \quad \hat{\pi}_t' \pi_t = 0, \quad \hat{Y}_t' Y_t = 0, \quad \hat{X}_t' X_t = 0$$

(Symbols with ˆ are slack vectors that added to LHS above turned them into equations)

$B_t(j)$ is the input/output vector of capacities, resources, and flows of all items (goods) needed for production and capacity formation in period t *except final consumer items*; $A_t(j)$ is the output/input vector of final consumer items in period t; and $D_t(j)$ is the output vector of capacities, resources, and intermediate goods left over or produced in period t for period $t + 1$. The model is then defined by five sets of relations numbered (1) through (5). The first two we refer to as the primal or physical flow constraints.

Primal Constraints: In (1) below, $Y_t \geq 0$ is the vector of aggregate production and investment levels to be determined in period t. In words, (1) states that the capacity, resources, intermediate items $B_t Y_t$, required for production and capacity formation at levels Y_t cannot exceed the amount of these items $D_{t-1} Y_{t-1}$ left over or produced by period $t-1$ activities for period t plus the vector k_t of these items exogenously supplied:

$$(1) \qquad B_t Y_t \leq D_{t-1} Y_{t-1} + k_t; \quad \text{corresp. dual } \sigma_t \geq 0.$$

The vector of dual prices corresponding to (1) is denoted by $\sigma_t \geq 0$, and the slack vector which turns (1) into an equation is denoted $\hat{\sigma}_t \geq 0$. According to the theory of Arrow and Debreu [1], production levels Y_t and prices σ_t will adjust until at equilibrium the complementary slackness conditions $\hat{\sigma}_t' \sigma_t = 0$ hold.

In (2) below, $X_t \geq 0$ is the vector of aggregate final consumption in period t measured in physical units. In words, (2) states that consumption cannot exceed $A_t Y_t$, the net output from production and investment less f_t, any fixed demand (like government plus any minimum floor provided to the final consumer and not paid for by income for consumption):

$$(2) \qquad -A_t Y_t + X_t \leq -f_t; \quad \text{corresp. dual } \pi_t \geq 0.$$

The corresponding vector of normalized discounted dual prices is denoted by $\pi_t \geq 0$, and the slack vector which turns (2) into an equation is denoted by $\hat{\pi}_t \geq 0$. At equilibrium $\hat{\pi}_t' \pi_t = 0$.

Dual Constraints: We assume that investors/producers require that a numeraire be selected in each period relative to which prices for various final consumer goods are measured before discounting it for use in their rate of return formulas. If so, we say that the prices $\bar{\pi}$ are "normalized." Prices $\sigma_t \geq 0$ and $\pi_t \geq 0$ for the dual constraints are defined to be *discounted period t prices*; moreover π_t is defined to be discounted *normalized period t prices*. Thus, $\pi_t = \delta^{t-1} \bar{\pi}_t$ where the discount factor is δ^{t-1} and $\bar{\pi}_t$ is the vector of normalized prices. The vector of unnormalized period t prices of final consumer items is denoted by p_t. We have no need for a symbol for prices on capacity, reserves, and intermediate goods relative to the unnormalized prices p_t but prices on these items relative to normalized prices $\bar{\pi}_t$ are denoted $\bar{\sigma}_t$.

Relation (3) below states that investors must receive at least their minimum rate of return $r = \delta^{-1} - 1$ or they won't invest. For $t < T$,

$$(3) \qquad -B_t' \sigma_t + A_t' \pi_t \leq -D_t' \sigma_{t+1}; \quad \text{corresp. primal } Y_t \geq 0.$$

The slack vector which turns (3) into an equation is denoted $\hat{Y}_t \geq 0$. It is in 1 to 1 correspondence[e] with primal variables $Y_t \geq 0$. At equilibrium, $\hat{Y}_t' Y_t = 0$.

In (4) below, $F_t(X_t)$ is the inverse of the expected aggregate demand function which we assume exists except for a scale factor to be determined that generates normalized period t prices $\bar{\pi}_t$ required by the rate-of-return formula (3):

(4) $-\pi_t + \delta^{t-1} F_t(\boldsymbol{X}_t) \leq 0;$ corresp. primal $\boldsymbol{X}_t \geq 0.$

The corresponding set of primal variables is $\boldsymbol{X}_t \geq 0$. When $\boldsymbol{X}_t > 0$, which is usually the case, this relation becomes an equation. The slack vector that turns (4) into an equation is denoted $\hat{\boldsymbol{X}}_t \geq 0$. At equilibrium $\hat{\boldsymbol{X}}_t' \boldsymbol{X}_t = 0$.

The Complementary Slackness Conditions are that all variables be non-negative and

(5) $\hat{\sigma}_t' \sigma_t = 0, \quad \hat{\pi}_t' \pi_t = 0, \quad \hat{\boldsymbol{Y}}_t' \boldsymbol{Y}_t = 0, \quad \hat{\boldsymbol{X}}_t' \boldsymbol{X}_t = 0.$

The model has $t = 1, 2, \ldots, T$ periods. For period $t = 1$, the term $D_0 Y_0$ is omitted in relation (1).

This completes the mathematical statement of the dynamic model. The remainder of this paper is concerned with deriving the form of the *inverse* aggregate demand function $F_t(\boldsymbol{X}_t)$, and the utility function $U(\boldsymbol{X}_1, \ldots, \boldsymbol{X}_t)$ for the full economy when it exists. Before doing so we note that if the economy were driven by an objective function of the form $U = \sum \delta^{t-1} U_t(\boldsymbol{X}_t)$, the Kuhn-Tucker conditions conditions derived by maximizing U subject to primal physical-flow conditions (1) and (2) would give rise to conditions (3), (4) and (5) where $F_t(\boldsymbol{X}_t) = \partial U_t / \partial \boldsymbol{X}_t$, see reference [7]. If the latter conditions hold for all t we say the vector functions $F_t(\boldsymbol{X}_t)$ in the context of the full model are *integrable*. If not, we say the model is non-integrable and no utility function for the economy exists. On the other hand, if the expected aggregate demand function for each period is integrable, we show that this implies that an objective function for the time-staged model exists when (and only when) the numeraire for measuring prices in each period has been suitably chosen.

Utility functions of individuals

The first assumption we make is that each final consumer has a utility function that is quadratic in the consumption variables and that he chooses his consumption vector by maximizing his utility function subject to his budget constraint. This specific functional form may be viewed as a second-order global approximation to whatever may be his true utility function.

Assumption 1. Individual i has a utility function $U^i(X^i)$ measuring the value i attaches to having a consumption vector X^i which can be represented by a general quadratic function of the form

(6) $U^i(X^i) = 2(M^i S^i) X^i - (X^i)' M^i (X^i) + \text{Constant}_i$

where vector $S^i > 0$ and matrix M^i is symmetric and positive definite, hence nonsingular.[f]

Without loss of generality, we may rescale the matrices M^i so that, letting $e' = (1, 1, \ldots, 1)$, their inverses H^i have the property

$$(7) \qquad e'H^i e = \sum_k \sum_l H^i(k, l) = 1, \quad H^i = (M^i)^{-1} \quad \text{for all } i.$$

Letting $\text{Constant}_i = -(S^i)'M^i S^i$, we can rewrite the utility function of i as

$$(8) \qquad U^i(X^i) = -(S^i - X^i)'M^i(S^i - X^i) < 0 \quad \text{for all } S^i - X^i \neq 0.$$

It is easy to see $U^i(X^i)$ in (8) is unconditionally maximized when $X^i = S^i$. Therefore, it is natural to assume that S^i is strictly positive and to refer to S^i as the "satiation" vector of individual i. We view the *income I* of an individual as an "authorization" to expend up to that amount for actual consumption. Should it happen that an individual's budget $I_i \geq p'S^i$, he maximizes his utility by buying his satiation vector S^i. The unexpended amount $I_i - p'S^i$, in this case, is not used.

Notation. For discussion involving a fixed period, we will usually omit the time subscript. Thus the consumption vector of the i-th consumer in period t is denoted by $X^i = X^i_t$; his *budget*, i.e., his personal income for consumption by $I = I_t$ measured in period t undiscounted dollars.[g] The vector of undiscounted prices is denoted by $p = p_t$. Occasionally when it is clear from the context that there is no confusion with the time subscript, we may denote the k-th component of X^i and p by X^i_k and p_k, otherwise by $X^i(k)$ and $p(k)$. We will use the symbol $\mathcal{J}$ to denote the identity matrix to avoid confusion with I which refers to personal income. The symbols α, λ, δ denote scalar constants. L.H.S. and R.H.S. are short for *left-hand side* and *right-hand side* of an equation or inequality. Boldface $\boldsymbol{X}_t$, $\boldsymbol{U}_t$, $\boldsymbol{I}_t$ are reserved for *aggregate* consumption, utility and income. The symbol $\mathcal{E}$ denotes expectation. The function $\mathcal{E}_i(a^i)$ for $i = (1, \ldots, n)$ has a special meaning: it is a function that generates the arithmetic mean of a^i.

Form of the individual demand functions. The budget constraint and nonnegativity constraint $X^i \geq 0$ for individual i in period t at fixed prices p (assumed to be strictly positive) are:

$$(9) \qquad p'X^i \leq I, \quad X^i, \quad p > 0,$$

where I is the income i has for consumption. Subject to (9), i maximizes his utility function $U^i(X^i)$. This is a special case of a quadratic programming problem [2]. We distinguish three cases: The *high* income case, the *standard* case that defines the *range of income of interest*, and the *low* income case. In the high income case, $I \geq p'S^i$ an individual i maximizes his utility by buying his satiation vector, i.e., $X^i = S^i$. Otherwise, the budget constraint is tight and the procedure begins by forming a Lagrangian and setting its partials to zero,

$$\text{(10)} \qquad \partial[U^i(x^I) - 2\lambda(p'x^I)]/\partial X^i = 0,$$

which is then solved to determine X^i as a function of λ; the expression for X^i as a vector function of λ is then substituted into (9) with the budget tight and solved for λ. If $X^i > 0$, then this is the standard case. The low case occurs, by definition, when the budget $I \leq I_i^*$ is so low that i maximizes his utility on the boundary of the non-negative orthant $X^i \geq 0$ by setting to zero one or more components of X^i.

For the "standard" case, we substitute the quadratic expression for $U^i(X^i)$ given by (6) into (10) and differentiate partially:

$$\text{(11)} \qquad M^i(S^i - X^i) = \lambda \cdot p.$$

Solving for $S^i - X^i$:

$$\text{(12)} \qquad S^i - X^i = \lambda \cdot H^i p, \quad \text{where } H^i = (M^i)^{-1}.$$

Note that the inverses $H^i = (M^i)^{-1}$ exist and are also *symmetric* and *positive definite*. We can now use the tight budge constraint to determine λ. Multiplying (12) by p' on the left and setting $p'X^i = I$, we can solve for λ and substitute back into (12). This yields (13) below, the *demand function of individual i* as a function of prices and income where λ, equal to the term in parentheses, is positive if the budget I is less than the income $p'S^i$ required to buy the satiation vector X^i. Note that $p'H^i p > 0$ follows from H^i being positive definite. It is easy to see that (13) below satisfies two properties of demand functions which hold when the budget constraint is tight: (a) $p'X^i = I$ and (b) X^i remains invariant if we rescale prices p and income I proportionally.

Theorem 1. *The demand function of individual i, for fixed prices p, is a piecewise linear function of consumption income I.*

(i) *For the "range of income of interest," the demand function is given by*

$$\text{(13)} \qquad S^i - X^i = \left(\frac{p'S^i - I}{p'H^i p}\right) H^i p, \quad I_i^* \leq I \leq I_i^{**} = p'S^i$$

(ii) *For $I \leq I_i^*$, one or more components $X^i(k) = 0$. As $I \to 0$, $X^i \to 0$.*

(iii) *For $I > I_i^{**} = p'$, the budget constraint is slack, and $X^i = S^i$ for all $I \geq I_i^{**}$.*

We will loosely refer to the income levels between $I^* = \max I_i^*$ and $I^{**} = \min p'S^i$ as the *range of income of interest*. It is [the] range of income for consumption in which no individual maximizes his utility on the boundary of the orthant $X^i \geq 0$ or has sufficient income to buy his satiation vector S^i. This range depends on the prices p. We think of this range as very broad, I^* representing extreme poverty and I^{**} as being very rich. As defined, this range is independent of i. Therefore, the form of the demand function for all i is given by (13) for $I^* \leq I \leq I^{**}$.

The next step is to determine the average demand vector of all individuals in [the] population with the same budget income I. *We assume that the utility function which people have is independent of the particular income which they happen to have.* Suppose there are n_I individuals at income level I. We need to have a way to assign the parameters (S^i, H^i) of the utility function to these n_I persons, sum their n_I demand functions and then average them to compute their average demand vector as a function of I.

We can achieve this independence by selecting a representative set of n possible (S^i, H^i) parameters and writing them as labels on n balls, $i = (1, \ldots, n)$, and placing the balls in an imaginary urn which we call the *population urn*. In making a random drawing from the urn, we think of each (S^i, H^i) as equally likely to be drawn. If it is desired to make it more likely to choose certain (S^i, H^i), this could be achieved by weighting the distribution of (S^i, H^i) in the urn or by replication of certain of the balls.

Assumption 2. *The Population Urn Assumption.* The set of utility functions of the n_I individuals in the population that happen to have the same personal income I for consumption is a random sample with replacement of size n_I taken from an "urn" containing a representative set of parameters (S^i, H^i), $i = (1, \ldots, n)$, of the utility functions of the whole population; moreover, we assume the distribution in the urn of the "satiation-level" parameters S^i is independent of the distribution of the price "cross-effect" parameters $H^i = (M^i)^{-1}$.

For any of the n_I individuals j, denote their expected S^j and X^j by $\bar{S}^I$ and $\bar{X}^I$, respectively. Our assumption that the distribution of the utility functions does not depend on I implies that this expected $\bar{S}^I$ is the same for all $I^* \leq I \leq I^{**}$ in this range and therefore $\bar{S}^I = \bar{S}$ where $\bar{S}$ is the arithmetic mean of the S^i in the population urn.

We will write the *arithmetic mean* of S^i in the population urn as $\mathcal{E}_i S^i$; it has the same value as the expected value of a single random drawing of S^i from the population urn. Similarly we will denote the arithmetic mean of any function $X(S^i, H^i)$ for (S^i, H^i) in the population urn as $\mathcal{E}_i X(S^i, H^i)$. For any of the n_I individuals j that have an income I in the range of income of interest, $I^* \leq I \leq I^{**}$, for any (S^i, H^i) that has been assigned to j from the urn, we know that (13) holds. Therefore taking the expectation of (13) we obtain (14) below.

Theorem 2. *For fixed prices* $p = p_t$,

(i) *for each individual* j *whose income level* I *is in the range of income of interest,* $\bar{X}^I$, *the expected value of the consumption vector* X^j *is a linear function of* I:

$$(14) \quad \bar{S} - \bar{X}^I = (p'\bar{S} - I) \cdot G(p), \quad \max I_i^* = I^* \leq I \leq I^{**} = \min p'S^i,$$

where

$$(15) \qquad\qquad G(p) = \mathcal{E}_i(p'H^i p)^{-1} \cdot H^i p$$

and $\mathcal{E}_i$ *denotes the arithmetic mean over* $i = 1, 2, \ldots, n$ *in the population urn.*

(ii) *As* I *decreases below* I^*, *it is more and more likely individuals* j *with this income will maximize their utility by setting components of* X^j *to zero and* $\bar{X}^I = \mathcal{E}X^j \to 0$.

(iii) *As* I *increases beyond* $I^{**} = \min p'S^i$, *it is more and more likely that individuals* j *with this income will maximize their utility by buying their randomly assigned satiation vectors, and* $\bar{X}^I = \mathcal{E}X^j$ *will level off to* $\bar{S}$.

The average demand, for some item k as a function [of] I, for all individuals whose consumption income is I is called an Engel curve. In [3] we present empirical data showing average consumption as a function of income for eight broad consumer categories (*Food, Clothing, Housing, Household Operation, Transportation, Recreation, Personal Care,* and *All Other*). The form of the observed Engel curves is generally consistent with same consumption income I is a linear function of I over the "range of income of practical interest."

Per capita demand as a function of per capita income. Given prices, per capita demand is derived from the expected demand of persons at various levels by convolution with the income distribution. Let $C_k(I)$ be the expected per capita consumption per year of item k by individuals at the same income level I. Let $\phi(I)$ be the density of individuals at income I. The per capita consumption of item k for the entire population and corresponding expected per capita income are given by

$$(16.1) \qquad\qquad \bar{X}(k) = \int_0^\infty C_k(I) \cdot \phi(I) dI,$$

$$(16.2) \qquad\qquad \bar{I} = \int_0^\infty I \cdot \phi(I) dI,$$

where $\bar{X}(k)$ denotes component k of $\bar{X}$. The symbol for expected *per capita* consumption vector $\bar{X}$ is to be distinguished from $\bar{X}^I$ which is the expected consumption vector of individuals whose income level is $I_i = I$. It would appear that the correspondence between $\bar{X}$ and $\bar{I}$ depends on the distribution of ϕ; *in fact it does not* for a broad range of $\bar{I}$.

Theorem 3. *If $C_k(I)$ is a linear function of I, then independent of the distribution of income $\phi(I)$, $\bar{X}_k = C_k(\bar{I})$, i.e., per capita consumption of item k is a linear function of per capita income $\bar{I}$, and this linear function is $C_k(\bar{I})$.*

Proof. Let $C_k(I) = a + bI$. Substituting into (16.1) and noting $\int \phi(I)dI = 1$ yields $\bar{X}_k = a + b\bar{I} = C_k(\bar{I})$. □

The hypothesis that $C_k(I)$ is a linear function of I is only true by Theorem 2 for a restricted range of income which we have referred to as the "broad" *range of income of interest*, $\max I_i^* = I^* \le I \le I^{**} = \min p'S^i$. Let us assume the distribution of income for consumption in the population is above the extreme poverty level $I^* = \max I_i^*$ and below being very rich, $I^{**} = \min p'S^i$. As time goes by, per capita income $\bar{I}$ will change (and likely increase) and the distribution of income $\phi(I)$ about $\bar{I}$ will change. As long as people at the same income level at the same prices buy in the same way in the future and the income distribution change is not so drastic that there are individuals with I outside the interval $I^* \le I \le I^{**}$, Theorem 3 states that $\bar{X}(k)$ is the *same* linear function of $\bar{I}$ as $X^I(k)$ is of I for some range $\bar{I}^* \le \bar{I} \le \bar{I}^{**}$ which we think of as quite broad. Therefore, we have established:

Theorem 4. *For fixed p,*

(i) *expected per capita consumption $\bar{X}$ is a linear function of per capita income $\bar{I}$ for a certain range of income $\bar{I}$, namely*

(17) $$\bar{S} - \bar{X} = (p'\bar{S} - \bar{I}) \cdot G(p), \quad \max \bar{I}^* \le \bar{I} \le \bar{I}^{**},$$

where $G(p) = H(p) \cdot p$ and $H(p) = \mathcal{E}_i(p'H^ip)^{-1} \cdot H^i$ is a symmetric positive-definite matrix whose elements depend on p and not on $\bar{I}$.

(ii) *If $\bar{I} < \bar{I}^*$, then some individuals j have $I_j < \min I_i$ for i in the population urn and there is a positive probability that these j will maximize their utility by setting some components of X^j to zero; as $\bar{I} \to 0, \bar{X} \to 0$.*

(iii) *If $\bar{I} > \bar{I}^{**}$, then for some individual's income I^j there is a positive probability that his assigned S^i satisfies $p'S^i < I_j$; these j will maximize their utility by buying their randomly assigned satiation vectors S^i; for sufficiently high $\bar{I}$, $\bar{X}$ will level off to $\bar{S}$.*

Our derived result of linearity *does not depend on the shape of the income function distribution or how this changes as per capita income increases or in the future* providing it does not rise so high that the range of the income distribution extends beyond $\min p'S^i$ or below I^*. Other authors have stated conditions that imply linear per capita demand, particularly Gorman [5] who found per capita demand to be *exactly* linear in income under very restrictive assumption on individual behavior. What we have shown is how linearity of the expected value of per capita demand can arise under very much weaker assumptions.

The expected *aggregate demand function* expresses consumption $X_t = P_t \cdot \bar{X}_t$ as a function of aggregate income $I_t = P_t \cdot \bar{I}_t$ and prices, where P_t is total size of the population in period t. We re-express Theorem 4:

$$(18) \quad S_t - X_t = (\pi_t' S_t - I_t) \cdot \mathcal{E}_i (\pi_t' H^i \pi_t)^{-1} \cdot H^i \pi_t, \quad P_t \cdot \bar{I}_t^* \leq I_t \leq P_t \cdot \bar{I}_t^{**},$$

where $S_t = P_t \cdot \bar{S}_t$, and $\pi_t = \delta^{t-1} \bar{\pi}_t$ are discounted normalized period t prices $\bar{\pi}_t$; aggregate income I_t is redefined to be aggregate consumption income measured in terms of π_t instead of p_t.   .

Now that we have our aggregate demand functions, we can ask whether they represent behavior which can be generated by maximizing some utility function over aggregate consumption.

Value of endowments. However, before we place $F_t(X_t)$, the inverse of this demand function into the time-staged model, we must first prove that the inverse demand function exists and also relate the I_t of the demand function to the value of endowments. The latter is important because the model does not provide any detail about how rents, wages, dividends, royalties, interest on loans, taxes, government doles, etc., get transferred to the final consumers for consumption. We meed to be assured that the model nevertheless implicitly provides a mechanism whereby the *total value* of endowments used for consumption are in fact transferred.

Theorem 5. *The value of endowments I_t used to produce consumption X_t in period t is exactly equal to $\pi_t' X_t$, the attained level of aggregate income used for consumption in period t.*

Proof. In terms of the prices of the model, the value of endowments available to period t is $\sigma_t'(D_{t-1} Y_{t-1} + k_t)$. If we subtract off the value used for fixed consumption $\pi_t' f_t$, less $\sigma_{t+1}' D_t Y_t$ the value passed down to period $t+1$, the net by definition is I_t:

$$(19.1) \qquad I_t = \sigma_t'(D_{t-1} Y_{t-1}) - \pi_t' f_t - \sigma_{t+1}' D_t Y_t$$

$$(19.2) \qquad = \sigma_t' B_t Y_t - \sigma_{t+1}' D_t Y_t - \pi_t' f_t$$

$$(19.3) \qquad = \pi_t'(A_t Y_t - f_t)$$

where (19.2) follows from (1) and (5), and (19.3) follows from (3) and (5). Therefore, by (2) and (5),

(19.4) $I_t = \pi'_t X_t$.

Thus, independent of the choice of the demand function, the primal conditions (1), (2) and the profitability conditions (3), and the complementarity conditions (5) imply that $I_t = \pi'_t X_t$ holds.   □

Existence of an inverse aggregate demand function and utility function

It would now appear to be an easy step to pass from the aggregate demand function (18) to the inverse demand function by finding an expression for π_t as a function $F_t(X_t)$, but it is not. In fact under certain conditions the inverse demand function $F_t(X_t)$ is not defined. When it is defined, we can prove that the aggregate demand function is integrable in the sense that there exists a $\bar{U}_t(X_t)$ which, maximized subject to an aggregate budget constraint $\pi'_t X_t = I^t$, implies the aggregate demand function (18). We will first present a necessary and sufficient condition for integrability of the aggregate demand function. This condition can also be derived as a special case of results found in the economic literature, see Varian [11]. The proofs of the main theorems will be found in [3]. We will then discuss what properties of the distribution of preference (S^i, H^i) of the n representative individuals is our imaginary population urn are sufficient to guarantee integrability.

The inverse demand function $F_t(X_t)$ is required to generate not just prices but prices $\bar{\pi}_t$ *normalized* by a numeraire needed for the rate of return formulas (3). However, there is more than one way to choose a numeraire. This could be the price of some item like food, or any homogeneous function of degree 1 in prices. One usual way to define normalized prices is $\bar{\pi}_t = p_t / \bar{e} p_t$ where $\bar{e} = (1/m, 1/m, \ldots, 1/m)$. If so defined, it can be shown that an objective function of the form $\sum \delta^{t-1} U_t(X_t)$ does not exist even though the aggregate demands for each period is integrable. However, if the numeraire is chosen in the alternative equally satisfactory way to be

(20) $\mathcal{G}_i(p'_t H^i p_t)^{1/2}$,

where $\mathcal{G}_i(a_i)$ denotes the geometric mean of $(a_1, a_2, \ldots, a_n)$, then the integrability in each time period implies an objective function $\sum \delta^{t-1} U_t(X_t)$ does exist which maximized subject to the physical constraints in turn implies the equilibrium solution.

Our immediate objective is to give necessary and sufficient conditions under which an inverse expected per capita demand function and per capita utility function exist for each period when the per capita demand function is given by (17). We find that a per capita utility function $\bar{U}(\bar{X})$ and an inverse demand function $F(\bar{X})$ exist if for all $i = 1, \ldots, n$ the ratio [h] of the highest to lowest eigenvalue of $\bar{H}^i = \bar{H}^{-1/2} H^i \bar{H}^{-1/2}$ is less than

$3 + 2\sqrt{2} \doteq 5.83$ for at least one positive definite matrix $\bar{H}$. The particular choice of positive definite $\bar{H}$ is arbitrary; choosing $\bar{H} = \mathcal{E}_i H^i$, however, gives us the property that if $H^i = \bar{H}$ for all i, then $\bar{H}^i = \mathfrak{I}$, the *identity*, and the ratio ρ_i of highest to lowest eigenvalue would be unity, implying that if H^i are close to $\bar{H}$, then the ratio would be close to unity and the condition would be satisfied. Moreover, the more randomly rotated the axes of the ellipsoids $p'H^i p = constant$ are with respect to each other, the higher the upper bound such that ρ_i below the bound implies $\bar{U}(\bar{X})$ exists.

While it is not unreasonable to assume that the orientations of these ellipsoids vary, nevertheless it is conceivable that the population of a country could be so highly polarized as to their consumption tastes at the same income level that a per capita utility function would not exist. We will present a simple example to illustrate this.

Definition of a utility function, integrability

In order for $\bar{U}(\bar{X})$ to qualify as a per capita utility function, we require $Z(v) = -\bar{U}(\bar{X})$, where $v = \bar{S} - \bar{X}$, to be a *convex function* twice differentiable (except possibly at $v = 0$) which attains a unique minimum subject to a budget constraint $p'\bar{X} = p'\bar{S} - J$, or equivalently $p' = J$ at a finite point $v = v^*$ where J measures the difference between the actual income and satiation income, rather than income itself. Therefore v^* is a function of p and J which we denote by $\bar{S} - \bar{X} = v(p, J)$ and call it the per capita *demand function* associated with the utility function $\bar{U}(\bar{X})$. Conversely, if we are given a per capita demand function such as

$$(21) \qquad \bar{S} - \bar{X} = (p'\bar{S} - \bar{I}) \cdot G(p),$$

or equivalently

$$(22) \qquad v(p, J) = J \cdot \mathcal{E}_i (p'H^i p)^{-1} \cdot H^i p,$$

we inquire if there exists a utility function with which the demand function is associated. If yes, we saw that the demand function is *integrable*.

We will, however, *restrict* the utility functions considered to those homogeneous in v of degree $+1$. Specifically we redefine a function $\bar{U}(\bar{X}) = -Z(v)$, $v = \bar{S} - \bar{X}$, to be a utility function, if (i) $Z(v)$ is twice differentiable for all v (except possibly at $v = 0$); (ii) $Z(v)$ is a homogeneous function in v of degree 1 along every ray, i.e., $Z(\alpha v) = \alpha Z(v)$ for all v, $\alpha \geq 0$; (iii) $Z(v)$ is strictly convex between any two points $v^1 \neq v^2$ satisfying the budget constraint $p'_i v = 1$:

$$(23) \quad \lambda Z(v^1) + \mu Z(v^2) > Z(\lambda v^1 + \mu v^2) \quad \text{for all } \lambda > 0, \ \mu > 0, \ \lambda + \mu = 1;$$

and (iv) $Z(v) > 0$ for all $v \neq 0$. Theorem 6 below implies that $Z(v)$ under this second definition qualifies as a utility function under the first definition.

Theorem 6. *Given any utility function $\bar{U}(\bar{X}) = -Z(v)$, the $\min Z(v)$ subject to the unit budget constraint $p'v = 1$ is attained at a finite point $v = v^*$ and is unique. Denoting $v^* = v(p, 1)$, the demand function associated with $Z(v)$ is $\bar{S} - \bar{X} = v(p, J) = J \cdot v(p, 1)$.*

Theorem 7. *Given any utility function $\bar{U}(\bar{X}) = -Z(v)$, the unique v that minimizes $Z(v)$ subject to the unit budget constraint $p'v = 1$ satisfies the first order condition:*

$$(24.1) \qquad \frac{1}{Z} \cdot \frac{\partial Z}{\partial v} = p.$$

Conversely, given any $v \doteq v^*$, there exists a unique p such that $\min Z$ subject to unit budget constraint $p'v = 1$ is attained at v^*, namely:

$$(24.2) \qquad \frac{1}{Z} \cdot \frac{\partial Z}{\partial v} \Big|_{v=v^*} = p.$$

Theorem 8. *A necessary condition for the existence of a utility function $\bar{U}(\bar{X}) = -Z(v)$, associated with the demand function*

$$(25) \qquad \bar{S} - \bar{X} = v = J \cdot \mathcal{E}_i(p'H^i p)^{-1} \cdot H^i p = J \cdot G(p),$$

is that the inverse function of $v = G(p)$, exists, namely,

$$(26) \qquad p = G^{-1}(v) = \frac{1}{Z} \frac{\partial Z}{\cdot} \partial v, \quad p'v = 1.$$

There are two ways that the function $v = G(p)$ can fail to have an inverse. The first is: given v, there exists no p that satisfies the equation $v = G(p)$. The second way it can fail is: given a particular v, there is more than one p satisfying the equation. We can prove that the first way can never happen and the second way can. However, under certain conditions that we will specify later, there is a unique solution for all choices of $v \neq 0$.

Theorem 9. *Given any $v \neq 0$, there are always one or more $p \neq 0$ satisfying*

$$(27) \qquad v = \mathcal{E}_i(p'H^i p)^{-1} \cdot H^i p, \quad v \neq 0.$$

The proof applies Brouwer's Fixed Point Theorem.

Theorem 10. *Given certain v and certain H^i, it is possible that there exist more than one p satisfying $v = G(p)$, implying $G^{-1}(v)$ does not exist in general.*

Proof. Let $n = 2$ where $i = 1, \ldots, n$ and let $m = 2$ where matrices H^i are $m \times m$. Let

$$(28.1) \ H^1 = \begin{pmatrix} 2.0 & -0.6 \\ -0.6 & 0.2 \end{pmatrix}, \quad H^2 = \begin{pmatrix} 0.2 & -0.6 \\ -0.6 & 2.0 \end{pmatrix}, \quad v = \begin{pmatrix} 0.5 \\ 0.5 \end{pmatrix}.$$

In the above case, it is not difficult to verify that there are three real solutions:

$$(28.2) \quad p = (1, 1), \quad p \doteq (0.48382, 1.51618), \quad p \doteq (1.51618, 0.48382).$$

Since these solutions satisfy $v = G(p)$, all three satisfy $p'v = 1$. $\square$

Theorem 11. *For some choices of H^i, $v = G(p)$ has an inverse $p = G^{-1}(v)$.*

Proof. Assume $H^i = \bar{H}$ for all i. It is easy to verify that the only p which satisfies (29.1) is given by (29.2):

$$(29.1) \qquad\qquad v = (p'\bar{H}p)^{-1} \cdot \bar{H}p,$$

$$(29.2) \qquad\qquad p = G^{-1}(v) = (v'\bar{H}^{-1}v)^{-1} \cdot \bar{H}^{-1}v. \quad \square$$

When $v = G(p)$ has an inverse, we make use of the following lemmas:

Lemma 1. *$v = G(p)$ and $p = G^{-1}(v)$ are homogeneous functions of degrees $\rho = -1$ and $1/\rho = -1$ in p and v respectively.*

Lemma 2. *The matrix $\partial v/\partial p'$ and its inverse $\partial p/\partial v'$ exist.*

Proof. $\partial v/\partial v = $ identity $= [\partial v/\partial p'] \cdot [\partial p/\partial v']$ from the theory of implicit functions. $\square$

Lemma 3. *The matrix $\partial p/\partial v'$ is symmetric.*

Lemma 4.

$$(30) \qquad\qquad p = -[\partial p/\partial v']v, \quad p' = -v'[\partial p/\partial v'].$$

The first part of the lemma follows from Euler's Theorem for homogeneous forms of degree -1; the second part follows from the first part and symmetry, see Lemma 3.

Lemma 5.

$$(31) \qquad\qquad p'\frac{\partial v}{\partial p'}p + (p'v)^2 = 0.$$

Theorem 12. *Given $v = G(p)$, a necessary condition that utility function $\bar{U}(\bar{X}) = -Z(v)$, exists is*

$$(32) \qquad\qquad q'\frac{\partial v}{\partial p'}q + (q'v)^2 = 0$$

for all $p \neq 0$ and $q \neq \alpha p$.

Theorem 13. *A sufficient condition that the inverse function, $p = G^{-1}(v)$ exists when $v = G(p) = \mathcal{E}_i(p'H^ip)^{-1} \cdot H^ip$ is given by (32).*

Theorem 14. *A sufficient condition that there exists a utility function $\bar{U}(\bar{X}) = -Z(v)$, $v = \bar{S} - \bar{X}$, associated with the per capita demand function $\bar{S} - \bar{X} = (p'\bar{S} - \bar{I}) \cdot G(p)$ is*

$$(33) \qquad q'\frac{\partial v}{\partial p'}q + (q'v)^2 = 0 \quad \forall q \neq \alpha p, \; p \neq 0,$$

where the function $Z(v)$ is the mapping $v \to Z$ defined by the following procedure:

Step 1. Find the unique p satisfying

$$(34.1) \qquad v = \mathcal{E}_i(p'H^ip)^{-1} \cdot H^ip.$$

Step 2. Find Z satisfying

$$(34.2) \qquad \log Z = -\tfrac{1}{2}\mathcal{E}_i(p'H^ip)$$

$$(34.3) \qquad Z = [(p'H^1p)(p'H^2p)\cdots(p'H^np)]^{-n/2}$$

$$(34.4) \qquad = \mathcal{G}_i(p'H^ip)^{-1/2}$$

Sufficient conditions for existence

Having found a necessary and sufficient condition that a per capita utility function exists, namely $q'\partial v/\partial pq + (q'v)^2 > 0$ for all $q \neq \alpha p$ holds, we now seek sufficient conditions on the distribution of H^i in the population urn that guarantee this condition is satisfied. Since $v = \mathcal{E}_i(p'H^ip)^{-1} \cdot H^ip$ and

$$(35) \qquad \frac{\partial v}{\partial p'} = \mathcal{E}_i\left[\frac{H^i}{p'H^ip} - \frac{H^ip \cdot p'H^i}{(p'H^ip)^2}\right], \quad p \neq 0,$$

we seek conditions on H^i so that for all $p \neq 0$, $q \neq \alpha \cdot p$:

$$(36) \qquad q'\frac{\partial v}{\partial p'}q + (q'v)^2 = \mathcal{E}_i\left[\frac{q'H^iq}{p'H^ip} - 2\frac{(q'H^ip)^2}{(p'H^ip)^2}\right] + \left[\mathcal{E}_i\frac{q'H^ip}{p'H^ip}\right]^2 > 0.$$

The purpose of Theorems 17 and 18 that follow is to show that the distribution of H^i in the population urn would have to be highly polarized, as in the example of Theorem 10, in order for condition (36) to fail. If $H^i = \bar{H}$ for all i, it is not difficult to show that (36) holds. Let $\bar{H}$ be any positive definite matrix, for example $\bar{H} = \mathcal{E}_iH^i$ where $\sum\sum H^i_{kl} = 1$. One measure of how much H^i differs from $\bar{H}$ is to form $\bar{H}^i = \bar{H}^{-1/2}H^i\bar{H}^{-1/2}$ and compare $\bar{H}^i$ to $\mathcal{I}$, the identity matrix. The eigenvalues of $\mathcal{I}$ are all unity and the ratio ρ_i of its highest to lowest eigenvalue is one. Therefore, we can study how much the ratio of the highest to lowest eigenvalues of $\bar{H}^i$ can differ from unity before condition (36) is violated.

Theorem 15. *Let $\bar{H}$ be any positive definite matrix and let $\bar{H}^i = \bar{H}^{-1/2} H^i \bar{H}^{-1/2}$, then condition (36) that a utility function exists is equivalent to finding conditions on $\bar{H}^i$ so that for all $p \neq 0$ and $q \neq 0$ and p orthogonal to q:*

$$(37) \qquad \mathcal{E}_i \left[\frac{q' \bar{H}^i q}{p' \bar{H}^i p} - 2 \frac{(q' \bar{H}^i p)^2}{(p' \bar{H}^i p)^2} \right] + \left[\mathcal{E}_i \frac{q' \bar{H}^i p}{p' \bar{H}^i p} \right]^2 > 0, \quad p'q = 0.$$

The last bracket expression of (37) is not likely to contribute much to the positivity of the L.H.S. For example, if $\bar{H} = \mathcal{E}_i H^i$ and $\bar{H}^i = \bar{H}$ for all i, then $\bar{H}^i = \mathcal{I}$, the identity, and the last term vanishes because $p'q = 0$.

Therefore, if we drop the second bracket, it is sufficient to only consider conditions on $\bar{H}^i$ that guarantee that the first bracket expression is positive. As an extreme or worst case scenario, we look for conditions on $\bar{H}^i$ that will guarantee *for every i* that t_i, the ith pair of terms of the first bracket, is positive:

$$(38) \quad t_i = \frac{(q' \bar{H}^i q)(p' \bar{H}^i p) - 2(q' \bar{H}^i p)^2}{(p' \bar{H}^i p)^2} > 0 \text{ for all } p \neq 0, \, q \neq 0, \, p'q = 0.$$

This is obviously sufficient to guarantee that (37) holds.

Theorem 16. *A utility function exists if, for each i,*

$$(39) \qquad t_i = \frac{q' D q}{p' D p} - 2 \frac{(q' D p)^2}{(p' D p)^2} > 0 \quad \text{for all } p'q = 0, \, p'p = 1, \, q'q = 1$$

where $D = D^i$ is the diagonal matrix whose diagonal elements are the m eigenvalues of $\bar{H}^i$.

Theorem 17. *A utility function exists if for every i the diagonal matrix $D = D^i$ of eigenvalues of $\bar{H}^i$ has the property*

$$(40.1) \qquad \qquad \min t_i = 1 - 2 \frac{(\rho_i - 1)^2}{(\rho_i + 1)^2} > 0,$$

where ρ_i is the ratio of the highest to lowest eigenvalue of $\bar{H}^i$ or equivalently when[i]

$$(40.2) \qquad \qquad \rho_i < 3 + 2\sqrt{2} \doteq 5.83.$$

In order for a utility function to exist it is sufficient that $\mathcal{E}_i t_i > 0$. Therefore the condition that $\min t_i > 0$ for each i is a worst case scenario that is far too stringent. On the other hand, we know for [the] case of $m = 2$, $n = 2$ that it is possible for $\mathcal{E}_i t_i < 0$, and this is true even if the term $[\mathcal{E}_i(q'\bar{H}^i p)/(p'H^i p)]^2$ is added to t_i, see counter example Theorem 10. In a large representative set of (S^i, H^i) in the population urn, we would expect for the set of ellipsoids $p'\bar{H}p = \text{constant}$ which can be rotated into one another to have somewhat randomly distributed orientations. If we rotate all such ellipsoids to H^i (or $\bar{H}^i$) to the position of the H^i with lowest index i, call it H, the effect is to rotate the p and q to a random position. Therefore, we need to consider for each such H,

$$(41) \quad f(p,q) = \mathop{\mathcal{E}}_{p,q}\left[\frac{q'Hq}{p'Hp} - 2\left(\frac{q'Hp}{p'Hp}\right)^2\right], \quad p'p = 1,\ q'q = 1,\ p'q = 0,$$

where $\mathop{\mathcal{E}}_{p,q}$ stands for expectation over p and q "randomly" distributed in some way. We, of course, do not know what is the true distribution of orientations of the ellipsoids $p'\bar{H}p = \text{constant}$ that can be rotated into one another. We can prove the following theorem when these orientations are uniformly distributed about the origin in R^m.

Theorem 18. *If the orientations of the ellipsoids $p'H^i p = \text{constant}$ that can be rotated into any particular H^i are uniformly distributed (or nearly so), then $\mathcal{E}_{p,q} f(p,q) > 0$ where $f(p,q)$ is defined by (41); moreover $\mathcal{E}t_i > 0$, implying that the expected per capita utility function exists.*

While the assumption of "uniformly distributed" is not realistic, the purpose of Theorem 18 is to illustrate that the more the orientations vary relative to one another, the higher the upper bound for ρ_i below which an expected per capita utility function exists. Theorem 17 and 18 suggest that in order for a per capita utility function to fail to exist the population would have to be highly polarized into large classes of people with very different consumption patterns at the same level of attained income.

Equivalent concave program

Having discovered conditions under which an expected aggregate demand function exists and is integrable, we now assume these conditions hold and turn to the time-staged model. We exhibit an optimization problem which will have a convex feasible set and concave maximand whenever aggregate demand is integrable. The solution to this optimization problem gives the equilibrium prices and aggregate flows for the underlying model. We also show a simplified approximate version of the optimization problem whose parameters can be estimated and large systems solved using commercially available software.

In order to discuss the optimization problem, define aggregate variables $X_t = P_t \bar{X}_t$, $S_t = P_t \bar{S}_t$, $U_t = P_t \bar{U}_t$, $I_t = P_t \cdot \bar{I}_t$ where P_t is the size of the population in period t. Let

(42)
$$p = G^{-1}(\bar{S}_t - \bar{X}_t).$$

It follows from (34.1), after rescaling for population size, [that]

(43)
$$U_t(X_t) = -P_t \cdot \mathcal{G}_t (p' H^i p)^{-1/2},$$

where $\mathcal{G}_t$ stands for [the] geometric mean of $(p' H^i p)^{-1/2}$ for $i = 1, \ldots, n$.

Theorem 19. *The equilibrium problem is equivalent to solving the concave program*

(44)
$$\max U(X) = \sum_{t=1}^{T} \delta^{t-1} U_t(X_t)$$

subject to $(X_t, Y_t) \geq 0$ and the primal flow conditions, $t = 1, \ldots, T$,

(45)
$$B_t Y_t \leq D_{t-1} Y_{t-1} + k_t,$$

(46)
$$-A_t Y_t + X_t \leq -f_t,$$

providing (i) the primal problem is feasible, (ii) the geometric mean of $(p'_t H^i p_t)^{1/2}$ for $i = 1, 2, \ldots, n$ is used as a numeraire for normalizing prices p_t, and (iii) the aggregate income $I_t = \pi'_t X_t$ associated with the optimal solution satisfies $P_t \cdot \bar{I}^* \leq I_t \leq P_t \cdot \bar{I}^{**}$, and (iv) $X_t > 0$. Under these conditions an equilibrium exists.

We are assuming a utility function for each period exists. The utility function, $U_t(X_t)$ defined by (42) and (43) is a homogeneous function of degree 1 in $P_t v = S_t - X_t$ which is strictly concave in v except along rays with $v = 0$ as origin. The concave program under these conditions has a finite optimal solution providing there is a feasible solution to physical constraints (45) and (46).

The condition that I_t is bounded between certain upper and lower limits is our way of saying that the demand function of all individuals i is of the form $S^i - X^i = (\pi' S^i - I)(\pi' H^i \pi)^{-1} \cdot H^i \pi$, which would not be the case if their budgets I were extremely low or extremely high.

In particular, if $X_t > 0$, then noting (24.1), (43), $Z = -\bar{U}_t$, and $v = \bar{S}_t - \bar{X}_t$,

(47.1)
$$\bar{\pi}_t = F_t(X_t) = \partial U_t / \partial X_t$$

(47.2)
$$= \partial \bar{U}_t / \partial \bar{X}_t = -\bar{U}_t \cdot p$$

(47.3)
$$= p / \mathcal{G}_i (p' H^i p)^{1/2}$$

(47.4)
$$= p_t / \mathcal{G}_i (p' H^i p)^{1/2}$$

where $\mathcal{G}_i$ denotes geometric mean. Therefore, the denominator $\mathcal{G}_i(p_t'H^ip_t)^{1/2}$ may be viewed as a numeraire for normalizing period t prices p_t.

Ideally normalized prices $\bar{\pi}_t$ should have the property that a unit amount of income should enable each individual i to purchase at prices $\bar{\pi}_t$ goods X^i whose *utility* to i is unity. In a certain geometric mean sense this is true when the numeraire $\mathcal{G}_i(p_t'H^ip_t)^{1/2}$ is used. For i in the population urn, let $-\hat{U}^i = [(S^i - X^i)'M^i(S^i - X^i)]^{1/2}$ be the negative utility to i, and J^i be the additional income needed to reach satiation S^i. It is not difficult to show $\mathcal{G}_i(-U^i) = \mathcal{G}_i(J^i)$, whence a unit amount of such additional income measured in normalized prices buys a unit amount of utility.

Theorem 20. *The existence of a utility function $U(X)$ depends on how the numeraire for period t prices used by the investor/producers in the rate-of-return formulas is defined.*

We prove in [3] that no objective function for the time-staged economic model exists if the numeraire for normalizing prices is $\bar{e}p_t$ where $\bar{e} = (1/m, 1/m, \ldots, 1/m)$.

Simplifying the form of the demand and utility functions

Our goal now is to replace the key factors $G(p) = \mathcal{E}_i[(p'H^ip)^{-1} \cdot H^ip]$ associated with the demand function and $-2\log Z = \mathcal{E}_i \log(p'H^ip)$ associated with the utility function by simpler expressions whose parameters are easier to estimate and then give reasons why these approximations may be very good. We use the symbol $\doteq$ to denote *approximately equal*.

Theorem 21. *The first-order approximation of $\log Z$ as a function of $p = G^{-1}(S_t - X_t)$ yields the approximation:*

$$(48) \qquad -\bar{U}_t(\bar{X}_t) = Z = \mathcal{G}_i(p'H^ip)^{-1/2} \doteq (p'\bar{H}p)^{-1/2},$$

for all p near $p_0' = (1, 1, \ldots, 1)$, where $\mathcal{G}_i$ stands for geometric mean and where positive definite H^i are rescaled so that $e'H^ie = 1$ for all i and $\bar{H} = \mathcal{E}_iH^i$.

We apply the above approximation to $-\partial(\log Z)/\partial p$ to obtain our approximation of the factor $G(p)$ of the demand function:

$$(49.1) \qquad G(p) = \mathop{\mathcal{E}}_{i}(p'H^ip)^{-1} \cdot H^ip = -\partial(\log Z)/\partial p$$
$$\doteq \tfrac{1}{2}\partial[\log(p'\bar{H}p)]/\partial p = (p'\bar{H}p)^{-1} \cdot \bar{H}p \text{ for all } p \text{ near } p_0$$

We therefore have the following approximations:
$$v \doteq (p'\bar{H}p)^{-1} \cdot \bar{H}p, \qquad p \doteq (v'Mv)^{-1} \cdot Mv,$$
$$(49.2)$$
$$-\bar{U}_t(\bar{X}_t) = Z \doteq (v'Mv) = (p'\bar{H}p)^{-1/2},$$

where $M = \bar{H}^{-1}$ and $v = \bar{S} - \bar{X}$. We now substitute these approximations into various demand function theorems and summarize them.

Demand functions of [an] individual with income I (Theorem 1):

$$(50.1) \qquad S^i - X^i = (p'\bar{S} - I)(p'H^i p)^{-1} \cdot H^i p$$

where $I_i^* \leq I \leq I_i^{**} = p'S^i$.

The approximation for Theorem 2, the expected per person demand function of individuals with income I, is

$$(50.2) \quad \bar{S} - \bar{X}^I = (p'\bar{S} - \bar{I})\mathcal{E}_i (p'H^i p)^{-1} \cdot H^i p \doteq (p'\bar{S} - I)(p'\bar{H}p)^{-1} \cdot \bar{H}p$$

where $\bar{I}^* \leq I \leq \bar{I}^{**} = \min p'S^i$, and H^i are rescaled so that $e'H^i e = 1$ and $\bar{H} = \mathcal{E}_i H^i$.

The approximation for Theorem 4, the expected per capita demand function, is

$$(50.3) \quad \bar{S} - \bar{X} = (p'\bar{S} - \bar{I})\mathcal{E}_i(p'H^i p)^{-1} \cdot H^i p \doteq (p'\bar{S} - \bar{I})(p'\bar{H}p)^{-1} \cdot \bar{H}p$$

where $\bar{I}^* \leq I \leq \bar{I}^{**}$.

The approximation for Theorem 14 is as follows: Denote $\exp(t) = e^t$ where e is the base of natural logarithms; the approximation of the per capita utility function $\bar{U}_t = \bar{U}_t(\bar{X}_t)$ for period t, is

$$(51.1) \qquad \bar{U}_t = -\exp[-\tfrac{1}{2}\mathcal{E}_i \log(p'H^i p)]$$

$$(51.2) \qquad \doteq -\exp[-\tfrac{1}{2}\log(p'\bar{H}p)] = -(p'\bar{H}p)^{-1/2} = -(v'M_t v)^{1/2}$$

$$(51.3) \qquad \doteq -[(\bar{S} - \bar{X})'M_t(\bar{S} - \bar{X}_t)]^{1/2}, \quad M_t = \bar{H}^{-1}.$$

Applying the approximation for the period t per capita utility function (50.3) to Theorem 19, after rescaling for population size, the equilibrium problem is equivalent to solving the concave program:

$$(52) \qquad \max U(X) \doteq -\sum_i \delta^{t-1}[(S_t - X_t)'M_t(S_t - X_t)]^{1/2},$$

subject to $(X_t, Y_t) \geq 0$ and the primal flow conditions $t = 1, \ldots, T$:

$$(53.1) \qquad B_t Y_t \leq D_{t-1}Y_{t-1} + k_t,$$

$$(53.2) \qquad -A_t Y_t + X_t \leq f_t,$$

where S_t, X_t, T_t are aggregate quantities, and where $M_t = \bar{H}_t^{-1}$, $\bar{H}_t = \mathcal{E}_i H_t^i$, and [the] H_t^i have been rescaled so that $\sum_k \sum_l H_t^i(k, l) = 1$.

Therefore if a feasible solution to the primal exists, an optimal feasible solution exists that satisfies the Kuhn-Tucker optimality conditions (3), (4), (5), which is the same as saying an equilibrium solution exists. The strict concavity implies that the values of X_t and π_t are unique, but those of Y_t and σ_t need not be unique.

Conclusions

The optimum value of time-staged objective $U(X)$ is the negative sum of discounted additional aggregate income (measured in normalized period t prices) needed to purchase the "satiation" vector over various periods t—the less additional income required the higher the "standard of living." This follows from Euler's Theorem

(54.1) $-U_t = P_t \cdot Z = P_t \cdot v'(\partial Z/\partial v)$

(54.2) $= P_t \cdot v'\bar{\pi} = P_t(\bar{\pi}'\bar{S}_t - \bar{I}_t).$

It is well known that an equilibrium problem can be restated as an optimization problem when all consumers are identical. We have shown that there exists an objective function which represents the aggregate behavior of the economy even under considerable variability of individual price cross-effect matrices H^i relative to $\mathcal{E}_i H^i = \bar{H}$. The ratio ρ_i of the highest to lowest eigenvalues of $\bar{H}^i = \bar{H}^{-1/2} H^i \bar{H}^{-1/2}$ can be as high as $3 + 2\sqrt{2}$ no matter how else they might vary from one another; indeed much higher if the ellipsoids $p' H^i p = $ constant are randomly oriented to some extent relative to one another. On the other hand, if individuals i in the population tend to be highly polarized as to their consumption tastes, as in the example of Theorem 10 with $\rho_1 = \rho_2 = 91$, an aggregate utility function may not exist.[j]

We conclude that the economy will grow if it has the resources and technology to grow and if it pays according to the aggregate "utility" function (52) to trade off lower consumption in earlier periods for considerably larger consumption in later periods.

References

[1] K. Arrow and G. Debreu, "Existence of an equilibrium for a competitive economy," *Econometrica* 22 (1954) 265–290.

[2] R.W. Cottle and G.B. Dantzig, "Complementary pivot theory of mathematical programming," *Linear Algebra and Its Applications* 1 (1968) 103-125.

[3] G.B. Dantzig, P.H. McAllister and J.C. Stone, "Deriving a utility function for the U.S. economy," Systems Optimization Laboratory, Department of Operations Research, Stanford University (October 1987).

[4] G. Debreu, *Theory of Value*, John Wiley & Sons, New York, 1959.

[5] W.M. Gorman, "Community preference fields," *Econometrica* 21 (1953) 63–80.

[6] D.W. Jorgenson, L.J. Lau and T.N. Stoker, "The transcendental logarithmic model of aggregate consumer behavior," in R.L. Baseman and G. Rhodes (eds.), *Advances in Economics*, Vol. 1, J.A.I. Press, Greenwich, 1982, pp. 97–238.

[7] H.W. Kuhn and A.W. Tucker, "Non-linear programming," *Econometrica* 19 (January 1951) 50–51 (abstract).[k]

[8] B.A. Murtagh and M.A. Saunders, "MINOS 5.0 user's guide," Systems Optimization Laboratory, Department of Operations Research, Stanford University, Technical Report 83-20 (December 1983).

[9] H. Scarf, "On the computation of economic equilibrium prices," in: *Ten Economic Studies in the Tradition of Irving Fisher*, John Wiley & Sons, New York, 1967.

[10] A. Sen, "Social choice and justice: A review article," *Journal of Economic Literature* 23 (1985) 1764–1776.

[11] H.R. Varian, *Microeconomic Analysis*, W.W. Norton & Co., New York, 1984. (Pages 135–137. discuss the integrability problem and Slutsky's condition.)

Part V: Linear Programming under Uncertainty

The four chapters that make up this part represent one of George Dantzig's central concerns: the solution of linear programs with uncertain data. The first is an early one that appeared in 1955, whereas the fourth was published in 1993 and is one of the most recent of all Dantzig's publications. In contrast to the standard linear programming problem, where all the problem data are assumed known and given, the ones considered here are assumed to exhibit some degree of randomness, enough so that the usual deterministic approach is deemed inappropriate.

The paper "Linear Programming under Uncertainty" is a truly seminal work. Virtually all research on this subject—or on *stochastic optimization* as it is sometimes called nowadays—can be traced back to this paper and another one written by E. M. L. Beale in the same year.[1] Dantzig credits discussions with A. Ferguson for stimulating this fruitful extension of linear programming. In the preceding year (1954), these two authors had produced a research memorandum advancing a linear programming formulation of the allocation of aircraft to airline routes. In that model, they assumed that the demand for the service was known. It was the more realistic uncertainty of the demand that prompted the investigation of how to deal with this broader class of problems.

In this paper, Dantzig presents a series of examples intermingled with the development of a theoretical approach to their solution. The first of these examples differs in spirit from the rest in that it involves randomness in the cost function and is dispensed with by replacing the random cost coefficients by their expected values and the caveat—expressed in a footnote citing the research of H. M. Markowitz—that this is not always an appropriate thing to do. The other examples are built around uncertainty of the right-hand side data (such as demands). Here we see the emergence of a two-stage recourse model and an algorithm for its solution. Models with more than two stages are discussed as well: first in an example, and then in general.

---

[1] The paper by Beale is "Minimizing a convex function subject to linear inequalities," *Journal of the Royal Statistical Society, Ser. B*, 17 (1955) 173–184. Beale's paper, part of a report of a "Symposium on Linear Programming," touches on linear programming, quadratic programming, and linear programming with random coefficient (i.e., under uncertainty). In a note added in proof, Beale says, "Ideas very similar to those of this section and some of the next have been put forward by Dantzig (1955) in Report P-596 of the Rand Corportation, Santa Monica, California, entitled 'Linear Programming Under Uncertainty.'"

The style of the second paper, "On the Solution of Two-stage Linear Programs under Uncertainty," by Dantzig and Madansky, contrasts rather sharply with that of the first. In this one, the two-stage problem is reintroduced and developed in an entirely theoretical way, and the multi-stage type of problem is also studied, both theoretically and algorithmically. In problems of the latter sort especially, the authors generate potentially very large-scale problems having a dual block-angular structure. This is a form to which the (not yet published) decomposition scheme of J. F. Benders (1962) would apply. The paper closes with an interesting proposal "for future consideration" regarding sampling from the distribution of the right-hand side vector (and thereby reducing the size of the problem).

The third paper of this set appeared nearly thirty years after the second. In the interim, Dantzig had several doctoral students, first at Berkeley and later at Stanford, who concentrated on stochastic programming. Foremost among these were Richard M. Van Slyke, Roger J-B. Wets, and John R. Birge. Also in the interim parallel computation emerged as a "hot topic." This seemed an attractive strategy for conquering the very large-scale optimization problems engendered in stochastic programming by the consideration of the outcomes of random events. In the paper "Parallel Processors for Planning under Uncertainty," Dantzig and Stanford colleague Peter Glynn combine this approach with the statistical variance-reduction technique called importance sampling. As they put it, "the idea behind importance sampling is to change the sampling procedure so that those events that matter more are sampled more."

Over and above the purely technical details of papers like this, one cannot fail to be impressed by the confluence of many streams of research activity: mathematical statistics, large-scale linear programming, energy modeling, and computer science.

The last paper in this set is "Multi-stage Stochastic Linear Programs for Portfolio Optimization." This is a joint effort with Gerd Infanger, with whom George Dantzig has worked closely for several years. As suggested by the title, the area of application of this work is the financial industry and specifically problems involving multi-period asset allocation. This, of course, is a setting in which random events with many outcomes abound. The multi-stage aspect of such a problem seriously compounds the explosion of its size. Dantzig and Infanger combine many computational techniques, including Benders decomposition and importance sampling (although not parallel processing), with stunning computational results.

Chapter 12

LINEAR PROGRAMMING UNDER UNCERTAINTY

GEORGE B. DANTZIG

The RAND Corporation, Santa Monica, Cal.

Summary [a]

The essential character of the general models under consideration is that activities are divided into two or more stages. The quantities of activities in the first stage are the only ones that are required to be determined; those in the second (or later) stages cannot be determined in advance since they depend on the earlier stages and the random or uncertain demands which occur on or before the latter stage. It is important to note that the set of activities are assumed to be *complete* in the sense that, whatever be the choice of activities in the earlier stages (consistent with the restrictions applicable to their stage), there is a possible choice of activities in the latter stages. In other words, *it is not possible to get in a position where the programming problem admits of no solution.*

The initial work on this paper was stimulated by discussions with A. Ferguson who proposed that linear programming method be extended to include the case of uncertain demands for the problem of optimal allocation of a carrier fleet to airline routes to meet an anticipated demand distribution. The application of the theory found in this paper to his problem (discussed later in Example 4) will be the subject of a separate joint paper. The case of certain demands was discussed earlier [4]. [b]

A complete computation procedure is given for a special class of two-stage linear programming models in which allocations in the first stage are made to meet an uncertain but known distribution of demands occurring in the second stage. This case, applicable to many practical problems, constitutes the principal part of the paper. Next, a class of models is considered where the activities are divided into two or more stages. The quantities of activities in the first stage are the only ones that can be determined in advance because those in the second and later stages depend on the outcome of random events. Theorems on convexity of the objective (cost) functions are established for the general m-stage case.

Example 1: *Minimum Expected Cost Diet.* A nutrition expert wishes to advise his followers on a minimum cost diet without prior knowledge of the prices [6]. Since the prices of food (except for general inflationary trends) are likely to show variability due to weather conditions, supply, etc., he wishes to assume a distribution of possible prices rather than a fixed price for each food, and determine a diet that meets specified nutritional requirements and minimizes expected costs. Let x_j be the quantity of the jth food purchased in pounds, p_j its price, and a_{ij} be the quantity of the ith nutrient (e.g., vitamin A) contained in a unit quantity of the jth food, and b_i the minimum quantity required by an individual for good health. Then the x_j must be chosen so that

$$(1) \qquad \sum_{j=1}^{n} a_{ij}x_j \geq b_i \qquad x_j \geq 0 \qquad (i = 1, 2, \cdots, m)$$

and the cost of the diet will be

$$(2) \qquad C = \sum_{j=1}^{n} p_j x_j.$$

The x_j are chosen before the prices are known so that the expected costs of such a diet are clearly

$$(3) \qquad \text{Exp}\, C = \sum_{j} \bar{p}_j x_j$$

where $\bar{p}_j$ is its expected price. Since the $\bar{p}_j$ are known in advance, the best choices of x_j are those which satisfy (1) and minimize (3). Hence in this case expected prices may be used in place of the distribution of prices, and the usual linear programming problem is solved.[1]

Example 2: *Shipping to an Outlet to Meet an Uncertain Demand.*

Let us consider a simple two-stage case: A factory has 100 items on hand which may be shipped to an outlet at the cost of $1 apiece to meet an uncertain demand d_2. In the event that the demand should exceed the supply, it is necessary to meet the unsatisfied demand by purchases on the local market at $2 apiece. The equations that the system must satisfy are

$$
\begin{aligned}
100 &= x_{11} + x_{12} \\
(4) \qquad d_2 &= x_{11} \qquad\quad + x_{21} - x_{22} \qquad\qquad (x_{ij} \geq 0) \\
C &= x_{11} \qquad\quad + 2x_{21}
\end{aligned}
$$

---

[1]In some applications, however, it may not be desirable to minimize the expected value of the costs if the decision has too great a variation in the actual costs. H. Markowitz [5] in his analysis of investment portfolios develops a technique for computing for each possible expected value the minimum variance. This enables the investor to sacrifice some of his expectation to control his risks.

where

x_{11} = number shipped from the factory;
x_{12} = number stored at factory;
x_{21} = number purchased on open market;
x_{22} = excess of supply over demand;
d_2 = unknown demand uniformly distributed between 70 and 80;
C = total costs.

It is clear that whatever be the amount shipped and whatever be the demand d_1, it is possible to choose x_{21} and x_{22} consistent with the second equation. The unused stocks $x_{12} + x_{22}$ are assumed to have no value or are written off at some reduced value (like last year's model automobiles when the new production comes in). To illustrate some of the concepts of this paper, a solution will be presented later.

Example 3: *A Three-Stage Case.*

For this purpose it is easy to construct an extension of the previous example by allowing the surpluses x_{12} and x_{22} to be carried over to a third stage, i.e.,

1st stage	$100 = x_{11} + x_{12}$				
2nd stage	$d_2 = x_{11}$	$+ \ x_{21} \ -$			
(5)	$70 =$	$- \ x_{12}$	$+ \ x_{23} + x_{24}$		
3rd stage	$d_3 =$		$+ \ x_{22} + x_{23}$	$+ \ x_{31} - x_{32}$	
	$C = x_{11}$	$+ \ 2x_{21}$	$+ \ x_{23}$	$+ \ 2x_{31}$	

where

x_{23} = number shipped from factory in 2nd stage;
x_{24} = number stored at factory in 2nd stage;
d_3 = unknown demand in 3rd stage uniformly distributed between 70 and 80;
x_{31} = number purchased on the open market in 3rd stage;
x_{32} = excess of supply over demand in 3rd stage.[2]

It will be noted that the distribution of d_3 is independent of d_2. However, the approach which we shall use will apply even if the distribution of d_3 depends on d_2. This is important in problems where there may be some postponement of the *timing of demand.* For example, it may be anticipated that the potential refrigerator buyers will buy in November or December. However, those buyers who failed to purchase in November will affect the demand distribution for December.

Example 4: *A Class of Two-Stage Problems.*

In the Ferguson problem and in many supply problems the total costs may be divided into two parts: first the costs of assigning various resources to several destinations j and second the costs (or lost revenues) incurred because of the failure of the total amounts $u_1,, u_2, \cdots, u_n$ assigned to meet demands at various destinations in unknown amounts $d_1, d_2, \cdots, d_n$, respectively.

The special class of two-stage programming problems we are considering has the following structure.[3] For the first stage:

$$(6) \qquad \sum_{j=1}^{n} x_{ij} = a_i \qquad\qquad (x_{ij} \geq 0)$$

$$(7) \qquad \sum_{i=1}^{m} b_{ij} x_{ij} = u_j$$

where x_{ij} represents the amount of ith resource assigned to the jth destination and b_{ij} represents the number of units of demand at destination j that can be satisfied by one unit of resource i. For the second stage

$$(8) \qquad d_j = u_j + v_j - s_j \qquad\qquad (j = 1, 2, \cdots, n)$$

where v_j is the shortage[4] of supply and s_j is the excess of supply.

The total cost function is assumed to be of the form

$$(9) \qquad C = \sum_{i=1}^{m} \sum_{j=1}^{n} c_{ij} x_{ij} + \sum_{j=1}^{n} \alpha_j v_j$$

i.e., depends linearly on the choice x_{ij} and on the shortages v_j (which depend on assignments u_j and the demands d_j).

Our objective will be to minimize total expected costs.[5] Let $\phi_j(u_j|d_j)$ be the minimum cost at a destination if the supply is u_j and the demand is d_j. It is clear that

$$(10) \qquad \phi_j(u_j|d_j) = \begin{cases} \alpha_j(d_j - u_j) & \text{if } d_j \geq u_j \\ 0 & \text{if } d_j < u_j \end{cases}$$

where α_j is the coefficient of proportionality. We shall now give a result due to H. Scarf.

---

[3]The remarks of this section apply if (6) and (7) are replaced more generally by $AX = a$, $BX = U$ where X is a vector of activity levels in the first stage, A and B are given matrices, a a given initial status vector, and $U = (u_1, u_2, \cdots, u_n)$.

[4]Equation (8) should be viewed more generally than simply as a statement about the shortage and excess of supply. In fact, given any u_j and d_j, there is an infinite range of possible values of v_j and s_j satisfying (8). For example, v_j might be interpreted as the amount obtained from some new source (perhaps at some premium price) and s_j the amount not used. When the cost form is as in (9), it becomes clear that in order for C to be a minimum the values of v_j and s_j will have the more restrictive meaning above.

[5]H. Markowitz in his analysis of portfolios considers the interrelation of the variance with the expected value. See [5].

Theorem: The expected value of $\phi_j(u_j|d_j)$ denoted by $\phi_j(u_j)$ is a convex function of u_j.

Proof: Let $p(d_j)$ be the probability density of d_j, then

$$\phi_j(u_j) = \alpha_j \int_{x=u_j}^{+\infty} (x - u_j)p(x)\,dx$$

(11)

$$= \alpha_j \int_{x=u_j}^{+\infty} xp(x)\,dx - \alpha_j u_j \int_{x=u_j}^{+\infty} p(x)\,dx$$

whence differentiating $\phi(u)$

(12) $$\phi_j'(u_j) = -\alpha_j \int_{x=u_j}^{+\infty} p(x)\,dx.$$

It is clear that $\phi_j'(u_j)$ is a non-decreasing function of u_j with $\phi_j''(u_j) \geq 0$ and that $\phi_j(u_j)$ is convex. An alternative proof (also due to Scarf) is obtained by applying a lemma which we shall use later on.

Lemma: If $\phi(x_1, x_2, \cdots, x_n|\theta)$ is a convex function over a fixed region Ω for every value of θ, then any positive linear combination of such functions is also convex in Ω.

In particular if θ is a random variable with probability density $p(\theta)$, then [the] expected value of ϕ

(13) $$\phi(x_1, x_2, \cdots x_n) = \int_{-\infty}^{+\infty} \phi(x_1, x_2, \cdots, x_n|\theta)p(\theta)\,d\theta$$

is convex. For example from (10), $\phi_j(u_j|d_j)$, plotted below, is convex.

(14)

From the lemma the result readily follows that $\phi_j(u_j|d_j)$ is convex.

From the basic theorem the expected value of the objective function is

(15) $$\text{Exp}\,C = \sum c_{ij}x_{ij} + \sum_{j=1}^{n} \alpha_j \phi_j(u_j)$$

where [the] $\phi_j(u_j)$ are *convex functions*. Thus the original problem has been reduced to minimizing (15) subject to (6), (7).

This permits application of a well-known device for *approximating* such a problem by a standard linear programming problem in the case [where] the objective function can be represented by a sum of convex functions.[c] See for example [3] or Charnes and Lemke, [2]. To do this one approximates the derivative of $\phi(u)$ in some sufficiently large range $0 \leq u \leq u_0$ by a step function

(16)

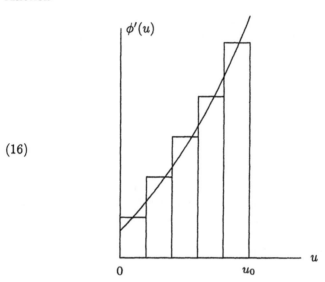

involving k steps where size of the ith base is a_i and its height is h_i, where $h_1 \leq h_2 \leq \cdots \leq h_k$ because ϕ is convex. An approximation for $\phi(u)$ is given by

(17)
$$\phi(u) \doteq \phi(0) + \text{Min} \sum_1^k h_i \Delta_i$$

subject to

(18)
$$u = \sum_{i=1}^k \Delta_i, \qquad 0 \leq \Delta_i \leq a_i.$$

Indeed, it is farily obvious that the approximation achieves its minimum by choosing $\Delta_1 = a_1$, $\Delta_2 = a_2$, $\cdots$ until the cumulative sum of the Δ_i exceeds u for some $i = r$; Δ_r is then chosen as the value of the residual with all remaining $\Delta_{r+i} = 0$. In other words, we have approximated an integral by the sum of rectangular areas under the curve up to u, i.e.,

(19)
$$\phi(u) = \phi(0) + \int_0^u \phi'(x)\,dx \doteq \sum_{i=1}^r h_i a_i + h_r \Delta_r.$$

The next step is to replace $\phi(u)$ by $\sum_1^k h_i\Delta_i$, u by $\sum_1^k \Delta_i$ in the programming problem and add the restrictions $0 \leq \Delta_i \leq a_i$. If the objective is minimization of total costs, it will of necessity, for whatever value of $u = \sum_1^k \Delta_i$ and $0 \leq \Delta_i \leq a_i$, minimize $\sum_1^k h_i\Delta_i$. Thus, this class of two-stage linear programming problems involving uncertainty can be reduced to a standard linear programming problem type problem. In addition, simplifying computational methods exist when variables have upper bounds such as $\Delta_i \leq a_i$; see [3].

Example 5: *The Two-Stage Problem with General Linear Structure.*

We shall prove a general theorem on convexity for the two-stage problem that forms the inductive step for the multi-stage problem. We shall say a few words about the significance of the convexity later on. The assumed structure of the general[6] two-stage model is

$$
\begin{aligned}
b_1 &= A_{11}X_1 \\
b_2 &= A_{21}X_1 + A_{22}X_2 \\
C &= \phi(X_1, X_2|E_2)
\end{aligned}
$$

(20)

where A_{ij} are known matrices, b_1 is a known vector of initial inventories. For example

$a_i = \sum_{j=1}^{n} x_{ij}$	here $b_1 = (a_1, a_2, \cdots, a_m)$
	here $X_1 = (x_{11}, \cdots, x_{1n}, x_{21}, \cdots, x_{2n}, \cdots, x_{mn})$
$d_j = \sum_{i=1}^{m} b_{ij}x_{ij} + v_j - s_j$	here $b_2 = (d_1, d_2, \cdots, d_n)$
$C = \sum \sum c_{ij}x_{ij} + \sum \alpha_j v_j$	here $X_2 = (v_1, v_2, \cdots, v_n, s_1, s_2, \cdots, s_n)$

b_2 [is] an unknown vector whose components are determined by a chance mechanism.[7] Mathematically, E_2 is a sample point drawn from a multi-dimensional sample space with known probability distribution; X_1 is the vector of nonnegative activity levels for the first stage, while X_2 is the vector of nonnegative activity levels for the second stage. It is assumed that whatever be the choice of X_1 satisfying the first-stage equations and whatever be the particular values of b_2 determined by chance, there exists at least one vector X_2 satisfying the second-stage equations. The total costs C of the program are assumed to depend on the choice of X_1, X_2, and parametrically on E_2. The basic problem is to choose X_1 and later X_2 in the second stage such that the expected value of C is a minimum.

Theorem: $\phi(X_1, X_2 | E_2)$ *is a convex function in X_1, X_2 whatever be X_1 in Ω_1, i.e., satisfying the 1st stage restrictions and whatever be X_2 in $\Omega_2 = \Omega_2(X_1 | b_2)$, i.e., satisfying the 2nd stage restrictions given b_2 and X_1,*

---

[6]A special case of the general model given in (2) is found in Example 4.

[7]The chance mechanism may be the "market," the "weather."

then there exists a convex function $\phi_0(X_1)$ such that the optimal choice of X_1 subject to $b_1 = A_{11}X_1$ is found by minimizing $\phi_0(X_1)$ where

$$\phi_0(X_1) = \underset{E_2}{\mathrm{Exp}} \; [\underset{X_2 \in \Omega_2}{\mathrm{Inf}} \; \phi(X_1, X_2 \,|\, E_2)],$$

(21)

$$\mathrm{Exp} \; C = \underset{X_1 \in \Omega_1}{\mathrm{Inf}} \; \phi_0(X_1);$$

the expectation (Exp) *is taken with respect to the distribution of E_2 and the greatest lower bound* (Inf)[8] *is taken with respect to all $X_2 = \Omega_2(X_1 \,|\, E_2)$.*

Proof:[9] In order to minimize the Exp $\phi_1(X_1, X_2 \,|\, E_2)$, it is clear that once X_1 has been selected, E_2 determined by chance, that X_2 must be selected so that $\phi(X_1, X_2 \,|\, E_2)$ is minimized for fixed X_1 and E_2. Thus, the costs for *given* X_1 and E_2 is given by

(22) $$\phi_1(X_1 \,|\, E_2) = \underset{X_2 \in \Omega_2}{\mathrm{Inf}} \; \phi(X_1, X_2) \,|\, E_2).$$

The expected cost for a *given* X_1 is then simply the expected value of $\phi_1(X_1 \,|\, E_2)$ and this we denote by $\phi_0(X_1)$. The optimal choice of X_1 to minimize expected costs C is thus reduced to choosing X_1 so as to minimize $\phi_0(X_1)$. There remains only to establish the convexity property. We shall show first that $\phi_1(X_1 \,|\, E_2)$ for bounded ϕ_1 is convex for X_1 in Ω_1. If true, then applying the lemma, the result that $\phi_0(X_1)$ is convex readily follows. Let us suppose that $\phi_1(X_1 \,|\, E_2)$ is not convex, then there exist three points in $\Omega_1 : X_1', X_1'', X_1''' = \lambda X_1' + \mu X_1'' \; (\lambda + \mu = 1, 0 \le \lambda \le 1)$ that violate the condition for convexity, i.e.,

(23) $$\lambda \phi_1(X_1' \,|\, E_2) + \mu \phi_1(X_1'' \,|\, E_2) < \phi_1(X_1''' \,|\, E_2)$$

or

(24) $$\lambda \phi_1(X_1' \,|\, E_2) + \mu \phi_1(X_1'' \,|\, E_2) = \phi_1(X_1''' \,|\, E_2) - \epsilon_0 \qquad \epsilon_0 > 0.$$

For any $\epsilon_0 > 0$, however, there exists X_2' and X_2'' such that

(25)
$$\phi_1(X_1' \,|\, E_2) = \phi(X_1', X_2' \,|\, E_2) - \epsilon_1 \qquad 0 \le \epsilon_1 < \epsilon_0$$
$$\phi_1(X_1'' \,|\, E_2) = \phi(X_1'', X_2'' \,|\, E_2) - \epsilon_2 \qquad 0 \le \epsilon_2 < \epsilon_0.$$

Setting $X_2''' = \lambda X_2' + \mu X_2''$ we note, because of the assumed linearity of the model (20), that $(\lambda X_2' + \mu X_2'') \in \Omega(\lambda X_1' + \mu X_1'' \,|\, E_2)$ and hence by [the] convexity of ϕ

(26) $$\lambda \phi(X_1', X_2' \,|\, E_2) + \mu \phi(X_1'', X_2'' \,|\, E_2) \ge \phi(X_1''', X_2''' \,|\, E_2)$$

---

[8] The greatest lower bound instead of minimum is used to avoid the possibility that the minimum value is not attained for any admissible point $X_2 \in \Omega_2$. In cases where the latter occurs, it should be understood that while there exists no X_i where the minimum is attained, there exists X_i for which values as close to minimum as desired are attained.

[9] This proof is along lines suggested by I. Glicksberg.

whence by (25)

(27) $\lambda\phi_1(X_1' \,|\, E_2) + \mu\phi_1(X_1'' \,|\, E_2) \geq \phi(X_1''', X_2''' \,|\, E_2) - \lambda\epsilon_1 - \mu\epsilon_2$

and by (24)

(28) $\phi_1(X_1''' \,|\, E_2) \geq \phi(X_1''', X_2''' \,|\, E_2) - \lambda\epsilon_1 - \mu\epsilon_2 + \epsilon_0$ $(0 \leq \lambda\epsilon_1 + \mu\epsilon_2 < \epsilon_0)$

which contradicts the assumption that $\phi_1(X_1''' \,|\, E_2) = \mathrm{Inf}\,\phi(X_1''', X_2 \,|\, E_2)$. The proof for unbounded ϕ is omitted.

Example 5: *The Multi-Stage Problem with General Linear Structure.* The structure is assumed is

$$b_1 = A_{11}X_1$$
$$b_2 = A_{21}X_1 + A_{22}X_2$$
$$b_3 = A_{31}X_1 + A_{32}X_2 + A_{33}X_3$$
(29) $$b_4 = A_{41}X_1 + A_{42}X_2 + A_{43}X_3 + A_{44}X_4$$
$$\cdots\cdots\cdots\cdots\cdots\cdots\cdots\cdots\cdots\cdots\cdots$$
$$b_m = A_{m1}X_1 + A_{m2}X_2 + A_{m3}X_3 + \cdots\cdots + A_{mm}X_m$$
$$C = \phi(X_1, X_2, \cdots, X_m \,|\, E_2, E_3, \cdots, E_m)$$

where b_1 is a known vector; b_i is a chance vector $(i = 2, \cdots, m)$ whose components are functions of a point E_i drawn from a known multi-dimensional distribution; A_{ij} are known matrices. The sequence of decisions is as follows: X_1, the vector of nonnegative activity levels in the 1st stage, is chosen so as to satisfy the first-stage restrictions $b_1 = A_{11}X_1$; the values of components of b_2 are chosen by chance by determining E_2; X_2 is chosen to satisfy the second-stage restrictions $b_2 = A_{21}X_1 + A_{22}X_2$, etc. iteratively for the third and higher stages. It is further assumed that

(1) The components of X_j are nonnegative;

(2) There exists at least one X_j satisfying the j-stage restraints, whatever be the choice of $X_1, X_2, \cdots, X_{j-1}$ satisfying the earlier restraints for the outcomes $b_1, b_2, \cdots, b_m$.

(3) The total cost C is a convex function of $X_1, X_2, \cdots, X_m$ which depends on the values of the sample points $E_2, E_3, \cdots, E_m$.

Theorem: An equivalent $(m-1)$-stage programming problem with a convex pay-off function can be obtained by dropping the mth-stage restrictions and replacing the convex cost function ϕ by

$$\phi_{m-1}(X_1, X_2, \cdots, X_{m-1} \mid E_2, \cdots, E_{m-1})$$

(30)
$$= \underset{E_m\ X_m \in \Omega_m}{\text{Exp Inf}} \quad \phi(X_1, X_2, \cdots, X_m \mid E_2, \cdots, E_m)$$

where Ω_m is the set of possible X_m that satisfy the mth-stage restrictions.

Since the proof of the above theorem is identical to the two-stage case, no details will be given. The fact that the cost function for the $(m-1)$-stage can be obtained from the mth stage is simply a consequence [of the fact] that optimal behavior for the mth stage is well defined, i.e., given any state, e.g., $(X_1, X_2, \cdots, X_{m-1})$ at the beginning of this stage, the best possible actions can be determined and the minimum expected cost evaluated. This is a standard technique in "dynamic programming." For the reader interested in methods built around this approach the reader is referred to R. Bellman's book on dynamic programming [1].

While the existence of convex functions has been demonstrated that permit reduction of an m-stage problem to equivalent $m-1, m-2, \cdots, 1$-stage problems, it appears hopeless that such functions can be computed except in very simple cases. The convexity theorem was demonstrated not as a solution to an m-stage problem but only in the hope that it will aid in the development of an efficient computational theory for such models. It should be remembered that any procedure that yields a local optimum will be a true optimum if the function is convex. This is important because multi-dimensional problems in which non-convex functions are defined over non-convex domains lead as a rule to [a] local optimum and an almost hopeless task, computationally, of exploring other parts of the domain for other extremes.

Solution for Example 2: *Shipping to an Outlet to Meet an Uncertain Demand.*

Let us consider the two-stage case given earlier (4). It is clear that, if supply exceeds demand [d] $(x_{11} > d_2)$, then $x_{21} = 0$ gives minimum costs and, if $x_{11} \leq d_2$,

(31)
$$\underset{x_{21}}{\text{Min}}\,\phi = \begin{cases} x_{11} & \text{if } x_{11} > d_2 \\ x_{11} + 2(d_2 - x_{11}) & \text{if } x_{11} \leq d_2 \end{cases}$$

Since d_2 is assumed to be uniformly distributed between 70 and 88

(32)
$$\underset{d_2}{\text{Exp}}\,\underset{x_{21}}{[\text{Min}\,\phi]} = \begin{cases} -x_{11} + 150 & \text{if } \quad x_{11} \leq 70 \\ 77.5 + \frac{1}{10}(75 - x_{11})^2 & \text{if } 70 < x_{11} \leq 80 \\ x_{11} & \text{if } 80 \leq x_{11} \end{cases}$$

This function is clearly convex and attains its minimum 77.5, which is the expected cost, at $x_{11} = 75$. Since $x_{11} = 75$ is in the range of possible values of x_{11} as determined by $100 = x_{11} + x_{12}$ this is clearly the optimal shipment. In this case it pays to ship $x_{11} = d_2 = 75$, the expected demand.

It can be shown by simple examples that one cannot replace, in general, the chance vectors b_i by $\bar{b}_i$, the vector of expected values of the components of b_i. Nevertheless, this procedure, which is quite common, probably provides an excellent starting solution for any improvement technique that might be devised. For example, in the problem of Ferguson (application of Example 4), using as a start the solution based on expected values of demand, it was an easy matter to improve the solution to an optimal one whose expected costs were 15% less.

Solution for Example 5: *The General Two-Stage Case.*

When the number [e] of possibilities for the chance vector b_2 is $b_2^{(1)}, b_2^{(2)}, \cdots,$ $b_2^{(k)}$ with probabilities $p_1, p_2, \cdots, p_k$, $(\sum p_i = 1)$, it is not difficult to obtain a direct linear programming solution for small k, say $k = 3$. Since this type of structure is very special, it appears likely that techniques can be developed to handle large k. For $k = 3$, the problem is equivalent to determining vectors X_1 and vectors $X_2^{(1)}, X_2^{(2)}, X_2^{(3)}$ such that

$$
\begin{aligned}
b_1 &= A_{11}X_1 \\
b_2^{(1)} &= A_{21}X_1 + A_{22}X_2^{(1)} \\
b_2^{(2)} &= A_{21}X_1 \qquad\qquad + A_{22}X_2^{(2)} \\
b_2^{(3)} &= A_{21}X_1 \qquad\qquad\qquad\qquad + A_{22}X_2^{(3)} \\
\mathrm{Exp}\,C &= \gamma_1 X_1 + p_1\gamma_2 X_2^{(1)} + p_2\gamma_2 X_2^{(2)} + p_3\gamma_3 X_2^{(3)} = \mathrm{Min}
\end{aligned}
$$

(33)

where for simplicity we have assumed a linear objective function.

References

[1] Bellman, R., *An Introduction to the Theory of Dynamic Programming,* The RAND Corporation, Report R-245, June, 1953.

[2] Charnes, A., and C.E. Lemke, *Minimization of Non-Linear Separable Functions,* Graduate School of Industrial Administration, Carnegie Institute of Technology, May, 1954.

[3] Dantzig, G., Notes on Linear Programming: Parts VIII, IX, X—Upper Bounds, Secondary Constraints, and Block Triangularity in Linear Programming, The RAND Corporation, Research Memorandum RM-1367, 4 October 1954.

[4] Ferguson, A.R., and G. Dantzig, *Notes on Linear Programming: Part XVI— The Problem of Routing Aircraft—A Mathematical Solution,* The RAND Corporation, Research Memorandum RM 1369, 1 September 1954.

[5] Markowitz, H., *Portfolio Selection*, thesis submitted to The University of Chicago, summer, 1953.

[6] Stigler, G.F., "The Cost of Subsistence," *Journal of Farm Economics*, Vol. 27, May 1945, pp. 303–314.

Chapter 13

ON THE SOLUTION OF TWO-STAGE
LINEAR PROGRAMS UNDER UNCERTAINTY

GEORGE B. DANTZIG

AND

ALBERT MADANSKY

THE RAND CORPORATION

1. Introduction

In this paper we shall study the program

$$(1) \qquad Ax + By = b, \qquad\qquad x \geq 0, \quad y \geq 0$$

where A and B are known $m \times n_1$ and $m \times n_2$ matrices, x and y are n_1- and n_2-dimensional vectors, and b is a random m-dimensional vector with known distribution. We wish to minimize with respect to x

$$(2) \qquad\qquad E \min_{y} (c'x + f'y),$$

where c and f are known n_1- and n_2-dimensional vectors, E denotes expectation taken with respect to the distribution of b, and prime denotes transpose.

As an example of a situation giving rise to such a program, consider the set of possible polyhedra given by $Ax = b$, where $x \geq 0$, when b is random. Here, in contrast to the usual case [6] where one minimizes $c'x$ subject to x lying in the intersection over b of these polyhedra, one is instead allowed, after selecting an x and subsequently observing b, to compensate with a vector $y \geq 0$ for infeasibility of the selected x at a penalty cost $f'y$, where $f \geq 0$. In this case By would be $y^+ - y^-$ and the vector y which yields the smallest penalty cost for each b and x would be composed of two parts,[a] $y^+ = b - Ax$, $y^- = 0$ if $b \geq Ax$ or $y^- = Ax - b$, $y^+ = 0$ if $b < Ax$. As choice of y depends on b as well as x, we alter the objective from minimizing $c'x$ to minimizing $c'x$ plus the expected smallest penalty cost.

Many short-range inventory problems can be expressed mathematically as such a program. The vector x may represent an inventory which is to be bought at a cost $c'x$ before the random demand b is observed. Once b is observed, one must compensate by a vector y, at cost $f'y$, for imbalances $(b - Ax)$ between the original inventory and the demand so as to satisfy (1). For example, coordinates of the vector y may represent the amount of additional inventory to be bought immediately to meet the excess of demand over supply or the amount of inventory to discard in case of an excess of inventory over demand.

As the structure of the problem involves a decision x to be made first, after which the random vector b is observed and a second decision y is made, we term this a *two-stage* problem. It may be that some coordinates of b are not random and that the corresponding equations do not involve y. We shall call these equations "fixed constraints" on x.

The structure of the matrices A and B may impose further constraints on x. For example, B may be a positive matrix, in which case $Ax + By = b$ and $y \geq 0$ imply $Ax \leq b$. We shall call such constraints "induced constraints." These constraints of course may depend on the value of the random vector b.

If some equations do not involve y but the corresponding subvector of b is random, we wish to restrict ourselves to the modified problem where we take as fixed restraints on x that x satisfies some specific one of all these equations. We further assume that, for each $x \geq 0$ and satisfying all existing fixed and all possible induced constraints and for each b, there exists a y such that (x, y) is feasible, that is, satisfies (1).

This last assumption may seem very restrictive, as it says that, given any feasible x and possible b, the set of linear equations $By = b - Ax$ must have a nonnegative solution. This assumption is motivated by the desire to solve a class of problem which can be expressed as the program given in (1) and where this assumption is necessary for the problem to have a solution. The constraints of this class of problems have the structure

(3)
$$
\begin{aligned}
A_{11}x \qquad &= b_1, \\
A_{21}x + A_{22}y &= b_2,
\end{aligned}
\qquad x \geq 0, \quad y \geq 0
$$

where b_1 is a known vector and b_2 is a random vector with known distribution. It is clear that these constraints can be written as those of the program (1) and that in this format, if the objective function for (3) is of the form (2), we have a two-stage program with fixed constraints on x. A further description of the underlying problem which gives rise to the structure in (3) and an example of such a problem are given in [2].

As an alternative to this assumption, we can define K as the convex set of the x such that each $x \in K$ is nonnegative and has an associated y for each b such that (x, y) is feasible. The problem is, then, to find $x \in K$

which minimizes $c'x + E \min_y f'y$. These x certainly satisfy all fixed and induced constraints.

2. Optimality conditions

Let us first study the program

(4) $$By = b - Ax, \qquad f'y = \min, \qquad\qquad y \geq 0$$

and its dual for each b, x. We assume the existence of a π which is feasible for the dual of the program given by (4) for each b, x. By the existence theorem for linear programming,[b] this assumption plus the feasibility property of the convex set K for the program given by (1) and (2) guarantees the existence of at least one optimal dual vector $\pi = \bar{\pi}(b, x)$ which maximizes $\pi'(b - Ax)$ subject to $\pi'B \leq f'$.

By the duality theorem

(5) $$\min_y f'y = \bar{\pi}'(b,x)(b - Ax),$$

so that

(6) $$\min_y c'x + f'y = c'x + \bar{\pi}'(b,x)(b - Ax) = C(b,x),$$

say, and

(7) $$EC(b,x) = c'x + E\bar{\pi}'(b,x)(b - Ax).$$

The optimal x is then the x that minimizes $EC(b,x)$ subject to $x \in K$. When for a given b and x there are many optimal π, we shall mean by $\bar{\pi}(b,x)$ any vector chosen from these optima, unless some explicit statement to the contrary is made.

Following is an immediate necessary condition for some vector $x = \bar{x}$ to be optimal.

THEOREM 1. *Let $\bar{x}$ be optimal and let $\bar{\pi}(b, x_1)$ be any vector which optimizes the dual of (4) for given b and $x = x_1$, where $x_1 \in K$. Then*

(8) $$[c' - E\bar{\pi}'(b,x_1)A]\bar{x} \leq [c' - E\bar{\pi}'(b,x_1)A]x_1.$$

PROOF. Since $\bar{x}$ is optimal and x_1 is feasible

(9) $$c'\bar{x} + E\bar{\pi}'(b,\bar{x})(b - A\bar{x}) \leq c'x_1 + E\bar{\pi}'(b,x_1)(b - Ax_1).$$

Also

(10) $$E\bar{\pi}'(b,\bar{x})(b - A\bar{x}) \geq E\bar{\pi}'(b,x_1)(b - A\bar{x})$$

since $\bar{\pi}'(b,\bar{x})$ optimizes the dual of (4) when $x = \bar{x}$. Hence

(11) $$c'\bar{x} + E\bar{\pi}'(b,x_1)(b - A\bar{x}) \leq c'x_1 + E\bar{\pi}'(b,x_1)(b - Ax_1).$$

The following lemmas enable us to obtain another necessary condition for some vector $x = x_0$ to be optimal.

LEMMA 1. $EC(b, x)$ *is a convex function of* x.

PROOF. It is easy to check directly from the definition of convexity that $C(b, x)$ is convex in x for each b [1]. Then $EC(b, x)$ is a convex function of x.

LEMMA 2. $[c' - E\bar{\pi}'(b, x_1)A]x + E\bar{\pi}'(b, x_1)b$ *is a support plane to* $EC(b, x)$ *at* $x = x_1$.

PROOF. Since at $x = x_1$ this plane intersects $EC(b, x)$, all we need show is that, for $x \neq x_1$,

$$(12) \quad [c' - E\bar{\pi}'(b, x_1)A]x + E\bar{\pi}'(b, x_1)b \leq [c' - E\bar{\pi}'(b, x)A]x + E\bar{\pi}'(b, x)b.$$

But this is true if and only if

$$(13) \qquad E\bar{\pi}'(b, x_1)(b - Ax) \leq E\bar{\pi}'(b, x)(b - Ax),$$

and this is so since $\bar{\pi}(b, x)$ is optimal for the dual of (4).

A consequence of these lemmas is the following theorem.

THEOREM 2. *Let* $\bar{x}$ *be a relative interior point of* K *and let* $EC(b, x)$ *be differentiable in the neighborhood of* $\bar{x}$. *Then there exists a* $\bar{\pi}(b, \bar{x})$ *such that* $c' - E\bar{\pi}'(b, \bar{x})A = 0$ *if and only if* $\bar{x}$ *is optimal.*

PROOF. Since the convex function $EC(b, x)$ is differentiable at $\bar{x}$, the supporting hyperplane

$$(14) \qquad z = [c' - E\bar{\pi}'(b, \bar{x})A]x + E\bar{\pi}'(b, \bar{x})b$$

is tangent to $EC(b, x)$ at $x = \bar{x}$. Hence

$$(15) \qquad \left.\frac{\partial EC(b, x)}{\partial x}\right|_{x=\bar{x}} = \left.\frac{\partial z}{\partial x}\right|_{x=\bar{x}} = c' - E\bar{\pi}'(b, \bar{x}) = 0$$

is a necessary condition for $\bar{x}$ to be optimal. As $\bar{x}$ is a relative interior point of K, it is also sufficient.

Returning once again to the program given in (4), let $\bar{y}(b, x)$ denote the solution of this program for given b, x. Then $\bar{\pi}'(b, x)$ and $\bar{y}(b, x)$ are saddle points of the function

$$(16) \qquad \Psi(y, \pi|x) = f'y + \pi'(b - Ax - By).$$

Let $\phi(x, y, \pi) = c'x + E\Psi(y, \pi|x)$. We then have the following results.

THEOREM 3. *Let* $\bar{x}$ *be optimal for the two-stage problem and* $\bar{y}(b, x)$, $\bar{\pi}(b, x)$ *be optimal for (4) and its dual. Then*

$$(17) \qquad \phi(\bar{x}, \bar{y}, \pi) \leq \phi(\bar{x}, \bar{y}, \bar{\pi}) \leq \phi(x, \bar{y}, \bar{\pi})$$

Conversely, if there exist vectors $\bar{x} \in K$ and $\bar{\pi}$ feasible for the dual of (4) *which satisfy* (17) *then $\bar{x}$ is optimal for the two-stage problem and $\bar{\pi}$ is optimal for the dual of* (4) *when $x = \bar{x}$.*

PROOF. Since $\Psi(\bar{y}, \pi|\bar{x}) \leq \Psi(\bar{y}, \bar{\pi}|\bar{x})$.

$$(18) \qquad \phi(\bar{x}, \bar{y}, \pi) = c'\bar{x} + E\Psi(\bar{y}, \pi|\bar{x}) \leq c'\bar{x} + E\Psi(\bar{y}, \bar{\pi}|\bar{x}) = \phi(\bar{x}, \bar{y}, \bar{\pi}).$$

Now write $\phi(x, \bar{y}, \bar{\pi})$ as

$$(19) \qquad \phi(x, \bar{y}, \bar{\pi}) = c'x + E\bar{\pi}'(b, x)(b - Ax) + E[f' - \bar{\pi}'(b, x)B]\bar{y}(b, x).$$

Since $\bar{\pi}(b, x)$ is optimal for the dual of (4), by the duality theorem $f' - \bar{\pi}'(b, x)B$ has the property that, if the ith coordinate of $\bar{y}(b, x)$ is positive, its ith coordinate is zero. This and the nonnegativity of $\bar{y}(b, x)$ imply that

$$(20) \qquad \phi(x, \bar{y}, \bar{\pi}) = c'x + E\bar{\pi}'(b, x)(b - Ax) = EC(b, x)$$

and, by optimality of $\bar{x}$

$$(21) \qquad\qquad \phi(\bar{x}, \bar{y}, \bar{\pi}) \leq \phi(x, \bar{y}, \bar{\pi}).$$

To prove the converse, we must first show that $\bar{\pi}(b, \bar{x})$ is optimal for the dual of (4). Then, since $\phi(x, \bar{y}, \bar{\pi}) = EC(b, x)$, it is immediately clear that $\bar{x}$ is optimal for the two-stage stochastic program.

Let $\pi^*(b, x)$ be optimal for the dual of (4). Then

$$(22) \qquad\qquad E\pi^{*'}(b, \bar{x})(b - A\bar{x}) \geq E\bar{\pi}'(b, \bar{x})(b - A\bar{x}),$$

and also

$$(23) \qquad\qquad [f' - \pi^{*'}(b, \bar{x})B]\bar{y}(b, \bar{x}) = 0.$$

But $\bar{\pi}(b, x)$ satisfies $\phi(\bar{x}, \bar{y}, \pi^*) \leq \phi(\bar{x}, \bar{y}, \bar{\pi})$, or

$$(24) \quad E\pi^{*'}(b, \bar{x})(b - A\bar{x}) \leq E\bar{\pi}'(b, \bar{x})(b - A\bar{x}) + E[f' - \bar{\pi}'(b, x)B]\bar{y}(b, \bar{x}).$$

If $\bar{\pi}(b, \bar{x})$ is not optimal, then $[f' - \bar{\pi}'(b, x)B]\bar{y}(b, \bar{x}) > 0$, and hence (24) contradicts (22).

This theorem is the analogue in the two-stage problem dealt with here of the duality theorem for the one-stage linear team decision problem under uncertainty given in [6]. Based on this theorem we can prove in general the following sufficient condition for optimality of $x = \bar{x}$.

THEOREM 4. *Let $\bar{\pi}(b, \bar{x})$ be optimal for the dual of* (4) *when $x = \bar{x}$. If for all $x \in K$, $[c' - E\bar{\pi}'(b, \bar{x})A]\bar{x} \leq [c' - E\bar{\pi}'(b, \bar{x})A]x$, then $\bar{x}$ is optimal for the two-stage problem.*

PROOF. Optimality of $\bar{\pi}(b, \bar{x})$ for the dual of (4) when $x = \bar{x}$ immediately yields the inequality

$$(25) \qquad \phi(\bar{x}, \bar{y}, \pi) \leq \phi(\bar{x}, \bar{y}, \bar{\pi}).$$

Now by definition, hypothesis, and noting the facts that $f' - \bar{\pi}'(b, x)B \geq 0$, $[f' - \bar{\pi}'(b, x)B]\bar{y}(b, x) = 0$ for all x, and $b - Ax - B\bar{y}(b, x) = 0$, we see that

$$
\begin{aligned}
\phi(\bar{x}, \bar{y}, \bar{\pi}) &= [c' - E\bar{\pi}'(b, \bar{x})A]\bar{x} + E\bar{\pi}'(b, \bar{x})b \\
&\leq [c' - E\bar{\pi}'(b, \bar{x})A]x + E\bar{\pi}'(b, \bar{x})b + E[f' - \bar{\pi}'(b, \bar{x})B]\bar{y}(b, x) \\
(26) \qquad &= c'x + Ef'\bar{y}(b, x) + E\bar{\pi}'(b, \bar{x})[b - Ax - B\bar{y}(b, x)] \\
&= c'x + Ef'\bar{y}(b, x) + E\bar{\pi}'(b, x)[b - Ax - B\bar{y}(b, x)] \\
&= \phi(x, \bar{y}, \bar{\pi}).
\end{aligned}
$$

Hence, by Theorem 3, $\bar{x}$ is optimal.

This indicates that if $\bar{x} \in K$ minimizes the linear form $[c' - E\bar{\pi}'(b, \bar{x})A]x$, it is optimal. It would be worthwhile to know whether the converse of Theorem 4 is true. We have established this converse if $EC(b, x)$ is differentiable and $\bar{x}$ exists and is an interior point of K, see Theorem 2. We shall consider later the finite case. A kind of converse of Theorem 4 is the following.

THEOREM 5. *Let $\bar{x}$ and $\bar{y}(b, \bar{x})$ be optimal for the two-stage problem for given b, and let $\bar{y}(b, x)$ and $\bar{\pi}(b, x)$ be optimal for (4) and its dual for given x. Then*

$$(27) \qquad E[((c', f') - \bar{\pi}'(b, \bar{x}))(A, B)][\bar{x}, \bar{y}(b, \bar{x})]$$
$$\leq E[((c'f') - \bar{\pi}'(b, \bar{x})(A, B)][x, \bar{y}(b, x)].$$

PROOF. It is seen from the definition of ϕ and the fact that $b - Ax - B\bar{y}(b, x) = 0$ that

$$(28) \qquad \phi[x, \bar{y}(b, x), \bar{\pi}(b, x)] = \phi[x, \bar{y}(b, x), \bar{\pi}(b, \bar{x})].$$

Now the right-hand member of (28) is the right member of (27), plus $E\bar{\pi}'(b, x)b$, and the left member of (28) is $\phi(x, \bar{y}, \bar{\pi})$, which by Theorem 4, is greater than or equal to $\phi(\bar{x}, \bar{y}, \bar{\pi})$, that is, the left member of (27) plus $E\bar{\pi}'(b, x)b$.

When there are only a finite number of possible b: $b_1, \cdots, b_N$, with associated probabilities $p_1, \cdots, p_N$, where $\sum_{i=1}^{N} p_i = 1$, then the two-stage program can be written as follows. Find $x, y_1, \cdots, y_N$ and min z satisfying

$$
\begin{aligned}
Ax + By_1 \qquad\qquad &= b_1 \\
Ax + \qquad By_2 \quad\; &= b_2 \\
\vdots \qquad\qquad \ddots \quad &\;\; \vdots \\
Ax + \qquad\qquad\quad\; &= b_N
\end{aligned}
$$

(29)

$$
c'x + p_1 f'y_1 + p_2 f'y_2 + \cdots + p_N f'y_N = z
$$

$$
x \geq 0,\ y_1 \geq 0,\ y_2 \geq 0,\ \cdots,\ y_N \geq 0
$$

As an application of the duality theorem and the optimality test of the simplex method in this special case, we obtain the following theorem.

THEOREM 5. *Let $\theta_i(\bar{x})$ be the ith subvector $(i = 1, \cdots, N)$ in the vector of prices associated with a basic solution $x = \bar{x}$, $y_i = \bar{y}_i$, $i = 1, \cdots, N$, for (29). Then $\bar{x}$, $\{\bar{y}_i\}$ is optimal if*

(30)
$$
c' - \sum_{i=1}^{N} \theta_i'(\bar{x})A \geq 0, \qquad [c' - \sum_{i=1}^{N} \theta_i'(\bar{x})A]\bar{x} = 0
$$

$$
p_i f' - \theta_i'(\bar{x})B \geq 0, \qquad [p_i f' - \theta_i'(\bar{x})B]\bar{y}_i = 0, \quad i = 1, \cdots, N.
$$

Further, if $\bar{x}$, $\{\bar{y}_i\}$ is optimal, then there exist prices $\theta_i(\bar{x})$ satisfying (30).[c]

We can easily prove Theorem 4 in the finite case.

THEOREM 4'. *Let $x = \bar{x}$ and suppose that there exist optimal prices $\bar{\pi}(b, \bar{x})$ for the program in (4) such that*

(31)
$$
c' - E\bar{\pi}'(b, \bar{x})A \geq 0, \qquad [c' - E\bar{\pi}'(b, \bar{x})A]\bar{x} = 0.
$$

Then $\bar{x}$ is optimal.

PROOF. Take

(32)
$$
\theta_i(\bar{x}) = p_i \bar{\pi}(b_i, \bar{x}).
$$

Then

(33)
$$
E\bar{\pi}'(b, x) = \sum_{i=1}^{N} p_i \bar{\pi}(b_i, \bar{x}) = \sum_{i=1}^{N} \theta_i(\bar{x}).
$$

Also, since $\bar{\pi}'(b_i, \bar{x})$ is optimal for the dual of (4), it satisfies

(34)
$$
f' - \bar{\pi}'(b_i, \bar{x})B \geq 0, \qquad [f' - \bar{\pi}'(b_i, \bar{x})B]\bar{y}(b_i, \bar{x}) = 0.
$$

Hence for $\bar{y}_i = \bar{y}_i(b_i, \bar{x})$, $\theta_i(\bar{x})$ so defined satisfies (30) and, by Theorem 5, $\bar{x}$ is optimal.

The converse of this theorem is also very easy to prove in the finite case.

Theorem 6. *Let $\bar{x}$ be optimal. Then there exist optimal prices $\bar{\pi}(b, \bar{x})$ for the program in* (4) *such that*

$$(35) \qquad c' - E\bar{\pi}'(b, \bar{x})A \geq 0, \qquad [c' - E\bar{\pi}'(b, \bar{x})A]\bar{x} = 0.$$

Proof. Let $\pi(b_i, \bar{x}) = \theta_i(\bar{x})/p_i$, where the $\theta_i(\bar{x})$ satisfy (30). Then we have $[f' - \pi'(b_i, \bar{x})B]\bar{y}_i = 0$, so that $\bar{y}_i = \bar{y}(b_i, \bar{x})$, and $\pi(b_i, \bar{x})$ is a set of optimal prices for (4).

It is interesting to contrast this necessary condition for the finite case with that of Theorem 2. In this case, not only is $c' - E\bar{\pi}'(b, \bar{x})A \geq 0$, but further if the ith coordinate of $\bar{x}$ is positive, then the ith coordinate of $c' - E\bar{\pi}'(b, \bar{x})A$ is zero. In the case dealt with in Theorem 2, all coordinates of $c' - E\bar{\pi}'(b, \bar{x})A$ are zero. Of course, in the finite case $EC(b, x)$ does not satisfy the conditions of Theorem 2 because here $\bar{x}$ is an extreme point of the convex region of interest, and $EC(, x)$ is not differentiable in the neighborhood of the extreme points of this convex region.

A simple example of a two-stage problem satisfying the conditions of Theorem 2 is the problem solved in [2]. There x' was a two-dimensional nonnegative vector (x_1, x_2) with fixed constraint $x_1 + x_2 = 100$ so that K was a line segment in the first quadrant, and b was distributed uniformly between 70 and 80, $EC(b, x)$ was differentiable at the optimum $\bar{x} = (75, 25)$, a relative interior point of K, and, though

$$(36) \qquad \bar{\pi}(b, x) = \begin{cases} (0, \pi_2), & b \leq x_1, \\ (2, \pi_2), & b > x_1, \end{cases}$$

was optimal for the dual of (4), where π_2 could take on any value, the particular $\bar{\pi}(b, \bar{x})$ for which Theorem 2 held had $\pi_2 = 0$.

3. Computational procedures

As the determination of an optimal y, given x and b, is a straightforward application of linear programming techniques to the program defined in (4), our objective is to find methods of determining an optimal x other than [by] solving the large program (29). As will be seen shortly, an application of the decomposition principle [4] to the dual of (29) will reduce the size of the problem greatly and will directly obtain for us only the optimal x and not the optimal set of y.

By virtue of Theorems 4' and 6, the problem dual to (29) can be expressed as

$$p_1 A'\pi_1 + p_2 A'\pi_2 + \cdots + p_N A'\pi_N \le c$$
$$B'\pi_1 \qquad\qquad\qquad\qquad\qquad \le f$$
$$B'\pi_2 \qquad\qquad\qquad \le f$$

(37)

$$\ddots \qquad\qquad \vdots$$
$$B'\pi_N \le f$$
$$p_1 b'\pi_1 + p_2 b'\pi_2 + \cdots + p_N b'\pi_N = \max$$

We now note that the dual problem is in standard form for the application of the decomposition algorithm [4] to solve the program. To utilize the algorithm, it is convenient to call the last N sets of inequalities in (37) a single subprogram and the first set of inequalities the master program. This will reduce the program from one with $n_1 + Nn_2$ to one with $n_1 + 1$ constraints.

For notational convenience in describing the algorithm, let $\tilde{B}$ be a $Nm \times Nn_2$ block diagonal matrix of the form

(38)
$$\tilde{B} = \begin{bmatrix} B & & 0 \\ & \ddots & \\ 0 & & B \end{bmatrix},$$

$\tilde{f}$ be a Nn_2-dimensional vector of the form $\tilde{f}' = [f' \cdots f']$, $\tilde{\pi}' = [\pi'_1 \cdots \pi'_N]$, $\tilde{A}' = [p_1 A' \cdots p_N A']$, and $\tilde{b}' = [p_1 b'_1 \cdots p_N b'_N]$. Then (37) can be rewritten as,

(39) $$\tilde{A}'\tilde{\pi} \le c, \qquad \tilde{B}'\tilde{\pi} \le \tilde{f}, \qquad \tilde{b}'\tilde{\pi} = \max.$$

Let $S = \{\tilde{\pi}|\tilde{B}'\tilde{\pi} \le \tilde{f}\}$ and let $W = \{\tilde{\pi}_1, \cdots, \tilde{\pi}_k\}$ be the set of extreme points of the convex set S. We assume here that S is a bounded set. The slight modification in the algorithm for unbounded S is given in [4]. Also let $P_j = \tilde{A}'\tilde{\pi}_j$ and $r_j = \tilde{b}'\tilde{\pi}_j$ for $j = 1, \cdots, k$. The extremal problem corresponding to (39) is to find numbers $\lambda_1, \cdots, \lambda_k$ such that

(40)
$$P_1\lambda_1 + P_2\lambda_2 + \cdots + P_k\lambda_k \le c$$
$$\lambda_1 + \lambda_2 + \cdots + \lambda_k = 1$$
$$r_1\lambda_1 + r_2\lambda_2 + \cdots + r_k\lambda_k = \max$$
$$\lambda_1 \ge 0, \ \lambda_2 \ge 0, \cdots, \lambda_k \ge 0.$$

Then, as is shown in [4], $\tilde{\pi} = \sum_{j=1}^{k} \lambda_j \tilde{\pi}_j$ solves (39).

Now this program has even more variables than (39), namely kNm; moveover k can be very large and hence not practical to determine W explicitly. However, (40) only has $n_1 + 1$ constraints and one need never carry more than $n_1 + 1$ variables in solving (40) when using the decomposition algorithm.

The algorithm is initiated once one has a feasible basis for (40), that is, $(n_1 + 1)$ vectors π_j, to determine the necessary $(n_1 + 1)$ vectors P_j and $(n_1 + 1)$ vectors λ_j which are positive and satisfy the constraints of (40). This may be obtained using phase one of the simplex method (see [4]). The prices for this basis are then determined and are used to generate those extreme points of S that appear promising and to suppress the others. This is done with each new basis formed during the process. In this case x will be the price vector for the first n_1 constraints and we will call z the price for the last constraint. When (40) is solved, the resulting price x is optimal for the original program (29).

As the algorithm is iterative, generating new prices with each iteration, we shall append the superscript t to x and z to denote the appropriate iteration. Given the initial feasible basis, we obtain concomitantly x^0 and z^0. To test optimality of x^0 and, if not optimal, to generate a new basis, one must first find $\tilde{\pi} = \tilde{\pi}^0$ which maximizes $\tilde{\pi}'(\tilde{b} - \tilde{A}x^0) - z^0$ subject to $\tilde{B}'\tilde{\pi} \leq \tilde{f}$. If $\tilde{\pi}^{0\prime}(\tilde{b} - \tilde{A}x^0) - z^0 \geq 0$, the algorithm is terminated, and x^0 solves (29). If not, a new column is added to the $n_1 + 1$ columns of the initial basis, namely,

$$(41) \qquad \begin{bmatrix} \tilde{A}'\tilde{\pi}^0 \\ 1 \end{bmatrix}$$

and its associated cost $\tilde{b}'\tilde{\pi}^0$ is added to the objective function. Using the simplex method, a new basis and new prices x^1, z^1 are determined, $\tilde{\pi} = \tilde{\pi}^1$ which maximizes $\tilde{\pi}'(\tilde{b} - \tilde{A}x^1) - z^1$ subject to $\tilde{B}'\tilde{\pi} \leq \tilde{f}$ is determined, and once again we test $\tilde{\pi}^1$ for optimality. The process terminates when for some iteration t and prices x^t, z^t, we have

$$(42) \qquad \max_{\tilde{B}'\tilde{\pi} \leq \tilde{f}} \tilde{\pi}'(\tilde{b} - \tilde{A}x^t) - z^t \geq 0.$$

Notice that all one needs to carry along in the computation are the columns of the current basis, $n_1 + 1$ in all. At iteration t, if (42) is not satisfied, the column

$$(43) \qquad \begin{bmatrix} \tilde{A}'\tilde{\pi}^t \\ 1 \end{bmatrix}$$

is added to the basis and the simplex method determines the appropriate column to remove from the basis and hence from consideration in subsequent calculation.

Since

$$(44) \qquad \tilde{b}'\tilde{\pi} = \sum_{i=1}^{N} p_i \pi'(b_i, x) b_i = E\pi'(b, x)b$$

and

$$(45) \qquad \tilde{\pi}'\tilde{A}x = \sum_{i=1}^{N} p_i \pi'(b_i, x) Ax = E\pi'(b, x) Ax,$$

we see that the test for optimality can be rewritten as

$$(46) \qquad \max_{\tilde{B}'\tilde{\pi}\leq\tilde{f}} E\pi'(b, x^t)b - E\pi'(b, x^t)Ax^t - z^t \geq 0.$$

Also, it can be shown that, at the optimal $\tilde{\pi}$

$$(47) \qquad z^t = \min_{\{y_i|x^t\}} \sum_{i=1}^{N} f'y_i$$

where $y_i \geq 0$ satisfies $By_i = b_i - Ax^t$. Since, for any feasible y_i and π_i of the subprogram,

$$(48) \qquad \min_{\substack{y_i\geq 0 \\ By_i=b_i-Ax}} f'y_i \geq 0 \max_{B'\pi(b_i,x)\leq f} p_i\pi'(b_i, x)(b - Ax),$$

summing (48) for $i = 1, \cdots, N$ yields (46) with the inequality reversed. Hence the test for optimality can be interpreted as checking whether equality holds in (46) or, substituting the value of z^t given in (47), whether $\{\pi(b_i, x^t), \; i = 1, \cdots, N\}$ satisfies

$$(49) \qquad E\min_{y} f'y = E\pi'(b, x^t))(b - Ax^t),$$

that is, is optimal for the dual of (4), and

$$(50) \qquad E\pi'(b, x^t)A \leq c.$$

In other words, the test for optimality of the decomposition algorithm is an implementation of the sufficient condition for optimality given in Theorem 4'.

As $EC(b, x)$ is a convex function of x defined over a convex set, the problem of minimizing $EC(b, x)$ is a problem of convex programming. The following procedure for solving this problem is an application of Lemma 2 and a technique due to Kelley [5] (see also [7]).

We assume here that aside from the condition $x \geq 0$, there are enough fixed and induced constraints on x so that x lies in a bounded convex polyhedron defined by, say, $\bar{A}x = \bar{b}$. The problem is then the following.

$$(51) \qquad \begin{aligned} \bar{A}x &= \bar{b}, \\ EC(b, x) &\leq z, \\ x &\geq 0, \\ z &= \min. \end{aligned}$$

To initiate the algorithm, let x^0 be feasible. Consider the linear program

(52)
$$\bar{A}x = \bar{b},$$
$$c'x + E\bar{\pi}'(b, x^0)(b - Ax) \leq z,$$
$$x \geq 0,$$
$$z = \min.$$

Let x^1 solve this program, and now consider the program

(53)
$$\bar{A}x = \bar{b},$$
$$c'x + E\bar{\pi}'(b, x^0)(b - Ax) \leq z,$$
$$c'x + E\bar{\pi}'(b, x^1)(b - Ax) \leq z,$$
$$x \geq 0,$$
$$z = \min.$$

Let x^2 solve this program.

One sees that on the kth iteration of this procedure one solves the program

(54)
$$\bar{A}x = \bar{b},$$
$$c'x + E\bar{\pi}'(b, x^i)(b - Ax) \leq z, \qquad i = 0, \cdots, k-1$$
$$x \geq 0,$$
$$z = \min.$$

Kelley has shown that $\lim_{k \to \infty} EC(b, x^k)$ is the minimum of $EC(b, x)$ though $\lim_{k \to \infty} x^k$ does not necessarily solve the convex program.

An alternative procedure [3] rewrites (51) as

(55)
$$\bar{A}x = \bar{b},$$
$$x \geq 0,$$
$$w + EC(b, x) = 0,$$
$$w = \max$$

and uses the decomposition principle with $\bar{A}x = \bar{b}$, $x \geq 0$ as the master program and $w + EC(b, x) = 0$ as the single subprogram.

The extremal problem which is equivalent to the master program is

(56)
$$\lambda_1 + \cdots + \lambda_k = 1,$$
$$(\bar{A}x^1)\lambda_1 + \cdots + (\bar{A}x^k)\lambda_k = \bar{b},$$
$$EC(b, x^1)\lambda_1 + \cdots + EC(b, x^k)\lambda_k = \min,$$

where $x^1, \cdots, x^k$ need not be feasible, provided some convex combination of them is. Once this program is solved and prices ρ_0^k, ρ^k are generated, one must solve the subprogram

(57)
$$w + EC(b, x) = 0,$$
$$w + \rho^{k\prime} \bar{A} x + \rho_0^k = \max$$

or equivalently, one must find $x = x^{k+1}$ such that

(58)
$$\delta_k(x) = EC(b, x) - \rho^{k\prime} \bar{A} x - \rho_0^k$$

is a minimum. If for all x

(59)
$$EC(b, x) \geq \rho^{k\prime} \bar{A} x + \rho_0^k$$

then $EC(b, x^{k+1})$ is minimal. If not, another column

(60)
$$\begin{bmatrix} 1 \\ \bar{A} x^{k+1} \end{bmatrix}$$

is added to (56), $EC(b, x^{k+1}) \lambda_{k+1}$ is added to the cost form in (56), and the algorithm is iterated. In [3] it is shown that $\lim_{k \to \infty} EC(b, x^k)$ is the minimum of $EC(b, x)$.

4. Discussion

It is well known (see, for example, [2]) that replacing the random b by its expected value is of little help in solving the stochastic linear program. However, we have seen from the above discussion that the expected value of the prices, for a given x, for the program given in (4) plays a critical role in solving the stochastic linear program. In fact roughly speaking, the vector $[c' - E\bar{\pi}'(b, \bar{x}) A]'$ acts as the gradient of the function $EC(b, x)$. An interesting area for future consideration is the effect of sampling from the distribution of b, estimating $E\bar{\pi}(b, x)$ and $E\bar{\pi}'(b, x)b$ for each value x generated by the iterative procedures given above, and using these estimates as $E\bar{\pi}(b, x)$ and $E\bar{\pi}'(b, x)b$ in those procedures.

Finally, we would like to acknowledge the valuable comments and suggestions of our colleagues D.R. Fulkerson and Philip Wolfe.

REFERENCES

[1] E.M.L. BEALE, "On minimizing a convex function subject to linear inequalities," *J. Roy. Statist. Soc., Ser. B*, Vol. 17 (1955), pp. 173–184.

[2] G.B. DANTZIG, "Linear programming under uncertainty," *Management Sci.*, Vol. 1 (1955), pp. 157–206.

[3] —————, "General convex objective forms," The RAND Corporation Paper, P-1664, 1959.[d]

[4] G.B. DANTZIG and P. WOLFE, "Decomposition principle for linear programs," *Operations Res.*, Vol. 8 (1960), pp. 101–111.

[5] J.E. KELLEY, JR., "The 'cutting plane' method for solving convex programs," to appear in *J. Soc. Indust. Appl. Math.*[e]

[6] R. RADNER, "The linear team: An example of linear programming under uncertainty," *Proceedings of the Second Symposium in Linear Programming*, Washington, D.C., 1955, pp. 381–396.

[7] P. WOLFE, "Accelerating the cutting plane method for nonlinear programming," The RAND Corporation Paper, P-2010, 1960.[f]

Chapter 14

PARALLEL PROCESSORS FOR PLANNING UNDER UNCERTAINTY

George B. DANTZIG and Peter W. GLYNN
Department of Operations Research, Stanford University, Stanford, CA 94305, USA

Abstract

Our goal is to demonstrate for an important class of multistage stochastic models that three techniques—namely nested decomposition, Monte Carlo importance sampling, and parallel computing—can be effectively combined to solve this fundamental problem of large-scale linear programming.

1. Hedging against uncertainty

An unresolved problem of great importance is that of finding an "optimal" solution to a linear program whose parameters (the coefficients and constant terms) are uncertain but whose distributions are known. The problem may be viewed as one of finding an optimal allocation of scarce resources and hence is fundamental to Operations Research, Control Theory, and Economics. If it could be solved in general, it would significantly advance man's ability to plan, schedule and control complex situations.

Industry and government routinely solve *deterministic* mathematical programs for planning and scheduling purposes, some involving thousands of variables with a linear or nonlinear objective and many thousands of inequality constraints. The solutions obtained are often ignored, however, because they do not properly hedge against future contingencies. It is relatively easy to reformulate models to include *uncertainty*. Because the resulting size of the system in practical applications can be enormous, the bottleneck has been (and still is) our capability to solve them.

Over the years, since the time it was first proposed independently by Dantzig and Beale in 1955 [14, 2], there has been progress in stochastic programming but on a disappointingly limited scale. However, with advances in the past ten years in computer technology, in techniques for solving large-scale models in general, and in simulation methods (particularly advanced sampling techniques), the research of specialists in the field of stochastic programming has appreciably accelerated. Workers in the field include such names in the United States as Birge, King, Nazareth, Rockafellar, and Wets; in Canada as Dempster, Gassmann, and Ziemba; in Brazil as Pereira; in Hungary as Prékopa; in Switzerland as Frauendorfer and Kall; at IIASA,[a] Russians such as Ermoliev and Gaivoronski. Specific references to their work will be given later.

Many important optimization problems involve complex systems that repeat a matrix pattern over time with variations in coefficients due to random events and the introduction of new technologies. For example, models of dynamic activities are often formulated as linear programs: the time-dependent nature of the system implies that the constraint matrices display a nearly block-triangular (staircase) structure. Staircase linear programs occur in many large-scale applications, in particular the modeling of multi-period economic or energy-related processes. Engineering applications such as the design of an exhaust nozzle of a jet engine can also be posed in this form. Thus, staircase linear programs have a matrix structure that arises in many problem contexts and therefore efficient methods for finding their solution is of great importance.

Although the simplex method is an extremely efficient algorithm for general linear programs, the number of iterations required to solve problems with staircase structure has been observed to be inordinately high. In addition, each iteration is more expensive than average because the basis factorizations tend to be more dense. On the other hand, interior methods have been observed to be more efficient than a general purpose simplex code when applied to staircase models. Even so, as the size of the system to be solved grows because the formulator increases the number of time steps or makes his model stochastic (or both), it becomes necessary to use solution methods based on decomposition and then employ one of several techniques that have been proposed for solving stochastic programs.

We favor coupling a nested dual-decomposition approach with Monte Carlo importance sampling and the assignment of the sampling tasks to Monte Carlo importance sampling. In this paper, we outline the role that parallel processors and importance sampling can play when combined with earlier results on decomposition.

2. Approaches to solving deterministic dynamic systems

Lower block-triangular matrix structures are typical for planning problems over time because activities initiated in period t have input and output coefficients in periods $t, t + 1, \ldots,$. For example, for $T = 3$ such a matrix has the form:

(1)
$$\begin{bmatrix} A_{11} & & \\ A_{21} & A_{22} & \\ A_{31} & A_{32} & A_{33} \end{bmatrix}$$

By the introduction of in-process inventories and other devices, linear programs of lower block-triangular type are mathematically equivalent to *staircase* or *multi-stage* problems of the form

Find Min Z and vectors $X_t \geq 0$, such that

$$
\begin{aligned}
b_1 &= A_1 X_1 \\
b_2 &= -B_1 X_1 + A_2 X_2 \\
&\;\;\vdots \qquad\qquad\qquad \ddots \\
b_t &= \qquad\qquad\qquad -B_{t-1} X_{t-1} + A_t X_t \\
&\;\;\vdots \qquad\qquad\qquad\qquad\qquad\qquad \ddots \\
b_T &= \qquad\qquad\qquad\qquad\qquad\qquad -B_{T-1} X_{T-1} + A_T X_T \\
(\text{Min})\ Z &= c_1 X_1 + c_2 X_2 + \cdots + c_{t-1} X_{t-1} + c_t X_t + \cdots + c_{T-1} X_{T-1} + c_T X_T
\end{aligned}
$$

(2)

where the matrices A_t, B_t and vectors b_t, c_t are given.

The decomposition approach to specially structured linear programs was suggested for the primal by Dantzig and Wolfe [23] and for the dual by Benders [4]; the first application of a nested form of decomposition is given in Dantzig [15], pp. 466–469. In applying dual decomposition to staircase dynamic systems, the original linear program is decomposed into a set of smaller linear programs, one for each time period. Each period communicates with the adjacent periods by "sending" its optimal solution to the following period, and its optimal price vector to the preceding period, where it is used to generate necessary conditions called Benders "cuts."

Various explanations have been advanced as to why standard techniques fail to perform efficiently on staircase problems. Because the dynamics of the system are known, techniques that take into account its special structure offer promise of greatly increasing computational efficiency. Research exploiting this approach has been encouraging. Among the methods for solving such systems are those of Dantzig and Wolfe [23], Glassey [42], and Ho and Manne [48], who suggested a primal nested decomposition approach that has been applied to large-scale modeling problems in the European Common Market by Ho and Loute [47], Bisschop and Meeraus [10b], Dantzig and Perold [22], Fourer [34–36], and Nishiya [64]. For a collection of papers relating to this subject, see Dantzig, Dempster, and Kallio [18].

The *dual* form of nested decomposition for staircase systems (which is one we use in our current work) has intuitive appeal because of its resemblance to certain "greedy" heuristics used by practical planners. The chief difference is the decomposition technique converges to an optimal solution. An important early work is that of Van Slyke and Wets [76]. Our more recent research along these lines began with Birge [5] and Dantzig [16], followed by major studies by Philip Abrahamson [1], Robert Wittrock [80], and Dan Scott [72] for the nonlinear case. These studies are concerned with enhancing the process of communication in the dual form of nested decomposition. Rather than sending the next period a single solution, each communicates a *family* of optimal solutions to the following period (and similarly for the information communicated to the preceding period).

Motivated by the prospect of greatly improved efficiency offered by the results of Wittrock and Abrahamson, Robert Entriken has been continuing their investigations of dual nested decomposition methods, particularly as they relate to vector processors and parallel processors. His results form part of his Ph.D. thesis. Earlier (experimental) computer implementations were only suitable for small test problems. More sophisticated software has been under development by Entriken, using modules of (Murtagh and Saunders [60]) the MINOS nonlinear programming system. Features include sparse LU factorization of the local bases, efficient ways to update the data structures that preserve the sparsity, techniques for increasing the numerical stability, and special staircase matrix partition generators. Experimentation on a number of large staircase test problems has been encouraging (Entriken [29]).

3. Stochastic case: Mathematical structure

For a wide class of stochastic planning problems, the values of b_t, B_{t-1}, A_t, c_t for $t > 1$ of model (2), described above, are not know to the planner with certainty at time 1 but would become known to him at some later time $\tau \leq t$. The value τ itself could be a random variable, and there could be a different τ for every element of the matrices and vectors. While the values of these matrices may not be known, their probability distribution may be given. In such problems, the planner wants to make a decision X_1; let random events happen; make a decision in period $t = 2$; let random events happen; make a decision in period $t = 3$, etc. He may wish to make the choice X_1 so that the expected value $E(Z)$ is minimum. For an extensive review of research on stochastic programming, see Birge and Wets [10a]. First, we give reasons why this *very general* class of stochastic problems is likely to remain intractable in the foreseeable future, with or without the availability of parallel processors. We then describe our plan to concentrate on an important class of practical stochastic problems, which are currently not practical to solve on serial-processor mainframes but which we believe could become so on multi-processor mainframes and parallel processors using our proposed techniques.

We begin with a review of the simplest *two-stage case,* first studied in Dantzig [14] and [15], and subsequently developed by R. Wets [75,77] and many others.

$$
\begin{aligned}
b_1 &= \quad A_1 X_1 \qquad\qquad , (X_1,\ X_2) \geq 0 \\
b_2 &= -B_1 X_1 + A_2 X_2
\end{aligned}
$$

(3)

$$
(\text{Min})\ Z = \quad c_1 X_1 +\ c_2 X_2
$$

where the first stage data (b_1, A_1, c_1) are known with certainty and (b_2, c_2, B_1, A_2) can take on possibly a continuum of values $b_2(\omega), c_2(\omega), B_1(\omega), A_2(\omega)$ with probability (density) distribution $p(\omega)$ for $\omega \in \Omega$, or a discrete probability distribution $p(\omega)$ for $\omega = 1, 2, \ldots, K$. The range of $\omega \in \Omega$ may therefore be continuous or it may be discrete, finite or infinite.

For (3), if the parameter ω takes on K distinct values, the problem of minimizing expected costs under uncertainty is tractable for K small. For example, if $K = 3$, the stochastic problem is equivalent to the deterministic linear program:

Find Min Z and vectors $X_1 \geq 0$, $X_2(\omega)$ for $\omega = 1, 2, 3$, such that

(4) $b_1\ =\quad A_1 X_1$

$\hspace{2em} b_2(1) = -B_1(1)X_1 + \quad A_2(1)X_2(1)$

(4.1) $b_2(2) = -B_1(2)X_1 \hspace{4em} + \quad A_2(2)X_2(2)$

$\hspace{2em} b_2(3) = -B_1(3)X_1 \hspace{8em} + \quad A_2(3)X_2(3)$

(4.2) $Z\ =\quad c_1 X_1 + p_2(1)c_2(1)X_2(1) + p_2(2)c_2(2)X_2(2) + p_2(3)c_2(3)X_2(3)$

To simplify the discussion, we may assume (without loss of generality in the bounded case) that $c_2(\omega) \geq 0$. Typically, this problem is solved using Benders [4] decomposition. The key idea in Van Slyke and Wets [76] is to replace the second-period constraints (4.1) and their objectives by a set of inequalities expressed only in terms of X_1 and a scalar variable θ_2, which are necessary conditions for feasible and optimal solutions to (4). θ_2 represents the second-period contribution to the objective Z. These necessary conditions (5.1), called "cuts," are added sequentially ($l = 1, 2, \ldots$) to the first-period problem until they become sufficient to solve (4). Cuts come in two "flavors": feasibility cuts and optimality cuts. The Master problem for Benders decomposition has the form:

(5)   MASTER PROBLEM: *Find* Min Z, $X_1 \geq 0$, θ_2,

$$b_1 = A_1 X_1 \qquad\qquad\qquad X_1 \geq 0$$

(5.1)   CUTS

$$g_1^l \leq G_1^l X_1 + \delta_2^l \theta_2 \qquad , \qquad l = 1, \ldots, L$$

$$\text{(Min)}\ Z = c_1 X_1 + \quad \theta_2,$$

where $\delta_2^l = 0$ in the case of feasibility cuts and $\delta_2^l = 1$ for optimality cuts. Assuming B_1 is the same for all ω, on any major iteration no more than $L \leq m_2$ of the constraints (5.1) will be tight, the rest may be dropped (possibly to be regenerated at a later iteration).

The solution $X_1 = X_1^*$ obtained is then "tested" for feasibility and optimality by solving the second period with $X_1 = X_1^*$. This is called the *subproblem* or "SUB" for short. The SUB decomposes into K independent sub-subproblems.

(6)   SUBPROBLEM: For ω in Ω, *find* Min $Z_2(\omega)$, $X_2(\omega) \geq 0$,

(6.1)

$$A_2(\omega) X_2(\omega) = b_2(\omega) + B_1(X_1^*),$$

$$c_2(\omega) X_2(\omega) = Z_2(\omega)\ \text{(Min)}$$

where $\Omega = \{\omega | \omega = (1, \ldots, K)\}$. These sub-subproblems are solved $\omega = 1, \ldots, K$.

If feasible, their expected value of Min $Z_2(\omega)$ is computed to test global optimality. If the test fails, the expected values

$$(6.2) \qquad g_1^{L+1} = \sum_\omega p_2(\omega) \pi_2(\omega) b_2(\omega), \qquad G_1^{L+1} = -\sum_\omega p_2(\omega) \pi_2(\omega) B_2(\omega)$$

are used to augment the cut conditions (5.1). If infeasible, then infeasibility prices are used in an analogous way. In the research of Wittrock, several extreme cuts are generated; in that of Abrahamson, in place of $B_1(X_1^*)$ several columns $B_1(X_1)$ for $X_1 = X_1^*, X_1^{**}, \ldots$, are passed to the next period at once and convex combinations are allowed; these can greatly speed up convergence.

4. Research restricted to a relevant class of stochastic programs

The two-stage case (4) represents the simplest application of parallel computers to stochastic programming. The general multi-stage case, using the corresponding "reduction" to the equivalent deterministic linear program almost always, even for $T = 3$, becomes intractable due to the proliferation of possible outcomes. This is illustrated in diagram (7).

Each node in the tree represents a point in time were a decision can be made. One of several contingencies can then happen, which are represented by the arcs branching out of the node. Corresponding to this, in the first stage we have only one set of constrains A, the same as in (4). In the second stage, we could have K more sets of constraints, shown as B, $C\,D$ above, but in general there could be infinitely many more. If each of these in turn has K outcomes, then in the third stage we have $K \times K$ more sets of constraints, shown as $(E\,F\,G\,H\,I\,J\,L\,M\,N)$. It is now easy to see why for $K = \infty$ or ω continuous, that the proliferation of cases is exponential in the number of stages and is out of hand.

(7)

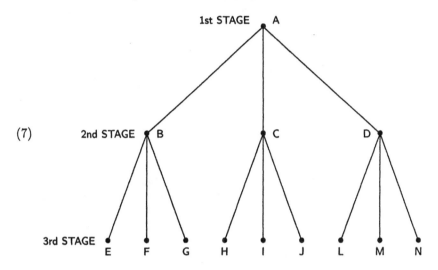

Even if the number of parallel processors available is large, it does not seem to be a practical way to solve the general class of such problems. Because these appear to be too general a class, we have been studying an important subclass of multi-stage uncertainty problems. Typical of such applications is the *facilities expansion planning problem under uncertainty.* It has a much more tractable structure.

A case in point is the fleet planning done by airlines. The problem is to plan over time the number of aircraft of various types to have in the fleet, together with the expansion of repair and passenger facilities at various airports. Within each time period (say one year), the fleet composition can be changed by buying new aircraft and selling obsolete ones, etc. Another good example is the *building of power stations and transmission lines for electric utilities.* For either example, the capacities in any period are used to meet an uncertain demand in period t as shown as random events $E^1(1), \ldots, E^t(\omega_t)$ in diagram (8).

In many such practical applications, it is required to lay out a schedule *here and now* of the amounts of future capacities (rather than *wait and see* what the future will look like and then decide). The here and now model, due to Madansky [58], assumes that installed facilities (capacities) will not be affected by any particular event that happens within a period, i.e., by a particular value of the uncertain demand or by a particular repair status of some facility. Only the *expected revenues and expected failures* (in some sense) to meet demands in the period affect the decision to invest in new facilities or to get rid of older ones.

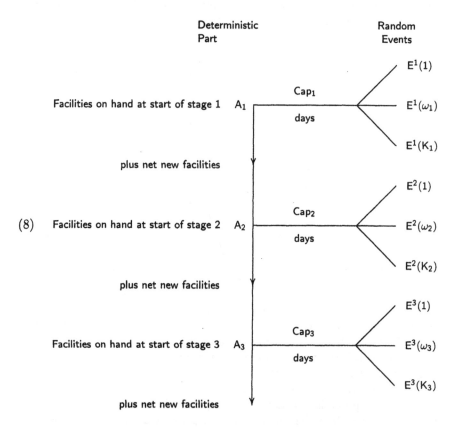

We illustrate the above concepts on an electric-power application that we use for test purposes. Corresponding to each scenario, ω is a vector listing the amount of capacities of transmission lines and generators that are not down for repair at various locations in the system. Typically, we assume that the values of these components are *independent* random variables. This basically means that we are asserting that generation/transmission failures in one part of the system happen independently of what occurs elsewhere. Equipment down for repair is repaired within a period and therefore does not affect the status of equipment available in the next period. Although this independence assumption simplifies much of the following discussion, the basic ideas and methods that we will be describing are equally pertinent to power systems in which generation/transmission failure is modeled in a dependent fashion.

For this class of problems, the mathematical structure for the facility expansion part of the model remains the same as (2), namely:

$$(9) \qquad b_t = -B_{t-1}X_{t-1} + A_tX_t, \quad \text{for } t = 1,\ldots,T \quad \text{and} \quad B_0X_0 \equiv 0,$$

where the X_t are the planned facilities (to be determined) for period t at a cost $\bar{Z} = \sum c_tX_t$, where b_t, A_t, B_t, c_t are all known with certainty. These form the "deterministic part" of (8). Relations (9) plus generated cuts form the dual Master problem.

The Benders subproblem breaks down into sub-subproblems, one for each period t and each $(\omega_t, \bar{\omega}_t)$ combination. The subproblem for period t is defined for some $X_t = X_t^*$ by first finding the vector of facilities F_t that the system owns at time t and Y_t, the amount of F_tX_t in repair and available for operations. Therefore,

$$(10) \qquad Y_t = \text{Diag}(\omega_t) \cdot F_tX_t, \quad \omega_t \in \Omega_t.$$

where $\text{Diag}(\omega_t)$ is a diagonal matrix with diagonal corresponding to ω_t, a random vector measuring the proportions of the components of F_tX_t not down for repair. The probability distribution of ω_t is assumed known. Letting $f_t(\bar{\omega}_t)$ be an uncertain demand, we then find optimal dual multipliers and $\text{Min}Z_t$ that solve (11) below for each random choice of right-hand side, i.e., for ω_t in Ω_t and $\bar{\omega}_t$ in $\bar{\Omega}_t$:

$$
\begin{aligned}
&DU_t = Y_t^*, \qquad U_t \geq 0, \ Y_t^* = \text{Diag}(\omega_t) \cdot FX_t^* \\
(11) \qquad &HU_t = f_t(\bar{\omega}_t), \quad \bar{\omega}_t \text{ in } \bar{\Omega}_t \\
&\bar{c}_tU_t = Z_t \ (\text{Min})
\end{aligned}
$$

where, given the randomly generated capacity vector $Y_t^* = \text{Diag}(\omega_t) \cdot FX_t^*$, demand $f_t(\bar{\omega}_t)$, and fixed matrices D, H, the vector of activities U_t that minimizes Z_t is found. The event $(\omega_t, \bar{\omega}_t)$ occurring with probability $p_t(\omega_t) \cdot \bar{p}_t(\bar{\omega}_t)$, is assumed known. These samples are used to estimate cuts of the form

$$(12) \qquad g_t^l \leq G_t^lX_t + \delta_{t+1}^l\theta_{t+1},$$

where g_t^l and G_t^l are generated by formulae corresponding to (6.2). The cost form

$$(13) \qquad Z = \sum_t (c_tX_t + \theta_{t+1}),$$

together with (9) and (12), form the MASTER PROBLEM.

5. Role of parallel processors

Thus, the method of solution we are working on for solving (8) uses parallel processors at each stage. These receive inputs X_t^* from the Master Problem and give back to the main program cuts (12) that are used to augment (9). If the cardinalities of $\omega_t, \bar{\omega}_t$ are small, this can be done exactly for each $\omega_t, \bar{\omega}_t$ combination. If these are large, then we propose that their expected values be estimated by *sampling* (discussion of which is the subject of the next section).

Note that the main Master Problem has the form of a deterministic stair-case system, which we solve using the dual nested decomposition approach described in detail in the Ph.D. theses of Abrahamson [1] and Wittrock [80], and as implemented by Entriken [29] for the deterministic case (and currently being modified to handle the stochastic case). The advantage of the dual decomposition approach is that the same parallel processors at each stage can be used effectively to provide information in the form of X_t^* for stage $t+1$ and pass back cuts from time stage t to stage $t-1$; the latter cuts are in addition to those given by (12) for $t-1$, which were generated by the random processes (10) and (11). The discussion which follows is for the $T = 2$ stage case.

Envision one computer at the MASTER level sequentially receiving as inputs cuts (5.1) and solving (5), (5.1) generating as an output $X_1 = X_1^*$. This process provides a *lower bound* for Min Z that keeps increasing.

Envision several parallel computers at the SUB level, each having as input the latest value of X_1^* and solving (6) in dual form for all possible choices of ω. When c_2, A_2 are the same for all ω, the dual of (6) is an LP with only the dual objective $b_2(\omega)$ changing; to provide cuts for the Master, the processors are used to determine the expected values of dual prices $\pi_2(\omega)$ and $Z_2(\omega)$ to obtain very good approximations. If it is practical, solve (6) for all ω, then via (6.2) and (5.1), solving (5) provides solutions to (6) which generate a valid cut and a correct *upper bound* estimate for Min Z. The difference between the lower bound and upper bound estimates is then used to test optimality of X_1^* for the original problem. The iterative process is terminated when the difference is deemed small enough.

6. Review of methods for obtaining approximate upper and lower bounds

An extensive review of methods of approximation, together with a list of references, can be found in Birge and Wets [10a]. See also Chapter 1 of Ermoliev and Wets, eds. [33]. For the cases where K is large, infinite, or ω is continuous, it is in general no longer possible to solve (6) for all ω. Recent research has therefore concentrated on techniques for obtaining a solution which is within an acceptable upper and lower bound of the true optimum. The essential difficulty is a numerical one of approximating the cost term: $E(Z_2) = \sum_\omega p_2(\omega)c_2(\omega)X_2^*(\omega)$, where $X_2^*(\omega)$ for $\omega = 1, 2, \ldots$, are the optimal solutions of the subproblem (6).

Typically, the random event ω is represented by points in a d-dimensional sample space, with the components of ω representing the random amounts of various facility capacities available for the operating system. It is therefore convenient to view ω as a d-dimensional vector varying over some range of values rather than ranging over an index set:

$$(14) \qquad\qquad \omega = (\omega_1, \omega_2, \ldots, \omega_d).$$

The jth sample point selected from the sample space will be denoted by $\omega = \omega^j$ and its ith component by ω_i^j. It is also convenient to let $p(\omega) = p_2(\omega)$, $c(\omega) = c_2(\omega)X_2^*$, and $\alpha = E(Z_2)$. Accordingly, we are interested in approximating the sum

$$(15) \qquad\qquad \alpha = \sum_\omega c(\omega)p(\omega).$$

If the d components of the vector ω vary continuously over their range of possible values in d-dimensional sample space, these sums take the form of a multiple integral $\int \int \int \cdots$, or if they vary over their range of discrete values, the take the form of multiple sums $\sum \sum \sum \cdots$.

One technique proposed by others for doing the approximations provides upper and lower bounds for the two-stage continuous case by discretizing the sample space Ω into cells and summing the function values at representative points within the cells over all cells. Some references are Huang et al. [49], Kall and Stoyan [52], Birge [6], Birge and Wets [9], and Frauendorfer and Kall [37]. These authors obtain lower bounds by applying Jensen's inequality. Upper bounds require an exponential number of function evaluations with respect to dimension d of the sample space[b] proposed an alternative scheme for obtaining upper bounds that requires solving "only" $O(m_2)$ linear programs. It replaces partitioning into cells by a method that seeks out an approximation using a small number of "positive" basis representations that span the space of columns associated with the second stage.

Another technique for doing the approximations which is closer in spirit to the one we follow is to sample from Ω randomly and to use sample information to guide the optimization algorithm. These include the stochastic quasi-gradient methods of Ermoliev [32] and Gaivoronski [28] They provide asymptotic convergence in the continuous case as the size of the sample $\to +\infty$. They do not provide any practical way to compute bounds.

7. Our sampling procedure and termination rules

Historical experience of numerical analysis, nevertheless, suggest that *Monte Carlo (random) sampling is the most efficient way to calculate the multiple integrals (or summations).* In other words, random sampling is the method of choice for integrating functions in higher dimensional space (Davis and Rabinowitz [24], Deák [25]).   Indeed, for higher dimensional space it may be the only way because, *generally speaking, the amount of computational effort (function evaluations) is relatively insensitive to dimension size*; this is to be contrasted with the schemes based on partitioning the space into cells and summing over values associated with representative points in the cells which grow exponentially with d, the dimension of the coordinate space within which the sample points in Ω are imbedded.

The sum we need to approximate in the two-stage case is (15). To do this, an independent random sample S of size s is drawn and the appropriately weighted mean is used for the upper bound estimate. By the law of large numbers, the distribution of such means, even for moderate size s, is approximately normally distributed about the true mean with $\sigma^2 = (1/s)$ (*population variance*). If this estimate of error turns out to be too high, the sample size is increased until the error of the estimate becomes tolerable.

When an acceptable sample size has been attained, an approximate cut based on the sample is generated. This cut would be a true cut if the variable θ is replaced by a $\theta(S)$ representing the subproblem objective when the universe when the universe of possible ω values and their relative probabilities are restricted to those of the sample S. Thus, the cut can be viewed as having all its coefficients correct except for the constant term g_t^l. We believe the error committed by the substitution of θ for $\theta(S)$, even for small size samples, is distributed about the same as standard error of the approximation of $E(Z_2)$ based on a sample of size s.

Based on an idea of Gerd Infanger, who has been collaborating with us, a distribution of lower bound estimates can be generated by randomly varying the g_t^l terms according to their approximately normal distributions and solving the master problem for each such selection. The mean of the thus generated lower bounds can then be used as the lower bound estimate. Such a mean is also approximately normally distributed, and its standard error can be estimated. Using standard statistical tests (appropriate variants of Student's t test), the upper and lower bounds can be tested to see if they differ significantly from a specified amount. If they test significantly different, another round of Benders decomposition is initiated. If not, the iterative process is terminated with X_1^* declared optimal. Should it turn out that the substitution of θ for $\theta(S)$ above can significantly bias the lower bound estimates, it will be necessary to find a way to estimate and adjust for the bias.

8. Variance reduction: Importance sampling

As the central limit theorem described above suggests, the convergence rate of Monte Carlo sampling (although dimension independent) can be quite slow, namely of the order $s^{-1/2}$ in the number of function evaluations, where s is the sample size. This puts a premium on the development and application of *variance reduction techniques* for computation of $E(Z_2)$. The idea here is to try to reduce the variance. This then reduces the error of the estimates in proportion to the reduction in standard deviation achieved. A particularly promising approach for obtaining significant variance reduction is to apply *importance sampling*.

In our test application to electric power, we expect the solution to hedge to some degree against contingencies in which significant facilities are disabled because of (random) failure. Loss of capacity due to failure reflects itself in the linear programming formulation primarily through constraints on expected unsupplied demand. Our test model has unsupplied demand constraints (called *reliability constraints*), which we treat as corresponding to a higher-order D-W or primal master so that the entire problem presented earlier is actually a sub to this primal master.[c] This master's dual variables are penalties (Lagrange Multipliers) which are used to weight the reliability constraints, which are then subtracted from the objective to form a modified objective for the primal master's sub. Because of safety margins built into the electric power systems application, significant capacity must be disabled for the unsupplied demand constraints to come into play. Clearly, this event typically has low probability because power systems are designed to be very reliable. Thus, the events that have a major impact on the solution's ability to hedge are precisely those events which will only rarely be picked up by a "naive" sampling procedure based on the original sampling frequencies. This, in turn, leads to a high variance in the estimator associated with naive sampling.

The idea behind importance sampling is to change the sampling procedure so that those events that matter more are sampled more. In the power systems context, this typically means that we sample contingencies in which multiple failures occur at a higher frequency than they occur naturally. Multiple failures lead to loss of significant system capacity, which in turn forces the solution to hedge properly to avoid such failures. Thus, importance sampling appears intuitively to be a useful tool in the power systems setting.

We now briefly describe the theory that underlies importance sampling. Let $q(\omega) > 0$ be any arbitrarily chosen (positive) probability mass function. Later, we say how $q(\omega)$ is chosen. We now re-express α in (15):

$$\text{(16)} \qquad \alpha = \sum_{\omega} \frac{c(\omega)}{q(\omega)} p(\omega) q(\omega)$$

$$\text{(17)} \qquad \alpha = E_q \frac{c(Y)}{q(Y)} p(Y).$$

where $Y = (Y_1, Y_2, \ldots, Y_d)$ is a random vector having a probability mass function $q(\cdot)$ (that is, $P(Y = y) = q(y)$), and E_q denotes expectation with respect to q. Let $Y = Y^j$ be the jth random sample point drawn with replacement. The variance of the above estimator of α based on a sample of size s is just:

$$(18) \qquad \mathrm{var}_q\left(\frac{1}{s}\sum_{j=1}^{s} c(y^j)\frac{p(y^j)}{q(y^j)}\right) = \frac{1}{s}\left(E_q\left[c(Y)^2\frac{p(Y)^2}{q(Y)^2}\right] - \alpha^2\right).$$

There is an obvious optimal choice of the mass function q, namely $q(y) = q^*(y)$, where

$$(19) \qquad q^*(y) = \frac{c(y) \cdot p(y)}{\displaystyle\sum_{\omega} c(\omega) \cdot p(\omega)}$$

We assume $c(y) \geq 0$ to simplify the discussion. In fact, the variance of $c(y))p(y)/q^*(y)$ is easily seen to be zero when c is non-negative. In other words, we obtain a perfect estimate for $E(Z_2)$ in just one observation!

Of course, this result, while true, is too good. The basic difficulty is that generating variates from $q^*(\cdot)$ is not practical because the denominator of q is the actual sum that we are trying to calculate. Nevertheless, the result provides a useful heuristic guide on how to choose a good sampling population q having two properties: (a) that $q(\omega)$ be roughly proportional to $c(\omega) \cdot p(\omega)$, and (b) that q be a kind of function with which it is easy to carry out calculations and easy to generate variates from q that are computationally inexpensive.

Suppose, for the sake of argument, that the function $c(\omega)$ is roughly *multiplicative in its arguments:*

$$(20.1) \qquad c(\omega) \approx c_1(\omega_1)\cdots c_d(\omega_d)$$

(The rougher this approximation is, the higher will be the variance of the estimator.) We then choose

$$(20.2) \quad q(\omega) = \left(\frac{c_1(\omega_1)p_1(\omega_1)}{\bar{c}_1}\right)\left(\frac{c_2(\omega_2)p_2(\omega_2)}{\bar{c}_2}\right)\cdots\left(\frac{c_d(\omega_d)p_d(\omega_d)}{\bar{c}_d}\right),$$

where $Ec_i(\omega_i) = \bar{c}_i$ is easily estimated by sampling the one-dimensional marginal distribution of ω_i. Sample points y^j for $j = 1,\ldots,s$ are selected independently choosing components Y_i^j according to their marginal distributions $c_i(y_i)p_i(y_i)/\bar{c}_i$. The arithmetic mean of the observed values $c(y^j)p(y^j)/q(y^j)$ for $j = 1, 2, \ldots, s$ is the estimate for α.

Although the multiplicative representation is easy to do calculations with, for our cost function application it turns out to be an unreasonable one, even as an approximation. A better heuristic is to assume that the cost function is better approximated by one that is roughly *additive in its arguments*, i.e.,

$$(21) \qquad c(\omega) \approx \sum_{i=1}^{d} c_i(\omega_i).$$

In this case, we can again reduce the computation of the joint mass function $q(\omega)$ to something involving the marginal distributions. The d-dimensional problem is then basically reduced to d one-dimensional problems. More specifically, if c takes on the additive form, then choose $q(\omega)$ as follows:

$$(22) \qquad q(\omega) = \frac{p(\omega)\sum_{i=1}^{d} c_i(\omega_i)}{\sum_{\omega} p(\omega)\sum_{k=1}^{d} c_k(\omega_k)}$$

$$= p(\omega)\sum_{i=1}^{d} \left(\frac{\bar{c}_i}{\sum \bar{c}_k}\right)\left(\frac{c_i(\omega_i)}{\bar{c}_i}\right).$$

where again $\bar{c}_i = Ec_i(\omega_i)$ is easily estimated by sampling the marginal distribution of ω_i. Finally, we write

$$(23) \qquad q(\omega) = \sum_{i=1}^{d} \left(\frac{\bar{c}_i}{\sum \bar{c}_k}\right)\left(\frac{p_i(\omega_i)c_i(\omega_i)}{\bar{c}_i} \cdot \prod_{k\neq i} p_k(\omega_k)\right).$$

The expression (17) for α becomes

$$(24) \qquad \alpha = \sum_{i=1}^{d} \frac{\bar{c}_i}{\sum \bar{c}_k} E_i\left(\frac{c(Y)p(Y)}{q(Y)}\right),$$

where E_i means that components y_i^j of sample points y^j is to be independently sampled according to the marginal distribution

$$q_i(\omega_i) = \frac{p_i(\omega_i)c_i(\omega_i)}{\bar{c}_i}$$

and all other components $k \neq i$ according to the marginal distribution $p_k(\omega_k)$. These expectations weighted by $\bar{c}_i/\sum \bar{c}_k$ yield α or the estimate of α when each E_i is estimated by sampling.

We now address the question of how to calculate the $c_i(\omega_i)$'s. This can be done by evaluating the cost function on a relatively small lattice of points, namely a set of lattice points along d coordinate directions:

$$(25) \qquad c_i(\omega_i) \approx c(\tau_1, \ldots, \tau_{i-1}, \omega_i, \tau_{i+1}, \ldots, \tau_d) - c(\tau_1, \ldots, \tau_i, \ldots, \tau_d),$$

where $(\tau_1, \ldots, \tau_i, \ldots, \tau_d)$ is arbitrarily chosen at some fixed set of values. This determines the c_i's up to the additive constant $c(\tau_1, \ldots, \tau_d)$. This additive constant can be disposed of by writing the cost function $c(\omega)$ as $c(\omega) = c(\tau_1, \ldots, \tau_d) + \Delta C(\omega)$. The function $\Delta C(\omega)$ is again of additive form, but has the advantage that we know a priori that we may take $\Delta c_i(\tau_i) = 0$. This eliminates the additive constant from the picture.

The degree of variance reduction obtained by applying this "additive importance sampling method" depends on the extent to which the true cost surface is fit by an additive representation. If the fit is poor, the variance estimate of the mean of the sample will be high. Experimental results based on the additive approach are described by M. Nakayama [61], who applied this method to our large-scale electric power system facilities test problem. It turned out to be a highly effective means of variance reduction. Indeed, the size of sample required to obtain the same size interval with the same degree of confidence of covering the true minimum value was 1/20,000 smaller using "importance" sampling than would have been the case using "naive" sampling.

9. Research in progress and future research

We have presented in detail the approach we are taking to solve the facilities expansion problem. Future research concerns (a) the tedious steps of software implementation, (b) testing on large "real-world" models, and (c) ways to improve the efficiency of the algorithms. Some of these tasks are:

TASK 1

The present version of the software program, developed by Entriken [29], solves a deterministic staircase linear program by nested dual decomposition. MINOS is used as a subroutine. A version of this code was tested on the parallel computers at Oak Ridge (see Entriken [30]). Dr. Gerd Infanger (from the Technical University, Austria),[d] Marvin Nakayama and Alamuru Krishna are setting up Entriken's code to run on the IBM 3090 multi-vector processor at Stanford. Without further modification, these versions will permit us to solve quite large problems that are staircase or staircase with a small amount of uncertainty. Martin Rinhart of the Computer Science Department is currently adapting the 3090 version to run on the Encore parallel processor at Stanford.

TASK 2

Introduce into both the IBM 3090 version and into the Encore version subroutines for doing the importance sampling, the generation of cuts, the estimation of the confidence intervals associated with the approximate optimal solution, the computation of standard errors, sample sizes, and stopping rules. As a preliminary step, Infanger has been running an APL version of our methodology on a Toshiba portable. The procedure has been tested on a "toy" model which he has developed, in which there is an electric power system onsisting of three generator demand nodes, three transmission links, and two time periods. We have been able to solve the deterministic equivalent of this problem with 1280 discrete values of the random variables and to compare the exact results with those obtained by importance sampling using a sample size of 20 and the additive first-order approximation (26). The empirical result so far is that very accurate results can be obtained for the toy problem with a sample size as small as 20.

TASK 3

Test the software developed above on our large-scale Electric Power System Model. This is a realistic multi-area prototype model comprising of six major utilities on the West Coast, covering an area from Canada to Mexico and some Rocky Mountain regions. We have a special version of the GAMS input generator, which inputs row and column indices in a form that can be used to conveniently partition the matrix into staircase and block-angular structures so that we can apply our decomposition code.

TASK 4

Theoretical problems: Future work will focus on ways to cut down the size of sample required to obtain a very close to optimal solution. Some of the topics of this research are: (1) For the higher-order Dantzig-Wolfe Master, can a small sample be used initially to obtain fairly good estimates of what penalty costs should be assigned to the reliability constraint? (2) Under what conditions can variances obtained from earlier Benders cycles be used to improve the standard error estimates of subsequent cycles? (3) We generate the approximate distribution of lower bounds from the Master by a supplementary Monte Carlo procedure which randomizes the RHS terms of the cuts. Can importance sampling be also used here effectively? (4) Is it possible to develop an approach that combines ours with those of Birge, Kall, King, Wets, Ziemba, and others?   (5) Generalize the notion of the additive first-order approximation (which currently guides the importance sampling) to a second-order approximation scheme based on second-order marginal distributions. (6) Explore the possibility of combining random sampling with one which always includes certain disaster scenarios, with the view of protecting the system from some of the rare but disastrous contingencies along the lines of Pereira et al. [66,66a]. (7) What is the best way to assign the different sample points to the parallel processors so that only a few iterations will be required to obtain the optimal solution of one sampled scenario, using as a warm start the optimal solution from the prior one?

References

[1]   P.G. Abrahamson, A nested decomposition approach for solving staircase linear programs, Technical Report SOL 83-4, Department of Operations Research, Stanford University, CA (1983).

[2]   E.M.L. Beale, On minimizing a convex function subject to linear inequalities, J. Roy. Statist. Soc. 17b(1955)173–184.

[3]   E.M.L. Beale, G.B. Dantzig and R.D. Watson, A first-order approach to a class of multi-time-period stochastic programming problems, Math. Progr. Study 27(1986)103–117.

[4]   J.F. Benders, Partitioning procedures for solving mixed-variab le programming problems, Numerische Mathematik 4(1962)238–252.

[5]   J.R. Birge, Solution method for stochastic dynamic linear programs, Technical Report SOL 80-29, Department of Operations Reseach, Stanford University, CA (1980).

[6]   J.R. Birge, Aggregation in stochastic linear programming, Math. Progr. 31(1984)25–41.

[7]   J.R. Birge, Decomposition and partitioning methods for multi-stage stochastic linear programs, Oper. Res. 33(1985)989–1007.

[8]   J.R. Birge and S.W. Wallace, A separable piecewise linear upper bound for stochastic linear programs, SIAM J. Control and Optimization 26(1988)725–739.

[9]   J.R. Birge and R.J.-B. Wets, Designing approximation schemes for stochastic optimization problems, in particular for stochastic programs with recourse, Math. Progr. Study 27(1986)54–102.

[10]   J.R. Birge and R.J.-B. Wets, Computing bounds for stochastic programming problems by means of a generalized moment problem, Math. Oper. Res. 12(1987)149–162.

[10a] J.R. Birge and R.J.-B. Wets, Sublinear upper bounds for stochastic programs with recourse, Math. Progr. 43(1989)131–149.

[10b] J.J. Bisschop and A. Meeraus, Towards successful modeling applications in a strategic planning environment, *Large-Scale Linear Programming*, Vol. 2, ed. G.B. Dantzig, M.A.H. Dempster and M.J. Kallio, CP-81-51, IIASA, Collaborative Proceedings Series, Laxenburg, Austria (1981) pp. 712–745.

[11]   P. Bratley, B. Fox and L. Schrage, *A Guide to Simulation* (Springer-Verlag, New York, 1983).

[12]   W.G. Cochran, *Sampling Techniques* (Wiley, New York, 1977).

[13]   K.J. Cohen and S. Thore, Programming bank portfolios under uncertainty, J. Bank Research 1(1970)42–61.

[14] G.B. Dantzig, Linear programming under uncertainty, *Mang. Sci.* 1(1955)157–206.

[15] G.B. Dantzig, *Linear Programming and Extensions* (Princeton University Press, Princeton, NJ, 1963)Chs. 22–25 and 28.

[16] G.B. Dantzig, Time-staged methods in linear programs, in: *Studies in Management Science and Systems*, Vol. 7: *Large-Scale Systems*, ed. Y.Y. Haims (North-Holland, Amsterdam, 1982) pp.19–30.

[17] G.B. Dantzig, Planning under uncertainty using parallel computing, *Ann. Oper. Res.* 14(1988)1–16.

[18] G.B. Dantzig, M.A.H. Dempster, and M.J. Kallio, eds., *Large-Scale Linear Programming*, Vols. 1, 2, IIASA Collaborative Proceedings Series, CP-81-51, IIASA, Laxenburg, Austria, 1981.

[19] G.B. Dantzig, P.W. Glynn, M. Avriel, J.C. Stone, R. Entriken and M. Nakayama, Decomposition techniques for multi-area transmission planning under uncertainty. Final report of EPRI Project RP 2940-1, prepared by Systems Optimization Laboratory, Operations Research Department, Stanford University, CA (1989).

[20] G.B. Dantzig and A. Madansky, On the solution of two-stage linear programs under uncertainty, in: *Proc. 4th Berkeley Symp. on Mathematical Statistics and Probability I*, ed. J. Neyman (1961) pp. 165–176.

[21] G.B. Dantzig, M.V.F. Pereira et al., Mathematical decompositoin techniques for power system expansion planning, EPRI EL-5299, Vols. 1–5, Electric Power Research Institute, Palo Alto, CA (1988).

[22] G.B. Dantzig and A.F. Perold, A basic factorization method for block triangular linear programs, Technical Report SOL 78-7, Department of Operations Research, Stanford University, CA (1979); *Sparse Matrix Proceedings*, ed. I.S. Duff and G.W. Stewart (SIAM, 1978) pp. 283–312.

[23] G.B. Dantzig and P. Wolfe, Decomposition principle for linear programs, *Oper. Res.* 8(1960)101–111.

[24] P.J. Davis and P. Rabinowitz, *Methods of Numerical Integration* (Academic Press, London, 1984).

[25] I. Deák, Multidimensional integration and stochastic programming in: *Numerical Techniques for Stochastic Optimization*, ed. Y. Ermoliev and R.J.-B. Wets (Springer-Verlag, Berlin, 1988) pp. 187–200.

[26] M.A.H. Dempster and E. Sole, Stochastic scheduling via stochastic control, Bernoulli 1(1987)783–788.

[27] J. Dupačová, Minimax approach to stochastic linear programming and the moment problem: Selected results, Zeitschrift für Angewandte Mathematik und Mechanik 58T(1978)466–467.

[28] J. Dupačová and R.J.-B. Wets, Asymptotic behavior of statistical estimators of optimal solutions of stochastic optimization problems, *Ann. Math. Statis.* 16(1988)1517–1549.

[29] R. Entriken, The parallel decomposition of linear programs, Ph.D. Dissertation, Department of Operations Research, Stanford University, CA (1989).

[30] R. Entriken, A parallel decomposition algorithm for staircase linear programs, Oak Ridge National Laboratory Report ORNL/TM 11011(1988).

[31] Y. Ermoliev, Stochastic quasi-gradient methods and their applications to systems optimization, Stochastics 9(1983)1–36.

[32] Y. Ermoliev, Stochastic quasi-gradient methods, in: *Numerical Techniques for Stochastic Optimization*, ed. Y. Ermoliev and R.J.-B. Wets (Springer-Verlag, Berlin, 1988) pp. 141–186.

[33] Y. Ermoliev and R.J.-B. Wets, eds., *Numerical Techniques for Stochastic Optimization* (Springer-Verlag, Berlin, 1988).

[34] R.H. Fourer, Solving staircase linear programs by the simplex method, 1: Inversion, Math. Progr. 23(1982)274–313.

[35] R.H. Fourer, Solving staircase linear programs by the simplex method, 2: Pricing, Math. Progr. 25(1983)251–292.

[36] R.H. Fourer, Staircase matrices and systems, SIAM Rev. 26(1984)1–70.

[37] K. Frauendorfer and P. Kall, A solution method for SLP recourse problems with arbitrary multivariate distributions – the independent case, Problems of Control and Information Theory 17(1988)177–205.

[38] A. Gaivoronski, Implementation of stochastic quasi-gradient methods, in: *Numerical Techniques for Stochastic Optimization*, Y. Ermoliev and R.J.-B. Wets, eds., (Springer-Verlag, Berlin, 1988) pp. 313–352.

[39] A. Gaivoronski and L. Nazareth, Combining generalized programming and sampling techniques for stochastic programs with recourse, in: *Planning Under Uncertainty for Electric Power Systems*, Proc. Workshop (in preparation), Department of Operations Research, Stanford University, CA (1989).

[40] H. Gassman and W.T. Ziemba, A tight upper bound for the expectation of a convex function of a multivariate random variable, Math. Progr. Study 27(1986)39–52.

[41] P.E. Gill, W. Murray, M.A. Saunders, J.A. Tomlin and M.H. Wright, On Newton-barrier methods for linear programming and on equivalence to Karmarkar's projective method, Technical Report SOL 85-9, Department of Operations Research, Stanford University, CA (1985).

[42] R. Glassey, Nested decomposition and multi-stage linear programs, Manag. Sci. 20(1973)282–292.

[43] P.W. Glynn and W. Whitt, Efficiency of simulation estimates (1988), submitted for publication.

[44] P.W. Glynn and D.L. Iglehart, Importance sampling for stochastic simulation (1988), submitted for publication.

[45] J.M. Hammersley and D.C. Handscomb, *Monte Carlo Methods* (Methuen, London 1964).

[46] J.K. Ho, T.C. Lee and R.P. Sundarraj, Decomposition of linear programs using parallel computation, Math. Progr. 42(1988)391–405.

[47] J.K. Loute and E. Loute, An advanced implementation of the Dantzig-Wolfe decomposition algorithm for linear programming, Discussion Paper 8014, Center for Operations Research and Econometrics (CORE), Belgium (1980).

[48] J.K. Ho and A.S. Manne, Nested decomposition for dynamic models, Math. Progr. 6(1974)121–140.

[49] C.C. Huang, W.T. Ziemba and A. Ben-Tal, Bounds on the expectation of a convex function of a random variable with applications to stochastic programming, Oper. Res. 25(1977)315–325.

[50] P.L. Jackson and D.F. Lynch, Revised Dantzig-Wolfe decomposition for staircase-structured linar programs, Technical Report 558, School of Operations Research and Industrial Engineering, Cornell University (1982), revised 1985.

[51] P. Kall, A. Ruszczyński and K. Frauendorfer, Approximation techniques in stochastic programming, in: ed. Y. Ermoliev and R.J.-B. Wets (Springer-Verlag, Berlin, 1988) pp. 33–64.

[52] P. Kall and D. Stoyan, Solving stochastic programming problems with recourse including error bounds, Mathematische Operationsforschung und Statistik, Series Optimization 13(1982)431–447.

[53] N. Karmarkar, A new polynomial-time algorithm for linear programming, Combinatorica 4(1984)373–395.

[54] A.J. King and R.J.-B. Wets, Epi-consistency of convex stochastic programs, Technical Report (Alan King, IBM Research Division, P.O. Box 218, Yorktown Heights, NY 10598, USA, 1989).

[55] S.S. Lavenberg and P.D. Welch, A perspective on the use of control variables to increase the efficiency of Monte Carlo simulation, Manag. Sci. 27(1981)322–335.

[56] F.V. Louveaux, Multistage stochastic programs with block-separable recourse, Math. Progr. Study 28(1986)48–62.

[57] F.V. Louveaux and Y. Smeers, Optimal investment for electricity generation: A stochastic model and a test problem, in: ed. Y. Ermoliev and R.J.-B. Wets *Numerical Techniques for Stochastic Optimization* (Springer-Verlag, Berlin, 1988) pp. 445–454.

[58] A. Madansky, Bounds on the expectation of a convex function of a multivariate random variable, Ann. Math. Statis. 30(1959)743–746.

[59] J. Mulvey and H. Vladimirou, Solving multistage investment problems: An application of scenario aggregation, Technical Report SOR 88-1, Princeton University, Princeton, NJ (1988).

[60] B.A. Murtagh and M.A. Saunders, MINOS User's Guide, Technical Report SOL 82-20, Department of Operations Research, Stanford University, CA (1983).

[61]   M. Nakayama, Section 6 in Dantzig, Glynn, Avriel et al. (1989).

[62]   L. Nazareth and R.J.-B. Wets, Algorithms for stochastic programs: The case of nonstochastic tenders, Math. Progr. Study 28(1986)1–28.

[63]   H. Niederreiter, Multidimensional numerical integration using pseudo random numbers, Math. Progr. Study 27(1986)17–38.

[64]   T. Nishiya, A basis factorization method for multi-stage linear programming with an application to optimal operation of an energy plant, Draft Report (1983).

[65]   J. Parida and A. Sen, A variational-like inequality for multifunctions with applications, J. Math. Analysis and Applications 124(1987)73–81.

[66]   M.F.V. Pereira and L.M.V.G. Pinto, Stochastic optimization for a multi-reservoir hydro-electric system – a decomposition approach, CEPAL (Centro del Pesquisas de Energia Electrica), Rio de Janeiro, Brazil (1983).

[66a] M.F.V. Pereira, M.V.G. Pinto, G.C. Oliveira and S.H.F. Cunha, A technique for solving LP problems with stochastic right-hand sides, CEPAL (Centro del Pesquisas de Energia Electrica), Rio de Janeiro, Brazil (1989), 13 pages.

[67]   A. Prékopa, Dynamic type stochastic programming models, in: *Studies in Applied Stochastic Programming*, ed. A. Prékopa (Hungarian Academy of Science, Budapest, 1978) pp. 179–209.

[68]   S.M. Robinson and R.J.-B. Wets, Stability in two-stage stochastic programming, SIAM J. Control and Optimization 25(1987)1409–1416.

[69]   R.T. Rockafellar and R.J.-B. Wets, Scenario and policy aggregation in optimization under uncertainty, Math. Oper. Res., to appear.

[70]   R.Y. Rubinstein and R. Marcus, Efficiency of multivariate control variates in Monte Carlo simulation, Oper. Res. 33(1985)661–677.

[71]   G. Salinetti and R.J.-B. Wets, On the convergence in distribution of measurable multifunctions (random sets), normal integrands, stochastic processes and stochastic infima, Math. Oper. Res. (1986)385–419.

[72]   D.M. Scott, A dynamic programming approach to time-staged convex programs, Technical Report SOL 85-3, Department of Operations Research, Stanford University, CA (1985).

[73]   B. Strazicky, Computational experience with an algorithm for discrete recourse problems, in: *Stochastic Programming*, ed. M. Dempster (Academic Press, London, 1980) pp. 263–274.

[74]   M.J. Todd, Probabilistic models for linear programming, Technical Report No. 836, School of Operations Research and Industrial Engineering, Cornell University, Ithaca, NY (1989).

[75]   R. Van Slyke and R.J.-B. Wets, Programming under uncertainty and stochastic optimal control, SIAM J. on Control and Optimization 4(1966)179–193.

[76] R. Van Slyke and R.J.-B. Wets, L-shaped linear programs with application to optimal control and stochastic programming, SIAM J. on Appl. Math. 17(1969)638–663.

[77] R.J.-B. Wets, Programming under uncertainty: The equivalent convex program, SIAM J. on Appl. Math. 14(1966)89–105.

[78] R.J.-B. Wets, On parallel processor design for solving stochastic programs, in: *Proc. 6th Mathematical Programming Symposium* (Japanese Mathematical Programming Society, Tokyo, 1985) pp. 13–36.

[79] R.J.-B. Wets, Large-scale linear programming techniques, in: ed. Y. Ermoliev and R.J.-B. Wets, *Numerical Techniques for Stochastic Optimization* (Springer-Verlag, Berlin, 1988) pp. 65–94.

[80] R.J. Wittrock, Advances in a nested decomposition algorithm for solving staircase linear programs, Technical Report SOL 83-2, Department of Operations Research, Stanford University, CA (1983).

Chapter 15

Multi-stage stochastic linear programs for portfolio optimization[*]

George B. Dantzig and Gerd Infanger

Department of Operations Research, Stanford University, Stanford, CA 94305-4022, USA

The paper demonstrates how multi-period portfolio optimization problems can be efficiently solved as multi-stage linear programs. A scheme based on a blending of classical Benders decomposition techniques and a special technique, called importance sampling, is used to solve this general class of multi-stochastic linear programs. We discuss the case where stochastic parameters are dependent within a period as well as between periods. Initial computational results are presented.

1. Introduction

Methods of Operations Research, especially Mathematical Programming methods, are receiving broader acceptance in the financial industry. The increasing complexities and inherent uncertainties in financial markets have led to the need for mathematical models supporting the decision making process. This paper addresses the portfolio selection problem. Since Markowitz [23], several models have been developed that allow one to determine portfolios with the highest expected returns for a given level of risk

---

*Research and reproduction of this report were partially supported by the Office of Naval Research Contract N00014-89-J-1659; the National Science Foundation Grants ECS-8906260, DMS-8913089, the Electric Power Research Institute Contract RP-8010-09, CSA-4O05335, and the Austrian Science Foundation, "Fonds zur Förderung der wissenschaftlichen Forschung," Grant J0323-Phy. Any opinions, findings, conclusions or recommendations expressed in this publication are those of the authors and do NOT necessarily reflect the views of the above sponsors. The comments of anonymous referees are gratefully acknowledged.

[22, 31, 34]. His model (and certain closely related ones) require the solution of a quadratic program. Other approaches model the stochastic nature of the problem directly as a stochastic program. For example, Mulvey [25] and Mulvey and Vladimirou [26, 27] formulate asset allocation problems as a stochastic network problem.

The use of stochastic programming techniques has been hampered until recently by the sheer size of practical problems when they are restated as deterministic linear problems. To solve them it was necessary that the number of scenarios representing uncertainties be kept small. Most models developed so far have been single-stage or single-period models, that is to say to the case where the decision making process and the future events (foresight) are restricted to a single time period. Only few attempts have been made to solve practical multi-stage decision making models whose future events are spread over several periods.

Multi-stage planning problems can often be formulated as linear programs with a dynamic matrix structure which, in the deterministic case, appear in a staircase pattern of blocks with non-zero submatrices. These blocks correspond to and are different for different time periods. In the stochastic case, the blocks of coefficients and right-hand sides in different time periods are functions of several parameters whose values vary stochastically with dependent and independent distributions which we assume to be known. The resulting problem is a multi-stage stochastic linear program. Even for problems with a small number of stochastic parameters per stage the size of multi-stage problems when expressed in equivalent deterministic form can get so large as to appear intractable. The simplest case and most studied is that with two stages. Stochastic linear programs were first introduced by Dantzig [4] and Beale [1]. Since then they have been studied by many authors, some recent references are Birge [3], Ermoliev [9], Frauendorfer [11], Higle and Sen [15], Kall [21], Pereira et al. [29], Rockafellar and Wets [32], Ruszczynski [33], and Wets [36]. See Ermoliev and Wets [10] for a survey of different ways proposed to solve the stochastic programs.

A new approach based on Benders decomposition and importance sampling was introduced by Dantzig and Glynn [5] and developed jointly by them and Infanger [18]. Our approach turned out to be very powerful. We demonstrated its power by solving several practical large-scale stochastic linear programs with numerous stochastic parameters. Infanger [19] and Dantzig and Infanger [6] report on computational results of large-scale problems with up to 52 stochastic parameters, where the deterministic equivalent problem—if attempted to express it explicitly—would have several billions of constraints.[a] These problems were two-stage problems or belonged to a restricted class of multi-stage problems which could be re-expressed in the two-stage framework.

2. The multi-period asset allocation problem

In this paper we formulate a class of multi-period financial asset allocation problems [26] and show how they can be solved by adaptations of multi-stage stochastic linear programming methodology and software.

At the initial time period 1 a certain amount of wealth is available to a decision maker in assets $i = 1, \ldots, n$ and in cash which we index as asset $n+1$. We denote x_i^0, $i = 1, \ldots, n+1$, to be the dollar value of the initially available assets. The decision maker has to decide each period how to arrange his portfolio to achieve [the] best return on his initial investment over time. We consider the problem in discrete time and define time steps $t = 1, \ldots, T$, e.g. by months, with T being the end of the planning horizon.

At each time period t the investor can either hold on to asset i, buy more, or sell off part (or all) of asset i. We denote [by] y_i^t the amount sold of asset i in period t and by x_i^t the amount of asset i held on to. Selling means decreasing the value x_i^t of asset i and increasing the value of cash, x_{n+1}^t. Also, the investor has the choice of using his resulting cash to buy certain amounts of assets i. The amount bought in period t is denoted by z_i^t.

Buying and selling causes transaction costs which we assume to be proportional to the amount of dollar value of asset traded. We denote by $100\nu_i$ the transaction costs (expressed as a percentage) associated with buying one unit of i and with $100\mu_i$ the transaction costs (expressed as a percentage) associated with selling off one unit of asset i. Buying one unit of asset i requires $1 + \nu_i$ units of cash, and selling one unit of asset i results in $1 - \mu_i$ units of cash.

Through buying and selling the investor can restructure his portfolio in each time period t. Once this t-th stage decision is made, the holdings x_i^t, $i = 1, \ldots, n+1$, can be calculated. The shares in the portfolio are then kept constant till the next time period. The value of x_i^t is affected by the returns on the market. For example, a portfolio x_i^t at time t changes its value to $R_i^t x_i^t$, where R_i^t denotes the return factors from period t to period $t+1$.

At time t, when the decision on rearranging the portfolio has to be made, returns R_i^t, for $i = 1, \ldots, n$, are not known to the decision maker with certainty. Only the return on cash, R_{n+1}^t, is assumed known. However, we assume we know the probability distributions of R_i^t. The problem is of the "wait-and-see" type. While the decision at t has to be made on the basis of distributions of future returns R_i^t, for $i = 1, \ldots, n$, $t = 1, \ldots, T$, the values of prior returns R_i^τ, for $i = 1, \ldots, n$, $\tau = 1, \ldots, t-1$, have already been observed. We denote by $R^t = R_i^t$, for $i = 1, \ldots, n$, the n-dimensional random vector with outcomes $r^t(\omega_t)$, $\omega_t \in \Omega_t$, by p^{ω_t} the corresponding probability and by Ω_t the set of all possible outcomes in t.

The random returns R_i^t of period t are mutually dependent and dependent on the random parameters of the previous period.

After the last period T no decision is made. Only the value of the portfolio is determined by adding all values of assets including the last period returns. We call this value v^T. The goal of the decision maker, however, is to maximize $Eu(v^T)$, the expected utility of the value of the portfolio after period T. The utility function $u(v^T)$ describes the way the investor views risk. If $u(v^T)$ is linear, it describes risk neutrality; if $u(v^T)$ is [nonlinear and] concave, it models risk averseness. Nonlinear utility functions require nonlinear programming techniques for the solution of the problem. Our methodology is not restricted to linear problems. However, for the sake of ease of computational speed we approximate the nonlinear function by a piecewise linear function with a sufficiently large number of linear segments.

In the model presented here we do not consider shortselling of assets, although this feature could be incorporated easily. Neither do we consider borrowing of cash, which also could be incorporated easily. The holdings of assets, as well as the amounts of assets sold or bought have to be positive. In general, there are also lower ($\underline{x}$) and upper ($\bar{x}$) bounds on holdings as well as on amounts of assets to be sold ($\underline{y},\bar{y}$) or to be bought ($\underline{z},\bar{z}$) which are given by the investor and/or by the market. E.g. a certain asset may only be available up to a certain amount or an investor wants to be a certain asset with at least a certain amount of dollar value in the portfolio. Therefore, in general we formulate $\underline{x}_i^t \le x_i^t \le \bar{x}_i^t, \underline{y}_i^t \le y_i^t \le \bar{y}_i^t, \underline{z}_i^t \le z_i^t \le \bar{z}_i^t$, where $\underline{x}_i^t \ge 0, \underline{y}_i^t \ge 0, \underline{z}_i^t \ge 0, x_i^0$ given for $i = 1,\ldots,n+1, t = 1,\ldots,T$.

We can now state the model:

$$t = 1,\ldots,T, \ i = 1,\ldots,n+1, \ r_i^0 x_i^0 \text{ given:}$$

$$-r_i^{t-1} x_i^{t-1} + \quad x_i^t + \qquad\qquad y_i^t - \qquad\qquad z_i^t = 0, \quad i = 1,\ldots n,$$

$$-r_{n+1}^{t-1} x_{n+1}^{t-1} + x_{n+1}^t - \sum_{i=1}^{n}(1-\mu_i)y_i^t + \sum_{i=1}^{n}(1+\nu_i)z_i^t = 0,$$

$$- \sum_{i=1}^{n+1} r_i^T x_i^T v^T = 0,$$

$$\max Eu(v^T)$$

$$\underline{x}_i^t \le x_i^t \le \bar{x}_i^t, \quad \underline{y}_i^t \le y_i^t \le \bar{y}_i^t, \quad \underline{z}_i^t \le z_i^t \le \bar{z}_i^t, \quad i = 1,\ldots,n, \quad t = 1,\ldots,T.$$

We describe correlation between asset returns using a factor model. Using factors is common in the financial industry (e.g. Perold [31]), hence historical data of various factors are commercially available. The idea of the factor model is to relate the vector of asset returns $R^t = (R_1, \ldots, R_n)'$ to factors $V^t = (V_1, \ldots, V_h)'$. While the number of assets, n, is large, e.g. a model should be able to handle about 500 to 3000 assets, the number of factors, h, is comparatively small. Factor models used in the financial industry typically involve no more than 20 different time series called factors. The factor matrix F ($n \times h$) relates R^t to V^t:

$$R^t = FV^t.$$

The coefficients of the factor matrix are estimated using regression analyses on historical data. By linear transformations of historical factors the transformed factors can always be determined in such a way that the factors V^t are orthogonal. These factors can then be interpreted as *independent* random parameters assumed normally distributed or log normally distributed. Using the factor model, stochastically dependent returns can be generated in the computer by using these stochastically independent factors. We denote [a value of] the random factor V_i^t by v_i^t, with corresponding probability $p(v_i^t)$, where $p(v_i^t) = \text{prob}(V_i^t = v_i^t)$.

We may also consider inter-period dependency. For example, we may wish to have a higher probability of having a high rate of return in period t if it was high in period $t - 1$ than if it was low in period $t - 1$. We can model this inter-period dependency as a Markovian type process applied directly on the factors:

$$v_i^t = v_i^{t-1} + \eta_i^t, \quad i = 1, \ldots, h.$$

The value of factor i in period t is the sum of the value of factor i in the previous period $t - 1$ plus some independent random variation of the factor in [period] t, denoted by η_i^t. The Markovian type model can be estimated based on historical data. Instead of having an additive effect as above, we may prefer to have a multiplicative effect by applying the Markovian process directly to the logs of the factors. We have not explored this alternative.

Most investors are risk averse. In this case $u(v^T)$ is a concave utility function. While we approximate the concave utility function with sufficient accuracy by a piece-wise linear one, it is also important and of interest to actually solve the nonlinear problem. This is the subject of future research. The methodology, which we present below, can be easily extended to nonlinear objective functions.

A linear utility function maximizes the expected returns. Using a linear utility function and simplifying the model by neglecting transaction costs and bounds on the holdings and turnovers, as well as the inter-period dependency of the return factors, leads to a model formulation in which the solution of the corresponding expected value problem (obtained by replacing the stochastic return factors by their expected values) is also optimal to the stochastic problem. In fact, in this case there is no carry-over of states from one period to the next, so that the myopic strategy of looking ahead one period is also optimal for the long-run multi-period model. See, for example, Hakansson [13,14] in this respect.

Multi-stage stochastic programs have a variety of possible applications in the area of finance. Besides the selection of equity portfolios, our approach can also be adapted to the selection of fixed income portfolios and to the pricing of options. In the latter applications, interest rates are one of the most important factors used to model returns or prices. References [20] and [24] point to an important effort involving the development of interest rate models. See Zenios [37] for designing large portfolios of mortgage-backed securities using two-stage stochastic programming models.

3. Multi-stage stochastic linear programs

As one can now see easily, the multi-period asset model proposed fits exactly into the framework of a general class of multi-stage stochastic linear programs with recourse. The factor model for generating dependent returns and the Markovian process for inter-period dependency define a special class of dependencies between stochastic parameters which we will exploit to solve the problem. Before doing so, we state the general problem and the methodology we have developed to solve it.

The multi-stage stochastic linear program can be formulated as follows:

$$\min z = c_1 x_1 + E(c_2 x_2^{\omega_2} + \cdots + E(c_{T-1} x_{T-1}^{\omega_{T-1},\ldots,\omega_2} + E(c_T x_T^{\omega_T,\ldots,\omega_2}))\cdots)$$

subject to

$$A_1 x_1 \qquad\qquad\qquad\qquad\qquad\qquad = b_1,$$

$$-B_1^{\omega_2} x_1 + \qquad\qquad\qquad\qquad A_2 x_2^{\omega_2} = b_2^{\omega_2},$$

$$\ddots \qquad\qquad\qquad \vdots$$

$$-B_{T-1}^{\omega_T} x_{T-1}^{\omega_T,\ldots,\omega_2} + \qquad A_T x_T^{\omega_T,\ldots,\omega_2} = b_T^{\omega_T},$$

$$x_1,\ x_2^{\omega_2},\ldots,\ x_{T-1}^{\omega_{T-1},\ldots,\omega_2},\ x_T^{\omega_T,\ldots,\omega_2} \geq 0$$

$$\omega_t \in \Omega_t,\ t = 2,\ldots,T.$$

The problem is the stochastic extension of a deterministic dynamic linear program. While the first stage parameters c_1, A_1, b_1 are known to the planner with certainty, the parameters of stages $2,\ldots,T$ are assumed known only by their distribution. We assume uncertainty in the coefficients of the transition matrices $B_t^{\omega_t}$, $t = 2,\ldots,T$, and the right-hand sides $b_t^{\omega_t}$, $t = 2,\ldots,T$, and assume the coefficients of the technology matrices A_t, $t = 2,\ldots,T$, and the objective function coefficients c_t, $t = 2,\ldots,T$, to be known with certainty. The goal of the planner is to minimize the expected value of present and future costs. Note that this formulation refers to a general class of multi-stage stochastic linear programming models and the multi-stage portfolio optimization problem is a sub-species of that class. We will state the correspondence between the parameters of the multi-stage stochastic linear program and the parameters of the portfolio optimization problem below. First we state the nature of the decision-making process in multi-stage stochastic programs.

The underlying "wait-and-see" decision making process is as follows: The decision maker makes a first stage decision $\hat{x}_1$ before observing any outcome of random parameters. Then he waits until an outcome of the second-stage random parameters gets realized. The second-stage decision then is made based on the knowledge of the realization ω_2 but without observing any outcome of random parameters of stages $2, \ldots, T$, and so forth. As the state (the actual outcome) is carried forward to the following period, the decision tree grows exponentially with the number of stages. We consider discrete distributions of random parameters with finite number of outcomes, e.g. $\omega_t \in \Omega_t$, $\omega_t = \{1, \ldots, K_t\}$, $t = 1, \ldots, T$. With K_t being the number of scenarios in period t, the total number of scenarios for all T stages is $\prod_{t=1}^{T} K_t$. The number K_t is expected to be large, as it is computed by the crossing of the sets of possible outcomes of the different random parameters within a period. E.g. the dimension of the random vector in period t is h_t and Ω_t^j contains k_t^j elements;[b] then $K_t = \prod_{j=1}^{h_t} k_t^j$. For example, in the asset allocation problem, consider the case of 20 factors, modeled as random parameters with 5 outcomes each: the number of scenarios per period is $5^{20} \approx 10^{14}$. If there are 3 periods, then the total number of scenarios grows to 10^{28}. The dimensions of an equivalent linear program of an asset allocation problem with a universe of about 500 assets is approximately 5×10^{30} rows and 1.5×10^{31} columns. It is of course impossible to write down this linear program explicitly.

It is clear that the multi-period asset allocation problem defined above is a special case of the multi-stage stochastic linear program. The correspondence is as follows: the vector x_t now denotes the vector of all decision variables (holdings, amount to be bought and to be sold) in period t. Uncertainty occurs only in the transition matrices B_{t-1} which contain in their diagonal the return factors R_i^{t-1}. Thus the product $B_{t-1}^{\omega_t} x_{t-1}$ gives the vector of holdings of each asset and of cash available for disposition in period t. The technology matrix A_t contains the coefficients according to the formulation of the transactions made in period t. The model formulated above follows a network structure. In period t, for each asset, the holding from the previous period, multiplied by the return factor, plus the amount bought, minus the amount sold, minus the holding at the end of the transaction of period t adds up to zero. Therefore A_t contains entries of "1" in the rows corresponding to the different assets for each decision variable. The last row of A_t accounts for cash and contains the loss factors corresponding to the transaction costs of buying or selling each asset. The right-hand sides $b_2, \ldots, b_T$ are zero, as well as the objective function coefficients $c_2, \ldots, c_{T-1}$. The right-hand side b_1 denotes the initial holdings of each asset and of cash, and the objective function coefficients c_T represent the piecewise linear utility of the wealth accumulated up to period T. We now describe the techniques we have developed to solve the multi-stage program.

4. Benders decomposition

A description of how Benders' [2] Decomposition Algorithm can be applied to solve stochastic linear programs can be found in Van Slyke and Wets [35] and Birge [3]. Using Benders decomposition we decompose the problem into subproblems of different stages t. In the most general case, where there is a dependency of stochastic parameters between stages, the number of subproblems is equal to the number of scenarios in each stage t. To distinguish one subproblem from another, each is indexed with $\omega_t, \ldots, \omega_2$, where ω_t is the random event in stage t and $\omega_{t-1}, \ldots, \omega_2$ is the path of previous events which gave rise to the particular subproblems in stage t.

For expository purposes, we assume initially the random events that happen in one stage are independent of those that happen in the next stage. For example, when the probability of having a high rate of return in period t is the same for all values of rate of return in period $t-1$. In the independent case, scenarios $\omega_{t+1} \in \Omega_{t+1}$ in period $t+1$ are identical for each scenario $\omega_t \in \Omega_t$ in period t. The history is only carried forward through optimal decisions $\hat{x}^{\omega_{t-1}, \ldots, \omega_2}$ from previous periods. In the special class of Markovian dependency which we described earlier, $B_t^{\omega_{t+1}\omega_t} = B_{t-1}^{\omega_t} + \epsilon_t^{\omega_{t+1}}$, where ϵ_t represents a matrix of random parameters independent of those in period $t-1$.

The idea of using Benders decomposition is to express in each stage, t, $t = 1, \ldots, T-1$, and scenario ω_t the expected future costs (the impact of stages $t+1, \ldots, T$) by a scalar θ_t and "cuts," necessary conditions for feasibility and optimality which are expressed only in terms of the stage t decision variables x_t and θ_t. Cuts are initially absent and then sequentially added to the stage t problems. Each scenario subproblem ω_t in stage t collects the information about expected future costs by means of the cuts. Clearly, in the case of the asset allocation problem, each stage subproblem of the decomposed multi-stage stochastic linear program represents the asset allocation decision to be made in the corresponding period, where the right-hand side $B_{t-1}^{\omega_t}\hat{x}_{t-1}$ represents the holdings of each asset and cash initially available in period t. The cuts represent an outer linearization of the future expected utility of wealth, expressed in terms of the decisions of holding, selling or buying assets in period t.

The relation between the stages and scenarios in the decomposed multi-stage problem is summarized as follows:

Stage 1 problem:

$$\min z_1 = \quad c_1 x_1 + \theta_1$$

subject to

$$\pi_1: \qquad A_1 x_1 \quad = b_1$$

$$\rho_1^{l_1}: \qquad -G_1^{l_1} x_1 + \theta_1 \geq g_1^{l_1}, \quad l_1 = 1, \ldots, L_1$$

$$x_1, \theta_1 \geq 0$$

Stage t, $t = 2, \ldots, T - 1$, problem:

$$\min z_t^{\omega_t} = \quad c_t x_t^{\omega_t} + \theta_t^{\omega_t}$$

subject to

$$\pi_t^{\omega_t}: \qquad A_t x_t^{\omega_t} \quad = b_t^{\omega_t} + B_{t-1}^{\omega_t} \hat{x}_{t-1}$$

$$\rho_t^{l_t, \omega_t}: \qquad -G_t^{l_t} x_t^{\omega_t} + \theta_t^{\omega_t} \geq g_t^{l_t}, \quad l_t = 1, \ldots, L_t$$

$$x_t^{\omega_t}, \theta_t^{\omega_t} \geq 0$$

Stage T problem:

$$\min z_T^{\omega_T} = c_T x_T^{\omega_T}$$

subject to

$$\pi_T^{\omega_T}: \qquad A_T x_T^{\omega_T} = b T^{\omega_T} + B_{T-1}^{\omega_T} \hat{x}_{T-1},$$

$$x_T^{\omega_T} \geq 0$$

$\min z_1$ represents the optimal objective function value in the first stage. x_1, θ_1 represent the optimal solution, the vector π_1 denotes the optimal dual prices associated to the original stage 1 constraints, and the scalars $\rho_1^{l_1}$ are the optimal dual prices associated to the cuts, which have been added so far in iterations $l_1, \ldots, L_1$. The optimal objective function values $\min z_t^{\omega_t} = \min z_t^{\omega_t}(\hat{x}_{t-1})$, and the optimal dual prices $\pi_t^{\omega_t} = \pi_t^{\omega_t}(\hat{x}_{t-1})$ associated to the original stage constraints in stages t, $t = 2, \ldots, T$, and the optimal dual prices $\rho_t^{l_t, \omega_t} = \rho_t^{l_t, \omega_t}(\hat{x}_{t-1})$ associated to the cuts in stages t, $t = 2, \ldots, T - 1$, are all dependent upon $\hat{x}_{t-1}$, the optimal solution passed as input from the previous stages $t - 1$. According to the scenario development in the previous stages, an optimal solution $\hat{x}_{t-1}$ is actually indexed by the scenario outcomes of all previous stages and is therefore denoted as $\hat{x}_{t-1}^{\omega_{t-1}, \ldots, \omega_2}$. For the sake of exposition, we suppress the scenario history and present the optimal solution of the subproblems in stage t, scenario ω_t as a function of the input $\hat{x}_{t-1}$.

We compute the expected future costs as $z_{t+1} = E_{\omega_{t+1}} z_{t+1}^{\omega_{t+1}}$, the right-hand sides of the cuts as $g_t^{l_t} = E_{\omega_{t+1}} (\pi_{t+1}^{\omega_{t+1}} b_{t+1}^{\omega_{t+1}} + \sum_{l_{t+1}=1}^{L_{t+1}} \rho_{t+1}^{l_{t+1} \omega_{t+1}} g_{t+1}^{l_{t+1}})$ and the coefficients of the cuts as $G_t^{l_t} = E_{\omega_{t+1}} \pi_{t+1}^{\omega_{t+1}} B_t^{\omega_{t+1}}$, where $\rho_T^{\omega T} = 0$, $G_T^{l_T} = 0$, and $g_T^{l_T} = 0$.

A subproblem in stage t and in scenario ω_t interacts with its predecessors and descendants by passing forward optimal solutions and backwards cuts. Benders decomposition splits the multi-stage problem into a series of two-stage relations which are overall connected by a nesting scheme. We call the stage t, scenario ω_t problem the current master problem. It receives from its ancestor in period $t-1$ a solution $\hat{x}_{t-1}$. The current scenario is determined by the outcome ω_t of the random parameters in stage t which are reflected in the right-hand side $b_t^{\omega_t} + B_{t-1}^{\omega_t} \hat{x}_{t-1}$. As stated above, $\hat{x}_{t-1}$ has a history. The history has to be considered when nesting several stages. Given and subject to $\hat{x}_{t-1}$ we solve the stage t problem in scenario ω_t and pass the obtained solution $\hat{x}_t^{\omega_t}$ to the descendant problems. By solving all problems $\omega_{t+1} \in \Omega_{t+1}$ (referred to as the universe case) we compute the expected value of the descendant stage costs $z_{t+1} = E_{\omega_{t+1}} z_{t+1}^{\omega_{t+1}}$ and the coefficients $G_t = E_{\omega_{t+1}} \pi_{t+1}^{\omega_{t+1}} B_t^{\omega_{t+1}}$ and the right-hand side $g_t = E_{\omega_{t+1}} (\pi_{t+1}^{\omega_{t+1}} b_{t+1}^{\omega_{t+1}} + \sum_{l_{t+1}=1}^{L_{t+1}} \rho_{t+1}^{l_{t+1} \omega_{t+1}} g_{t+1}^{l_{t+1}})$ of a cut. The cut is added to the current master problem (stage t, scenario ω_t problem) and by solving the problem again, another trial solution is obtained.

The optimal solution of the current master problem in stage t, scenario ω_t, gives a lower bound, and the expected cost of the trial solution gives an upper bound of the expected costs of all scenarios descendant from the stage t, scenario ω_t. If [the] lower bound and [the] upper bound are sufficiently close, the current master problem is said to represent the future expected cost and contains (by means of a sufficient number of cuts) all the information needed from future scenarios. In this case we say *the current master is balanced* with its descendant problems.

Note that the current master problem represents the expected future costs only subject to the trial solution $\hat{x}_{t-1}$ which was passed from its ancestor and subject to the scenario ω_t. Note also that we have implicitly assumed that the descendant problems in stage $t + 1$ are also balanced with their descendant problems in stage $t + 2$ by means of having collected a sufficient number of cuts to represent the expected costs of descendant scenarios from $t + 2$ on, and so forth. However, note that the solution of the current stage t scenario ω_t problem gives a lower bound on the expected costs of all scenarios descendant from the stage t scenario ω_t problem regardless of having collected a sufficient number of cuts. We shall exploit this fact.

Two properties of cuts are crucial for the solution procedure:

(1) *In the case of independence of stochastic parameters between stages:*

The cuts derived from any trial solutions $\hat{x}_t^{\omega_t}$ are valid cuts for all subproblems $\omega_t \in \Omega_t$. E.g. the cut: $\theta_t \geq E_{\omega_{t+1}} \pi_{t+1}^{\omega_{t+1}} B_t^{\omega_{t+1}} x_t + E_{\omega_{t+1}} (\pi_{t+1}^{\omega_{t+1}} b_{t+1}^{\omega_{t+1}} + \sum_{l_{t+1}=1}^{L_{t+1}} \rho_{t+1}^{l_{t+1}\omega_{t+1}} g_{t+1}^{l_{t+1}})$ is a constraint whose coefficients do not depend on x_t, hence is valid for all values of x_t. To see this, note $\pi_{t+1}^{\omega_{t+1}} = \pi_{t+1}^{\omega_{t+1}}(\hat{x}_t)$ and $\rho_{t+1}^{\omega_{t+1}} = \rho_{t+1}^{\omega_{t+1}}(\hat{x}_t)$ are optimal dual prices that do depend on $\hat{x}_t$ for optimality, but they remain *dual feasible* independent of the values of the right-hand side as a function of $\hat{x}_t$. The validity of the cuts depends only on the dual feasibility of the $\pi_{t+1}^{\omega_{t+1}}$ and $\rho_{t+1}^{\omega_{t+1}}$. It represents an outer linearization of the future expected cost function $z_{t+1}(x_t)$, evaluated at $\hat{x}_t$. Different scenarios ω_t in stage t are distinguished by different right-hand sides of the original stage t constraints, e.g. $A_t x_t = b_{t-1}^{\omega_t} + B_{t-1}^{\omega_t} \hat{x}_{t-1}$. The set of cuts $-G_t^{l_t} x_t + \theta_t \geq g_t^{l_t}$, $l_t = 1, \ldots, L_t$, represents an outer linearization of the expected future costs independent of scenarios $\omega_t \in \Omega_t$. The outer linearization defined by the set of cuts equals the expected future cost function, if $E z_{t+1}^{\omega_{t+1}}(\hat{x}_t) = \hat{\theta}_t$, where $\hat{\theta}_t$ is the value of θ_t corresponding to the solution $\hat{x}_t$ of any stage t problem. If $E z_{t+1}^{\omega_{t+1}}(\hat{x}_t^{\omega_t}) = \hat{\theta}_t^{\omega_t}$, $\omega_t \in \Omega_t$, then a sufficient number of necessary cuts have been generated to represent the expected future costs for all solutions $\hat{x}_t^{\omega_t}$ of scenarios $\omega_t \in \Omega_t$ in stage t, and we say stage t is balanced with stage $t+1$.

(2) In the case of dependency of stochastic parameters between stages:
Cuts now depend on scenario ω_t in period t. Sharing of cuts between different scenario subproblems $\omega_t \in \Omega_t$ is no longer directly possible. However, for additive dependency (e.g. Markovian type dependency) *up to three stages*, cuts can be easily adjusted to different scenarios. For example in the case of the Markovian type dependency which we introduced in the multiperiod asset allocation problem we may model $B_t^{\omega_{t+1},\omega_t} = B_{t-1}^{\omega_t} + \epsilon_t^{\omega_{t+1}}$, for $t = 1, 2$, and $B_t^{\omega_{t+1}} = \epsilon_t^{\omega_{t+1}}$, for $t = 3, \ldots, T-1$ (additive dependency up to stage 3 and independence thereafter). Here ϵ_t represents a matrix whose elements are functions of random parameters which are independent of the period $t-1$ random parameters. (The elements of ϵ_t are the inter-stage independent part of the random returns and are generated by the product $F\eta_t$.) For example, in the case of the additive dependency up to three stages and independence of all further stages, a cut in stage 2 scenario ω_2 has the form: $\theta_2 \geq [(E_{\omega_3} \pi_3^{\omega_3}) B_2^{\omega_2} + E_{\omega_3} \pi_3^{\omega_3} \epsilon_2^{\omega_3}] x_2 + E_{\omega_3} \pi_3^{\omega_3} b_2^{\omega_3}$. It can be easily seen that the coefficients of the cut consist of a part independent of scenarios ω_2 and a dependent part. The cut can be adjusted to different scenarios $\omega_2 \in \Omega_2$ by adding the scenario dependent part $(E_{\omega_3} \pi_3^{\omega_3}) B_2^{\omega_2}$ according to scenario ω_2. This requires storing of the expected value of the dual variables $E_{\omega_3} \pi_3^{\omega_3}$. Sharing of cuts in the case of additive dependency for more than three stages seems at best difficult, as in this case also the dual feasible regions of stages 3 till T depend on the scenario history, and therefore dual feasibility of the optimal dual variables for different scenario

history is not automatically guaranteed.

Taking advantage of the above stated properties we actually only need to store one subproblem per stage t. For different scenarios ω_t and different solutions $\hat{x}_{t-1}$ passed from the previous stage we determine the right-hand side accordingly. The cuts are valid for all scenarios $\omega_t \in \Omega_t$ in the case of independence of the stochastic parameters between stages or are adjusted in the gradient according to the actual scenario ω_t in the case of Markovian type dependency between stages. Therefore it is easily possible to generate any ω_t subproblem. Future information is represented in the cuts which have been generated so far and can be efficiently used in any scenario $\omega_t \in \Omega_t$ independently of which scenario originated it.

5. Multidimensional integration

The computation of the expected future costs z_{t+1}, the coefficients G_t and the right-hand side g_t of the cuts requires the computation of multiple integrals or multiple sums. The expected value of the second stage costs in period $t + 1$ (we suppress the index t for this discussion), e.g. $z = Ez^\omega = E(C)$, is an expectation of functions $C(v^\omega)$, $\omega \in \Omega$, where $C(v^\omega)$ is obtained by solving a linear program. V (in general) is an h-dimensional random vector parameter, e.g. $V = (V_1, \ldots, V_h)$, with outcomes $v^\omega = (v_1, \ldots, v_h)^\omega$. For example, V_i represents the value of the i-th factor v_i^ω, the observed random outcome. The vector v^ω is also denoted by v, and $p(v^\omega)$ alias $p(v)$ denotes the corresponding probability. Ω is the set of all possible random events and is constructed by crossing the sets of outcomes $\omega = \Omega_1 \times \Omega_2 \times \cdots \times \Omega_h$. With P being the probability measure under the assumption of independence, the integral $EC(V) = \int C(v^\omega)P(d\omega)$ takes the form of a multiple integral $EC(V) = \int \cdots \int C(v)p(v)dv_1 \cdots dv_h$, or, in case of discrete distributions, the form of a multiple sum $EC(V) = \sum_{v_1} \cdots \sum_{v_h} C(v)p(v)$, where $p(v) = p_1(v_1) \cdots p_h(v_h)$.

The number of terms in the multiple sum computation becomes astronomically large, and therefore the evaluations of multiple sums by direct summation is not practical. This is especially true because function evaluations are computationally expensive since the evaluation of each term in the multiple sum requires the solution of a linear program. In the following we discuss a scheme for estimating the expected values with a sufficiently low estimation error without having to evaluate each term.

6. Importance sampling

Monte Carlo methods are recommended to compute multiple integrals or multiple sums for higher h-dimensional sample spaces [8, 12]. Suppose $C^\omega = C(v^\omega)$ are independent random variates of v^ω, $\omega = 1, \ldots, n$, with expectation z, where n is the sample size. An unbiased estimator of z with variance $\sigma_{\bar{z}}^2 = \sigma^2/n$, $\sigma^2 = var(C(V))$ is

$$\bar{z} = (1/n) \sum_{\omega=1}^{n} C^{\omega}.$$

Note that the standard error decreases with $n^{-0.5}$, and the convergence rate of $\bar{z}$ to z is independent of the dimension of the sample space h. We rewrite $z = \sum_{\omega \in \Omega} C(v^{\omega}) p(v^{\omega})$ as

$$\sum_{\omega \in \Omega} \frac{C(v^{\omega}) p(v^{\omega}) q(v^{\omega})}{q(v^{\omega})}$$

by introducing a new probability mass function $q(v^{\omega})$ and we obtain a new estimator of z

$$\bar{z} = \frac{1}{n} \sum_{\omega=1}^{n} \frac{C(v^{\omega}) p(v^{\omega})}{q(v^{\omega})}$$

by sampling from $q(v^{\omega})$. the variance of $\bar{z}$ is given by

$$var(\bar{z}) = \frac{1}{n} \sum_{\omega \in \Omega} \left(\frac{C(v^{\omega}) p(v^{\omega})}{q(v^{\omega}} - z \right)^2 q(v^{\omega}).$$

Choosing $q^*(v^{\omega}) = C(v^{\omega}) p(v^{\omega}) / (\sum_{\omega \in \Omega} C(v^{\omega}) p(v^{\omega}))$ would lead to $var(\bar{z}) = 0$, which means one could get a perfect estimate of the multiple sum from only one estimation. Practically, however, this is useless since to compute $q(v^{\omega})$ we have to know $z = \sum_{\omega \in \Omega} c^{\omega} p(v^{\omega})$, which is what we are trying to compute in the first place.

The result, however, helps to derive a heuristic for choosing q. It should be proportional to the product $C(v^{\omega}) p(v^{\omega})$ and should have a form that can be integrated easily. Thus, a function $\Gamma(v^{\omega}) \approx C(v^{\omega})$ is sought which can be integrated with less effort than $C(v^{\omega})$. Additive and multiplicative (in the components of the stochastic vector v) approximation functions and combinations of these are potential candidates for our approximations. Especially for financial investment problems, we have been getting good results using $C(V) \approx \sum_{i=1}^{h} C_i(V_i)$. We compute q as

$$q(v^{\omega}) \approx \frac{C(v^{\omega}) p(v^{\omega})}{\sum_{i=1}^{h} \sum_{\omega \in \Omega_i} C_i(v^{\omega}) p_i(v^{\omega})}.$$

In this case one has to compute only h one-dimensional sums instead of one h-dimensional sum. The variance reduction depends on how well the approximation function fits the original cost function. If the original cost function has the property of additivity (separability), the multiple sum can be computed exactly by h one-dimensional sums. If the additive model is a bad approximation of the cost function, the only "price" that has to be paid is increasing the sample size. If the observed variance is too high using a starting sample size, the sample size is adjusted higher. Actually, we use a variant of the additive approximation function. By introducing $C(\tau)$, the costs of a base case, we make the model more sensitive to the impact of the stochastic parameters v.

$$\Gamma(V) = C(\tau) + \sum_{i=1}^{h} \Gamma_i(V_i), \quad \Gamma_i(V_i) = C(\tau_1, \ldots, \tau_{i-1}, V_i, \tau_{i+1}, \ldots, \tau_h) - C(\tau).$$

We denote this as a marginal cost model. τ can be any arbitrarily chosen point of the set of values v_i, $i = 1, \ldots, h$. For example, we choose τ_i as that outcome of V_i which leads to the lowest costs, ceteris paribus.

Summarizing, the importance sampling scheme has two phases: the preparation phase and the sample phase. In the preparation phase, we explore the cost function $C(V)$ at the margins to compute the additive approximation function $\Gamma(V)$. For this process $n_{prep} = 1 + \sum_{i=1}^{h}(k_i - 1)$ subproblems have to be solved. Using $\Gamma(V)$, we compute the approximate importance density

$$q(v^\omega) = \frac{\Gamma(v^\omega)p(v^\omega)}{C(\tau) + \sum_{i=1}^{h} \sum_{\omega \in \Omega_i} \Gamma_i(v^\omega)p(v^\omega)}$$

Next, we sample n scenarios from the importance density and, in the sample phase, solve n linear programs to compute the estimation of $\bar{z}$ using the Monte Carlo estimator. We compute the gradient G and the right-hand side g of the cut using the same sample points at hand from the expected cost calculation. See Infanger [19] for the computation of the cuts and details of the estimation process.

We apply importance sampling directly on the independent random variations η_t of the factors. In the case of inter-stage independence, we translate an observation η_t into the random outcome of the vector of factors, $v_t = \eta_t$, in the case of inter-period dependency up to three stages, according to the additive dependency model, we translate an observation η_t into the random outcome of the vector of factors, $v_t = \eta_t + v_{t-1}$. We then compute the corresponding random outcome of returns, $r_t = Fv_t$ according to the factor model. By doing so we obtain a random outcome of the matrix B_t, as B_t contains the returns r_t in its diagonal.

7. The algorithm

By solving a sample of subproblems ω_{t+1} according to the importance sampling scheme, we compute estimates of the expected future costs $z_{t+1}^{\omega_t}$, the gradients $G_t^{l_t}$ and the right-hand sides $g_t^{l_t}$ of the cuts in each stage t and scenario ω. The objective function value of the solution of each stage t, scenario ω_t subproblem gives a valid lower-bound estimate of the expected costs $z_t^{\omega t} = c_t \hat{x}_t^{\omega t} + \hat{\theta}_t^{\omega t}$ subject to scenario ω_t and subject to $\hat{x}_{t-1}$, the (optimal) solution passed forward from the previous stage. The obtained lower-bound estimate is the tightest lower bound that can be generated, if in stage $t = 1$ a sufficient number of cuts have been added to represent the expected future costs with respect to stage $t + 1$ for all scenarios $\omega_{t+1} \in \Omega_{t+1}$, and is a weaker lower-bound estimate if there is not a sufficient number of cuts.

We are especially interested in the lower-bound estimate of the first stage costs which we obtain by solving the first stage problem. If the first stage problem is balanced with the second stage, that is, if the cuts added so far to the first stage problem fully represent the expected second stage costs, and if the second stage is balanced with the third stage for all scenarios $\omega_2 \in \Omega_2$ and all values of $\hat{x}_1$, passed to it from the first stage, and so forth till stage $T - 1$, then the solution of the first stage problem is the optimum solution of the multi-stage stochastic linear program. In this case the lower-bound estimate of z_1 takes on the value of the total expected costs of the multi-stage problem.

To obtain an upper bound of the total expected costs of the multi-stage problem, we evaluate the expected costs of the current first stage trial solution $\hat{x}_1$. This can be accomplished by sampling paths from stages $2, \ldots, T$. For a reference, see Pereira and Pinto [30]. To efficiently sample a small number of paths to obtain an accurate estimate of the expected costs associated with $\hat{x}_1$, we also use importance sampling. We define a path $\hat{s}^\omega = (\hat{x}_1, \hat{x}_2, \ldots, \hat{x}_T)^\omega$, $\omega \in \Omega$, where $\Omega = \Omega_2 \times \Omega_3 \times \cdots \times \Omega_T$, as a sequence of optimal solutions $\hat{x}_t^{\omega t}$ of stage t scenario ω_t problems, $t = 2, \ldots, T$, and $\hat{x}_1$ being the first stage trial solution. A path is computed by observing the "wait-and-see" requirements: We pass $\hat{x}_1$ to the second stage and solve the second stage problem for scenario ω_t and obtain the optimal solution $\hat{x}^{\omega_2}$. Next we pass the obtained second stage solution $\hat{x}^{\omega_2}$ to the third stage and solve the third stage problem for scenario ω_3 to obtain $\hat{x}_3^{\omega_3}$. We continue in this way until we obtain $\hat{x}_T^{\omega_T}$ in stage T. Note that when solving the stage t problem no future outcomes $\omega_{t+1}, \ldots, \omega_T$ are used. All future information at each stage is solely represented by means of the cuts added in stage t so far. The cost of a path $\hat{s}^\omega$, $C(\hat{s}^\omega)$, is given by $C(\hat{s}^\omega) = \sum_{t=1}^{T} c_t \hat{x}_t^{\omega t}$. The expected value of the costs of all paths $\hat{s}^\omega$, $\omega \in \Omega$, $E\hat{s}^\omega$, gives an upper bound to the costs of a trial solution $\hat{x}_1$.

We sample paths by applying the importance sampling scheme to the dimensional space of size $\sum_{t-2}^{T} h_t$ of all random parameters $V_{i_t}^t$, $i_t = 1, \ldots, h_t$, $t = 2, \ldots, T$. For sampling paths the importance density $q(V)$ is computed based on the additive marginal approximation function analogous to the way it was defined earlier:

$$\Gamma(V) = C(\tau) + \sum_{t=1}^{T}\sum_{i=1}^{h} C(\tau_{1,1},\ldots,\tau_{t,i_t-1},V_{t,i_t},\tau_{t,i_t+1},\ldots,\tau_{T,h_T}) - C(\tau).$$

where $V = (V_1^1,\ldots,V_{h_1}^1,V_1^2,\ldots,V_{h_T}^T)$ and $\tau = (\tau_1^1,\ldots,\tau_{h_1}^1,\tau_1^2,\ldots,\tau_{h_t}^T)$. Sampling paths $\omega \in \Omega$ according to this importance sampling scheme we obtain an equal number of sample points $\omega_t \in \Omega_t$ in stages $t = 2,\ldots,T$. At these sample points we define the current stage t scenario ω_t subproblems and generate cuts to be added at stages $t = 1,\ldots T_1$ by employing importance sampling as described above for cuts.

The overall procedure works as follows: Solving the stage 1 problem in iteration 1 we obtain a trial solution $\hat{x}_1$ and a lower-bound estimate of the expected costs z_1. Now we employ the path sampling procedure to obtain an upper-bound estimate of the expected costs z_1. It the upper-bound estimate and the lower-bound estimate are within a given optimality tolerance, we call the first stage solution the optimal solution of the multi-stage problem, and quit. Otherwise, we generate cuts in stages $1,\ldots,T-1$. The path sampling procedure used for the upper-bound estimate has produced sample points $\omega_t \in \Omega_t$ in stages $t = 2,\ldots,T$ with corresponding ancestor solutions $\hat{x}_4$ and $\hat{x}_t^{\omega_t}$ in stages $t = 2,\ldots,T-1$ to be passed to the current stage t scenario ω_t problem. Starting at stage $T-1$ and moving backwards till stage 1 we take each sample problem ω_t in stage t and finally the stage 1 problem as the current master problem and compute cuts by sampling again $\omega_{t+1} \in \Omega_{t+1}$ descendant problems until each scenario problem ω_t in stage t is balanced with stage $t+1$ with regard to ancestor solutions $\hat{x}_{t-1}$ which have been passed from stage $t-1$. Arriving at stage 1 we obtain a new solution $\hat{x}_1$ and a new lower-bound estimate. We continue as defined above by sampling new paths for the upper-bound estimate. Finally, after a finite number of iterations, upper- and lower-bound estimates will be sufficiently close. Upper- and lower-bound estimates can be seen as the sum of i.i.d. random terms which for sample sizes of 30 or more can be assumed normally distributed with known (derived from the sampling process) variances. A 95% confidence interval of the obtained solution is computed.

8. Computational experience

Computational results of using Benders decomposition and importance sampling for two-stage asset allocation problems can be found in Infanger [19] and Dantzig and Infanger [6], where we report on the solution of test problems with up to 52 stochastic parameters and a number of universe scenarios of more than 10^{24}. These problems were formulated as two-stage stochastic programs. Using importance sampling and sample sizes between

200 and 600, very accurate results were obtained, e.g. the estimated 95% confidence interval was less than 0.8% on each side based on the optimal objective function value. Additional tests on these examples showed that the ratio of variance reduction obtained by using importance sampling versus crude (naive) Monte Carlo sampling was about 10^{-6}.

Inspired by these results we implemented an earlier version of the methodology described above for the multi-stage case which did not consider dependency between stages. Instead of the path sampling procedure for obtaining upper bounds, we implemented a procedure where we sampled points rather than paths, which required the handling of an exponentially expanding decision tree. Therefore, even when we used very small sample sizes, the number of stages that was practical to solve was limited.

We did test up to 3-stage problems. FI3 is a 3-stage test problem derived from a 2-stage financial portfolio problem found in Mulvey and Vladimirou [26]. The problem is to select a portfolio which maximizes expected returns in future periods taking into account the possibility of revising the portfolio in each period. There are transaction costs and bounds on the holdings and turnovers. Our test problem covers a planning horizon of 3 periods whereas the original Mulvey-Vladimirou test problem was a 2-stage problem which compressed all future periods into a single second stage. They solved the stochastic problem by restricting the number of scenarios in Ω.

We assumed the returns of the stocks in the future periods to be independent stochastic parameters with 3 outcomes each. With 13 assets with uncertain returns, the problem had 26 stochastic parameters instead of 39 because after the last stage decision was made, the expected money-value of the portfolio can be evaluated. The number of universe scenarios was 2.5×10^{12}. (The deterministic equivalent formulation of the problem has more than 10^{14} rows and a similar number of columns.) We obtained an estimated optimal solution of the 3-stage stochastic problem using a sample size of only 50 per stage. The optimal objective function value was estimated to be 1.10895 with an estimated 95% confidence interval off 0.004% on the left side and 0.001% on the right side of the obtained objective function value. Thus the optimal objective value lies within $1.10881 \le z^* \le 1.10895$ with 95% probability. Note how small the confidence interval is.

9. Conclusion

We have demonstrated how real-world multi-period asset allocation problems can be efficiently solved as multi-stage stochastic linear programs using our approach of combining Benders decomposition and importance sampling. The numerical results obtained so far are very promising: We obtained very accurate solutions for a 3-stage asset allocation problem using remarkably small sample sizes.

References

[1] E.M.L. Beale, On minimizing a convex function subject to linear inequalities, J. Roy. Stat. Soc. 17b (1955) 173–184.

[2] J.F. Benders, Partitioning procedures for solving mixed-variable programming problems, Numer. Math. 4 (1962) 238–252.

[3] J.R. Birge, Decomposition and partitioning methods for multi-stage stochastic linear programming, Oper. Res. 33 (1985) 989–1007.

[4] G.B. Dantzig, Linear programming under uncertainty, Manag. Sci. 1 (1955) 197–206.

[5] G.B. Dantzig and P.W. Glynn, Parallel processors for planning under uncertainty, Ann. Oper. Res. 22 (1990) 1–21.

[6] G.B. Dantzig and G. Infanger, Large-scale stochastic linear programs: Importance sampling and Benders decomposition, Technical Report SOL 91-4, Department of Operations Research, Stanford University (1991).

[7] G.B. Dantzig and A. Madansky, On the solution of two-staged linear programs under uncertainty, *Proc. 4th Berkeley Symp. on Mathematical Statistics and Probability I,* ed. J. Neyman (1961) pp. 165–176.

[8] P.J. Davis and P. Rabinowitz, *Methods of Numerical Integration* (Academic Press, London, 1984).

[9] Y. Ermoliev, Stochastic quasi-gradient methods and the applications to systems optimization, Stochastics 9 (1983) 1–36.

[10] Y. Ermoliev and R.J. Wets (eds.) *Numerical Techniques for Stochastic Optimization* (Springer, 1988).

[11] K. Frauendorfer, Solving SLP recourse problems with arbitrary multivariate distributions—The dependent case, Math. Oper. Res. 13 (1988) 377–394.

[12] P.W. Glynn and D.L. Iglehart, Importance sampling for stochastic simulation, Manag. Sci. 35 (1989) 1367–1392.

[13] N.H. Hakansson, Optimal myopic portfolio policies, with and without serial correlation of yields, J. Bus. 44 (1971) 324–334.

[14] N.H. Hakansson, Convergence to isoelastic utility and policy in multiperiod portfolio choice, J. Fin. Econ. 1 (1974) 201–224.

[15] J.L. Higle and S. Sen, Stochastic decomposition: An algorithm for two stage linear programs with recourse, Math. Oper. Res. 16 (1991) 650–669.

[16] J.K. Ho and E. Loute, A set of staircase linear programming test problems, Math. Prog. 20 (1981) 245–250.

[17] J.K. Ho and A.S. Manne, Nested decomposition for dynamic models, Math. Prog. 6 (1974) 121–140.

[18] G. Infanger, Monte Carlo (importance) sampling within a Benders decomposition algorithm for stochastic linear programs, Technical Report SOL 89-13R, Department of Operations Research, Stanford University 1990.

[19] G. Infanger, Monte Carlo (importance) sampling within a Benders decomposition algorithm for stochastic linear programs, Extended Version: Including large-scale results, Ann. Oper. Res. 39 (1992) 41–67.

[20] R.A. Jarrow, Pricing interest rate options, in: *Handbooks in Operations Research and Management Science,* eds. R. Jarrow, V. Maksimovic and W.T. Ziemba. (Elsevier, Amsterdam, 1995) pp. 251–272.

[21] P. Kall, Computational methods for two stage stochastic linear programming problems, Z. angew. Math. Phys. 30 (1979) 261–271.

[22] H. Konno, Piecewise linear risk function and portfolio optimization, J. Oper. Res. Soc. Japan 33 (1990) 139–155.

[23] H. Markowitz, *Portfolio Selection: Efficient Diversification of Investments* (Wiley, New York, 1959).

[24] T.A. Marsh, Term structure of interest rates and the pricing of fixed income claims and bonds, in: *Handbooks in Operations Research and Management Science,* eds. R.A. Jarrow, V. Maksimovic and W.T. Ziemba. (Elsevier, Amsterdam, 1995) pp. 273–314.

[25] J.M. Mulvey, Nonlinear network models in finance, Adv. Math. Prog. Fin. Planning I (1987) 253–271.

[26] J. M. Mulvey and H. Vladimirou, Stochastic network optimaization models for investment planning, Ann. Oper. Res. 20 (1989) 187–217.

[27] J. M. Mulvey and H. Vladimirou, Applying the progressive hedging algorithm to stochastic generalized networks, Ann. Oper. Res. 31 (1991) 399–424.

[28] B.S. Murtagh and M.A. Saunders, MINOS User's User's Guide, SOL 82-20, Department of Operations Research, Stanford University, Stanford, CA (1983).

[29] M.V. Pereira, L.M.V.G. Pinto, G.C. Oliveira, and S.H.F Cunha, A technique for solving LP-problems with stochastic right-hand sides, CEPEL, Centro del Pel Pesquisas de Energia Eletria, Rio de Janieiro, (1989).

[30] M.V. Pereira and L.M.V.G. Pinto, Stochastic dual dynamic programming, Technical Note, DEE-PUC/RJ — Catholic University of Rio de Janeiro, Caixa Postal 38063 Gávea, Rio de Janeiro RJ CEP 22452 Brazil (1989).

[31] A. Perold, Large-scale portfolio optimization, Manag. Sci. 30 (1984) 1143–1160.

[32] R.T. Rockafellar and R.J. Wets, Scenario and policy aggregation in optimization under uncertainty, Math. Oper. Res. 16 (1991) 119–147.

[33] A. Ruszczynski, A regularized decomposition method for minimizing a sum of polyhedral functions, Math. Prog. 35 (1986) 309–333.

[34] W.F. Sharpe, Capital asset prices: A theory of market equilibrium under conditions of risk, J. Finance 19 (1964) 425–442.

[35] R. Van Slyke and R.J. Wets, L-shaped linear prorams with applications to optimal control and stochastic programming, SIAM J. Appl. Math. 17 (1969) 638–663.

[36] R.J. Wets, Programming under uncertainty: The equivalent convex program, SIAM J. Appl. Math. 14 (1966) 89–105.

[37] S.A. Zenios, A model for portfolio management with mortgage backed securities, Ann. Oper. Res. 43 (1993) 337–356.

Part VI: Network Optimization

The presence of networks in everyday life is a common experience. This helps to make the statements of some network optimization problems easy for the nonspecialist to comprehend, even if the details of theory and computation must be left to others. Everyone can relate to the problem of getting from point A to point B in the fastest, shortest, or generally least costly way. Everyone who has set out (by car) with a long list of errands must occasionally think about the best order in which to arrange them. Everyone who has spent some time on a crowded freeway has a sense of the notions of flow and arc capacity. This part brings together three papers by George Dantzig and coauthors that address simply stated and easily understood problems belonging to the category of network optimization problems. The kinds of applications that motivated these papers have more to do with military logistics and industrial processes than with consumers' shopping sprees.

In their landmark paper "Solution of a Large-Scale Traveling-Salesman Problem," George Dantzig, Ray Fulkerson, and Selmer Johnson tackled a problem that was, by virtue of its size, a very challenging problem for its day. The traveling salesman problem (or TSP as it is known) begins with a network of n nodes and $n(n-1)$ arcs, and a known distance between each pair of distinct nodes, i.e., the length of the corresponding arc.[1] The nodes of the network are commonly called cities. The TSP is to find a tour of the cities having minimal length that visits each city except for the initial one exactly once. If the cities are denoted $1, 2, \ldots, n$, then a tour of the required type will be a sequence of cities $i_1, i_2, \ldots, i_n, i_{n+1}$ where $i_1 = i_{n+1}$ and when $1 \leq j, k \leq n$ and $j \neq k$, then $i_j \neq i_k$. Of course, the length of the tour is the sum of the lengths of the arcs connecting successive arcs that make up the tour.

In this paper, an optimal solution is found for a TSP based on 49 cities: Washington, D.C., and 48 others all located in different states of what are sometimes called "the lower 48 states." The real work of the problem focuses on 42 cities because there are 7 eastern-seaboard cities in the list for which a portion of the required tour is clear. Dantzig, Fulkerson, and

---

[1]In this paper, and in the literature generally, the matrix of arc lengths is assumed to be *symmetric*; thus, the problem is properly called the symmetric traveling salesman problem (STSP).

Johnson developed a linear programming approach to the problem and incorporated information about the structure of feasible region (later known technically as the traveling salesman polytope) to solve the problem. This achievement stood for many years and inspired further work on the problem which benefited greatly from advances in computing equipment and the further study of the TSP. [2]

In another early paper, "On the Max-Flow Min-Cut Theorem of Networks," Dantzig and Fulkerson produced a constructive proof for a result due to Lester Ford and Ray Fulkerson which had been done in a nonconstructive way. That result, called the "max-flow min-cut" theorem is a consequence of the duality theorem in linear programming. The emphasis put here on the constructive proof reflects an interesting philosophical position that had much greater currency in the mid-1950s than it does today, probably because we now take the issue for granted.

In its simplest form, the maximal flow problem is about sending a single commodity (the flow) through a network from a node designated as the source (or origin) to another designated node called the sink (or destination) so that the amount allocated to arcs does not exceed a known upper limit (the capacity) and such that with the exception of the source and the sink, the amount of flow entering a node must equal the amount leaving the node (a conservation constraint). Because the network is connected, flow that leaves the source must eventually enter the sink. The amount that arrives at the sink is to be maximized. This verbal statement of the problem results in a linear programming problem whose solution gives an allocation of flow to individual arcs that is consistent with the imposed constraints (the arc capacities and the conservation equations) and gives the largest amount of flow that can enter the sink. The latter number is called the "max flow" (value). Another problem, posed with respect to the same network, is concerned with sets of arcs called cuts. One begins by partitioning the nodes of the network into two disjoint sets, one containing the source, the other containing the sink. The collection of all arcs with the property that one endpoint in one set and the other endpoint in the other set is called a cut, and the sum of the arc capacities of its elements is the capacity of the cut. The min-cut problem asks for a partitioning of the nodes of the network (as described above) such that the capacity of the induced cut is minimal, hence the term min-cut. The min-cut problem gives rise to a linear programming problem which happens to be dual to that of the max-flow problem. The duality theorem ensures that the max-flow value equals the min-cut capacity. Solution of either problem with

---

[2]For a lively and very informative account of the history of the traveling salesman problem, see the chapter simply called "History" by A. J. Hoffman and Philip Wolfe in *The Traveling Salesman Problem* (edited by E. L. Lawler, J. K. Lenstra, A. H. G. Rinnooy Kan, and D. B. Shmoys), New York: John Wiley & Sons, 1985.

the simplex algorithm (a decidedly constructive procedure) will produce an optimal solution of the other.

As noted above, finding the shortest route in a network is a problem we deal with informally all the time, but without giving very much thought to checking our solutions for optimality. Dantzig's paper, "On the Shortest Route Through a Network," is the last of this group on network optimization problems.

In addressing this problem, Dantzig acknowledges that "this problem has been solved the same way by many authors." He merely claims to be refinining previously published proposals, that of E. F. Moore being the closest, at least insofar as using the strategy of "fanning out" from a given origin is concerned. (This is in contrast to a "depth-first" strategy.) The algorithm assumes as already given the sorting of the arc lengths in ascending order, and this work is not counted in assessing the computational effort that the algorithm entails. Dantzig notes that the algorithm obtains the shortest route from the origin to every node of the (n-node) network using $n(n-1)/2$ comparisons and less than half this amount to a particular node. For a more recent evaluation of shortest route algorithms, see the references cited in Editor's Note a to Chapter 18.

Chapter 16

SOLUTION OF A LARGE-SCALE TRAVELING-SALESMAN PROBLEM [*]

G. Dantzig, R. Fulkerson and S. Johnson

The Rand Corporation, Santa Monica, California

It is shown that a certain tour of 49 cities, one in each of the 48
states and Washington, D.C., has the shortest road distance.

THE TRAVELING-SALESMAN PROBLEM might be described as follows: Find the shortest route (tour) for a salesman starting from a given
city, visiting each of a specified group of cities, and then returning to the
original point of departure. More generally, given an n by n symmetric
matrix $D = (d_{IJ})$, where d_{IJ} represents the 'distance' from I to J, arrange
the points in a cyclic order in such a way that the sum of the d_{IJ} between consecutive points is minimal. Since there are only a finite number
of possibilities (at most $1/2 (n - 1)!$) to consider, the problem is to devise
a method of picking out the optimal arrangement which is reasonably efficient for fairly large values of n. Although algorithms have been devised
for problems of a similar nature, e.g., the optimal assignment problem,[3,7,8]
little is known about the traveling-salesman problem. We do not claim
that this note alters the situation very much; what we shall do is outline

---

[*] HISTORICAL NOTE: The origin of this problem is somewhat obscure. It appears to have been discussed informally among mathematicians at mathematics
meetings for many years. Surprisingly little in the way of results has appeared in
the mathematical literature.[10] It may be that the minimal-distance tour problem
was stimulated by the so-called Hamiltonian game[1] which is concerned with finding the number of different tours possible over a specified network. The latter
problem is cited by some as the origin of group theory and has some connections
with the famous Four-Color Conjecture.[9] Merrill Flood (Columbia University)
should be credited with stimulating interest in the traveling-salesman problem
in many quarters. As early as 1937, he tried to obtain near optimal solutions in
reference to routing of school buses. Both Flood and A.W. Tucker (Princeton
University) recall that they heard about the problem first in a seminar talk by
Hassler Whitney at Princeton in 1934 (although Whitney, recently queried, does
not seem to recall the problem). The relations between the traveling-salesman
problem and the transportation problem of linear programming appear to have
been first explored by M. Flood, J. Robinson, T. C. Koopmans, M. Beckmann,
and later by I. Heller and H. Kuhn.[4,5,6]

a way of approaching the problem that sometimes, at least, enables one to find an optimal path and prove it so.[a] In particular, it will be shown that a certain arrangement of 49 cities, one in each of the 48 states and Washington, D.C., is best, the d_{IJ} used representing road distances as taken from an atlas.

In order to try the method on a large problem,[b] the following set of 49 cities, on in each state and the District of Columbia, was selected:

1. Manchester, N. H.	18. Carson City, Nev.	34. Birmingham, Ala,
2. Montpelier, Vt.	19. Los Angeles, Calif.	35. Atlanta, Ga.
3. Detroit, Mich.	20. Phoenix, Ariz.	36. Jacksonville, Fla.
4. Cleveland, Ohio	21. Santa Fe, N. M.	37. Columbia, S. C.
5. Charleston, W. Va.	22. Denver, Colo.	38. Raleigh, N. C.
6. Louisville, Ky.	23. Cheyenne, Wyo.	39. Richmond, Va.
7. Indianapolis, Ind.	24. Omaha, Neb.	40. Washington, D. C.
8. Chicago, Ill.	25. Des Moines, Iowa	41. Boston, Mass.
9. Milwaukee, Wis.	26. Kansas City, Mo.	42. Portland, Me.
10. Minneapolis, Minn.	27. Topeka, Kans.	A. Baltimore, Md.
11. Pierre, S. D.	28. Oklahoma City, Okla.	B. Wilmington, Del.
12. Bismarck, N. D.	29. Dallas, Tex.	C. Philadelphia, Penn.
13. Helena, Mont.	30. Little Rock, Ark.	D. Newark, N. J.
14. Seattle, Wash.	31. Memphis, Tenn.	E. New York, N. Y.
15. Portland, Ore.	32. Jackson, Miss.	F. Hartford, Conn.
16. Boise, Idaho	33. New Orleans, La.	G. Providence, R. I.
17. Salt Lake City, Utah		

The reason for picking this particular set was that most of the road distances between them were easy to get from an atlas. The triangular table of distances between these cities (Table I) is part of the original one prepared by Bernice Brown of The Rand Corporation. It gives $d_{IJ} = \frac{1}{17}(d'_{IJ} - 11)$,[*] $(I, J = 1, 2, \cdots, 42)$, where d'_{IJ} is the road distance in miles between I and J. The d_{IJ} have been rounded to the nearest integer. Certainly such a linear transformation does not alter the ordering of the tour lengths, although, of course, rounding could cause a tour that was not optimal in terms of the original mileage to become optimal in terms of the adjusted units used in this paper.

We will show that the tour (see Fig. 16) through the cities 1, 2, $\cdots$, 42 is this order is minimal for this subset of 42 cities. Moreover, since in driving from city 40 (Washington, D. C.) to city 41 (Boston, Massachusetts) by the shortest road distance one goes through $A, B, \cdots, G$, successively, it follows that the tour through 49 cities 1, 2, $\cdots$, 40, $A, B, \cdots, G$, 41, 42 in that order is also optimal.

---

[*] This particular transformation was chosen to make the d_{IJ} of the original table less than 256, which would permit compact storage of the distance table in binary representation; however, no use was made of this.

PRELIMINARY NOTIONS

Whenever the road from I to J (in that order) is traveled, the value $x'_{IJ} = 1$ is entered into the I, J element of a matrix; otherwise $x'_{IJ} = 0$ is entered. A (directed) tour through n cities can now be thought of as a permutation matrix of order n which represents an n-cycle (we assume $n > 2$ throughout). For example, for $n = 5$, the first matrix displayed below

$$\|x'_{IJ}\| = \begin{Vmatrix} 0 & 1 & 0 & 0 & 0 \\ 0 & 0 & 0 & 1 & 0 \\ 0 & 0 & 0 & 0 & 1 \\ 0 & 0 & 1 & 0 & 0 \\ 1 & 0 & 0 & 0 & 0 \end{Vmatrix}, \qquad \|x'_{IJ}\| = \begin{Vmatrix} 0 & 1 & 0 & 0 & 0 \\ 1 & 0 & 0 & 0 & 0 \\ 0 & 0 & 0 & 0 & 1 \\ 0 & 0 & 1 & 0 & 0 \\ 0 & 0 & 0 & 1 & 0 \end{Vmatrix},$$

is a tour since it represents visiting the cities in the 5-cycle (1 2 4 3 5), while the other matrix is not a tour since it represents visiting the cities by means of two sub-cycles (1 2) and (3 4 5).

It is clear that all representations for directed tours satisfy the relations

$$\sum_I x'_{IJ} = \sum_J x'_{IJ} = 1, \qquad x'_{II} = 0, \qquad x'_{IJ} \geq 0.$$

The matrix may be made into a triangular array by reflecting the numbers above the diagonal in the diagonal. The sum of corresponding elements is denoted $x_{IJ} = x'_{IJ} + x'_{JI}$. Then the matrices above become

$$\|x_{IJ}\| = \begin{Vmatrix} \cdot & & & & \\ 1 & \cdot & & & \\ 0 & 0 & \cdot & & \\ 0 & 1 & 1 & \cdot & \\ 1 & 0 & 1 & 0 & \cdot \end{Vmatrix}, \qquad \|x_{IJ}\| = \begin{Vmatrix} \cdot & & & & \\ 2 & \cdot & & & \\ 0 & 0 & \cdot & & \\ 0 & 0 & 1 & \cdot & \\ 0 & 0 & 1 & 1 & \cdot \end{Vmatrix}.$$

Consequently, the sum along the Kth row plus the sum along the Kth column must now be 2. This may be written

$$(1) \qquad \sum_{J<I=K} x_{IJ} + \sum_{I>J=K} x_{IJ} = 2, \qquad (K = 1, \cdots, n; \ x_{IJ} \geq 0)$$

This device yields a representation for undirected tours and is the one used throughout this paper. It will be noted that the second array above does not represent a tour but nevertheless satisfies the relation (1).

For undirected tours, the symbol x_{IJ} will be treated identically with x_{JI} so that we may we may rewrite (1) as

$$(2) \qquad \sum_{j<k=N} x_{IJ} = 2, \qquad (x_{IJ} \geq 0; \ I = 1, 2, \cdots, n; \ I \neq J; \ x_{IJ} \equiv x_{JI})$$

TABLE I

ROAD DISTANCES BETWEEN CITIES IN ADJUSTED UNITS

The figures in the table are mileages between the two specified numbered cities, less 11, divided by 17, and rounded to the nearest integer.

	1	2	3	4	5	6	7	8	9	10	11	12	13	14	15	16	17	18	19	20	21	22	23	24	25	26	27	28	29	30	31	32	33	34	35	36	37	38	39	40	41
2	8																																								
3	39	45																																							
4	37	47	9																																						
5	50	49	21	15																																					
6	61	62	21	20	17																																				
7	58	60	16	17	18	6																																			
8	59	66	15	26	31	17	10																																		
9	62	60	20	31	26	22	15	5																																	
10	81	66	25	50	31	63	35	24	20																																
11	103	107	40	62	72	68	61	46	41	23																															
12	108	117	62	66	77	63	57	51	46	26	11																														
13	145	149	66	104	71	99	61	88	84	63	49	40																													
14	181	185	104	144	77	135	99	124	120	105	85	76	35																												
15	187	191	140	150	114	137	91	130	125	90	90	81	41	10																											
16	161	170	146	156	84	142	115	104	105	105	72	64	34	31	27																										
17	142	146	120	130	53	130	110	111	110	90	83	59	29	53	48	21																									
18	174	178	101	124	46	115	97	123	118	107	93	84	54	46	35	26	27																								
19	185	186	133	138	69	129	123	117	128	118	101	72	46	69	58	35	43	31																							
20	164	165	142	143	71	130	126	124	110	104	86	101	59	93	58	58	45	42	26																						
21	137	139	120	143	66	106	106	106	104	77	56	97	64	90	60	62	56	53	49	30																					
22	117	122	94	96	51	80	78	62	84	50	34	82	49	82	60	58	45	61	66	55	32																				
23	114	118	77	80	46	68	62	63	61	61	28	77	43	77	45	36	27	59	81	81	54	29																			
24	85	89	44	78	34	62	52	61	59	50	34	45	34	74	64	84	56	52	75	75	71	40	12																		
25	77	80	36	48	35	41	27	34	38	38	28	36	29	72	66	84	56	62	72	79	64	36	9	8																	
26	87	89	44	40	40	34	30	44	44	46	36	40	40	78	88	98	66	59	69	71	39	33	42	33	11																
27	91	93	48	50	48	32	39	49	49	54	33	45	47	77	84	97	75	76	67	54	62	39	21	36	21	3															
28	105	106	62	64	64	46	51	56	53	61	46	51	53	85	84	98	70	67	64	62	67	54	32	39	30	27	20														
29	111	113	69	71	69	51	53	59	57	57	49	60	71	96	98	109	84	84	69	67	70	70	36	42	36	31	28	20													
30	91	92	50	51	50	30	34	43	43	49	60	81	103	103	112	90	88	88	81	62	67	73	54	46	39	31	28	48	8												
31	83	85	42	43	38	22	32	38	36	51	81	99	121	99	115	90	88	73	67	59	65	64	39	38	36	27	31	46	15	8											
32	89	91	44	50	44	26	32	44	48	63	96	95	124	112	123	100	86	64	64	56	50	53	37	43	37	39	44	38	25	25	12										
33	95	97	41	43	43	34	30	48	43	76	137	91	159	136	150	123	92	80	59	53	53	62	50	46	46	49	54	40	30	33	23	11									
34	74	76	42	41	34	35	34	36	46	66	91	117	151	128	155	104	98	78	66	58	67	66	53	54	50	56	62	56	41	34	24	14	9								
35	67	69	35	37	35	30	33	35	40	83	117	91	155	133	171	125	92	82	65	56	65	60	71	62	66	71	54	50	45	41	32	24	23	18							
36	74	76	30	41	35	44	41	41	56	102	137	110	179	176	176	144	98	88	60	50	62	74	79	69	74	60	62	58	53	46	38	32	24	29	17						
37	57	59	46	61	36	38	38	60	60	99	137	98	172	151	176	129	108	88	67	53	67	80	82	72	77	64	67	60	56	48	45	38	38	27	21	12					
38	45	46	41	34	20	48	48	53	49	96	131	99	171	144	163	100	113	75	62	54	64	88	88	78	84	65	62	58	54	53	49	45	38	24	13	13	9				
39	35	37	35	26	18	46	46	51	40	93	129	97	176	159	164	109	95	64	56	41	66	92	92	80	80	60	64	71	77	64	54	46	32	24	24	21	15	6			
40	29	33	30	21	18	40	40	45	45	87	135	101	171	166	182	123	118	71	60	62	67	98	107	88	84	62	65	64	64	71	41	38	38	32	38	27	41	32	25		
41	3	11	41	37	47	63	63	66	63	83	139	105	150	164	176	129	113	86	67	60	60	80	116	88	86	78	88	88	80	74	77	54	45	45	45	54	48	38	40	40	32
42	5	12	55	41	53	64	61	61	66	84	113	111	150	186	192	166	147	180	167	140	124	119	90	87	90	94	107	114	94	86	92	98	80	74	77	74	60	48	38	32	6

The problem is to find the minimum of the linear form

$$(3) \qquad\qquad D(x) = \sum_{I > J} d_{IJ} x_{IJ},$$

where the $x_{IJ} = 0$ or 1 and the $x_{IJ} = 1$ form a tour, and where the summation in (3) extends over all indices (I, J) such that $I > J$.

To make a linear programming problem out of this (see ref. 2) one needs, as we have observed, a way to describe tours by more linear restraints than that given by (2). This is extremely difficult to do as illustrated by the work of I. Heller[4] and H. Kuhn.[6] They point out that such relations always exist. However, there seems to be no simple way to characterize them and for moderate size n the number of such restraints appears to be astronomical. In spite of these difficulties, this paper will describe the techniques we have developed which have been successful in solving all the problems we have tried by this approach. A surprising empirical observation is the use of only a trivial number of the many possible restraints to solve any particular problem. To demonstrate the procedure, we shall attempt to use direct elementary proofs even though they were originally motivated in many places by linear programming procedures.

There are possibly four devices we have used which have greatly reduced the effort in obtaining solutions of the problems we have attempted.

First of all, we use undirected tours. This seems to simplify the characterization of the tours when n is small and certainly cuts down the amount of computation, even for large n. Secondly, and this is decisive, we do not try to characterize the tours by the complete set of linear restraints, but rather impose, in addition to (2), just enough linear conditions on the x_{IJ} to assure that the minimum of the linear form (3) is assumed by some tour. For the 49-city problem and also for all the smaller problems we have considered, such a procedure has been relatively easy to carry through by hand computation. This may be due in part to the fact that we use a simple symbolism which permits direct representation of the algebraic relationships and manipulations on a map of the cities. This third device speeds up the entire iterative process, makes it easy to follow, and sometimes suggests new linear restraints that are not likely to be obtained by less visual methods. Finally, once a tour has been obtained which is nearly optimal, a combinatorial approach, using the map and listing possible tours which have not yet been eliminated by the conditions imposed on the problem, may be advantageous. This list can be very much shorter than one would expect, due to the complex interlocking of the restraints. However, except for short discussion in the section below, "An Estimation Procedure," this method will not be described in detail although it has worked out well for all examples we have studied.

An important class of conditions that tours satisfy, which excludes many non-tour cases satisfying (2), are the 'loop conditions.' These are linear inequality restraints that exclude sub-cycles or loops.   Consider a non-tour solution to (2) which has a subtour of $n_1 < n$ cities; we note that the sum of the x_{IJ} for those links (I, J) in the subtour is n_1. Hence we can eliminate this type of solution by imposing the condition that the sum of x_{IJ} over all links (I, J) connecting cities in the subset S of n_1 cities be less than n_1, i.e.

$$(4) \qquad\qquad\qquad \sum_S x_{IJ} \leq n_1 - 1$$

where the summation extends over all (I, J) which I and J in the n_1 cities S. From (2) we note that two other conditions, each equivalent to (4), are

$$(5) \qquad\qquad\qquad \sum_{\bar{S}} x_{IJ} \leq n - n_1 - 1,$$

where $\bar{S}$ means the summation extends over all (I, J) such that neither I nor J is in S, and

$$(6) \qquad\qquad\qquad \sum_{S\bar{S}} x_{IJ} \geq 2,$$

where $S\bar{S}$ means that the summation extends over all (I, J) such that I is in S and J is not in S.

There are, however, other more complicated types of restraints which sometimes must be added to (2) in addition to an assortment of loop conditions in order to exclude solutions involving fractional weights x_{IJ}. In the 49-city case we needed two such conditions. However, later when we tried the combinatorial approach, after imposing a few of the loop condition, we found we could handle the 49-city problem without the use of the special restraints and this would have led to a shorter proof of optimality. In fact, we have yet to find an example which could not be handled by using only loop conditions and combinatorial arguments.

THE METHOD

The technique will be illustrated by a series of simple examples.

Example 1

First consider a five-city map forming a regular pentagon of unit length per side and with length $1/2 (\sqrt{5}+1) \doteq 1.7$ on a diagonal (Fig. 1). Suppose

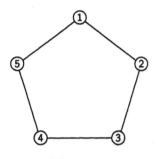

FIGURE 1

that the problem is to minimize (3) subject only to (2). Start with a tour
which is conjectured to be optimal, obviously (1 2 3 4 5). In this case the
values of x_{IJ}, denoted $\bar{x}_{IJ}$, are $\bar{x}_{12} = \bar{x}_{23} = \bar{x}_{34} = \bar{x}_{45} = \bar{x}_{51} = 1$ and all
other $\bar{x}_{IJ} = 0$. The variables x_{IJ} corresponding to links on the tour are
called "basic variables." The length of the tour given by the linear form
(3) for $x = \bar{x}$ is $D(\bar{x}) = 5$. There are five equations in (2). Multiply each
by a parameter π_I to be determined, and then subtract the sum from (3).
Thus, we are led to

$$D(x) = \sum_{I>J} d_{IJ}x_{IJ} = \sum_{I=1}^{n} \pi_I \left(\sum_{J=1}^{n} x_{IJ} - 2 \right) \qquad (x_{IJ} \equiv x_{JI};\ I \neq J)$$

$$= -\sum_{I>J} (\pi_I + \pi_J - d_{IJ})x_{IJ} + 2\sum_{1}^{n} \pi_I.$$

Denote the coefficient of x_{IJ} by δ_{IJ} so that

(7) $\qquad D(x) = -\sum_{I>J} \delta_{IJ}x_{IJ} + 2\sum_{1}^{n} \pi_I, \qquad (\delta_{IJ} = \pi_I + \pi_J - d_{IJ})$

Now determine the five π_I values so that δ_{IJ} corresponding to basic variables vanish:

(8) $\qquad\qquad\qquad\qquad \delta_{IJ} = 0, \qquad\qquad\qquad$ (for $\bar{x}_{IJ} = 1$)

i.e., if the link (I, J) is on the tour in question. Note that to solve for the
π_I we have five linear equations in five unknowns.

If now we set $x_{IJ} = \bar{x}_{IJ}$ in (7), then $\bar{x}_{IJ}\delta_{IJ} = 0$ for *all* (I, J) and

(9) $\qquad\qquad\qquad\qquad D(\bar{x}) = 2\sum_{1}^{n} \pi_I = 5.$

Subtracting (9) from (7) we have finally

(10) $\qquad\qquad\qquad D(x) - D(\bar{x}) = -\sum_{I>J} \delta_{IJ}x_{IJ}.$

For the regular pentagon $\pi_I = 1/2$ for $I = 1, 2, 3, 4, 5$ solves (8), so $\delta_{IJ} = 1/2(1 - \sqrt{5}) < 0$ on a diagonal, i.e., $\delta_{IJ} \leq 0$ for every (I, J). Thus, the right side of (1) is always nonnegative or $D(x) \geq D(\bar{x})$ for all x satisfying (2), and in particular other tours are longer than the tour represented by $\bar{x}$.

Example 2

Next, take another five-city problem whose map is not a regular pentagon (Fig. 2). We start with the tour (1, 2 3 4 5) of length $D(\bar{x}) = 32$ where the basic variables take on the values $\bar{x}_{12} = \bar{x}_{23} = \bar{x}_{34} = \bar{x}_{45} = \bar{x}_{51} = 1$ and all other $\bar{x}_{IJ} = 0$. Repeat the steps in the previous problem leading to (10)

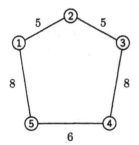
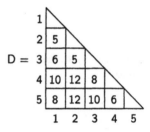

$$D = \begin{array}{c|ccccc} & & & & & \\ 1 & & & & & \\ 2 & 5 & & & & \\ 3 & 6 & 5 & & & \\ 4 & 10 & 12 & 8 & & \\ 5 & 8 & 12 & 10 & 6 & \\ \hline & 1 & 2 & 3 & 4 & 5 \end{array}$$

FIGURE 2

where, as before, calculate the π_I by setting $\delta_{IJ} = 0$ for δ_{IJ} corresponding to basic variables x_{IJ}. The five equations that the π_I must satisfy are

$$\pi_1 + \pi_2 = 5, \quad \pi_2 + \pi_3 = 5, \quad \pi_3 + \pi_4 = 8, \quad \pi_4 + \pi_5 = 6, \quad \pi_5 + \pi_1 = 8.$$

By alternately subtracting and adding these equations one obtains

$$2\pi_1 = d_{12} - d_{23} + d_{34} - d_{45} + d_{51} = 5 - 5 + 8 - 6 + 8 = 10,$$

or

$$\pi_1 = 5, \quad \pi_2 = 0, \quad \pi_3 = 5, \quad \pi_4 = 3, \quad \pi_5 = 3.$$

The factors π_I which multiply equations (2) to form (10) are called "potentials."[*] There is one such potential associated with each city I, and these are readily computed by working directly on the map of the cities (see Fig. 3).

To form other δ_{IJ}, add the π_I and π_J of city I and city J and subtract off the distance d_{IJ} between them. In this case we note that except for $\delta_{31} = 5 + 5 - 6 = +4$, all the other δ_{IJ} are ≤ 0.

---

[*] The term potential is used by T. C. Koopmans in an analogous connection for the transportation problem.[5]

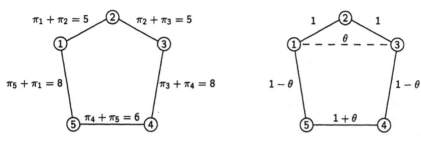

FIGURE 3   FIGURE 4

We see from (10) that if x_{31} were to take on a positive value, $x_{31} = \theta$, the other nonbasic variables remaining at zero, this may lead to a better solution. We let θ be the largest value consistent with (2). Thus the weights x_{IJ} must add up to 2 on links from each city and no weight is negative. However, in setting $x_{31} = \theta$ we adjust only the basic set of variables, leaving all other nonbasic variables at zero value. This is worked put on the map shown in Fig. 4. Here the maximum value of θ is 1, and this leads to a 3-cycle (1 2 3) and a 2-cycle (4 5) (Fig. 5).

This is not a tour, so we add a loop condition which excludes this solution but which is satisfied by all tours. In this case $x_{45} \leq 1$ or

$$(11) \qquad\qquad x_{45} + y_6 - 1 = 0, \qquad\qquad (y_6 \geq 0)$$

is such a condition. Accordingly, we start over again using the five equations (2) and the sixth equation (11). This time we will need six basic variables and it will be convenient to have x_{13} (the one we set equal to θ previously) included with those associated with the tour. Thus, the

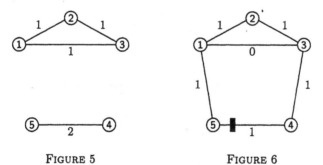

FIGURE 5   FIGURE 6

starting solution is as follows: The basic variables have values $x_{12} = x_{23} = x_{34} = x_{45} = x_{51} = 1$, $x_{13} = 0$. All other $x_{IJ} = 0$. This solution is shown in Fig. 6. The presence of an upper bound on x_{45} or relation (11) is depicted in Fig. 6 by a block symbol on (4, 5). We now multiply equation (11) by π_6, add it to $\sum\limits_{I=1}^{5} \pi_I \left(\sum\limits_{J=1}^{5} x_{IJ} - 2 \right)$, subtract the sum from $\sum d_{IJ}x_{IJ}$ and collect terms in x_{IJ} as before. The result is

$$(12) \qquad \sum_{I>J} d_{IJ}x_{IJ} = -\sum_{I>J} \delta_{IJ}x_{IJ} + 2\sum_{I=1}^{5} \pi_I + \pi_6(1 - y_6)$$

where $\delta_{IJ} = \pi_I + \pi_J - d_{IJ}$ except $\delta_{45} = \pi_4 + \pi_5 - (d_{45} - \pi_6)$.

Now determine the six values of π_I by setting $\delta_{IJ} = 0$ corresponding to basic variables x_{IJ}:

$$(13) \qquad \delta_{12} = \delta_{23} = \delta_{34} = \delta_{45} = \delta_{51} = \delta_{13} = 0,$$

from which it follows that

$$(14) \qquad D(x) - D(\bar{x}) = \sum \delta_{IJ}x_{IJ} - \pi_6 y_6$$

To evaluate π_I we note that there are six equations in six unknowns. These are shown on the map below (Fig. 7). The three conditions about the triangular loop (1 2 3) permit us to solve for π_1, π_2, π_3. Branching out from the triangle we get next π_4 and π_5 and finally π_6. Thus, we determine first that $2\pi_1 = d_{12} - d_{23} + d_{31} = 5 - 5 + 6$ so that $\pi_1 = 3$, $\pi_2 = 2$, $\pi_3 = 3$. Working down, $\pi_4 = 5$, $\pi_5 = 5$. Thus, $\pi_4 + \pi_5 = -\pi_6 + 6$, so $\pi_6 = -4$. These values are shown adjacent to each city in Fig. 7.

With these values of π_I all remaining $\delta_{IJ} = (\pi_I + \pi_J - d_{IJ}) \leq 0$; hence, with $\pi_6 < 0$ we have the right side of (14) always positive, so the tour (1 2 3 4 5) is minimal. This illustrates the use of the simplest of loop conditions, namely, an upper bound on the variable x_{45}.

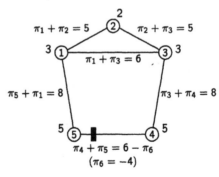

FIGURE 7

Example 3

Here we consider a six-city case (Fig. 8) where the optimal tour is not our initial choice. Let the starting tour be (1 2 3 4 5 6) of length $D(\bar{x}) = 23$. If we proceed as before, relation (8) implies that the π_I satisfy the relations shown in Fig. 8. In this case (and this is generally true for

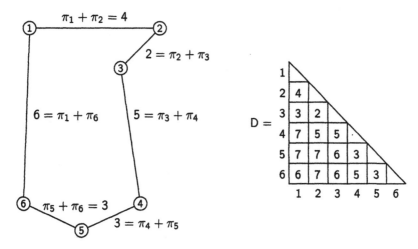

FIGURE 8

loops with an even number of links) the sum of equations on links $(1,2)$, $(3,4)$, $(5,6)$ is identical with the sum for $(2,3)$, $(4,5)$, $(6,1)$ except for different constant terms, so that the system of equations in π_I is inconsistent.

This difficulty can be avoided if the following general rule is followed: the set of basic variables must be so selected that when the remaining x_{IJ} are fixed, the values of the basic variables are uniquely determined. This means the matrix of coefficients of the basic variables is nonsingular (i.e., their determinant is nonvanishing). Since the π_I satisfy a system of equations whose coefficient matrix is the transpose of this matrix, the π_I will be uniquely determined also. In the six-city case, one may augment the system (2) with the additional upper-bound condition

$$(15) \qquad\qquad x_{45} + y_7 = 1 \qquad\qquad (y_7 \geq 0)$$

and select x_{13} as a basic variable in addition to the basic variables x_{IJ} corresponding to (I, J) on the tour. Then, letting π_7 be the weight associated with restriction (15), the π_I satisfy [the] relations in Fig. 9.

The value of $\pi_1 = 5/2$ can be determined from the odd loop $(1\ 2\ 3)$ by alternately adding and subtracting the equations around the loop. The others can then be evaluated immediately. In this case, we have, analogous to (14),

$$(16) \qquad\qquad D(x) - D(\bar{x}) = -\sum \delta_{IJ}x_{IJ} - \pi_7 y_7,$$

where $\delta_{IJ} = 0$ if x_{IJ} is a basic variable and $\delta_{IJ} = \pi_I + \pi_J - d_{IJ}$ otherwise. Since $\delta_{46} = 3$, increasing the value of x_{46} to θ (while all other nonbasic variables remain zero), with corresponding adjustments in the basic variables, will yield $D(x) - D(\bar{x}) = -3\theta < 0$. In Fig. 10 it is seen that the largest

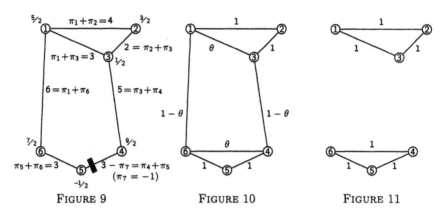

FIGURE 9   FIGURE 10   FIGURE 11

value of $\theta = 1$ and the resulting solution is Fig. 11, which is not a new tour, but two loops. However, we can exclude this solution by imposing the additional restriction satisfied by all tour solutions

$$(17) \quad x_{12} + x_{23} + x_{31} \leq 2, \quad \text{or} \quad x_{12} + x_{23} + x_{31} + y_8 = 2, \quad (y_8 \geq 0)$$

since in Fig. 11 the inadmissible solution has $x_{12} + x_{23} + x_{31} = 3$. We now start all over again augmenting relations (2) by (15) and (17). Let the basic variables be the same as before but include x_{46} (i.e., the one we set equal to θ in Fig. 10). Let π_I for $1, 2, \cdots, 8$ be the weights assigned to these relations respectively in forming $D(x) - D(\bar{x})$; then the π_I satisfy the relations shown in Fig. 12, where the loop condition (17) is symbolized by the dotted loop in the figure.

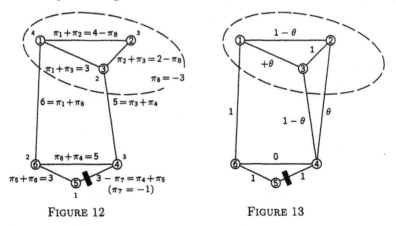

FIGURE 12   FIGURE 13

The value of $\pi_6 = 2$ may be evaluated from the odd loop (6 4 3 2 1) by alternately adding and subtracting the equations in π_I shown on this loop.

The other π_I can then be immediately determined. This time

(18) $$D(x) - D(\bar{x}) = -\sum \delta_{IJ} x_{IJ} - \pi_7 y_7 - \pi_8 y_8$$

where $\delta_{IJ} = 0$ for x_{IJ} a basic variable and $\delta_{IJ} = \pi_I + \pi_J - d_{IJ}$ otherwise. Since $\delta_{24} = 1$ while all other $\delta_{IJ} \leq 0$, we set $x_{24} = \theta$; then the adjustments in the values of the basic variables necessary to satisfy (2), (15), (17) are

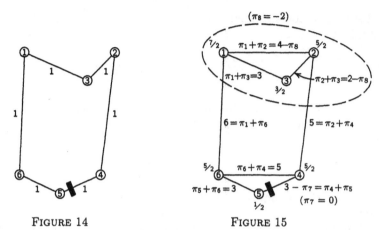

FIGURE 14   FIGURE 15

shown in Fig. 13 and the new solution for $\theta = 1$ is a new tour $\bar{\bar{x}}$ with length $D(\bar{\bar{x}}) = D(\bar{x}) - 1 = 22$, Fig. 14. We may now drop $x_{34} = 0$ from the basic set of variables (or alternatively x_{12}) and replace it by x_{24} as a new basic variable. This yields the relations for π_I of Fig. 15. The expression for $D(x) - D(\bar{\bar{x}})$ is similar to (18). It can now be tested that all $\delta_{IJ} \leq 0$ corresponding to non-basic x_{IJ}, and the coefficients of y_7 and y_8 are $\pi_7 \leq 0$, $\pi_8 \leq 0$, so that the new tour is established as optimal.

AN ESTIMATION PROCEDURE

In any linear programming problem with bounded variables, an estimate is available of how much a basic solution differs from an optimal solution.[c] Let $D(x)$ represent a linear form to be minimized and let $D(\bar{x})$ be the value for some basic solution $\bar{x}$ where variables $(x_1, x_2, \cdots, x_{n'})$, represented by the symbol x, satisfy a system of equations as well as bounds $0 \leq x_J \leq r_J$. If the equations are multiplied by weights π_I and subtracted from $D(x)$, then (as we have noted earlier)

(19) $$D(x) - D(\bar{x}) = -\sum_{J=1}^{n'} \delta_J x_J \qquad (x_J \geq 0)$$

where π_I are chosen such that $\delta_J = 0$ if the corresponding x_J is a basic variable. We may now split the right side of (19) into positive and negative parts and obtain a lower bound for the difference by dropping the positive part, i.e.,

$$(20) \quad D(x) - D(\bar{x}) = -\sum_{\delta_J > 0} \delta_J x_J - \sum_{\delta_J \leq 0} \delta_J x_J \quad (x_J \geq 0)$$

$$(21) \quad D(x) - D(\bar{x}) \geq -\sum_{\delta_J > 0} \delta_J x_J \geq -E, \quad (E \geq 0)$$

where $-E$ is some estimate for the negative part. By setting $x_J = r_J$, we obtain in particular

$$(22) \quad D(x) - D(\bar{x}) \geq -\sum_{\delta_J > 0} \delta_J x_J.$$

For the traveling-salesman problem the variables x_{IJ} must be either 0 or 1 if x represents a tour. From (20), no link (I, J) can occur in an optimal tour if

$$(23) \quad \delta_{IJ} < -E,$$

hence all corresponding variables x_{IJ} can be dropped from further consideration.

During the early stages of the computation, E may be quite large and very few links can be dropped by this rule; however, in the latter stages often so many links are eliminated that one can list all possible tours that use the remaining admissible links. By extending this type of combinatorial argument to the range of values of the 'slack' variables y_K, it is often possible at an earlier stage of the iterative algorithm to rule out so many of the tours that direct examination of the remaining tours for minimum length is a feasible approach.

THE 49-CITY PROBLEM[*]

The optimal tour $\bar{x}$ is shown in Fig. 16. The proof that it is optimal is given in Fig. 17. To make the correspondence between the latter and its programming problem clear, we will write down in addition to 42 relations in non-negative variables (2), a set of 25 relations which suffice to prove that $D(x)$ is a minimum for $\bar{x}$. We distinguish the following subsets of the 42 cites:

$$S_1 = \{1, 2, 41, 42\} \qquad\qquad S_5 = \{13, 14, \cdots, 23\}$$
$$S_2 = \{3, 4, \cdots, 9\} \qquad\qquad S_6 = \{13, 14, 15, 16, 17\}$$
$$S_3 = \{1, 2, \cdots, 9, 29, 30, \cdots, 42\} \qquad S_7 = \{24, 25, 26, 27\}.$$
$$S_4 = \{11, 12, \cdots, 23\}$$

[*] As indicated earlier, it was possible to treat this as a 42-city problem.

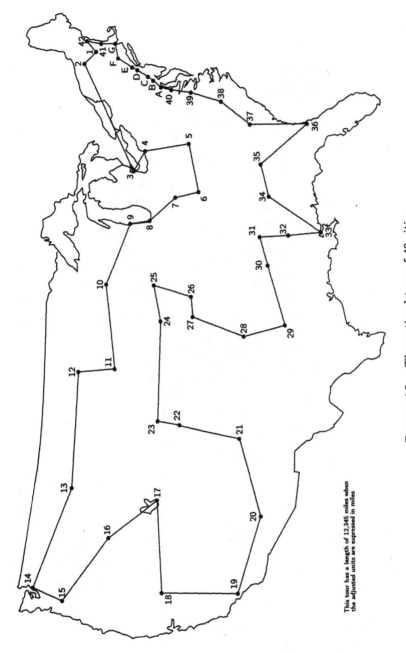

This tour has a length of 12,345 miles when the adjusted units are expressed in miles

FIGURE 16. The optimal tour of 49 cities.

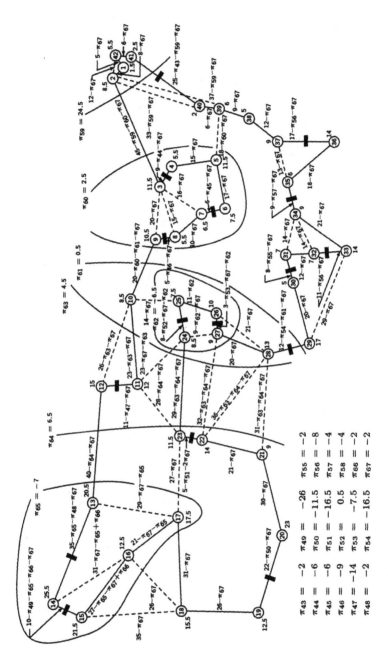

FIGURE 17. Only the right-hand side of the equations satisfied by π_I are shown on the map; the left-hand side on line (I, J) is $\pi_I + \pi_J$. Dotted links (I, J) correspond to additional basic variables x_{IJ}.

Except for two inequalities which we will discuss in a moment, the programming problem may now be written as the following 65 relations:†

$$\sum_J x_{IJ} = 2 \ (I = 1, \cdots, 42), \qquad x_{41,1} \le 1, \qquad x_{4,3} \le 1, \qquad x_{7,6} \le 1,$$

$$x_{9,8} \le 1, \qquad x_{12,11} \le 1, \qquad x_{14,13} \le 1, \qquad x_{15,14} \le 1, \qquad x_{20,19} \le 1,$$

$$x_{23,22} \le 1, \qquad x_{25,24} \le 1, \qquad x_{27,26} \le 1, \qquad x_{29,28} \le 1, \qquad x_{31,30} \le 1,$$

$$x_{33,32} \le 1, \qquad x_{35,34} \le 1, \qquad x_{37,36} \le 1, \qquad \sum_{S_1, \bar{S}_1} x_{IJ} \ge 2, \qquad \sum_{S_2, \bar{S}_2} x_{IJ} \ge 2,$$

$$\sum_{S_3, \bar{S}_3} x_{IJ} \ge 2, \qquad \sum_{S_4, \bar{S}_4} x_{IJ} \ge 2, \qquad \sum_{S_5, \bar{S}_5} x_{IJ} \ge 2, \qquad \sum_{S_6} x_{IJ} \le 4, \qquad \sum_{S_7} x_{IJ} \le 3.$$

The remaining two relations (66 and 67) are perhaps most easily described verbally.

66: $x_{14,15}$ minus the sum of all other x_{IJ} on links out of 15, 16, 19, except for $x_{18,15}, x_{18,16}, x_{17,16}, x_{19,18}$ and $x_{20,19}$, is not positive.

67: $\sum a_{IJ} x_{IJ} \le 42$, where $a_{23,22} = 2$, $a_{26,25} = 0$, all other $a_{IJ} = 1$ except $a_{IJ} = 0$ if x_{IJ} is a non-basic variable and either (a) I is in S_3, J not in S_3, or (b) I or J is 10, 21, 25, 26, 27, or 28.‡

These two inequalities are satisfied by all tours. For example, if a tour were to violate the first one, it must have successively $x_{15,14} = 1$, $x_{18,16} = 1$, but also $x_{19,18} = 1$, a contradiction. The argument that each tour satisfies the second inequality is similar. If a tour x exists with $\sum a_{IJ} x_{IJ} > 42$, then clearly $x_{23,22} = 1$, and also $x_{10,9} = x_{29,28} = 1$, since by (a) these are the only links connecting S_3 and $\bar{S}_3$ having non-zero a_{IJ}. (See Fig. 17 to distinguish between basic and non-basic variables.) Moreover, since $a_{26,25} = 0$, it follows from (b) that $x_{25,10} = x_{25,24} = x_{27,26} = x_{28,26} = 1$. Again, (b) and the fact that $x_{28.21} = 0$ imply $x_{21,20} = x_{22,21} = 1$. Now look at city 27. There are three possibilities: $x_{27,24} = 1$, $x_{27,22} = 1$, or $x_{28,27} = 1$. But each of these contradicts the assumption that x is a tour.

These relations were imposed to cut out fractional solutions which satisfy all the conditions (2) and (4). A picture of such a fractional solution, which gives a smaller value for the minimizing form than does any tour, is shown in Fig. 18. Notice that it does not satisfy relation 67.

We assert that if the weights π_I are assigned to these restraints in the order presented above, then the values as given in Fig. 17 satisfy $\delta_{IJ} = 0$ for all variables x_{IJ} in the basis. With these values of π_I in the expression for $D(x) - D(\bar{x})$, all $\delta_{IJ} \le 0$ corresponding to variables x_{IJ} and

---

† $\sum_{S, \bar{S}} x_{IJ}$ means the sum of all variables where only one of the subscripts I or J is in S. $\sum_S x_{IJ}$ means the sum of all variables such that I and J are in S—see relations (4), (5), (6).

‡ We are indebted to I. Glicksberg of Rand for pointing out relations of this kind to us.

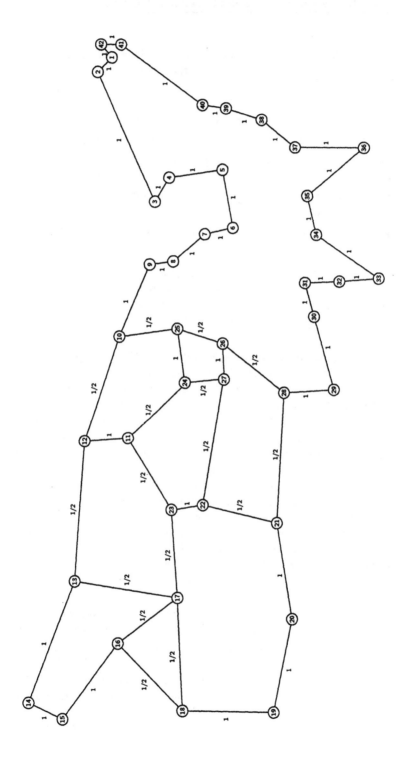

FIGURE 18. A fractional solution x satisfying all loop conditions with $\sum d_{IJ}x_{IJ} = 698$.

π_{43}, π_{44}, $\cdots$, π_{67} corresponding to variables y_{43}, y_{44}, $\cdots$, y_{67} are appropriately positive or negative (positive if its y occurs with a minus sign in the relation, negative otherwise) with the exception of $\pi_{52} = 1/2$ where $x_{25,24} + y_{52} = 1$. This proves, since $E = 1/2$ and all the d_{IJ} are integers, that $\bar{x}$ is minimal. The length $D(\bar{x})$ is 699 units, or 12,345 miles except for rounding errors.

It can be shown by introducing all links for which $\delta \geq -1/2$ that $\bar{x}$ is the unique minimum. There are only 7 such links in addition to those shown in Fig. 17, and consequently all possible tying tours were enumerated without too much trouble. None of them proved to be as good as $\bar{x}$.

CONCLUDING REMARK

It is clear that we have left unanswered practically any question one might pose of a theoretical nature concerning the traveling-salesman problem; however, we hope that the feasibility of attacking problems having a moderate number of points has been successfully demonstrated, and that perhaps some of the ideas can be used in problems of a similar nature.

REFERENCES

[1] W. W. R. BALL, *Mathematical Recreations and Essays*, as rev. by H. S. M. Coxeter, 11th ed., Macmillan, New York, 1939.

[2] G. B. DANTZIG, *The Generalized Simplex Method for Minimizing a Linear Form under Linear Inequality Restraints*, Rand Research Memorandum RM-1264 (April 5, 1954).

[3] G. B. DANTZIG, "Application of the Simplex Method to a Transportation Problem," *Activity Analysis of Production and Allocation*, T. C. Koopmans, Ed., Wiley, New York, 1951.

[4] I. HELLER, "On the Problem of Shortest Path Between Points," I and II (abstract), *Bull. Am. Math. Soc.* **59**, 6 (November, 1953).

[5] T. C. KOOPMANS, "A Model of Transportation," *Activity Analysis of Production and Allocation*, T. C. Koopmans, Ed., Wiley, New York, 1951.

[6] H. W. KUHN, "The Traveling-Salesman Problem," to appear in the *Proc. Sixth Symposium in Applied Mathematics* of the American Mathematical Society, McGraw-Hill, New York.

[7] D. F. VOTAW AND A. ORDEN, "Personnel Assignment Problem," *Symposium on Linear Inequalities and Programming*, Comptroller, Headquarters U. S. Air Force (June 14–16, 1951).

[8] J. VON NEUMANN, "A Certain Zero-sum Two-person Game Equivalent to the Optimal Assignment Problem," *Contributions to the Theory of Games II*, Princeton University Press, 1953.[d]

[9] W. T. TUTTE, "On Hamiltonian Circuits," *London Mathematical Society Journal* XXI, Part 2, No. 82, 98–101 (April, 1946).

[10] S. VERBLUNSKY, "On the Shortest Path Through a Number of Points," *Proc. Am. Math. Soc.* II, 6 (December, 1951).

Chapter 17

ON THE MAX-FLOW MIN-CUT THEOREM OF NETWORKS

G.B. Dantzig and D.R. Fulkerson

Introduction

The problem discussed in this paper arises naturally in the study of transportation networks. Roughly stated, it is as follows. Consider a network connecting two nodes by way of a number of intermediate nodes, and suppose the arcs and nodes can handle certain designated amounts of traffic per unit time. Assuming a steady state condition, find a maximal flow of traffic from one given node (the source) to the other (the sink).

For example, let the network be that of Figure 1

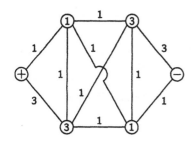

Figure 1

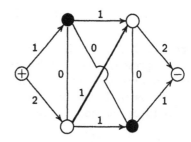

Figure 2

where the source and sink are denoted by + and − respectively, with flow capacities of the arcs and nodes as indicated. A maximal flow from source to sink is shown in Figure 2. Notice that the quantity of flow leaving the source (or entering the sink) is equal to the sum of capacities of the two nodes and one arc which are emphasized in the figure, and that this collection of nodes and arcs forms a "cut" in the network; i.e., meets every chain from source to sink.

A nonconstructive proof based on convexity arguments has been given in an unpublished manuscript[a] by L.R. Ford, Jr. and one of the present writers (D.R. Fulkerson) that the maximal flow value, relative to a given source and sink, attainable in any network is equal to the minimal sum of capacities on arcs and nodes constituting a cut. Our aim is to formulate the problem of finding a maximal flow as a linear programming problem (§1) and to deduce the max flow min cut theorem from the dual problem (§3). In §4 we observe that a combinatorial form of this theorem yields Menger's theorem [5, p. 244] concerning linear graphs.[b]

§1. The Programming Problem

There various ways of formulating the flow problem as a linear programming problem. One way[1], convenient from both a computational and theoretical viewpoint, is as follows. Set up the pseudo transporation array

$$
\begin{array}{cccccc}
 & & & & & \text{Totals} \\
\begin{bmatrix}
-x_{00} & x_{01} & x_{01} & \cdots & x_{0n} \\
x_{10} & -x_{11} & x_{12} & \cdots & x_{1n} \\
x_{20} & x_{21} & -x_{22} & \cdots & x_{2n} \\
\vdots & \vdots & \vdots & \ddots & \\
x_{n0} & x_{n1} & x_{n2} & & -x_{nn}
\end{bmatrix}
& \begin{matrix} 0 \\ 0 \\ 0 \\ \vdots \\ 0 \end{matrix}
\end{array}
$$

Totals   0   0   0 $\cdots$ 0

schematizing the equations

(1a) $$-x_{ii} + \sum_{j,\, j \neq i} x_{ij} = 0 \qquad (i = 0, 1, \ldots, n)$$

(1b) $$-x_{jj} + \sum_{i,\, i \neq j} x_{ij} = 0 \qquad (j = 0, 1, \ldots, n),$$

where $x_{ij} \geq 0$ $(i, j = 1, \ldots, n;\ i \neq j)$ denotes the flow from node i to node j, x_{ii} represents the total flow through not i, $x_{0j} \geq 0$ $(j = 1, \ldots,)$ is the flow from the source to node j, and $x_{i0} \geq 0$ is the flow from node i to the sink. Thus x_{00} is the total flow through the network and the problem is to maximize x_{00} subject to (1a), (1b), and

(2) $$x_{ij} + x_{ji} \leq c_{ij} \qquad (c_{ij} = c_{ji})$$

$$x_{ii} \leq c_{ii}$$
(3) $$x_{i0} \leq c_{i0} \qquad (i, j = 1, \ldots, n),$$
$$x_{0j} \leq c_{j0}$$

(4) $$x_{ij} \geq 0 \qquad (i, j = 1, \ldots, n),$$

---

[1]A. Hoffman has given a different formulation of the problem which also yields the max flow min cut theorem. While the techniques employed in his approach are similar to those of this paper, he uses an entirely different set of variables which are of interest in themselves.

where the c's are given non-negative constants. We have formally included all variables x_{ij} in the problem; arcs not present in the network have $c_{ij} = 0$.

Because of (2), we refer to this as the undirected problem: that is, except for source and sink arcs, the direction of flow is not specified in the arcs.

Given an undirected problem, it is easy to describe an equivalent directed problem. Simply replace each undirected arc by a pair of oppositely directed arcs, each with capacity equal to that of the original arcs. That the two problems are equivalent follows from the fact that given any $x = (x_{ij})$ satisfying (1), (3), (4) and

$$
(2') \qquad \begin{aligned} x_{ij} &\le c_{ij} \\ x_{ji} &\ge c_{ji} \end{aligned} \qquad (c_{ij} = c_{ji})
$$

a flow x' of equal value is obtained by setting

$$
\begin{aligned}
x'_{i0} &= x_{i0} & (i = 0, \ldots, n) \\
x'_{0j} &= x_{0j} & (j = 0, \ldots, n) \\
x'_{ij} &= \max\left(x_{ij} - x_{ji},\ 0 \right) & (i, j = 1, \ldots, n) \\
x'_{ii} &= \sum_{\substack{j=1 \\ j \ne i}}^{n} \min\left(x_{ij},\ x_{ji} \right) & (i = 1, \ldots, n)
\end{aligned}
$$

Thus (2) may be replaced by $(2')$ without changing the value of a maximal flow.

A cut in an undirected network has been defined as a collection of arcs and nodes meeting every chain joining source and sink; a cut in a directed network is similarly defined as a collection of directed arcs and nodes meeting every directed chain from source to sink. The value of a cut in either case is the sum of the capacities of all its member nodes and arcs. One proves easily that the minimal cut value is the same for an undirected network and its equivalent directed network. Thus, to prove the max flow min cut theorem, it suffices to consider directed networks only. Accordingly, we shall make no further use of the condition $c_{ij} = c_{ji}$ in $(2')$.

Let us now rewrite the inequalities $(2')$, (3), as

$$
(5) \qquad x_{ij} + y_{ij} = c_{ij}, \quad y_{ij} \ge 0 \quad (i, j = 0, 1, \ldots, n)
$$

where, to avoid special cases, we have included a sufficiently large upper bound of c_{00} on the variable; for example, choose

$$
c_{00} > \sum_{i=1}^{n} c_{i0}.
$$

Then the problem is to maximize x_{00} subject to (1a), (1b), (4), and (5).

§2. Bases

We turn momentarily to the question of what constitutes a basis,[2] in order to note that the Hitchcock-Koopmans transportation theory carries over to the flow problem.

There are $(n+1)^2 + 2(n+1) - 1$ linearly independent equations in the set (1a), (1b), (5), since one of the set (1a), (1b), is redundant. Drop the first equation of (1a) as the redundant one, and denote by X_{ij}, Y_{ij} the column vectors of the coefficient matrix of the remaining equations corresponding to the variables x_{ij}, y_{ij}, respectively.

It is clear that at least one of X_{ij}, Y_{ij} must belong to any basis B. Thus the pairs ij fall into one of three classes:

$$\alpha : \quad \text{those } ij \text{ for which } X_{ij} \in B, \quad Y_{ij} \in B;$$
$$\beta : \quad \text{those } ij \text{ for which } X_{ij} \in B, \quad Y_{ij} \notin B;$$
$$\gamma : \quad \text{those } ij \text{ for which } X_{ij} \notin B, \quad Y_{ij} \in B.$$

The number of pairs ij of type α is always $2n + 1$. For if there are k of type α, hence $(n+1)^2 - k$ of types β and γ, then $2k + (n+1)^2 - k = (n+1)^2 + 2(n+1) - 1$, $k = 2n + 1$. Moreover, it is impossible to find among the pairs of type α a subset of the form

$$i_1 j_1, \; i_1 j_2, \; i_2 j_2, \; i_2 j_3, \; \ldots, \; i_k j_k, \; i_k j_1$$

where the i's and j's are distinct among themselves, as otherwise the column vectors X_{ij}, Y_{ij} corresponding to these pairs can easily be shown to be dependent.

These two statements together imply that B can be arranged in triangular form, just as in the Hitchcock-Koopmans case. To see this, it is convenient to associate a linear graph G with B, and to look at the problem of finding the basic solution corresponding to B in terms of this graph.[3]

---

[2] Let $\sum_{j=1}^{n} a_{ij} x_j = b_i$, $x_j \geq 0$ $(i = 1, \ldots, m)$ be the constraints of a linear programming problem, and suppose $A = (a_{ij})$ has rank m. A set of m linearly independent columns of A is a "basis", the corresponding x_j are "basic variables". The vector $\hat{x} = (\hat{x}_1, \ldots, \hat{x}_n)$ obtained by assigning non-basic variables zero values is called a "basic solution." If $\hat{x}$ has non-negative components, it is termed a "basic feasible solution". Geometrically, basic feasible solutions correspond to extreme points of the convex set defined by the constraints.

[3] There are several alternative ways one can view the equation-solving process in terms of a linear graph. Since the equations came from such a graph, one way would be to use the original network. This appears to be most efficient for hand-computation. Another way, in terms of the array (1), can be developed as in [3]. A third way, the one we adopt, is suggested as in [2]. In all of these, the notion of "basis" in the programming sense is closely related to the notion of "tree" in the graph sense.

Let $a_0, \ldots, a_n, b_0, \ldots, b_n$ be the nodes of G; the arcs of G are those $a_i b_j$ for which ij is of type α. As we have seen, G has $2n+1$ arcs containing no cycles. It is therefore a tree. Call a node of G which has only once arc on it an "end-node." There are at least two such.

We associate with node $a_i(b_j)$ of G the equation

$$-x_{ii} + \sum_{j,\, j \neq i} x_{ij} = 0 \quad \left(-x_{jj} + \sum_{i,\, i \neq j} x_{ij} = 0 \right).$$

Now locate an end-node, say a_k, and let its arc be $a_k b_\ell$. Since for pairs ij of type β, $y_{ij} = 0$, $x_{ij} = c_{ij}$, and similarly $x_{ij} = 0$, $y_{ij} = c_{ij}$ for pairs of type γ, all the variables of the equation

$$-x_{kk} + \sum_{j,\, j \neq k} x_{kj} = 0$$

are determined but one, $x_{k\ell}$, and thus its value may be found immediately. Then use (5) to get $y_{k\ell} = c_{k\ell} - x_{k\ell}$. Delete a_k and $a_k b_\ell$ from G, leaving a tree, and repeat the procedure. After $2n+1$ steps, the values of all variables are determined.

Notice that only addition and subtraction are required. Thus, if the c_{ij} are integral, so are the values of all variables in the basic solution, hence in a basic feasible solution. We will make use of this fact in the concluding section.

§3. Simplex Criterion and the Dual Problem

Let u_i, v_j, w_{ij} be the multipliers (dual variables) corresponding to the equations (1a), (1b), (5), respectively, in applying the simplex algorithm. Then the conditions for an optimal basis B^* are:

(6a) $-u_i - v_i + w_{ii} \geq \delta_{i0}$ ($\delta_{00} = 1$, $\delta_{i0} = 0$ for $i > 0$)

(6b) $u_i + v_j + w_{ij} \geq 0$ ($i \neq j$)

(6c) $w_{ij} \geq 0$

with equality holding in (6a), (6b), if the corresponding $X_{ij} \in B^*$, in (6c) if $Y_{ij} \in B^*$. Ignoring the redundant equation amounts to taking $u_0 = 0$. Then, since $X_{00}, Y_{00} \in B^*$,[4] $w_0 0 = 0$, $v_0 = -1$. For all other pairs ij of type α, $w_{ij} = 0$, and the equations $u_i + v_j = 0$ hold. It follows that all $u_i = 0$ or 1, all $v_j = 0$ or -1. (A convenient way to see this is to associate the variable $u_i(v_j)$ with the node $a_i(b_j)$ of the graph G^* corresponding to

---

[4]Our choice of c_{00} implies that $Y_{00} \in B$ for any B yielding a basic feasible solution; also clearly $X_{00} \in B^*$ except possibly in the trivial case where the maximal flow over the network is zero. The assertion is valid in general, however, as otherwise all multipliers have zero value, violating (6a) with $i = 0$.

B^* and the equations $u_i + v_j = 0$ to the arcs of G^*.) Substituting these values into (6a), (6b), to determine the w_{ij} corresponding to $Y_{ij} \notin B^*$ and noting (6c) shows that all $w_{ij} = 0$ or 1.

The dual programming problem is to minimize $\sum c_{ij} w_{ij}$ subject to (6a) – (6c), and the multipliers corresponding to an optimal primal solution solves the dual problem. Thus

$$\text{(7)} \qquad\qquad \max x_{00} = \min \sum c_{ij} w_{ij} = \sum_\sigma c_{ij}$$

where σ is that set of pairs ij corresponding to $w_{ij} = 1$; in terms of the network, σ is some subset of those (directed) arcs and nodes which are at capacity in the flow x. We claim that σ is a cut. For suppose all c_{ij}, $ij \notin \sigma$, are increased by $\epsilon > 0$. This does not change the solution to the dual, hence cannot increase the flow in the network. But if there were some directed chain from source to sink not meeting σ, the maximal flow value would be increased by at least ϵ. Thus σ is a cut, and since it is clear that no flow can exceed the value of any cut, the proof of the max flow min cut theorem is complete.

§4. Menger's Theorem

Given an arbitrary linear graph G, let I_1. I_2 be two disjoint sets of nodes of G. Menger's theorem states that the maximal number of pairwise node-disjoint chains joining I_1 to I_2 is equal to the minimal number of nodes necessary to separate I_1 from I_2. To deduce this theorem from the max flow min cut theorem, join all the nodes of I_1 to a new node, the sink; then assign unit capacity to each of the old nodes, infinite capacity to each arc. Menger's theorem now follows by selecting a maximal flow x with integral components.

Bibliography

[1] DANTZIG, G. B., "Application of the simplex method to a transportation problem," *Activity Analysis of Production and Allocation*, Cowles Commission monograph No. 13, T. C. Koopmans, Ed., John Wiley & Sons, Inc., New York, (1951), pp. 359–373.

[2] KOOPMANS, T. C., and REITER, S., "A model of transportation," *Activity Analysis of Production and Allocation*, Cowles Commission monograph No. 13, T. C. Koopmans, Ed., John Wiley & Sons, Inc., New York, (1951), pp. 222–259.

[3] FLOOD, M. M., "On the Hitchcock distribution problem," *Pac. Jour. Math.* 3, No. 2 (1953), pp. 369–386.

[4] HITCHCOCK, F. L., "The distribution of a product from several sources to numerous localities," *Jour. Math. Physics* 10 (1941), pp. 224–230.

[5] KÖNIG, D., *Theorie der Endlichen und Unendlichen Graphen*, Chelsea Publishing Co., New York, 1956.

G. B. Dantzig
D. R. Fulkerson

The RAND Corporation

Chapter 18

ON THE SHORTEST ROUTE THROUGH A NETWORK

GEORGE B. DANTZIG

The RAND Corporation

The chief feature of the method is that it fans out from the origin working out the shortest path to one new node from the origin and never having to backtrack. No more than $n(n-1)/2$ comparisons are needed to find the shortest route from a given origin to all other nodes and possibly less between two fixed nodes.

Except for details and bias of various authors towards a particular brand of proof, *this problem has been solved the same way by many authors.* This paper *refines* these proposals to give what is believed to be the shortest procedure for finding the shortest route when it is little effort to arrange distances in increasing order by nodes or to skip consideration of arcs into nodes whose shortest route to the origin has been determined earlier in the computation.

In practice the number of comparisons is much less than indicated bounds because *all* arcs leading to nodes previously evaluated are deleted from further consideration. A further efficiency can be achieved in the event of ties by including least distances from origin to many nodes simultaneously during the fanning out process. However, these are shown as separate steps to illustrate the underlying principle.

The purpose of this paper is to give what is believed to be the shortest procedure for obtaining the shortest route from a given origin to all other nodes in the network or to a particular destination point. The method can be interpreted as a slight refinement of those reported by Bellman, Moore, Ford, and the author in [1], [2], [3], [4], and those proposed by Gale and Fulkerson in informal conversations.[a] It is similar to Moore's method of fanning out from the origin. However, its special feature—which is believed to be new—is that the fanning out is done one point at a time and the distance assigned is final.

It is assumed (a) that one can write down without effort for each node the arcs leading to other nodes in increasing order of length and (b) that it is no effort to ignore an arc of the list if it leads to a node that has been reached earlier. It will be shown that no more than $n(n-1)/2$ comparisons are needed in an n-node network to determine the shortest routes from a given origin to all other nodes and less than half this number for a shortest route to [a] particular node. The basic idea is as follows:

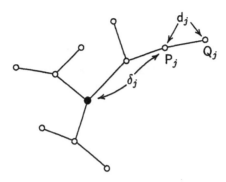

FIG. 1

Suppose at some stage k in the computing process the shortest distances to k of the nodes from some origin are known as well as the paths. Call the set of these points S.

(1) Let P_j be one of the nodes in S,
(2) let δ_j be its least distance to the origin •,
(3) let Q_j be the nearest node to P_j not in S,
(4) let d_j be the distance from P_j to Q_j.

Choose as the $k+1$ point, Q_s, where s satisfies

$$\delta_s + d_s = \min(\delta_j + d_j) \qquad\qquad j = 1, 2, \cdots, k$$

The minimum distance of Q_s to the origin is $\delta_s + d_s$ and the best path to the origin is via P_s. The reason is obvious, for if the best path from Q_s were via some other j in S or via several other points not in S and then via some other j in S, then the distance is at least $\delta_j + d_j \geq \delta_s + d_s$. In case of ties for minimum, several such nodes Q_s could be determined at the same time and the process made more efficient.

It will be noted that the minimum requires only k comparisons for a decision as to the $k+1$st point. Hence in an n node network no more than

$$1 + 2 + \cdots + (n - 1) = n(n - 1)/2$$

comparisons are needed.

In practice the number of comparisons can be considerably less than this bound because after several stages one or more of the nodes in S have only arcs leading to points in S [in the 8-node example below only a total of 16 comparisons was needed instead of $7 \times 8/2 = 28$ comparisons].

If the problem is to determine only the shortest path from a given origin to a given terminal, the number of comparisons may often be reduced by fanning out from the origin and the terminal simultaneously—adding alternatively one point at a time to sets S about the origin and S' about the terminal.

Once the shortest distance from a node to origin is evaluated, the node is conceptually connected directly to the origin by a hypothetical arc with the specified shortest distance and disconnected from all arcs leading to other nodes evaluated earlier. Nodes whose shortest distance to the terminal which have been determined are similarly treated. Once the origin is reached by either fanning system the process terminates.

Example

Distances on links of the network are as indicated.

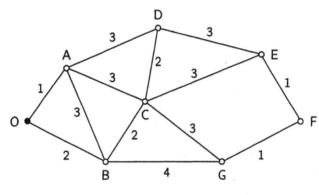

FIG. 2

Arrange in ascending order the nodes by distances to a given node

(O)	(A)	(B)	(C)	(D)	(E)	(F)	(G)
OA-1	AB-3	BC-2	CB-2	DC-2	EF-1	FE-1	GF-1
OB-2	AC-3	BA-3	CD-2	DA-3	EC-3	FG-1	GC-3
	AD-3	BG-4	CA-3	DA-3	ED-3		GB-4
			CG-3				
			CE-3				

Step 1. *Choose path* OA; place its distance 1 above A column, delete all arcs *into* A.

Step 2. Compare OB-2 and AB-(3 + 1) and *choose path* OB: place its distance 2 above B column, delete all arcs *into* B.

Step 3. Compare AC-(3 + 1), AD-(3 + 1), BC-(2 + 2), and because of ties *choose paths* AC (*or* BC) *and* AD; place distance 4 above C column, delete all arcs *into* C *and* D.

Step 4. Compare BG-(4 + 2), CG-(3 + 4), DE-(3 + 4) and *choose path* BG, place its distance 6 above G column, delete all arcs *into* G.

Step 5.   Compare CE-(3 + 4), DE-(3 + 4), GF-(1 + 6) and *choose path* CE (*or* DE), GF; place distance 7 above E and F columns, delete all arcs *into* E *and* F.

Step 6.   Compare EF-(1 + 7), GF-(1 + 6) and *choose path* GF, place its distance 7 above F column, delete all arcs *into* F.

Because of ties many of the steps were carried on simultaneously.

The shortest paths from the origin to other nodes are along paths OA, OB, AC, AD, BG, CE, GF with alternative BC for AC and DE for CE.

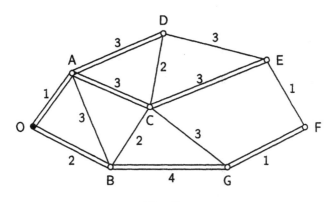

FIG. 3

References

[1] BELLMAN, RICHARD, "On a Routing Problem," *Q. Appl. Math.,* Vol. XVI, No. 1, April 1958, pp. 87–90.

[2] DANTZIG, GEORGE B., "Discrete Variable Extremum Problems," *JORSA,* Vol. 5, No. 2, April 1957, pp. 266–277.

[3] MOORE, E.F., "The Shortest Path Through a Maze," unpublished mimeographed report, 16 pages.[b]

[4] FORD, L. R. JR., "Network Flow Theory," RAND Paper P-923, 1956.

Part VII: Integer Programming and Linear Inequalities

This part contains only two papers, one on integer linear programming, the other on a method of solving linear inequalities. At first blush, the grouping may seem somewhat artificial, but, as should become clear, that would not be an entirely correct interpretation.

Linear programming problems in which all (or some of the) variables must be integers are called (mixed) integer linear programs. The inclusion of integrality as a restriction on variables places these optimization problems in a different—and generally much more difficult—class. On a certain level, integer programs would seem to have much in common with systems of diophantine equations; these have a very long history going back to ancient times. Some of this history is briefly summarized by Alexander Schrijver in *Theory of Linear and Integer Programming* (Chichester: John Wiley & Sons, 1986). Yet despite more than two millenia of interest in the subject, little of what has come down to us from before the mid-1950s is used in solving integer programs.

The paper on integer linear programming chosen for this part is "On the Significance of Solving Linear Programming Problems with Some Integer Variables." This is not George Dantzig's only publication on this subject, nor is it his first. Indeed, it can be said that the 1954 paper by Dantzig, Fulkerson, and Johnson (Chapter 16) on the traveling salesman problem contains elements of integer programming through the introduction of what are called valid inequalities. Dantzig advanced more ideas along these lines in a solely authored note published in 1959.

What is distinctive about the present integer programming paper (Chapter 19) is its exclusive focus on the *formulation* of difficult combinatorial problems as linear programs in which at least some of the variables are required to have integer values. This article was written during a time when activity in the integer linear programming field was in its infancy. It is evident that the writings of Martin Beale and Ralph Gomory had a stimulating effect on George Dantzig. In this paper, after plugging the work of Beale and Gomory, Dantzig brings his modeling ingenuity to bear on "a host of difficult, indeed seemingly impossible, problems of a nonlinear, nonconvex, and combinatorial character." One might expect such a paper to have appeared in a mathematics journal, but it did not. Instead, this article went to *Econometrica*, as a sequel to an earlier integer programming paper published there by Harry Markowitz and Alan Manne.

The paper "Fourier-Motzkin Elimination and its Dual" by George Dantzig and Curtis Eaves, is dedicated to the memory of Theodore S. Motzkin, a leading investigator of the theory of inequalities in modern times. Motzkin's inaugural dissertation "Beiträge zur Theorie der linearen Ungleichungen" (Contributions to the Theory of Linear Inequalities) anticipated the development of linear programming by about fourteen years. This scholarly and systematic work investigates several topics; one of them is the question of solvability or unsolvability of linear inequality systems.[1] Motzkin's dissertation includes a technique for determining whether a given system of this type has a solution. As he notes, this approach can be traced to , Fourier (1823), Dines (1918), and Stokes (1931). (See the comments in the Editor's Notes to Chapter 20.) Using this method, one eliminates variables individually but is left with a larger number of linear inequalities in fewer variables.

In their paper, Dantzig and Eaves review the Fourier-Motzkin elimination procedure and a theorem on necessary and sufficient conditions for the existence of a solution to a linear inequality system (the proof of which is attributable to Harold Kuhn), and then derive Motzkin's Transpositionssatz (op. cit. Satz D 6, p. 51), which deals with a pair of linear homogeneous systems. Roughly speaking, the theorem states that exactly one of the systems has a solution. Because of their connection with the theory of dual linear programs, these inequality systems have come to be called dual systems (Motzkin called them "komplementär").

A salient feature of a pair of dual systems is that there is a one-to-one correspondence between the variables of one system and the linear inequalities of the other (which system comes first is immaterial from this standpoint). Each step of the Fourier-Motzkin elimination procedure yields a "reduced system" as described above. For this new system, there is a corresponding dual system. By virtue of the previously mentioned one-to-one correspondence, it is reasonable to imagine a procedure that begins with the dual system, eliminates one of its constraints, and introduces more variables along with corresponding coefficients in the linear system. This view of the procedure is what Dantzig and Eaves call the dual of Motzkin elimination. What is remarkable about this is that they apply it to schemes for generating all integer solutions of a linear program with integer data.

---

[1] It is interesting to speculate about what might have happened if Motzkin had known about the linear programming problem in 1933. It seems safe to say he would have developed duality theory and then made the observation that solving a linear program (and its dual) is tantamount to solving an appropriate system of linear inequalities.

Chapter 19

ON THE SIGNIFICANCE OF SOLVING LINEAR PROGRAMMING PROBLEMS WITH SOME INTEGER VARIABLES

By George B. Dantzig

Recent proposals by Gomory and others for solving linear programs involving integer-valued variables appear sufficiently promising that it is worthwhile to systematically review and classify problems that can be reduced to this class and thereby solved. Historically, nonlinear, nonconvex and combinatorial problems are areas where classical mathematics almost always fails. It is therefore significant that the reduction can be made for problems involving multiple dichotomies and k-fold alternatives which include problems with discrete variables, nonlinear separable minimizing functions, conditional constraints, global minimum of general concave functions and combinatorial problems such as the fixed charge problem, traveling salesman problem, orthogonal latin square problems, and map coloring problems.

RECENTLY R. Gomory developed a theory of automatically generating "cutting planes" which permits efficient solution of linear programs in integers in a finite number of steps [7]. This approach has been generalized to a case where some variables are continuous and some are constrained to be integers, by E. M. L. Beale [1], and in a more direct way by Gomory [8], see also [3]. Small scale test problems have been successfully computed. The procedure is so promising that it is relevant to review systematically and to classify problems that can be reduced to this class. We shall show that a host of difficult, indeed seemingly impossible, problems of a nonlinear, nonconvex, and combinatorial character are now open for direct attack.

The cutting plane approach was first proposed and its power demonstrated by successfully solving an example of a large scale traveling salesman problem by Fulkerson, Johnson, and the author [5]. Markowitz and Manne explored this technique further in [10] and pointed out how it could be applied to solve problems involving nonlinear objective forms (separable in the variables but not convex).

In Section 1 we shall give a general description of the cutting plane approach and then describe the principles for solving several general problems. In the later sections these principles will be applied to several well-known problems. The outline for the paper is as follows:

1. GENERAL PRINCIPLES

(a) *The Method.* The cutting plane method consists in first solving the linear programming problem without the integer constraints. If the optimum solution happens to satisfy these conditions, all is well. If not, then additional linear inequality constraints (called cutting planes) are added to the system in such a way as to remove the non-admissible extreme point solution and yet retain all admissible solutions (e.g., those having integer values). In principle, that this could be done has been known for some time. For example, a plane that does through all neighboring vertices of the non-admissible extreme point can be used as a cutting plane in the case where all variables must have values 0 or 1. Such a procedure, however, has been regarded as probably too slow, and actual problems until recently were solved using more efficient cutting planes whose validity depended on special arguments. This weakness has been overcome by the recent proposals which generate cutting planes in an efficient manner. It is the author's belief that now it is only a matter of time before a subroutine for integer and partial integer solutions will be part of electronic computer simplex codes.

Let us now turn to the main subject of this paper: types of problems that are reducible to linear programs some or all of whose variables are integer-valued.

Quite often in the literature papers will appear which formulate a problem in L.P. (linear programming) form except for certain side conditions such as $x_1 \cdot x_2 = 0$, or the sum of terms of this type such as $x_1 \cdot x_2 + x_3 \cdot x_4 = 0$, which imply for nonnegative variables that at least one variable in each pair must be zero. Superficially this seems to place the problem in the area of quadratic programming. However the presence of such conditions can change entirely the character of the problem (as we shall see in a moment) and should serve as a warning to those who would apply willy-nilly a general nonlinear programming method. If we graph (as below) the conditions $x_1 \cdot x_2 = 0$, $x_1 \geq 0$, $x_2 \geq 0$, $x_1 + x_2 \geq 1$, the double lines depict the domain of feasible solutions. It will be noted that this domain has *two disconnected parts*. If there are many such *dichotomies* in a larger problem, the result can be a domain of feasibles solution with many disconnected parts or connected nonconvex regions. For example, k pairs of variables in which one is zero might lead to 2^k disconnected parts. Usual mathematical approaches can guarantee at best a local optimum solution to such problems, i.e., a solution which is optimum only over some connected convex part.

It has been well known that by special devices the local optimum solutions could be avoided in many cases by the introduction of integer-valued variables, but this has only been of passing interest until the recent developments rendered this approach practical. Our purpose here will be to systematize this knowledge.

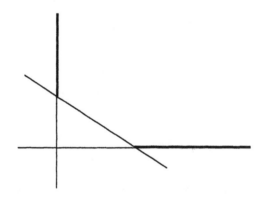

(b) *Dichotomies.* Let us begin with the important class of problems that have "*either-or*" conditions. For such a problem to be computationally difficult, there must be many sets of such conditions. Let us focus our attention on one of them, say either

(1) $\qquad\qquad\qquad G(x_1, x_2, \ldots, x_n) \geq 0$

or

(2) $\qquad\qquad\qquad H(x_1, x_2, \ldots, x_n) \geq 0$

must hold for values of $(x_1, x_2, \ldots, x_n)$ chosen over some set S. We do not exclude the case of both holding if this is possible. For example, a contractor in a bid might stipulate either $x_1 \geq \$10,000$ or $x_1 = 0$. If all bids are nonnegative so that $x_1 \geq 0$, then we can write either

$$x_1 - 10{,}000 \geq 0$$

or

$$- x_1 \qquad\qquad \geq 0$$

From other considerations it may be known that no bid can exceed \$1,000,000 so that the set S of interest is $0 \leq x_1 \leq 1{,}000{,}000$.

We now assume that lower bounds for the functions G and H are known for all values of $(x_1, x_2, \ldots, x_n)$ in S. If L_G is a lower bound for G, and L_H for H, then for $\delta = 1$ the condition

$$(3) \qquad\qquad G(x_1, x_2, \ldots, x_n) - \delta L_G \geq 0$$

holds for all values of $(x_1, x_2, \ldots, x_n)$ in S. Similarly for $\delta = 0$ the condition

$$(4) \qquad\qquad H((x_1, x_2, \ldots, x_n) - (1 - \delta)L_H \geq 0$$

holds for all values of $(x_1, x_2, \ldots, x_n)$ in S. For our example we would have

$$x_1 - 10{,}000 - \delta(-10{,}000) \geq 0$$

and

$$-x_1 - (1 - \delta)(-1{,}000{,}000) \geq 0.$$

The *either-or* condition (1, 2) can now be replaced by

$$(5) \qquad\qquad G(x_1, x_2, \ldots, x_n) - \delta L_g \geq 0,$$
$$(6) \qquad\qquad H(x_1, x_2, \ldots, x_n) - (1 - \delta)L_H \geq 0,$$
$$(7) \qquad\qquad\qquad\qquad 0 \leq \delta \leq 1,$$

where δ is an integer variable. The effect of $\delta = 1$ is to *relax* the G condition when H holds and of $\delta = 0$ is to *relax* H when G holds. If G and H are linear functions we have reduced the *either-or* condition to three simultaneous linear inequalities in which the variable δ must be 0 or 1.

A dichotomy can be used to describe an L-shaped region (nonconvex); for example, $x_1 \geq 0$; $x_2 \geq 0$; $x_1 \leq 2$; $x_2 \leq 2$; and *either* $x_1 \leq 1$ *or* $x_2 \leq 1$. We replace this by

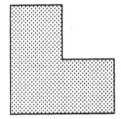

$$0 \leq x_1 \leq 1 + \delta,$$
$$0 \leq x_2 \leq 2 - \delta,$$
$$0 \leq \delta \leq 1 \quad (\delta = 0, 1)$$

If now a problem contains not one but several such pairs of dichotomies (1) and (2), each one would be replaced by a simultaneous set (5), (6), (7) in integer variables δ_i.

(c) *k-fold Alternatives.* More generally suppose we have a set of conditions

(8)
$$G_1(x_1, x_2, \ldots, x_n) \geq 0,$$
$$G_2(x_1, x_2, \ldots, x_n) \geq 0,$$
$$\vdots$$
$$G_p(x_1, x_2, \ldots, x_n) \geq 0.$$

Suppose a solution is required in which at least k of the conditions must hold simultaneously. We replace (8) by

(9)
$$G_1(x_1, x_2, \ldots, x_n) - \delta_1 L_1 \geq 0,$$
$$G_2(x_1, x_2, \ldots, x_n) - \delta_2 L_2 \geq 0,$$
$$\vdots$$
$$G_p(x_1, x_2, \ldots, x_n) - \delta_p L_p \geq 0.$$

Where L_i is the lower bound for $G_i(x)$ for $x = (x_1, x_2, \ldots, x_n)$ in S, and δ_i are integer-valued variables satisfying

(10)
$$\delta_1 + \delta_2 + \cdots + \delta_p = p - k$$

and

(11)
$$0 \leq \delta_i \leq 1.$$

An example of this type of problem might occur if one wishes to find the minimum over the shaded regions described by $G_1 \geq 0$, $G_2 \geq 0, G_3 \geq 0$, and at least two of the conditions $G_4 \geq 0$, $G_5 \geq 0$, $G_6 \geq 0$ as in (12).

(12)
$$G_j = G_j(x).$$

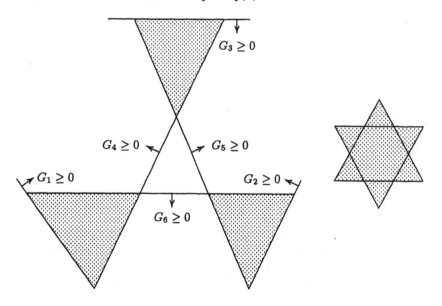

(d) *Selection from Many Pairs of Regions.* The six-pointed "Star of David" region shown on the right in (12) can best be described by a dichotomy in which a point must be taken from one of two triangles. It is only when there are many such pairs to be chosen at the same time that the problem becomes significant. In general we might have several pairs of regions $(R_1, R_1'), (R_2, R_2'), \ldots, (R_n, R_n')$, and the solution point x must lie in *either R_i or R_i'* for each i. For each pair R and R' we proceed as follows. Let region R be described by a set of inequalities $G_1(x) \geq 0, G_2(x) \geq 0, \ldots, G_n(x) \geq 0$, and R' by $H_1(x) \geq 0, H_2(x) \geq 0, \ldots, H_n(x) \geq 0$. The condition that the point must selected from either the first or second region can be written

$$
\begin{aligned}
G_1(x) - \delta L_1 \geq 0, &\qquad H_1(x) - (1-\delta)L_1' \geq 0, \\
G_2(x) - \delta L_2 \geq 0, &\qquad H_2(x) - (1-\delta)L_2' \geq 0,
\end{aligned}
$$

(13)

$$
\vdots
$$

$$
\begin{aligned}
G_n(x) - \delta L_n \geq 0, &\qquad H_n(x) - (1-\delta)L_n' \geq 0, \\
0 \leq \delta \leq 1 \quad (\delta = 0 \text{ or } 1),
\end{aligned}
$$

where L_i, L_i' are lower bounds for G_i and H_i. The more general case of selection from several regions can be done by introducing several δ_i as in (10) and (11).

(e) *Discrete Variable Problems.* Suppose that a variable is constrained to take one of several values: $x_1 = a_1$ or $x_1 = a_2$, ... or $x_1 = a_k$ and at the same time several other variables are also constrained in the same way. It would be a formidable task to test all the combinations. Instead we replace each k-fold dichotomy by

(14)
$$
x_1 = a_1\delta_1 + a_2\delta_2 + \cdots + a_k\delta_k,
$$

(15)
$$
\delta_1 + \delta_2 + \cdots + \delta_k = 1, \quad (\delta_j = 0 \text{ or } 1).
$$

Similarly let $x = (x_1, x_2, \ldots, x_n)$ represent a vector which may only take on specified vector values $x = a^1$ or $x = a^2$, or $x = a^3 \ldots$ This may be replaced by

(16)
$$
x = a^1\delta_1 + a^2\delta_2 + \cdots + a^k\delta_k,
$$

(17)
$$
\delta_1 + \delta_2 + \cdots + \delta_k = 1, \quad (\delta_j = 0 \text{ or } 1).
$$

This device permits the replacement of a nonlinear function $F_{ij} = F_{ij}(x_j)$, in a system $\sum_{j=1}^{n} F_{ij}(x_j) = 0$ for $(i = 1, 2, \ldots, m)$, by a sprinkling of representative values of x_j, say $x_j = x_j^r$ where $r = 1, 2, \ldots, k$. In this case the vector is the set of values $(F_{1j}, F_{2j}, \ldots, F_{mj})$ for some value $x_j = x_j^r$.

(f) *Nonlinear Objective Problems.* Suppose the objective form can be written [a]

$$(18) \qquad \sum_{j=1}^{n} \varphi_j(x_j) = z \text{ (Min)}$$

where φ_j is nonlinear and nonconvex. Let each $\varphi(x)$ be approximated by a broken line function. These define a set of intervals $i = 1, 2, \ldots, k$ of width h_i and slopes s_i for the approximating chords. We now define y_i as the amount of overlap of the interval from 0 to x with interval i.[b] Then

$$(19) \qquad x = y_1 + y_2 + \cdots + y_k$$

and $\varphi(x)$ is given approximately by

$$(20) \qquad \varphi(x) \doteq b_0 + s_1 y_1 + s_2 y_2 + \cdots + s_k y_k$$

where

$$(21) \qquad 0 \le y_i \le h_i \qquad\qquad (i = 1, 2, \ldots, k)$$

In the case of *convex* φ, the procedure is to replace x and $\varphi(x)$ by (19) and (20) and conditions (21). Here the slopes are monotonically increasing so that

$$(22) \qquad s_1 \le s_2 \le \cdots \le s_k.$$

For a fixed x, $\varphi(x)$ would be minimum if y_1 is chosen maximum and if for y_1 maximum, y_2 is chosen maximum, etc. In other words for the minimizing solution the y_i's are the overlap of the ith interval with the interval 0 to x and all is well.

However if $\varphi(x)$ is *not convex* as in (27), then simple replacement of x and $\varphi(x)$ would result for fixed x in y_i with smaller slopes being maximized first. In this case the segments that comprise y_i would be disconnected and our approximation for $\varphi(x)$ would no longer be valid.[c] It is clear however that the figure labeled here as (27) is what was intended. In order to avoid this we impose the condition that

$$(23) \qquad \text{either} \quad h_i - y_i = 0 \quad \text{or} \quad y_{i+1} = 0,$$

which implies that unless y_i is maximum, $y_{i+1} = 0$, and if y_i is maximum, then $y_{i+1} > 0$ is possible. We rewrite this condition

$$(24) \qquad \text{either} \quad y_i - h_i \ge 0 \quad \text{or} \quad -y_{i+1} \le 0,$$

and then replace it formally by

(25)
$$\begin{cases} y_i - h_i - (-h_i)\delta_i \geq 0 \qquad\qquad (i = 1, 2, \ldots, k-1), \\ -y_{i+1} - (-h_{i+1})(1 - \delta_i) \geq 0, \\ 0 \leq \delta_i \leq 1 \quad \delta_i = 0 \text{ or } 1. \end{cases}$$

Upon substitution of $\delta_i' = 1 - \delta_i$ (25) simplifies to

(26)
$$\begin{cases} y_i \geq h_i\delta_i', \\ y_{i+1} \leq h_{i+1}\delta_i', \\ 0 \leq \delta_i' \leq 1 \qquad (\delta_i' = 0, 1) \end{cases}$$

The above procedure for the nonconvex case was discussed in the paper of Markowitz and Manne and Markowitz [10]. The convex case will be found in [4] and [2].

(27)

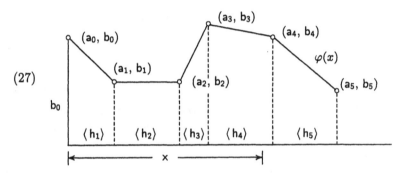

A second method based on (16) is worth noting. Any point on the curve $\varphi(x)$ can be represented as a weighted average of two *successive* breakpoints. Hence we may replace x and $\varphi(x)$ by

(28)
$$\begin{cases} x = \lambda_0 a_0 + \lambda_1 a_1 + \cdots + \lambda_k a_k \qquad (0 \leq \lambda_i \leq 1), \\ \varphi(x) = \lambda_0 b_0 + \lambda_1 b_1 + \cdots + \lambda_k b_k, \\ 1 = \lambda_0 + \lambda_1 + \cdots + \lambda_k, \end{cases}$$

and then impose the conditions that all $\lambda_i = 0$ except for one pair λ_i and λ_{i+1}. For $k = 4$ this may be expressed by

(29)
$$\begin{aligned} \lambda_0 &\leq \delta_0, \\ \lambda_1 &\leq \delta_0 + \delta_1, \\ \lambda_2 &\leq \quad\;\; \delta_1 + \delta_2, \\ \lambda_3 &\leq \quad\qquad \delta_2 + \delta_3, \\ \lambda_4 &\leq \quad\qquad\quad\; \delta_3 + \delta_4, \\ \lambda_5 &\leq \quad\qquad\qquad\quad\; \delta_4, \end{aligned}$$

where the δ_i are integer-valued variables satisfying

(30)
$$\delta_0 + \delta_1 + \delta_2 + \delta_3 + \delta_4 + \delta_5 = 1 \qquad (\delta_i = 0, 1).$$

Indeed it will be noted that when $\delta_{i_0} = 1$ for some $i = i_0$, the inequalities involving λ_{i_0} and λ_{i_0+1} are relaxed, but the remainder satisfy $\lambda_i \leq 0$ since their $\delta_i = 0$ by (30).

(g) *Conditional Constraints.* Suppose x and y are functions of several variables $(x_1, x_2, \ldots, x_n)$ for which upper bounds U_x and lower bounds L_x and L_y are known. We wish to impose condition such as

$$(31) \qquad\qquad x > 0 \Longrightarrow y \geq 0.$$

We can write this as

$$(32) \qquad\qquad \text{either} \quad x > 0, \; y \geq 0 \quad \text{or} \quad x \leq 0$$

which we rewrite as

$$(33) \qquad \begin{cases} x \geq \delta L_x, \\ y \geq \delta L_y, \\ x \leq (1 - \delta) U_x \quad (\delta = 0, 1), \end{cases}$$

where the first inequality is written ($\geq$) instead of ($>$) because the condition $y \geq 0$ is automatically relaxed for $x = 0$ by selecting $\delta = 1$.

We can now elaborate this to impose conditions such as

$$(34) \qquad\qquad \begin{aligned} x > 0 &\Longrightarrow u \geq 0, \\ x < 0 &\Longrightarrow w \geq 0, \end{aligned}$$

which may be written as

$$(35) \qquad \begin{aligned} x &\geq \delta_1 L_x, \\ u &\geq \delta_1 L_u, \\ x &\leq \delta_2 U_x, \\ w &\geq \delta_2 L_w, \\ \delta_1 + \delta_2 &= 1 \quad (\delta_i = 0, 1) \end{aligned}$$

For example, suppose in a T-period program we wish to complete a specified work load by the earliest period possible. Let x_t be the cumulative sum of activity levels from the tth period through the last period T; then we wish to arrange matters so that $x_t = 0$ for the smallest t. In this case we can define for $t = 1, 2, \ldots, T$

$$(36) \qquad\qquad \delta_t = 0 \Longrightarrow x_t = 0$$

which we may rewrite as

$$(37) \qquad\qquad x_t \leq \delta_t U_t \quad (\delta_t = 0, 1)$$

where U_t is an upper bound for x_t, and determine Min z where

$$(38) \qquad\qquad z = \delta_1 + \delta_2 + \cdots + \delta_T.$$

(h) *Finding a Global Minimum of a Concave Function.*[1] Suppose the concave function $Z = Z(x_1, x_2, \ldots, x_n)$ is to be minimized over a region R. We shall assume R convex for convenience here, noting that the devices discussed earlier extend the domain to the wide class expressible by *either-or* conditions. We suppose R to be given, after a suitable change in variables, in standard linear programming form

$$(39) \qquad\qquad Ex = e, \quad x \geq 0$$

where E is a given $m \times n$ matrix and e a given m-component vector.

This is intrinsically a difficult problem because the concave function could have local minima at many, indeed at *all*, the extreme points of R.

The concave function Z may be given explicitly or be given implicitly. For example, suppose vector y and quantity z for *fixed* x is given by

$$(40) \qquad \begin{aligned} Fy &= f + \bar{E}x, \quad y \geq 0, \\ z &= ax - \operatorname*{Min}_{y|x} \beta y, \end{aligned}$$

where $\bar{E}$ and F are given matrices and f, a, and β are given vectors. This is the situation discussed in the application of these methods to [6]. Here, however, we shall suppose that Z can reasonably be approximated at all points x in R by the minimum Z of a *finite set of k tangent planes*,

$$(41) \qquad Z = a_{i1}x_1 + a_{i2}x_2 + \cdots + a_{in}x_n - b_i \qquad (i = 1, 2, \ldots, k),$$

to the surface $Z = Z(x)$. The problem reduces to choosing min Z where Z must satisfy at least one of the conditions

$$(42) \qquad \begin{aligned} Z - [a_{11}x_1 + a_{12}x_2 + \cdots + a_{1n}x_n - b_1] &\geq 0, \\ Z - [a_{21}x_1 + a_{22}x_2 + \cdots + a_{2n}x_n - b_2] &\geq 0, \\ \vdots \\ Z - [a_{k1}x_1 + a_{k2}x_2 + \cdots + a_{kn}x_n - b_k] &\geq 0, \end{aligned}$$

which we may rewrite as

$$(43) \qquad \begin{aligned} Z - [a_{i1}x_1 + a_{i2}x_2 + \cdots + a_{in}x_n] &\geq -M\delta_i \quad (i = 1, 2, \ldots, k), \\ \delta_1 + \delta_2 + \cdots + \delta_k &= 1 \quad (\delta_i = 0 \text{ or } 1) \end{aligned}$$

where $-M$ is some assumed lower bound for the differences. This solution depends on the approximation of the function $Z = Z(x)$ by k hyperplanes.

---

[1] This application developed jointly with Philip Wolfe.

The solution given in [6], for the case where Z is given implicitly by (40), requires finding x, y, min z, and auxiliary variables $\pi = (\pi_1, \pi_2, \ldots, \pi_m)$ and $\eta_j \geq 0$, for $j = 1, 2, \ldots, n'$ satisfying

$$Ex = e, \quad Fy = f + \bar{E}x, \quad z = \alpha x - \beta y,$$
(44)
$$\pi F_j + \eta_j = \beta_j \qquad (j = 1, 2, \ldots, n'),$$
$$\text{either} \quad \eta_j \leq 0 \text{ or } \quad y_j \leq 0,$$

where $\pi = (\pi_1, \pi_2, \ldots, \pi_{m'})$ is a row vector, F_j is the jth column of F, and β_j is the jth component of β.

2. FIXED CHARGE PROBLEM

Earlier we described a problem required that either the order $x = 0$ or $x \geq a$. In this and many other problems there is an underlying notion of a fixed charge that is independent of the size of the order. In this case $x = a$ represents the break-even point to the bidder. In general the cost C is characterized by

(45)
$$C = \begin{cases} kx + b & \text{if } x > 0 \\ 0 \end{cases}$$

where b is the fixed charge. We may write this in the form

(46)
$$C = kx + \delta b \quad (\delta = 0, 1)$$

where $x = 0$ if $\delta = 0$, which we impose by

(47)
$$x \leq \delta U$$

and

(48)
$$0 \leq \delta \leq 1 \quad (\delta = 0, 1),$$

where U is some upper bound for x. A discussion of the fixed charge problem including this device will be found in the paper by Warren Hirsch and the author [9].

3. THE TRAVELING SALESMAN PROBLEM

We shall give two formulations of this well-known problem. Let $x_{ijt} = 1$ or 0 according to whether the tth directed arc on the route is from node i to node j or not. The conditions

(49)
$$\sum_{i,j} x_{ijt} = 1 \qquad (t = 1, 2, \ldots, n)$$

(50) $$\sum_{j,t} x_{ijt} = 1 \qquad\qquad (i = 1, 2, \ldots, n)$$

(51) $$\sum_{i,t} x_{ijt} = 1 \qquad\qquad (j = 1, 2, \ldots, n)$$

(52) $$\sum_{i,j} d_{ij} x_{ij} = z \text{ (Min)}$$

express that (1) there is only one tth directed arc, (2) there is one directed arc leaving node i, (3) there is only one directed arc into node j, and (4) the length of the tour is minimum. It is not difficult to see that an integer solution to this system is a tour.

In the paper by Fulkerson, Johnson, and the author the case of a symmetric distance $d_{ij} = d_{ji}$ was formulated with only two indices. Here $x_{ij} = x_{ji} = 1$ or 0 according to whether the route from i to j or from j to i was traversed at some time on a route or not. The conditions

(53) $$\sum_{i} x_{ij} = 2 \qquad\qquad (j = 1, 2, \ldots, n)$$

(54) $$\sum_{i,j} d_{ij} x_{ij} = z \text{ (Min)}$$

express the condition that the sum of the number of entries and departures from each node is two. These conditions are not enough to characterize a tour even though the x_{ij}'s are restricted to be integers in the interval,

(55) $$0 \le x_{ij} \le 1,$$

since sub-tours like

(56)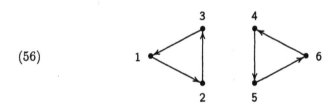

also satisfy the conditions. However if so-called loop conditions discussed in [5] like

(57) $$x_{12} + x_{23} + x_{31} \le 2$$

are imposed (in the same manner that cutting planes are introduced as required), these will rule out integer solutions which are not admissible.

4. THE ORTHOGONAL LATIN SQUARE PROBLEM[2]

A latin square consists of n sets of objects (1), (2), ..., (n) assigned to an $n \times n$ square array so that no object is repeated in any row or column. Two latin squares are orthogonal such as

(58)
$$
\begin{array}{ccc}
(1)\ (2)\ (3) & : & (2)\ (3)\ (1) \\
(2)\ (3)\ (1) & : & (1)\ (2)\ (3) \\
(3)\ (1)\ (2) & . & (3)\ (1)\ (2)
\end{array}
$$

if the n^2 pairs of corresponding entries are all different. It was conjectured by Euler[d] that there are no orthogonal latin squares for certain n. In spite of a great deal of research by leading mathematicians, the case for $n = 10$, has never been settled. It has been suggested informally by David Gale that the proposed method be tried in this area.

The formulation is straightforward and well known. Let $x_{ijkl} = 0$ or 1 according to whether the pair (i,j) is assigned to row k, column l or not. The condition that the pair is assigned to only one location is given by

(59)
$$\sum_{k,l} x_{ijkl} = 1 \qquad (i,j = 1,2,\ldots,n).$$

The condition that at least one is assigned to each location k, l is:

(60)
$$\sum_{k,l} x_{ijkl} = 1.$$

The conditions that i and j appear only once in the first and second latin square respectively in column l is given by

(61)
$$\sum_{j,k} x_{ijkl} = 1 \qquad (i,l = 1,2,\ldots,n),$$
$$\sum_{i,k} x_{ijkl} = 1 \qquad (j,l = 1,2,\ldots,n).$$

Similarly, the conditions that i and j appear only once in the first and second latin square respectively in row k is given by

(62)
$$\sum_{j,l} x_{ijkl} = 1 \qquad (i,k = 1,2,\ldots,n),$$
$$\sum_{i,l} x_{ijkl} = 1 \qquad (j,k = 1,2,\ldots,n).$$

[2]Recently R. C. Bose and S. S. Shrikhande proved that Euler's famous conjecture about the non-existence of Orthogonal Latin Squares of certain even orders was *false*. E. T. Parker has constructed a pair of Orthogonal Latin Squares of order 10. For further information the reader is referred to Abstract 558-27 of the August 1959 Notices of the American Mathematical Society.

It is interesting to note that every pair of subscripts that is possible out of four are summed to form each of the six sets of n^2 equations. For $n = 10$ there are 600 equations, which are too many for a general linear programming code to handle at the present time. With some short cuts introduced, however, it might be tractable in the near future.

5. FOUR-COLORING A MAP (IF POSSIBLE)[e]

A famous unsolved problem is to prove or disprove that any map in the plane can be colored using at most four colors so no two regions having a boundary in common (other than a point) have the same color. We shall give two ways to color constructively a particular map, if possible. This does not contribute anything to a proof of the truth or falsity of that conjecture except that an efficient way for solving particular problems on an electronic computer may provide a counter example.

Without difficulty it can be arranged (as below) so

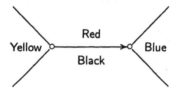

that three regions have at most one point in common which will be called a node. There will be, accordingly, three directed arcs leading from any node i to other nodes j. It is well known that if it is possible to four-color a map then (and this will be true conversely) it is possible to treat the nodes as cities and the arcs as routes between cities and be able either to make a tour of all the cities or to make a group of mutually exclusive sub-tours of the cities in several *even* (sub-cycle) loops as shown below.

We may associate with each such even cycle sub-tour, directed arcs that reverse their direction as we pass from node to node.

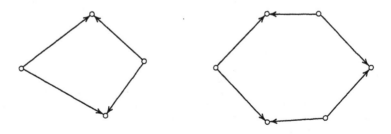

This means the nodes i can be classified into two classes: those which have two arcs pointing away from them and those that have two arcs pointing towards them. Let us set $x_{ij} = 1$ if an arc is part of a sub-tour in the direction of the arrow; otherwise $x_{ij} = 0$. Hence

(63) $$0 \leq x_{ij} \leq 1.$$

It is understood that only arcs (i, j) and variables x_{ij} are considered corresponding to regions that have a boundary in common. All arcs (i, j) that do not correspond to boundaries are omitted in the constraints.

The conditions

(64) $$\sum_j x_{ij} = 2\delta_i \quad (\delta_i = 0, 1)$$

express the fact that there must be two arcs on some sub-tour leading away from node i if $\delta_i = 1$; otherwise there are none. The conditions

(65) $$\sum_i x_{ij} = 2 - 2\delta_i$$

state there must be two arcs on some sub-tour leading into node i if $\delta_i = 0$, and otherwise none. The three sets of conditions (63), (64), and (65) are those of a *bounded transportation problem* and will be integers (at an extreme point) if δ_i are integers. This would seem to imply that it is only necessary to assume that the δ_i are integers and the x_{ij}'s will come out automatically integral in an extremizing solution without further assumptions. Since the objective form is open to choice by choosing it in a nondegenerate way, however, it is clear that the extreme point solution with integral x_{ij}'s would be determined by the process.

A second formulation suggested informally by R. Gomory is straightforward. Let the regions be $r = 1, 2, \ldots, R$, and let t_r be an integer-valued variable such that

$$0 \leq t_r \leq 3,$$

the four values $t = 0, 1, 2, 3$ corresponding to the four colors. If regions r and s have a boundary in common, their colors must be different. Hence for each such pair

(66) $$t_r - t_s \neq 0.$$

This may be written in *either-or* form:

(67) $$\text{either} \quad t_r - t_s \geq 1 \quad \text{or} \quad t_s - t_r \geq 1$$

which we may rewrite as

$$
(68) \quad
\begin{aligned}
t_r - t_s &\geq 1 - 4\delta_{rs} \quad (\delta_{rs} = 0, 1) \\
t_s - t_r &\geq -3 + 4\delta_{rs}.
\end{aligned}
$$

The RAND Corporation

REFERENCES

[1] BEALE, E. M. L.: "A Method of Solving Linear Programming Problems when some but not all of the Variables must take Integral Values," *Statistical Research Group,* Princeton, approximate date March 1958.

[2] CHARNES, ABRAHAM AND CARLETON E. LEMKE: "Minimization of Non-linear Separable Convex Functionals," *Naval Research Logistics Quarterly,* Vol. 1, No. 4, December 1954, pp. 301–312.

[3] DANTZIG, GEORGE B.: *On Integer and Partial Integer Linear Programming Problems,* The RAND Corporation, Paper P-1410, June 20, 1958.

[4] DANTZIG, GEORGE B.: "Recent Advances in Linear Programming," *Management Science,* Vol. 2, No. 2, January 1956, pp. 131–144.

[5] DANTZIG, GEORGE B., D. R. FULKERSON AND SELMER JOHNSON: "Solution of a Large-Scale Traveling-Salesman Problem," *Journal of the Operations Research Society of America,* November 1954, No. 4, pp. 393–410.

[6] DANTZIG, GEORGE B.: *Solving Two-Move Games with Perfect Information,* The RAND Corporation, Paper P-1459, August 11, 1958.

[7] GOMORY, RALPH: "Essentials of an Algorithm for Integer Solutions to Linear Programs," *Bulletin of the American Mathematical Society,* Vol. 64, No. 5, 1958.

[8] GOMORY, RALPH: Same subject as Reference 1. Paper in preparation based on research at the RAND Corporation, July 1958.

[9] HIRSCH, WARREN M. AND GEORGE B. DANTZIG: *The Fixed Charge Problem,* The RAND Corporation, Paper P-648, December 1, 1954.

[10] MARKOWITZ, H. M. AND A. S. MANNE: "On the Solution of Discrete Programming Problems," *Econometrica,* Vol. 25, No. 1, January 1957, p. 19.

Chapter 20

FOURIER-MOTZKIN ELIMINATION AND ITS DUAL [*]

GEORGE B. DANTZIG AND B. CURTIS EAVES

Department of Operations Research, Stanford University, Stanford, California 94305

DEDICATED TO THE MEMORY OF THEODORE S. MOTZKIN

Research on linear inequalities systems prior to 1947 consisted of isolated efforts by a few investigators. A good case in point is the elimination technique for reducing the number of variables in the system. A description of the method can be found in Fourier [1], Dines [2], and Motzkin [3]. It differs from its analog for systems of equations in that (unfortunately) each step in the elimination can greatly increase the number of inequalities in the remaining variables. For years the method was referred to as the *Motzkin* Elimination Method. However, because of the odd grave-digging custom of looking for artifacts in long forgotten papers, it is now known as the *Fourier-Motzkin* Elimination Method and perhaps will eventually be known as the *Fourier-Dines-Motzkin* Elimination Method.[a]

Given a system of inequalities: Find $x = (x_1, \ldots, x_n)$ such that[b]

$$(1) \qquad \sum_{j=1}^{n} a_{ij} x_j \geq b_i, \qquad i = 1, \ldots, m$$

One may partition it into three sets of inequalities according to whether the coefficients of x_1 are positive, negative, or zero. This permits rewriting (1) in the form:

$$(2) \qquad \begin{cases} x_1 \geq D_1(\bar{x}) \\ \vdots \\ x_p \geq D_p(\bar{x}) \end{cases} \begin{cases} x_1 \leq E_1(\bar{x}) \\ \vdots \\ x_q \leq E_q(\bar{x}) \end{cases} \begin{cases} 0 \geq F_1(\bar{x}) \\ \vdots \\ 0 \geq F_r(\bar{x}) \end{cases}$$

[*] Research and reproduction of this report was partially supported by the Office of Naval Research under contract N-00014-67-A-0112-001, U.S. Atomic Energy Commission Contract AT(0403) PA #18, National Science Foundation Grants GP 31393, and GP 34559, and Army Research Office—Durham DAHC-71-C-0041.

where $D_i(\bar{x})$, $E_j(\bar{x})$, $F_k(\bar{x})$ are linear functions of $\bar{x} = (x_2, \ldots, x_n)$. It may be solved by first solving the *reduced* system: Find $\bar{x}$ satisfying

(3)
$$D_i(\bar{x}) \leq E_j(\bar{x}) \quad i = 1, \ldots, p, \quad j = 1, \ldots, q, \quad k = 1, \ldots, r$$
$$0 \leq F_k(\bar{x}),$$

and then finding an x_1, satisfying

(4)
$$\max_i D_i(\bar{x}) \leq x_1 \leq \min_j E_j(\bar{x}),$$

where x_1 always exists providing there exists an $\bar{x}$ satisfying (3).

Proof. Given any $(x_1, \bar{x})$ satisfying (2), it is is clear that (3) and (4) must hold. Conversely, given any $\bar{x}$ satisfying (3), then $\max D_i(\bar{x}) \leq \min E_j(\bar{x})$ and we can always find an x_1 satisfying (4), hence $(x_1, \bar{x})$ satisfies (1).

System (3) is said to be the result of "eliminating" x_1 from system (2). If $p + q \leq 4$, the reduced system contains one less variable and no more inequalities. If $p > 2$, $q > 2$, $r = 0$, however, the process of elimination will greatly increase the number of inequalities. This is the chief reason given why it is not used as a practical solution method. It is worth noting, however, that (3) has special structure and that this might be used to advantage to develop it into a practical computational procedure.

Since (3) is a linear inequality system also, one could next proceed to eliminate x_2, etc., until one has eliminated all but a single variable, say x_n. The original system is solvable if and only if the final system $x_n \leq \alpha_i$, $x_n \geq \beta_j$, $0 \leq \gamma_k$ for $i = 1, \ldots, p'$, $j = 1, \ldots, q'$, $k = 1,, \ldots, r'$ is consistent, i.e., iff $\alpha_i - \beta_j \geq 0$ and $\gamma_k \geq 0$ for all i, j, k. Another way to state this is:

FEASIBILITY THEOREM. *A necessary and sufficient condition that system* (1) *is solvable, is there exist no set of weights* $(y_1 \geq 0, y_2 \geq 0, \ldots, y_m \geq 0)$ *such that*

(5)
$$\sum_{i=1}^{m} y_i b_i > 0 \quad and \quad \sum_{i=1}^{m} y_i a_{ij} = 0, \quad for \quad j = 1, \ldots, n.$$

Proof. Assume a solution x to (1) exists and there exists weights $y_i \geq 0$ satisfying (5); then (1) implies

(6)
$$\sum_{j=1}^{n} \left(\sum_{i=1}^{m} y_i a_{ij} \right) x_j \geq \sum_{i=1}^{m} y_i b_i, \quad y_i \geq 0,$$

or $0x \geq \sum y_i b_i > 0$, a contradiction. Thus the condition is necessary.

Assume no solution x to (1) exists; then note each system generated by the elimination process, for example (3) from (2), is formed by *nonnegative* linear combinations of the inequalities of the previous system which in turn were formed by nonnegative linear combinations of the system one before that, etc., back to the original system (1). Thus the condition for non-solvability, $\alpha_i - \beta_j < 0$ or $\gamma_k < 0$ for some i, j, or k (referred to earlier), could be derived directly by some nonnegative linear combination of the inequalities of the original system.

This remarkably simple proof[c] of the feasibility theorem based on Fourier-Motzkin elimination is due to Kuhn [4]. From it one can derive easily (by trivial algebraic manipulations) the fundamental Duality Theorem of linear programming, Farkas Lemma, the various theorems of the alternatives, and the well-known

MOTZKIN TRANSPORTATION THEOREM.[d] *Given the dual homogeneous linear program in partitioned form*

(7)
$$Primal : A_I x_I + A_{II} x_{II} = 0, \qquad (x_I, x_{II}) \geq 0,$$
$$Dual : \quad yA_I \leq 0, \qquad yA_{II} \leq 0,$$

then either there exists a solution to the dual such that $yA_I < 0$ (i.e., holds strictly in all components) or there exists a solution to the primal such that $x_I \neq 0$.

Proof. A solution to the dual such that $yA_I < 0$ implies there exists a y such that

(8)
$$yA_I \leq -e, \qquad e = (1, 1, \ldots, 1)$$
$$yA_{II} \leq 0.$$

If no such y exists satisfying (8), then by the feasibility theorem, there exists weights $x_I \geq 0$, $x_{II} \geq 0$ such that $A_I x_I + A_{II} x_{II} = 0$ and $-e^T x_I < 0$, i.e., $x_I \neq 0$.

THE DUAL OF FOURIER-MOTZKIN ELIMINATION.[e] Suppose we are given the homogeneous linear program

(9)
$$x_1 - D_i \bar{x} \geq 0 \quad i = (1, \ldots, p)$$
$$-x_1 + E_j \bar{x} \geq 0 \quad j = (1, \ldots, q)$$
$$F_k \bar{x} \geq 0 \quad k = (1, \ldots, r)$$

where $\bar{x} = (x_2, \ldots, x_n)$ and D_i, E_j, F_k are $1 \times n$.[f] The elimination of x_1 from (9) yields

(10)
$$(E_j - D_i)\bar{x} \geq 0, \qquad \text{for all } i, j$$
$$F_k \bar{x} \geq 0, \qquad \text{for all } k.$$

On the other hand the homogeneous dual of (9) is: to find $u_i \geq 0$, $v_j \geq 0$,

$w_k \geq 0$ such that

$$\text{(a)} \qquad \sum_{i=1}^{p} u_i - \sum_{j=1}^{q} v_j = 0,$$

(11)

$$\text{(b)} \qquad -\sum_{i=1}^{p} u_i D_i + \sum_{j=1}^{q} v_j E_j + \sum_{k=1}^{r} w_k F_k = 0;$$

and the homogeneous dual of (10) is: to find $\lambda_{ij} \geq 0$, $w_k \geq 0$ such that:

$$\text{(12)} \qquad \sum_{i=1}^{p} \sum_{j=1}^{q} \lambda_{ij}(E_j - D_i) + \sum_{k=1}^{r} w_k F_k = 0.$$

Since (9) and its eliminated form (10) are in a sense equivalent systems, it seems natural to expect that their duals (11) and (12) are also equivalent in the same sense; i.e., from any solution to (11) we can derive a solution to (12) and conversely. Note that (11) has n equations corresponding to the n components of x_j whereas (12) has $n - 1$ equations but would have (in general) far more variables. This suggests we have at hand a technique for reducing the number of equations in a linear program. Let us give a direct proof of this for the *non*-homogeneous system:

Find $u_i \geq 0$, $v_j \geq 0$, $w_k \geq 0$ satisfying:

$$\text{(a)} \qquad \sum_{i=1}^{p} u_i - \sum_{j=1}^{q} v_j = 0,$$

(13)

$$\text{(b)} \qquad -\sum_{i=1}^{p} u_i D_i + \sum_{j=1}^{q} v_j E_j + \sum_{k=1}^{r} w_k F_k = g.$$

Let us introduce pq new variables $\lambda_{ij} \geq 0$ by setting

$$u_i = \sum_{j=1}^{q} \lambda_{ij}, \qquad i = 1, \ldots, p,$$

(14)

$$v_j = \sum_{i=1}^{p} \lambda_{ij}, \qquad j = 1, \ldots, q.$$

Note that, if u_i and v_j satisfy (13a), it is always easy to find $\lambda_{ij} \geq 0$ satisfying (14). Even if $u_i \geq 0$ and $v_j \geq 0$ are constrained to be *integers*, it is easy to find *integer* $\lambda_{ij} \geq 0$ satisfying (14). Substituting (14) into (13) we note that (13a) is automatically satisfied and we obtain the reduced system:

Find $\lambda_{ij} \geq 0$, $w_k \geq 0$ such that

$$(15) \qquad \sum_{i=1}^{p} \sum_{j=1}^{q} \lambda_{ij}(E_j - D_i) + \sum_{k=1}^{r} w_k F_k = g.$$

Conversely note that, if we have a solution to (15), we can, by regrouping the terms and substituting u_i and v_j for the resulting expressions λ_{ij}, obtain a solution to (13). The solution will be in integers if λ_{ij} is integral.

To apply the technique to a system of equations in nonnegative variables, it is necessary to have one equation with a zero constant term to play the role of (13a) or to create an equation with a zero constant term by replacing one of the equations by some appropriate linear combination of the equations of the system. This will yield an equation of the form

$$(16) \qquad \sum_{i=1}^{p} \alpha_i u_i - \sum_{j=1}^{q} \beta_i v_j = 0, \qquad \alpha_i \geq 0, \quad \beta_j \geq 0,$$

and we could obtain a system of the form (13) by a change of units. This may conveniently be done by replacing (14) by

$$(17) \qquad \begin{aligned} \alpha_i u_i &= \sum_{j=1}^{q} \lambda_{ij}, \quad i = 1, \ldots, p, \\ \beta_j v_j &= \sum_{i=1}^{p} \lambda_{ij}, \quad j = 1, \ldots, q. \end{aligned}$$

where $\alpha_i \geq 0$, $\beta_j \geq 0$, $\lambda_{ij} \geq 0$, $u_i \geq 0$, $v_j \geq 0$.

APPLICATION OF THE DUAL OF THE MOTZKIN ELIMINATION TO INTEGER PROGRAMS: Given the system[g]

$$(18) \qquad \begin{aligned} \sum_{j=1}^{n} a_{ij}x_j &= b_i, \quad i = (1, \ldots, m) \\ x_j &\geq 0 \quad j = (1, \ldots, n) \end{aligned}$$

where the a_{ij}'s and b_i's are integer we describe two schemes, 1 and 2, for generating all solutions $x = (x_1, \ldots, x_n)$ which are integer, that is, have integer components. Scheme 1 requires that the a_{ij} be nonnegative, whereas Scheme 2 requires no additional assumptions.

Scheme 1 for Generating all Integer Solutions

First let us assume that system (18) is 0–1, that is, all a_{ij}'s and b_i's are 0 or 1; hence we can assume that all b_i's are 1, since otherwise, we obviously have an infeasible or redundant system.

If $m = 1$, the set of solutions is evident, if $a_{ij} = 1$ a typical solution is

$$
(19) \qquad x_i = \begin{cases} 1 & i = j \\ 0 & \text{if} \quad i \neq j \quad \text{and} \quad a_{1i} \neq 0. \\ \text{arbitrary} & a_{1i} = 0 \end{cases}
$$

Now assume $m > 1$. Subtract row one from row two to obtain an equation of the form

$$
(20) \qquad \sum_I x_i = \sum_J x_j \qquad I \cap J = \emptyset.
$$

Introduce the variables λ_{ij} for $(i, j) \in I \times J$ and replace x_i for $i \in I$ and x_j for $j \in J$ in the system (18) by

$$
(21) \qquad \begin{aligned} x_i &= \sum_{j \in J} \lambda_{ij} \\ x_j &= \sum_{i \in I} \lambda_{ij}. \end{aligned}
$$

If some λ_{ij} has a coefficient exceeding 1, clearly $\lambda_{ij} = 0$ in a solution. Finally delete the first row $(i = 1)$ in (18). We have now reduced the original 0–1 system in m rows to a 0–1 system in $m - 1$ rows. Repeating this process until there is but one row, then, by generating all solutions, and by back-substitution, one gets all solutions to the original system (18).

This scheme for the 0–1 system, if properly implemented, appears to yield a reasonable technique for enumerating all solutions (especially if there are not too many solutions and equations).

Scheme 2 for Generating all Integer Solutions

We suppose that the data of (18) is integer. Either some b_i is 0, or one can scale (with integers) rows one and two and subtract them to get an expression of form

$$
(22) \qquad \sum_{i \in I} \alpha_i x_i = \sum_{j \in J} \beta_j x_j \qquad I \cap J = \emptyset.
$$

Suppose for (22) that we have the following example:

$$
(23) \qquad (u_1 + 2u_2) - (v_1 + v_2 + v_3) = 0.
$$

Let us rewrite this

$$
(24) \qquad (u_1 + u_2 + u_3) - (v_1 + v_2 + v_3) = 0,
$$

where $u_2 = u_3$ and set as above[h]

(25)
$$u_i = \sum_{j=1}^{3} \lambda_{ij}, \quad i = 1, 2, 3,$$

$$v_j = \sum_{i=1}^{r} \lambda_{ij}, \quad j = 1, 2, 3.$$

The resulting integer reduced system is in $\lambda_{ij} \geq 0$ (as before) except that we have the additional condition $u_2 = u_3$ which, in terms of λ_{ij}, becomes

(26) $(\lambda_{21} + \lambda_{22} + \lambda_{23}) - (\lambda_{31} + \lambda_{32} + \lambda_{33}) = 0.$

But (26) is in *exactly* the form we need for the integer reduction. We accordingly can introduce additional integer variables $\mu_{ij} \geq 0$, where

(27)
$$\lambda_{2i} = \sum_{j=1}^{3} \mu_{ij}, \quad i = 1, 2, 3,$$

$$\lambda_{3j} = \sum_{i=1}^{3} \mu_{ij}, \quad j = 1, 2, 3.$$

Back-substituting into (25), we have the desired integer substitution in terms of 12 auxiliary variables:

(28)
$$u_1 = \sum_{j=1}^{3} \lambda_{1j},$$

$$u_2(= u_3) = \sum_{i=1}^{3} \sum_{j=1}^{3} \mu_{ij},$$

$$v_1 = \lambda_{11} + \sum_{j=1}^{3} \mu_{1j} + \sum_{i=1}^{3} \mu_{i1},$$

$$v_2 = \lambda_{12} + \sum_{j=1}^{3} \mu_{2j} + \sum_{i=1}^{3} \mu_{i2},$$

$$v_3 = \lambda_{13} + \sum_{j=1}^{3} \mu_{2j} + \sum_{i=1}^{3} \mu_{i3}.$$

By setting $\mu_{12} + \mu_{21} = \bar{\mu}_{12}$, $\mu_{13} + \mu_{31} = \bar{\mu}_{13}$, $\mu_{32} + \mu_{23} = \bar{\mu}_{23}$, we could simplify the above substitution to one involving nine nonnegative integer variables λ_{1i}, μ_{ii}, $\bar{\mu}_{ij}$, where $i, j = 1, 2, 3$ and $i \neq j$.

The problem in general of finding substitutions to replace (14) so as to reduce a linear system in nonnegative *integer* variables to few equations is under study and will be the subject of a subsequent paper.

APPENDIX

Our purpose here is to show that a system of form (18) where the a_{ij}'s and b_i's are nonnegative integers has an equivalent 0–1 system.

Consider the system with one equation:

$$4x + 3y + 2z = 6$$

(29)

$$x \geq 0, \ y \geq 0, \ z \geq 0$$

and the corresponding system in detached coefficient form:

(30)

$$
\begin{array}{cccccccccccc}
x_1 & x_2 & x_3 & y_1 & y_2 & y_3 & y_4 & z_1 & z_2 & z_3 & z_4 & z_5
\end{array}
$$

$$
\begin{bmatrix}
1 & 0 & 0 & 1 & 0 & 0 & 0 & 1 & 0 & 0 & 0 & 0 \\
1 & 1 & 0 & 1 & 1 & 0 & 0 & 1 & 1 & 0 & 0 & 0 \\
1 & 1 & 1 & 1 & 1 & 1 & 0 & 0 & 1 & 1 & 0 & 0 \\
1 & 1 & 1 & 0 & 1 & 1 & 1 & 0 & 0 & 1 & 1 & 0 \\
0 & 1 & 1 & 0 & 0 & 1 & 1 & 0 & 0 & 0 & 1 & 1 \\
0 & 0 & 1 & 0 & 0 & 0 & 1 & 0 & 0 & 0 & 0 & 1
\end{bmatrix}
=
\begin{bmatrix}
1 \\ 1 \\ 1 \\ 1 \\ 1 \\ 1
\end{bmatrix}
$$

$$x_i \geq 0, \ i = (1, \ldots, 3), \quad y_i \geq 0, \ i = (1, \ldots, 4), \quad z_i \geq 0, \ i = (1, \ldots, 5).$$

We will call (30) the 0–1 form of (29). Note that (30) is generated so that the number of equations, 6, is equal to the right-hand side of (29), and so that the column corresponding to x_i has 1's in positions i to $i + a$ where $1 + a = 4$ is the coefficient of x in (29), and $i = 1, \ldots, k$ where $k + a = 6$, etc., for y_i and z_i. One can readily see that if (20) is solved with integer x_i, y_i, and z_i's then

(31) $$x = \sum x_i, \quad y = \sum y_i, \quad z = \sum z_i$$

is an integer solution of (29). Further if (x, y, z) is an integer solution of (29) then there is an integer solution of (30) where (31) holds.

THEOREM. *The expanded 0–1 form of a linear equation with nonnegative integer data and variables is totally unimodular. All extreme solutions are integral.*

Proof. By totally unimodular we mean that each submatrix of the coefficient matrix (as that in (30)) had determinant 0 or ±1. Consider a submatrix, by subtracting row $j + 1$ from j for $j = 1, \ldots$, we get a network matrix; it is well known that such matrices are totally unimodular and the result follows. (Veinott and Wagner [5] made extensive use of this feature. Note that if we augment the system by including an $i = 0$ equation which is the negative sum of equations $i = 1, \ldots$, we see that a solution corresponds to a directed path from $i = 0$ to $i = 6$.)

Next consider the example

(32)
$$4x_1 + \sum_{i=2}^{n} a_i x_i = 6$$

$$1x_1 + \sum_{i=2}^{n} a_i x_i = 2.$$

One could proceed much as above to generate a 0–1 system for (32) as (30) was for (29). Here we get the detached coefficient formi0.8exi

(33)
$$
\begin{array}{c}
x_1 \; x_2 \; x_3 \; x_4 \; x_5 \; x_6 \\
\begin{bmatrix}
1 & 0 & 0 & 1 & 0 & 0 \\
1 & 1 & 0 & 1 & 1 & 0 \\
1 & 1 & 1 & 1 & 1 & 1 \\
1 & 1 & 1 & 1 & 1 & 1 \\
0 & 1 & 1 & 0 & 1 & 1 \\
0 & 0 & 1 & 0 & 0 & 1
\end{bmatrix}
\;+\cdots=\;
\begin{bmatrix}
1 \\ 1 \\ 1 \\ 1 \\ 1 \\ 1
\end{bmatrix}
\\[2ex]
\begin{bmatrix}
1 & 1 & 1 & 0 & 0 & 0 \\
0 & 0 & 0 & 1 & 1 & 1
\end{bmatrix}
\qquad\quad
\begin{bmatrix}
1 \\ 1
\end{bmatrix}
\end{array}
$$

$$x_i \geq 0 \quad i = (1, \ldots, 6)$$

These techniques of generating (30) and (33) from (29) and (32) can be applied in general to get a 0–1 system with integer $a_{ij} \geq 0$ and b_i. Observe that the derived 0–1 system can be arbitrary orders of magnitude larger than the original system. Unfortunately, it is easy to construct examples where (33) has nonintegral extreme points; hence (33) is not in general unimodular.

REFERENCES[j]

[1] J.B.J. FOURIER, Solution d'une question particulière du calcul des inégalités, (1826), and extracts from "Histoire de l'Académie" (1823, 1824), Oeuvres II, pp. 317–328 (French Academy of Sciences).

[2] L.L. DINES, Systems of Linear Inequalities, *Ann. of Math.* 20 (1918–1919), 191-199.

[3] T.S. MOTZKIN, Beiträge zur Theorie der linearen Ungleichungen, Doctoral Thesis, University of Basel, 1934.[k]

[4] H.W. KUHN, Solvability and Consistency for Linear Equations and Inequalities, *Amer. Math. Monthly* 43 (1956), 217–232.

[5] ARTHUR F. VEINOTT, JR. AND HARVEY M. WAGNER, Optimal Capacity Scheduling, *Operations Res.* 10 (1962), 518–532.

Part VIII: Nonlinear Programming

Nonlinear programming is concerned with continuous optimization problems in which there is a nonlinear element: in the objective function, in the constraints, or in both. Quadratic programming, the subject of the opening chapter of this part, deals with nonlinear programming problems that are arguably the closest in spirit to those of linear programming. One can rightly think of quadratic programming as an *extension* of linear programming. Indeed, this chapter is drawn from George B. Dantzig's seminal book *Linear Programming and Extensions* (the other chapters of this anthology are based on material published in scholarly journals). By definition, a quadratic programming problem calls for the minimization (or maximization) of a quadratic function with linear side conditions, that is, linear equations and/or linear inequalities.

Minimizing a function subject only to a system of equations is regarded as a classical problem that is often associated with the name of Joseph-Louis Lagrange (1736–1813). The problem of minimizing a quadratic function of variables required to satisfy a system of linear equations has long been a well understood special case. For instance, one finds key ideas on this in Harris Hancock's *Theory of Maxima and Minima* (1917), a paper by H. B. Mann (1943), Paul Samuelson's *Foundations of Economic Analysis* (1947), and a paper by Gerard Debreu (1952). During the twentieth century—certainly from the 1930s onward—researchers increasingly recognized the necessity of modeling optimization problems with unilateral (i.e., inequality) constraints, possibly in addition to equality constraints. In line with the paper "Nonlinear Programming" by Harold W. Kuhn and Albert W. Tucker in 1951, Robert M. Dorfman coined the term "quadratic programming" in his little monograph, *Application of Linear Programming to the Theory of the Firm*, based on his doctoral dissertation.

Unlike the linear programming problem, where an optimal solution (if one exists) can be sought among the *basic* solutions of the constraints, a nonlinear programming problem—and in particular a quadratic programming problem—can have a *nonbasic* optimal solution (only). What is special about a quadratic programming problem, as Edward Barankin and Robert Dorfman observed in 1958, is that if the problem has an optimal solution, then it is part (that is, a subvector) of a basic solution of the equations that arise as first-order necessary conditions of optimality for the problem. Because these conditions are mainly linear and need to be satisfied anyway, one is, at least in theory, brought back to finding basic solutions of a particular kind. This justifies the inclusion of quadratic programming among the extensions of linear programming.

Dantzig's "Quadratic Programming" is a product of the early 1960s. The algorithm it proposes was strongly influenced by two papers published a few years earlier by Harry Markowitz and Philip Wolfe (see Chapter 21 for details). At that stage, only *convex* quadratic programming problems were considered. The impact of Wolfe's "Simplex Method for Quadratic Programming" was especially notable, in part because its implementation as a computer program involved only a slight modification of an existing linear programming code, a definite advantage from the labor standpoint. Wolfe accomplished this by using what could be called a *restricted basis approach*, thereby pioneering the notion of "complementary pivoting." Yet Wolfe's algorithm suffered from separate treatment of the strictly convex and ordinary convex cases. Dantzig strove to remove these distinctions. He accomplished this, but in a limited way, by focusing on a special kind of convex quadratic function: one having no linear term, only a quadratic form. Minimizing a convex quadratic form on a nonempty polyhedral feasible set presents no difficulties regarding the *existence* of an optimal solution. When the objective function is of the standard type, that is, the sum of a linear form and a quadratic form, it is possible for the objective function to be unbounded below and hence for there to be no optimal solution to the problem. Dantzig (quite literally) left the treatment of this issue as an exercise. Independently, Andrew Whinston and Cornelius van de Panne published a paper in 1964 that did so with a simplex algorithm for quadratic programming that extends the one given here.

The second paper of this part is considerably more theoretical than the first, although the kind of information it seeks to provide is no less practical. Recognizing the obvious fact that an optimal solution to a mathematical programming problem will depend on the constraints of the problem and its objective function, one might naturally ask for insight on how the optimal solution would vary as the data that specify the problem are varied. Abstract as this investigation of stability may seem, it was nonetheless motivated by work on the chemical equilibrium problem (see Chapter 9) and has theoretical significance in that framework. But the problem of finding chemical equilibrium compositions is by no means the only potential area of application for the analysis presented in this paper. Economics and game theory are disciplines in which some of the same issues are encountered.

One of the technical matters that must be confronted in a study such as this is the very real possibility that an optimization problem might have multiple optima. Under such circumstances, asking for continuous variation of the *set* of optimal solutions calls for suitable machinery to give meaning to this process. The authors address these needs.

Chapter 21

24-4. QUADRATIC PROGRAMMING

Although a convex quadratic objective function can be treated by the methods of §24-1 and can be reduced to the convex separable case discussed in §24-3, the linear nature of its partial derivatives has given rise to an elegant theory important in its own right.[a] It is doubtful at this writing that the full potential of this theory has been realized.

Quadratic programs can arise in several ways; four listed by Wolfe in his [1959-1] paper are as follows:

Regression: To find the best least-squares fit to given data, where certain parameters are known a priori to satisfy linear inequalities constraints.

Efficient Production: Maximization of profit, assuming linear production functions and linearly varying marginal costs [Dorfman 1951-1].

Minimum Variance: To find the solution of a linear program with variable cost coefficients which will have given expected costs and minimum variance [Markowitz 1956-1, 1959-1].

Convex Programming: To find the minimum of a general convex function under linear constraints and quadratic approximation [White, Johnson, and Dantzig 1958-1].

Historically, it was Barankin and Dorfman [1958-1] who first pointed out that, if the linear Lagrangian conditions of optimality were combined with those of the original system, the optimum solution was a basic solution in the enlarged system with the property that only one of certain pairs of variables were in the basic set. Markowitz [1956-1, 1959-1], on the other hand, showed that it was possible to modify the enlarged system and then parametrically generate a class of basic solutions with the above special property which converged to the optimum in a finite number of iterations. Finally, Wolfe [1959-1] proved that an easy way to do this is by slightly modifying the simplex algorithm so as not to allow a variable to enter the basic set if its "complementary" variable is already in the set. Thus, by modifying a few instructions in a simplex code for linear programs, it was possible to solve a convex quadratic program! We shall present here a variant of Wolfe's elegant procedure. The chief difference is that ours is more nearly a strict analogue of the simplex method; it has a tighter selection rule and a monotonically decreasing objective.

Preliminaries.

Before stating the problem, let us note that every quadratic form can be conveniently expressed in terms of a *symmetric matrix* associated with its coefficients. For example, for $n = 3$ variables,

$$(1) \quad Q(x) = c_{11}c_1^2 + c_{22}x_2^2 + c_{33}x_3^2 + 2c_{12}x_1x_2 + 2c_{23}x_2x_3 + 2c_{13}x_1x_3$$

$$= [x_1, x_2, x_3] \begin{bmatrix} c_{11} & c_{12} & c_{13} \\ c_{12} & c_{22} & c_{23} \\ c_{13} & c_{23} & c_{33} \end{bmatrix} \begin{bmatrix} x_1 \\ x_2 \\ x_3 \end{bmatrix} = x^T C x$$

where T stands for *transpose*.

DEFINITION: A quadratic form is called *positive definite* if $x^T C x > 0$ for all $x \neq 0$; it is called *positive semi-definite* if $x^T C x \geq 0$ for all x.

Problem: Find $x = (x_1, x_2, \ldots, x_n) \geq 0$ and Min $Q(x)$ satisfying

$$(2) \qquad Ax = b \qquad\qquad A = [a_{ij}] \qquad\qquad (i = 1, 2, \ldots, m)$$
$$x^T C x = Q(x) \qquad\quad C = [c_{ij}] \qquad\qquad (j = 1, 2, \ldots, n)$$

where $Q(x)$ is a convex quadratic function.

LEMMA 1: $x^T C x$ *is convex if and only if it is positive semi-definite.*

PROOF: Assume $x^T C x$ is a convex function. To prove $x^T C x \geq 0$, suppose on the contrary that, $(x^0)^T C x^0 < 0$ for some $x = x^0$. Then for $x' = -x^0$, it is also true that $(x')^T C x' < 0$ and for any convex combination, x^*, of x^0 and x' we have $(x^*)^T C x^* < 0$ because $x^T C x$ is convex. In particular, for $x^* = \frac{1}{2}x^0 + \frac{1}{2}x'$ we have $(\frac{1}{2}x^0 + \frac{1}{2}x')^T C(\frac{1}{2}x^0 + \frac{1}{2}x') < 0$ or $(0)^T C(0) < 0$, a contradiction, since $\frac{1}{2}x^0 + \frac{1}{2}x' = 0$.

The convexity of a positive semi-definite form follows from Lemma 2 below because a linear transform, $\bar{x}$, of the variables x reduces $Q(x)$ to a sum of convex functions in $\bar{x}$.

LEMMA 2: *If $x^T C x$ is positive semi-definite, there exists a nonsingular matrix E such that a change of variables $x = E\bar{x}$ yields*

$$(3) \qquad\qquad x^T C x = \sum_1^n \lambda_j \bar{x}_j^2 \qquad\qquad (\lambda_j \geq 0)$$

where $\lambda_j \geq 0$ is the jth diagonal element of a diagonal matrix $E^T C E$.

PROOF: Select any variable, say x_1, with $c_{11} > 0$. (See first exercise below.) Express $Q(x)$ as a quadratic polynomial in x_1 and "complete the square"; thus

$$(4) \qquad x^T C x = c_{11} x_1^2 + 2 x_1 \sum_{j=2}^{n} c_{1j} + \sum_{i=2}^{n} \sum_{j=2}^{n} c_{ij} x_i x_j,$$

$$= \frac{1}{c_{11}} \left[\sum_{j=1}^{n} c_{1j} x_j^2 \right]^2 - \left[\sum_{j=2}^{n} c_{1j} x_j^2 \right]^2 + \sum_{i=2}^{n} \sum_{j=2}^{n} c_{ij} x_i x_j,$$

$$= \frac{1}{c_{11}} \bar{x}_1^2 + \sum_{i=2}^{n} \sum_{j=2}^{n} c'_{ij} x_i x_j$$

where $\bar{x}_1 = \sum_{j=1}^{n} c_{1j} x_j$ and $c'_{ij} = (c_{11} c_{ij} - c_{1i} c_{1j})/c_{11}$. The process may now be repeated using the quadratic expression in $(x_2, \ldots, x_n)$ on the right. The process terminates in $k \le n$ steps. Set $\bar{x}_j = x_j$ and $\lambda_j = 0$ for $j = k+1, \ldots, n$.

EXERCISE: Show that either $c_{11} > 0$ or all $c_{11} = c_{12} = \cdots c_{1n} = 0$ in a positive semi-definite quadratic form.

EXERCISE: Show that the determinants of all principal minors of C are positive if $Q(x)$ is positive definite, in particular $c_{11} > 0$.

EXERCISE: Show that if $k = n$, $Q(x)$ is positive definite; and that if $k < n$, it is semi-definite.

EXERCISE: Complete the proof of Lemma 1.

Optimality Conditions.

Let A_j, C_j denote the jth columns of A and C, respectively, and let [b]

$$(5) \qquad y_j = C_j^T x - \pi A_j \qquad\qquad (\pi = \pi_1, \pi_2, \ldots, \pi_m)$$

THEOREM 1: *A solution $x = x^0$ is minimal if there exist $\pi = \pi^0$ and $y = y^0$ such that*

$$(6) \qquad A x^0 = b, \qquad x^0 \ge 0$$

$$(7) \qquad y_j^0 = C_j^T x^0 - \pi^0 A_j \ge 0 \qquad\qquad (j = 1, 2, \ldots n)$$

$$(8) \qquad y_j^0 = 0 \quad \text{if } x_j^0 > 0$$

PROOF: Rewrite $Q(x)$ in the form

$$(9) \quad Q(x) - Q(x^0) = 2 \sum_{j=1}^{n} \left[\sum_{i=1}^{n} c_{ij} x_i^0 \right] (x_j - x_j^0) + \sum_{j=1}^{n} \sum_{i=1}^{n} c_{ij} (x_i - x_i^0)(x_j - x_j^0)$$

$$= 2 \sum_{j=1}^{n} (C_j^T x^0)(x_j - x_j^0) + (x - x^0)^T C (x - x^0)$$

Let $x \geq 0$ be any solution satisfying $Ax = b$, then

(10)
$$A(x - x^0) = \sum_{j=1}^{n} A_j(x_j - x_j^0) = 0$$

Multiplying on the left by $2\pi^0$ and subtracting from (9) yield

(11)
$$Q(x) - Q(x^0) = 2\sum_{j=1}^{n}(C_j^T x^0 - \pi^0 A_j)(x_j - x_j^0) + (x - x^0)^T C(x - x^0)$$
$$= 2\sum_{j=1}^{n} y_j^0(x_j - x_j^0) + (x - x^0)^T C(x - x^0)$$

For the class of solutions with the property $y_j^0 = 0$ for $x_j > 0$, (11) simplifies to

(12)
$$Q(x) - Q(x^0) = 2\sum_{j=1}^{n} y_j^0 x_j + (x - x^0)^T C(x - x^0)$$

Note that (12) holds by (8) and $y_j^0 \geq 0$ holds by (7), thus all terms in (12) are nonnegative, therefore $Q(x) \geq Q(x^0)$.

Improving a Non-optimal Solution.

Consider the system

(13)
$$\begin{aligned} Ax &= b \qquad\qquad (x \geq 0) \\ Cx - A^T \pi^T - I_n y &= 0 \end{aligned}$$

where $x^T Cx$ is assumed to be positive semi-definite. Let x^0, π^0, y^0 be a basic feasible solution associated with a basic set *with the complementarity property*, namely, for each j either x_j or y_j, but not both, is in the basic set. We shall assume further that the right-hand side has been perturbed to ensure that all basic solutions are nondegenerate. Note that neither π nor y is sign restricted; only $x \geq 0$ is required for a feasible solution to (13); an optimal solution will have been obtained if $y_j \geq 0$ and $x_j y_j = 0$ for all j.

THEOREM 2: *If a basis is complementary and $y_s^0 < 0$, then any increase of the non-basic variable x_s, with adjustment of only the basic variables, generates a class of solutions x', π', y', such that^c $x^T Cx$ decreases as long as $y_s' < 0$.*

PROOF: Let x be any solution in the class above, i.e., generated by increasing x_s; in particular, let x' be generated by $x_s = x_s'$. Analogous to (11), $Q(x) - Q(x') = 2y_s'(x_s - x_s') + (x - x')^T C(x - x')$ since for all $j \neq s$ either $x_j = x_j' = 0$ if x_j is non-basic or if x_j is basic $y_j = y_j'$ by the complementarity assumption. The adjusted values of the basic variables are linear functions of x_s, hence it follows that $(x - x') = (x_s - x_s')v$ where v

is a *constant vector*. Hence $Q(x)-Q(x') = (x_s-x'_s)[2y'_s+(x_s-x'_s)^T(v^TCv)]$ and it is clear that, if $y'_s < 0$, the right-hand side is negative for sufficiently small $(x_s - x'_s) > 0$.

Moreover for $Q(x)$ to decrease with an increase of $x_s \geq 0$ from, say, x'_s to x''_s, it must be accompanied by $y'_s < y''_s$ because

$$Q(x'') - Q(x') = 2(x''_s - x'_s)y'_s + (x''_s - x'_s)^2 v^T Cv$$

and, by interchanging the roles of x' and x'',

$$Q(x') - Q(x'') = 2(x'_s - x''_s)y'_s + (x''_s - x'_s)^2 v^T Cv$$

whence $2(y''_s - y'_s) = 2(x''_s - x'_s)v^TCv \geq 0$. But $v^TCv \neq 0$ because $v^TCv = 0$ implies $Cv = 0$ for positive semi-definite forms (see the last exercise following proof of Lemma 2), and if $Cv = 0$, then from (9), $Q(x'')-Q(x') = 2(x''_s-x'_s)(x')^TCv+(x''_s-x'_s)^2v^TCv = 0$ which contradicts $Q(x'') < Q(x')$; we conclude that $y''_s > y'_s$.

As in the simplex method, we require that all solutions generated by increasing x_s and adjusting the basic variables remain feasible, i.e., $x_j \geq 0$ for all j. In this process, either y_s attains the value zero first, and thus can be dropped from the basic set, or the value of some basic x_r attains the zero value first and is dropped.

THEOREM 3: *If x_r drops as basic variable, introduction of y_s either causes x^TCx to decrease (and some x_{r_1} or y_s to be dropped) or causes x^TCx to stay fixed and y_s to be dropped; if x_{r_1} is dropped, this theorem may be reapplied; if y_s is dropped either initially or upon increase of y_r Theorem 2 may be reapplied.*

PROOF: Our proof is completely general; however, for convenience we will illustrate it on system (14)

(14)

	x_1	x_2	x_3	x_4	x_5	$-\pi_1$	$-\pi_2$	y_1	y_2	y_3	y_4	y_5	Constants
	a_{11}	a_{12}	a_{13}	a_{14}	a_{15}								b_1
	a_{21}	a_{22}	a_{23}	a_{24}	a_{25}								b_2
	c_{11}	c_{12}	c_{13}	c_{14}	c_{15}	a_{11}	a_{12}	-1					0
	c_{21}	c_{22}	c_{23}	c_{24}	c_{25}	a_{21}	a_{22}		-1				0
	c_{31}	c_{32}	c_{33}	c_{34}	c_{35}	a_{31}	a_{32}			-1			0
	c_{41}	c_{42}	c_{43}	c_{44}	c_{45}	a_{41}	a_{42}				-1		0
	c_{51}	c_{52}	c_{53}	c_{54}	c_{55}	a_{51}	a_{52}					-1	0
B_1	•	•	•	•	★	•	•				•		
B'_1	•	•	•	•	•	•	•			★	•		

Let system (14) in vector form be

(15) $P_1x_1 + P_2x_2 + P_3x_3 + P_4x_4 + P_5x_5 + (P_6\pi_1 + P_7\pi_2)$

$$+\bar{P}_1y_1 + \bar{P}_2y_2 + \bar{P}_3y_3 + \bar{P}_4y_4 + \bar{P}_5y_5 = P_0$$

We suppose that we have on some cycle a basis B and a basic feasible complementary solution (x^0, π^0, y^0) with basic variables x_1, x_2, x_3, x_4, π_1, π_2, y_5 and the value of $y_5 = y_5^0 < 0$. In this case, x_5 will be the new basic variable and we assume that x_4 will drop. This yields a new basis B'. In (14), the heavy dots ($\bullet$) indicate that the column is in the basis B, and the star indicates that the column P_5 associated with x_5 is replacing a vector P_4 of the basis B to form basis B'; see second row of dots. The dropping of x_4 automatically requires that y_4 become the new basic variable for the basis following B'; see $\star$ in the B' row of (14).

Let the representation of both P_5 and $\bar{P}_4$ in terms of the basis B be:

$$(16) \qquad P_5 = P_1\alpha_1 + P_2\alpha_2 + P_3\alpha_3 + P_4\alpha_4 + (P_6\alpha_6 + P_7\alpha_7) + \bar{P}_5\bar{\alpha}_5$$

$$(17) \qquad \bar{P}_4 = P_1\lambda_1 + P_2\lambda_2 + P_3\lambda_3 + P_4\lambda_4 + (P_6\lambda_6 + P_7\lambda_7) + \bar{P}_5\bar{\lambda}_5$$

We first show that $\lambda_4 \leq 0$ in (17). Setting $\lambda = (\lambda_1, \lambda_2, \lambda_3, \lambda_4)$, the first six rows of representation (17) yield (18) and (19):

$$(18) \qquad [a_{11}\, a_{12}\, a_{13}\, a_{14}]\lambda^T \qquad\qquad = \quad 0$$
$$\qquad\qquad\quad [a_{21}\, a_{22}\, a_{23}\, a_{24}]\lambda^T \qquad\qquad = \quad 0$$

$$(19) \qquad \begin{bmatrix} c_{11}\, c_{12}\, c_{13}\, c_{14} \\ c_{21}\, c_{22}\, c_{23}\, c_{24} \\ c_{31}\, c_{32}\, c_{33}\, c_{34} \\ c_{41}\, c_{42}\, c_{43}\, c_{44} \end{bmatrix}\lambda^T + \begin{bmatrix} a_{11} \\ a_{12} \\ a_{13} \\ a_{14} \end{bmatrix}\lambda_6 + \begin{bmatrix} a_{21} \\ a_{22} \\ a_{23} \\ a_{24} \end{bmatrix}\lambda_7 = \begin{bmatrix} 0 \\ 0 \\ 0 \\ -1 \end{bmatrix}$$

Multiplying (19) by λ on the left and denoting the square matrix by C_4 yield, by (18), $\lambda C_4 \lambda^T = -\lambda_4$. Since $\lambda C_4 \lambda^T$ is positive semi-definite (C_4 is a principal minor of C), $\lambda C \lambda^T \geq 0$ and $\lambda_4 \leq 0$.[d]

Case $\lambda_4 < 0$: Our objective is to show that, if x_4 drops out of the basic set upon introduction of x_5 into the basic set and if the non-basic complementary variable to x_4, namely y_4, is subsequently increased (with adjustment of the values of the new basic variables), then x_5 and y_5 will continue to increase and $x^T C x$ to decrease as long as y_5 remains negative. This assumes $\lambda_4 < 0$. (Later, for the case $\lambda_4 = 0$, we shall show that x_5 and $x^T C x$ will remain unchanged by y_5 will decrease to zero when y_4 is increased in value.) Let the representation of P_4 in terms of the basis B' be

$$(20) \qquad \bar{P}_4 = P_1\lambda_1' + P_2\lambda_2' + P_3\lambda_3' + P_5\lambda_5' + (P_6\lambda_6' + P_7\lambda_7') + \bar{P}_5\bar{\lambda}_5'$$

and let the basic solution[e] associated with B' be

$$(21) \qquad P_0 = P_1x_1' + P_2x_2' + P_3x_3' + P_5x_5' + (P_6\pi_6' + P_7\pi_7') + \bar{P}_5y_5'$$

We observe that in the representation (16) of P_5 in terms of B, the weight α_4 on P_4 is positive (since x_4 decreased when x_5 increased). Since (20) is obained by eliminating P_4 from (16) and (17) and since $\lambda_4 < 0$ and $\alpha_4 > 0$, it follows that $\lambda_5' < 0$. If $y_4 = \theta > 0$ units of $\bar{P}_4$ are introduced into the solution and the values of the basic variables are adjusted, we obtain from (20) and (21),

$$(22) \quad P_0 = P_1(x_1' - \theta\lambda_1') + \cdots + P_3(x_3' - \theta\lambda_3') + P_3(x_5' - \theta\lambda_5') + \cdots$$
$$+\bar{P}_4\theta + \bar{P}_5(y_5' - \theta\bar{\lambda}_5')$$

Thus $x_5 = x_5' - \theta\lambda_5'$ will increase when $y_4 = \theta > 0$ is increased since $\lambda_5' < 0$. Moreover, we may adopt the point of view for the purpose of the proof, that it is the increase in x_s that is "causing" the increase in y_4 (instead of the other way around), so that we are, in fact, repeating the situation just considered of increasing x_5 and adjusting the other "basic" variables, except here y_4 is in the basic set instead of x_4. It follows, therefore, as before, that an increase in x_5 decreases $x^T C x$ as long as y_5 remains negative in value in the adjustment of the basic solution by the increase of x_5.

Case $\lambda_4 = 0$: On the other hand, if $\lambda_4 = 0$ in (17), then we must set [f] $\lambda_i = \lambda_i'$ in (20) because the representation of $\bar{P}_4$ is the same, whether in terms of B or B'; hence, $\lambda_5' = 0$. In this case $\lambda C_4 \lambda^T = -\lambda_4 = 0$ and therefore, because C is positive semi-definite, $C_4 \lambda = 0$. In addition, $\lambda = 0$ must hold because $\lambda \neq 0$ implies a dependence of the first four columns of (18) and (19) which is *impossible* because then the square array of coefficients of (18) and (19), and in turn B, would be singular. Setting $\lambda_1', \ldots, \lambda_5' = 0$ in (20) and (21), we observe (and this holds in general) that $\bar{P}_4$ is dependent only on the columns of π_i and of y_j, and therefore the values of $x_j' - \theta\lambda_j'$ remain unchanged in (21) with increasing values of $y_4 = \theta$.

Because the y_j are not sign restricted, y_4 can be increased until y_5 is dropped out of the basic set at value zero (since all x_j values are unaffected). Hence, in this shift of basis there is no change in the value of $x^T C x$; however, the introduction of y_4 into the basic set and the dropping of y_5 give rise to a new basic set that satisfies the complementarity property. We may thus reapply Theorem 2 to reduce $x^T C x$.

The Quadratic Algorithm.

Step I. Initiate: Let x^0 be a basic feasible solution for $Ax = b$, $x \geq 0$. with basic variables $x_{j_1}, x_{j_2}, \ldots, x_{j_m}$; choose for the initial set of basic variables x_j for the enlarged problem these x_{j_i}, the complements y_j of the non-basic x_j, and the set of π_i.

Step II. For the values of y_j^0 of the basic solution, determine Min $y_j^0 = y_s^0$. If $y_s^0 \geq 0$, *terminate; the solution is optimal.* If $y_s^0 < 0$, introduce into the basic set x_s; if y_s drops from the basic set, repeat Step II. Go to Step III if x_r drops.

Step III. Introduce y_r into basic set. If y_s drops, return to Step II; otherwise, if some x_{r_s} drops, repeat Step III with r_s playing the role of r.

THEOREM 4. *The iterative process is finite.*

EXERCISE: Prove Theorem 4.

EXERCISE: Extend the results of this section to cover the case of a convex objective form consisting of mixed quadratic and linear terms.

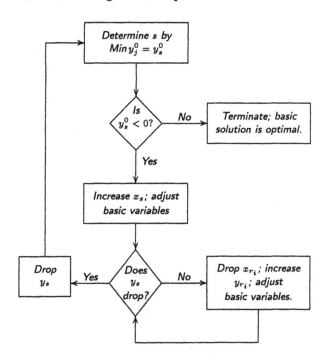

Figure 24-4-I. Flowchart of the quadratic programming algorithm.

Bibliography.

Barankin, E. W., and R. Dorfman, 1958-1. *On Quadratic Programming*, University of California Publications in Statistics, Vol. 2, No. 13, University of California Press, Berkeley, California, 1958. pp. 285–318.

Dorfman, R., 1951-1. *Application of Linear Programming to the Theory of the Firm*, University of California Press, Berkeley, California, 1951, 98 pp.

Markowitz, H. M., 1956-1. "The Optmization of a Quadratic Function Subject to Linear Constraints," The RAND Corporation, Research Memorandum RM-1438, February 21, 1955; also the RAND Corporation, Paper P-637, June 17, 1955. Published in *Naval Res. Logist. Quart.*, Vol. 3, 1956.

Markowitz, H. M., 1959-1. *Portfolio Selection: Efficient Diversification of Investments*, John Wiley & Sons, New York, 1959, 344 pp.

White, W. B., S. M. Johnson, and G. B. Dantzig, 1958-1. "Chemical Equilibrium in Complex Mixtures," *J. Chem. Phys.*, Vol. 28, No. 5, May, 1958, pp. 751–755.

Wolfe, Philip, 1959-1. "The Simplex Method for Quadratic Programming," *Econometrica*, Vol. 27, No. 3, July, 1959.

Chapter 22

On the Continuity of the Minimum Set of a Continuous Function

George B. Dantzig, Jon Folkman, and Norman Shapiro

The Rand Corporation, Santa Monica, California

In this paper we are concerned with the question: How does the solution of a constrained minimization problem vary when the constraints and/or the objective function are varied? In particular we ask for the conditions on the constraints, objective function, the manner in which the constraints are varied, for the minimum (or more precisely, the point at which the minimum is attained) to vary in some sort of continuous manner.

This question arose in some work on chemical equilibrium theory. The equilibrium composition of a chemical system can be determined as the composition which minimizes the Gibbs free energy function subject to the constraints imposed by the mass balance laws. The continuity of the equilibrium composition as a function of the free energy function and the mass balance constraints is of interest for two reasons. First, the continuity of this function is equivalent to the stability of the constrained minimization problem. Stability is of crucial importance in determining the equilibrium composition by numerical methods. Second, this function must be continuous in order for the assumption of instantaneous equilibrium in a slowly changing dynamic chemical system to be valid.

Functions defined as the solutions of constrained minimization problems are also encountered in such areas as economics and game theory. The continuity of these functions is of interest for much the same reasons as in the case of chemical equilibrium theory.

One difficulty in treating this question is that the minimum may not be unique. We resolve this difficulty in two ways: (1) by dealing with the set of minima and using an appropriate notion for the variation of a set, (2) by finding conditions for the continuous variation of the minimum, whenever it is unique.

It turns out that the variation of the objective function offers little difficulty and can be dealt with in two theorems. Thus, we concentrate largely on the dependence of the set of minima (or of the unique minimum) on the constraint set.

In Part I we deal with the general problem. In Part II we deal with the special case that the constraint set is defined by linear inequalities and equations. That is, we ask for conditions that the set of points, x, which minimize $f(x, p)$ subject to the constraint that $ax \leq b$, is a continuous function of the parameters p, the matrix a, and the vector b. Here f is a real-valued function defined on $E^n \times P$, where P is the space in which p varies.[a]

I. The General Problem

Section I.1

Let $\{A_n\}$ be a sequence of subsets of a metric space X. We define the outer limit, $\overline{\lim}_{n \to \infty} A_n$, by

$$\overline{\lim_{n \to \infty}} A_n = \{x \in X \mid x = \lim_{i \to \infty} x_{n_i}, \text{ where } \{n_i\} \text{ is an infinite sub-}$$
$$\text{sequence of the integers and } x_{n_i} \in A_{n_i}\}.$$

We define the inner limit, $\underline{\lim}_{n \to \infty} A_n$, by

$$\underline{\lim_{n \to \infty}} A_n = \{x \in X \mid x = \lim_{n \to \infty} A_n, \text{ where } x_n \in A_n \text{ for all but a}$$
$$\text{finite number of } n \}$$

If $\overline{\lim}_{n \to \infty} A_n = \underline{\lim}_{n \to \infty} A_n$ we say that the limit, $\lim_{n \to \infty} A_n$, exists and set

$$\lim_{n \to \infty} A_n = \overline{\lim_{n \to \infty}} A_n = \underline{\lim_{n \to \infty}} A_n.$$

If Y is any subset of X, then $\bar{Y}$ is the topological closure of Y and Bndry Y is the boundary of Y.

The following properties follow immediately from the definitions. We let I denote the set of all infinite subsequences $\{n_i\}$ of the positive integers.

(I.1.1)
$$\overline{\lim_{n \to \infty}} A_n = \bigcup_{n_i \in I} \underline{\lim_{i \to \infty}} A_{n_i},$$

(I.1.2)
$$\underline{\lim_{n \to \infty}} A_n = \bigcup_{n_i \in I} \overline{\lim_{i \to \infty}} A_{n_i},$$

(I.1.3)
$$\overline{\lim_{n \to \infty}} A_n = \bigcap_{m=1}^{\infty} \left(\overline{\bigcup_{n=m}^{\infty} A_n} \right),$$

(I.1.4) $\overline{\lim_{n \to \infty}} A_n$ and $\underline{\lim_{n \to \infty}} A_n$ are closed

If $A_n \subset B_n$ for all sufficiently large n, then

(I.1.5) $\overline{\lim_{n \to \infty}} A_n \subset \overline{\lim_{n \to \infty}} B_n$ and $\underline{\lim_{n \to \infty}} A_n \subset \underline{\lim_{n \to \infty}} B_n$.

If $A_n = A$ for all sufficiently large n, then

(I.1.6) $\lim_{n \to \infty} A_n$ exists and is equal to $\bar{A}$.

If $\{A_n\}$ is a sequence of convex subsets of E^n, then

(I.1.7) $\underline{\lim_{n \to \infty}} A_n$ is convex.

Suppose that F is a set-valued function[b] from the metric space X to the metric space Y. That is, suppose the domain of F is X and that the range of F consists of subsets of Y. We define F^* to be the function which is defined for those $x \in X$ for which $F(x)$ contains exactly one element, and $F^*(x)$ is defined to be that element. Following Berge [1, p. 111], we say that F is *closed at the point* $x_0 \in X$ if, for all sequences $\{x_n\} \subset X$ and $\{y_n\} \subset Y$ satisfying $x_n \to x_0$, $y_n \to y_0$, $y_n \in F(x_n)$, we have $y_0 \in F(x_0)$. With the above terminology this becomes: For all sequences $\{x_n\} \subset X$ with $x_n \to x_0$, we have

$$\overline{\lim_{n \to \infty}} F(x_n) \subset F(x_0).$$

We say that F is *closed* if it is closed at each point $x \in X$.

Note that the associated single-valued function F^* need not be continuous even though F is closed. For example, the set-valued function from the reals to the reals given by

$$F(x) = \begin{cases} \{1/x\} & \text{if} \quad x \neq 0, \\ \{0\} & \text{if} \quad x = 0 \end{cases}$$

is closed, but F^* is discontinuous at zero.

If φ is a real-valued function on a metric space X and H is a subset of X, we define $M(\varphi \mid H)$ to be the subset of H where φ achieves its minimum. More precisely,

$$M(\varphi \mid H) = \{x \in H \mid \varphi(x) = \inf\{\varphi(y) \mid y \in H\}\}.$$

Note that $M(\varphi \mid H)$ may be thought of as the set of solutions of a constrained minimization problem. If H is a set-valued function from a metric space T to X, then $M(\varphi \mid H(t))$ a set-valued function from T to X. We will be interested in finding conditions for this function to be a closed function of t and for the associated point-valued function $M^*(\varphi \mid H(t))$ to be continuous.

The remainder of this section is devoted to several results which we will find useful in the sequel. Most readers will prefer to defer them until completing the rest of the paper.

THEOREM I.1.8. *Let X be a metric space and let $\{A_n\}$ be a sequence of connected subsets of X. Let U be an open subset of X with compact boundary. If $\underline{\lim}_{n\to\infty} A_n$ is nonempty and $\overline{\lim}_{n\to\infty} A_n \subset U$, then $A_n \subset U$ for all sufficiently large n.*

PROOF. Let

$$x \in \lim_{n\to\infty} A_n \subset \overline{\lim}_{n\to\infty} A_n \subset U.$$

There is a sequence $\{x_n\}$ with $x_n \to x$ and $x_n \in A_n$ for n large. Hence $x_n \in A_n \cap U$ for n large. Suppose the conclusion does not hold. Then we can find a sequence $\{n_i\}$ and points $y_i \in A_{n_i}$ such that $y_i \notin U$.

For i sufficiently large, $x_{n_i} \in A_{n_i} \cap U$ and $y_{n_i} \in A_{n_i} - U$. Hence, since A_{n_i} is connected, there is a point $z_i \in A_{n_i} \cap \text{Bndry } U$. Now Bndry U is compact so a subsequence of the z_i converges to a point $z \in \text{Bndry } U$. But

$$z \in \overline{\lim}_{n\to\infty} A_n \subset U. \qquad \text{Q.E.D.}$$

THEOREM I.1.9. *Let X be a locally compact metric space and let $\{A_n\}$ be a sequence of connected subsets of X. If $\underline{\lim}_{n\to\infty} A_n$ is nonempty and $\overline{\lim}_{n\to\infty} A_n$ is compact, then $\overline{\lim}_{n\to\infty} A_n$ is connected.*

PROOF. Suppose not. Then there are disjoint open sets $U, V \subset X$ such that $\overline{\lim}_{n\to\infty} A_n \subset U \cup V$, and $U \cap \overline{\lim}_{n\to\infty} A_n$ and $V \cap \overline{\lim}_{n\to\infty} A_n$ are both nonempty. Since $\overline{\lim}_{n\to\infty} A_n$ is compact and X is locally compact, we may choose U and V so that $\overline{U \cup V}$ is compact. Hence Bndry $(U \cup V)$ is compact. By Theorem I.1.8, $A_n \subset U \cup V$, for n sufficiently large.

Let $x \in \underline{\lim}_{n\to\infty} A_n$ and let $x_n \to x$ with $x_n \in A_n$ for n sufficiently large. We have $in \lim_{n\to\infty} A_n \subset U \cup V$, so we may assume $x \in U$. Then, for n sufficiently large, $A_n \subset U \cup V$ and $x_n \in A_n \cap U$. Since A_n is connected, $A_n \subset U$ for n sufficiently large. Hence $\overline{\lim}_{n\to\infty} A_n \subset \bar{U}$. But $\bar{U} \cap V = \emptyset$, so this contradicts the assumption that $V \cap \overline{\lim}_{n\to\infty} A_n$ is nonempty. Q.E.D.

THEOREM I.1.10. *Let $\{A_n\}$ be a sequence of subsets of the metric space X. Let U be an open subset of X and suppose that*

$$(\lim_{n\to\infty} A_n) \cap \bar{U} \subset \overline{(\lim_{n\to\infty} A_n) \cap U}.$$

Then

$$(\varliminf_{n\to\infty} A_n \cap \bar{U}) = (\varliminf_{n\to\infty} A_n) \cap \bar{U}.$$

PROOF. $A_n \cap \bar{U} \subset A_n$ and $A_n \cap \bar{U} \subset \bar{U}$, so by (I.1.5) and (I.1.6),

$$(\varliminf_{n\to\infty} A_n \cap \bar{U}) \subset (\varliminf_{n\to\infty} A_n) \cap \bar{U}.$$

By assumption,

$$(\varliminf_{n\to\infty} A_n) \cap \bar{U} \subset \overline{(\varliminf_{n\to\infty} A_n) \cap U}.$$

Let $x \in (\varliminf_{n\to\infty} A_n) \cap U$. Then $x = \lim_{n\to\infty} x_n$, where $x_n \in A_n$ for n sufficiently large and $x \in U$. Therefore, $x_n \in A_n \cap U \subset A_n \cap \bar{U}$ for n sufficiently large, so $x \in \varliminf_{n\to\infty}(A_n \cap \bar{U})$. This set is closed, so

$$\overline{(\varliminf_{n\to\infty} A_n) \cap U} \subset (\varliminf_{n\to\infty} A_n) \cap \bar{U}. \qquad\qquad \text{Q.E.D.}$$

THEOREM I.1.11. *Let y be a point in E^m and let $\{H_n\}$ be a sequence of nonempty closed subsets of E^m. There is a nonnegative convex function φ defined on E^m such that $M(\varphi \mid E^m) = \{y\}$ and $M(\varphi \mid H_n) = \{x_n\}$ for some $x_n \in H_n$. Furthermore, given any such φ, if $y \in \varliminf_{n\to\infty} H_n$, then $y = \lim_{n\to\infty} x_n$.*

PROOF. We construct a sequence $\{x_n\}$ of points in E^m, a sequence $\{A_n\}$ of real numbers, and a sequence $\{\varphi_n\}$ of functions on E^m such that each sequence is defined for $0 \le n < \infty$, $x_0 = y$, and such that for $n \ge 0$:

(1) $$A_n > 0,$$

(2) $$A_{n+1} \le \tfrac{A_n}{10},$$

(3) $$A_n\|y - x_n\| \le \tfrac{1}{2^n},$$

(4) $$\varphi_n(x) = \sum_{i=0}^{n} A_i\|x - x_i\|,$$

(5) $$x_{n+i} \in M(\varphi_n \mid H_{n+1}),$$

where $\| \cdot \|$ denotes the usual norm in E^m.

Set $x_0 = y$, $A_0 = 1$, and $\varphi_0(x) = \|x - x_0\|$. Suppose that x_i, A_i, and φ_i are defined for $0 \le i \le n$. The $M(\varphi_n \mid H_{n+1})$ is nonempty because H_{n+1} is closed and nonempty, and for any real number b, $\{x \in E^m \mid \varphi_n(x) \le b\}$ is bounded. Choose $x_{n+1} \in M(\varphi_n \mid H_{n+1})$. Choose A_{n+1} to be any real number satisfying (1), (2), and (3). Define φ_{n+1} by (4).

We now define

$$\varphi(x) = \lim_{n\to\infty} \varphi_n(x) = \sum_{n=0}^{\infty} A_n\|x - x_n\|.$$

To show that this limit exists it suffices to show that

$$\lim_{n\to\infty} \sum_{i=n}^{\infty} A_i\|x - x_i\| = 0.$$

But

$$\sum_{i=n}^{\infty} A_i\|x - x_i\| \le \left(\sum_{i=n}^{\infty} A_i\right)\|x - y\| + \sum_{i=n}^{\infty} A_i\|y - x_i\|$$

which tends to zero as $n \to \infty$ by virtue of (2) and (3). Since φ is the pointwise limit of non-negative convex functions, it is non-negative and convex.

Let $H_0 = E^m$ and we will show that φ achieves its minimum on H_n uniquely at x_n for $n \ge 0$. Note that if we set $\varphi_{-1} = 0$, then (5) holds for $n = -1$. Let $x \in H_n$, $x \neq x_n$. Then

$$\varphi(x) - \varphi(x_n) = \varphi_{n-1}(x) - \varphi_{n-1}(x_n) + A_n\|x - x_n\|$$

$$+ \sum_{i=n+1}^{\infty} A_i(\|x - x_i\| - \|x_n - x_i\|)$$

$$\ge \varphi_{n-1}(x) - \varphi_{n-1}(x_n) + A_n\|x - x_n\|$$

$$+ \sum_{i=n+1}^{\infty} A_i(\|x - x_i\| - \|x_n - x\| - \|x - x_i\|)$$

$$= \varphi_{n-1}(x) - \varphi_{n-1}(x_n) + \left(A_n - \sum_{i=n+1}^{\infty} A_i\right)\|x_n - x\|$$

$$\ge \varphi_{n-1}(x) - \varphi_{n-1}(x_n) + \tfrac{8}{9}A_n\|x - x_n\|$$

by (2). Hence, by (5)

$$\varphi(x) - \varphi(x_n) \ge \tfrac{8}{9}A_n\|x_n - x\| > 0.$$

This proves the first part of the theorem.

Now suppose $y \in \underline{\lim}_{n\to\infty} H_n$. Then there is a sequence $\{y_n\}$ with $y_n \in H_n$ and $y_n \to y$. Since φ is convex on E^m, it is continuous, so $\varphi(y_n) \to \varphi(y)$. But $\varphi(y_n) \ge \varphi(x_n)$, so $\varphi(x_n) \to \varphi(y)$. But $\varphi(y_n) \ge \varphi(x_n) \ge \varphi(y)$, so $\varphi(x_n) \to \varphi(y)$. Let $\epsilon > 0$. Let

$$\delta = \min\{\varphi(x) \mid x \in E^m, \|x - y\| = \epsilon\} - \varphi(y).$$

The minimum exists because φ is continuous and the set

$$\{x \in E^m \mid \|x - y\| = \epsilon\}$$

is compact. Furthermore, $\delta > 0$ because φ achieves its minimum uniquely at y. Let N be so large that $|\varphi(x_n) - \varphi(y)| < \delta$ for $n \ge N$.

Suppose that for some $n \geq N$, $|x_n - y| \geq \epsilon$. Then there is a t with $0 < t \leq 1$ such that if $x = tx_n + (1 - t)y$, then $\|x - y\| = \epsilon$. Hence

$$\begin{aligned}\varphi(y) + \delta \leq \varphi(x) &\leq t\varphi(x_n) + (1 - t)\varphi(y) \\ &< t(\varphi(y) + \delta) + (1 - t)\varphi(y) \\ &\leq \varphi(y) + \delta.\end{aligned}$$

This is a contradiction. Therefore, $\|x_n - y\| < \epsilon$ for $n \geq N$, so $x_n \to y$.

Q.E.D.

Section I.2

In this section we obtain necessary and sufficient conditions on the variation of φ and of H so that $M(\varphi \mid H)$ varies in a closed manner. We first obtain a necessary condition on the variation of H, assuming φ to be an arbitrary but fixed continuous function.

THEOREM I.2.1. *Let T and X be metric spaces, and let H be a set-valued function from T to X. Suppose that for every continuous $\varphi : X \to R$ the set valued function*

$$t \to M(\varphi \mid H(t))$$

is closed at the point $t_0 \in T$. Then, for every sequence $\{t_n\} \subset T$ with $t_n \to t_0$, $\underline{\lim}_{n \to \infty} H(t_n)$ is either empty or equal to $H(t_0)$.

PROOF. Let $\{t_n\} \subset T$ be a sequence with $t_n \to t_0$. Suppose $\underline{\lim}_{n \to \infty} H(t_n)$ is nonempty. Then there is an $x_0 \in \underline{\lim}_{n \to \infty} H(t_n)$ and $x_0 = \lim_{n \to \infty} x_n$ where $x_n \in H(t_n)$ for n sufficiently large. Define $\varphi : X \to R$ by

$$\varphi(x) = \inf_n d(x, x_n),$$

where d is the metric in X. We have $\varphi(x) \geq 0$ for all x, $\varphi(x_n) = 0$ and $x_n \in H(t_n)$ for n large, so $x_n \in M(\varphi \mid H(t_n))$ for n large. Consequently, since φ is continuous, $t \to M(\varphi \mid H(t))$ is closed at t_0, so

$$x_0 = \lim x_n \in \underline{\lim} M(\varphi \mid H(t_n)) \subset M(\varphi \mid H(t_0)) \subset H(t_0).$$

Therefore, $\underline{\lim}_{n \to \infty} H(t_n) \subset H(t_0)$.

Suppose that $\underline{\lim}_{n \to \infty} H(t_n) \neq H(t_0)$. Then there is a point $x_0' \in H(t_0)$ with $x_0' \notin \underline{\lim}_{n \to \infty} H(t_n)$. Hence there is an $\epsilon > 0$ and an infinite subsequence $\{n_i\}$ of the positive integers such that

$$d(x_0', H(t_{n_i})) \geq \epsilon \quad \text{for all } i.$$

Define $\psi : X \to R$ by

$$\psi(x) = \min(d(x, x_0'), \inf_n d(x.x_n) + \epsilon).$$

For $x \in H(t_{n_i})$, $\psi(x) \geq \epsilon$. Now $\psi(x_{n_i}) = \epsilon$, so $x_{n_i} \in M(\psi \mid H(t_n))$. Since $\lim_{i \to \infty} t_{n_i} = t_0$, we have

$$x_0 = \lim_{i \to \infty} x_{n_i} \in \varlimsup_{i \to \infty} M(\psi \mid H(t_{n_i})) \subset M(\psi \mid H(t_0)).$$

But

$$\psi(x_0) = \lim_{i \to \infty} \psi(x_{n_i}) = \epsilon > 0 = \psi(x_0')$$

and $x_0' \in H(t_0)$, so this is a contradiction. Q.E.D.

We now prove the converse of Theorem I.2.1 in a strengthened form.

THEOREM I.2.2. *Let H be a set-valued function from the metric space T to the metric space X. Let $t_0 \in T$ and suppose that for every sequence $\{t_n\} \subset T$ with $t_n \to t_0$, $\varliminf_{n \to \infty} H(t_n)$ is either empty or equal to $H(t_0)$. Let $\{\varphi_n\}$ and φ be continuous real-valued functions on X such that $\varphi_n \to \varphi$ uniformly on compact sets. Then, for each sequence $\{t_n\} \subset T$ with $t_n \to t_0$,*

$$\varlimsup_{n \to \infty} M(\varphi_n \mid H(t_n)) \subset M(\varphi \mid H(t_0)).$$

In particular, taking $\varphi_n = \varphi$ for all n, the set-valued function

$$t \to M(\varphi \mid H(t))$$

is closed at t_0.

PROOF. $\{t_n\} \subset T$ with $t_n \to t_0$. Suppose $x_0 \in \varlimsup_{n \to \infty} M(\varphi_n \mid H(t_n))$. Then $x_0 = \lim_{n \to \infty} x_n$ where $x_n \in M(\varphi_n \mid H(t_n))$ for n large. We have $x_0 \in \varlimsup_{n \to \infty} H(t_n)$, so $\varliminf_{n \to \infty} H(t_n) = H(t_0)$. Let $x_0' \in H(t_0)$. Then $x_0' = \lim_{n \to \infty} x_n'$, where $x_n' \in H(t_n)$ for n large. Hence, $\varphi_n(x_n) \leq \varphi_n(x_n')$ for n large.

The set consisting of the points $\{x_n\}$, $\{x_n'\}$, x_0, and x_0' is the union of two convergent sequences together with their limits, so it is compact. Now $\varphi_n \to \varphi$ uniformly on compact sets. Consequently,

$$\varphi(x_0) = \lim_{n \to \infty} \varphi_n(x_n) \leq \lim_{n \to \infty} \varphi_n(x_n') = \varphi(x_0').$$

Since this holds for every $x_0' \in H(t_0)$, $x_0 \in M(\varphi \mid H(t_0))$. Q.E.D.

COROLLARY I.2.3. *Suppose that the functions $\{\varphi_n\}$ and φ in Theorem I.2.2 have the form*

$$\varphi_n(x) = \psi(x, p_n),$$

$$\varphi(x) = \psi(x, p_0).$$

where ψ is a continuous real-valued function on $X \times P$, P is a metric space, $\{p_n\}$ and p_0 are points in P with $p_n \to p_0$. Then

$$\lim_{n \to \infty} M(\varphi_n \mid H(t_n)) \subset M(\varphi \mid H(t_0)).$$

PROOF. It suffices to show that $\varphi_n \to \varphi$ uniformly on compact subsets of X. Let $Q \subset X$ be compact and let $\epsilon > 0$. For each $x \in Q$ there is a neighborhood U_x of x in X and a neighborhood V_x of p_0 in P such that

$$|\psi(y, p) - \psi(x, p_0)| < \frac{\epsilon}{2}$$

for $y \in U_x$ and $p \in V_x$. The $\{U_x\}_{x \in Q}$ form a covering of Q. Let $U_{x_1}, \ldots, U_{x_n}$ be a finite subcovering. Let $V = V_{x_1} \cap \cdots \cap V_{x_n}$. Now V is a neighborhood of p_0, so there is an N such that $p_n \in V$ for $n \geq N$. Let $x \in Q$ and let $n \geq N$. Then $x \in U_{x_i}$, for some i and $p_n, p_0 \in V \subset V_{x_i}$. Hence

$$|\varphi_n(x) - \varphi(x)| = |\psi(x, p_n) - \psi(x, p_0)|$$
$$\leq |\psi(x, p_n) - \psi(x_i, p_0)| + |\psi(x_i, p_0) - \psi(x, p_0)| < \epsilon.$$

Q.E.D.

If H is a set-valued function from the metric space T to the metric space X, Theorems I.2.1 and I.2.2 give necessary and sufficient conditions on H for the set-valued function $t \to M((\varphi \mid H(t))$ to be closed for every continuous $\varphi : X \to R$.

Furthermore, taken together with Corollary I.2.3, they imply, roughly speaking, that if the variation of H is such that $M(\varphi \mid H)$ varies in a closed manner for each fixed, continuous φ, then $M(\varphi \mid H)$ varies in a closed manner if φ is allowed to vary by means of a parameter in which it is continuous. The next corollary treats the case of fixed H and variable φ. This result has a simple and direct proof and is almost certainly known, although we have not found a reference.

COROLLARY I.2.4. *Let H be a metric space. Let φ_n and φ be continuous real-valued functions on H such that $\varphi_n \to \varphi$ uniformly on compact sets, then*

$$\lim_{n \to \infty} M(\varphi_n \mid H) \subset M(\varphi \mid H).$$

PROOF. Clear from Theorem I.2.2.   Q.E.D.

Section I.3

In this section we find conditions for $M^*(\varphi \mid H(t))$ to be a continuous function of t. Our results on this problem apply only in a much more limited context.

THEOREM I.3.1 *Let H be a set-valued function from the metric space T to E^n. Suppose that $H(t)$ is closed for each $t \in T$. Let T' be the subset of T consisting of those points t for which $H(t)$ is nonempty.*

Let $t_0 \in T'$. Suppose that for every non-negative convex $\varphi : E^n \to R$ the function

$$t \to M^*(\varphi \mid H(t))$$

is continuous at t_0 if t_0 is in its domain. Then for every sequence $\{t_m\} \subset T'$ with $t_m \to t_0$,

$$\lim_{m \to \infty} H(t_m) = H(t_0).$$

PROOF. Let $\{t_m\} \subset T'$ be a sequence with $t_m \to t_0$. We first show that $\overline{\lim}_{m \to \infty} H(t_m) \subset H(t_0)$. Let $y_0 \in \limsup_{m \to \infty} H(t_m)$. Then $y_0 \in \underline{\lim}_{i \to \infty} H(t_{m_i})$ for some infinite subsequence $\{m_i\}$ of the positive integers. Applying Theorem I.1.11 with $H_1 = H(t_0)$ and $H_{i+1} = H(t_{m_i})$ for $i > 0$, we obtain a non-negative convex function $\varphi : E^n \to R$ with

$$M^*(\varphi \mid H(t_{m_i})) = x_i, \qquad M^*(\varphi \mid H(t_0)) = x_0,$$

and

$$x_i \to y_0.$$

Since $t \to M^*(\varphi \mid H(t))$ is continuous at t_0,

$$y_0 = \lim_{i \to \infty} x_i = \lim_{i \to \infty} M^*(\varphi \mid H(t_m)) = M^*(\varphi \mid H(t_0)) = x_0 \in H(t_0).$$

Now we show that

$$H(t_0) \subset \underline{\lim}_{m \to \infty} H(t_m).$$

Since

$$\underline{\lim}_{m \to \infty} H(t_m) \subset \overline{\lim}_{m \to \infty} H(t_m)$$

by (I.1.2), this will complete the proof.

Let $y_0 \in H(t_0)$ and apply Theorem I.1.11 with $H_m = H(t_m)$. We obtain a convex function φ with

$$M^*(\varphi \mid H(t_m)) = x_m$$

and

$$M^*(\varphi \mid E^n) = y_0.$$

Since $y_0 \in H(t_0)$ and $\varphi(y_0) \leq \varphi(x)$ for all $x \in E^n$, $y_0 = x_0$. Therefore,

$$y_0 = M^*(\varphi \mid H(t_0)) = \lim_{m \to \infty} M^*(\varphi \mid H(t_m)) \in \varliminf_{m \to \infty} M(\varphi \mid H(t_m))$$
$$\subset \varliminf_{m \to \infty} H(t_m).$$

Q.E.D.

As the following example shows, the converse of Theorem I.3.1 is false.

EXAMPLE. Let $T = [0, \infty)$ and $E^n = E^2$. Let

$$H(t) = \begin{cases} \{(t,0), (t, -1/t)\} & \text{if} \quad t > 0, \\ \{(0,0)\} & \text{if} \quad t = 0. \end{cases}$$

Then $T' = T$ and $\lim_{n \to \infty} H(t_n) = H(t)$ whenever $t_n \to t$. If we define $\varphi : E^2 \to R$ by

$$\varphi(x_1, x_2) = e^{x_2},$$

then φ is convex and non-negative and

$$M(\varphi \mid H(t)) = \begin{cases} \{(t, -1/t)\} & \text{if} \quad t > 0, \\ \{(0,0)\} & \text{if} \quad t = 0. \end{cases}$$

Hence $M^*(\varphi \mid H(t))$ is defined for all $t \in T$, but it is discontinuous at $t = 0$. We now prove two restricted converses of Theorem I.3.1.

THEOREM I.3.2. *Let H, T, and T' be as in Theorem I.3.1. Suppose that $H(t)$ is connected for each $t \in T'$. Let $t_0 \in T'$ and suppose that $H(t_0)$ is compact and, for every sequence $\{t_n\} \subset T'$ with $t_n \to t_0$, we have $\lim_{n \to \infty} H(t_n) = H(t_0)$. If $\varphi : E^n \to R$ is continuous, then the function*

$$t \to M^*(\varphi \mid H(t))$$

is continuous at t_0 if t_0 is in its domain.

(Note. Theorem I.3.2 does not assume that φ is convex.)

PROOF. Suppose t_0 is in the domain of $M^*(\varphi \mid H)$. Let $\{t_n\}$ be a sequence of points in the domain of $M^*(\varphi \mid H)$ with $t_n \to t_0$. Then

$\{t_n\} \subset T'$, so $\lim_{n\to\infty} H(t_n) = H(t_0)$. Now $H(t_0)$ is compact, so it is contained in a bounded open set U of E^n. We have

$$\varliminf_{n\to\infty} H(t_n) = H(t_0) \neq \emptyset \quad \text{and} \quad \varlimsup_{n\to\infty} H(t_n) = H(t_0) \subset U.$$

The boundary of U is a closed bounded subset of E^n, so is compact. Hence, by Theorem I.1.8, $H(t_n) \subset U$ for n sufficiently large.

The sequence $\{M^*(\varphi \mid H(t)n))\}$ is bounded, so if it does not converge to $M^*(\varphi \mid H(t_0))$ then there is an infinite sequence $\{n_i\}$ such that $M^*(\varphi \mid H(t_{n_i})) \to x_0$, where $x_0 \neq M^*(\varphi \mid H(t_0))$. Now $t_{n_i} \to t_0$, so by Theorem I.2.2

$$x_0 \in \varliminf_{i\to\infty} M(\varphi \mid H(t_{n_i})) \subset M(\varphi \mid H(t_0)) = \{M^*(\varphi \mid H(t_0))\}.$$

This is a contradiction. Hence $M^*(\varphi \mid H(t_n)) \to M^*(\varphi \mid H(t_0))$.   Q.E.D.

Recall that a real-valued function φ on E^n is *quasi*-convex if, for every real a, the set of x for which $\varphi(x) \leq a$ is convex. Every convex function is quasi-convex.

THEOREM I.3.3 *Let H, T, and T' be as in Theorem I.3.1. Suppose $H(t)$ is closed and convex for every $t \in T$. Let $t_0 \in T'$ and suppose that for every sequence $\{t_m\} \subset T'$ with $t_m \to t_0$, $\lim_{m\to\infty} H(t_m) = H(t_0)$. Let φ be a continuous, quasi-convex^c function on E^n. If $M(\varphi \mid H(t_0))$ is nonempty and $M(\varphi \mid H(t_0)) \subset U$ where U is a bounded open subset of E^n, then $M(\varphi \mid H(t)) \subset U$ for all t in some neighborhood of t_0.*

PROOF. Let $M = M(\varphi \mid H(t_0))$. Now M is closed and bounded so it is compact. Hence, since $M \subset U$, $d(M, E^n - U) = \epsilon > 0$. Let

$$V = \{x \in E^n \mid d(M, x) < \epsilon\}.$$

We have $M \subset V \subset U$ and V is an open bounded subset of E^n.

The set $H(t_0) \cap V \subset H(t_0) \cap \bar{V}$ which is closed, so

$$\overline{H(t_0) \cap V} \subset H(t_0) \cap \bar{V}$$

Let $x \in H(t_0) \cap \bar{V}$. Then $d(x, M) \leq \epsilon$ and, since M is compact, $d(x, M) = d(x, y)$ for some $y \in M \subset H(t_0)$. Let $0 < \lambda < 1$. Then $\lambda y + (1 - \lambda)x \in H(t_0)$ because $H(t_0)$ is convex. Furthermore,

$$d(\lambda y + (1 - \lambda)x, M) \leq d(\lambda y + (1 - \lambda)x, y) = (1 - \lambda)d(x, y) < \epsilon,$$

so $\lambda y + (1 - \lambda)x \in V$. Therefore,

$$x = \lim_{\lambda\downarrow 0}(\lambda y + (1 - \lambda)x) \in \overline{H(t_0) \cap V}.$$

Hence,

$$H(t_0) \cap \bar{V} = \overline{H(t_0) \cap V}.$$

Suppose the conclusion of Theorem I.3.3 does not hold. Then there is a sequence $\{t_m\} \subset T$ with $t_m \to t_0$ such that $M(\varphi \mid H(t_m))$ is not contained in U. Hence $M(\varphi \mid H(t_m))$ is nonempty, so $\{t_m\} \subset T'$.

Let $\hat{T}$ be the subspace of T' consisting of the points $\{t_m\}$ and the point t_0. Let $\hat{H}$ be the set-valued function from $\hat{T}$ to E^n given by $\hat{H}(t) = H(t) \cap \bar{V}$. If $\{\hat{t}_m\} \subset \hat{T} \subset T'$ is a sequence with $\hat{t}_m \to t_0$, then

$$\varlimsup_{m \to \infty} H(\hat{t}_m) = \varliminf_{m \to \infty} H(\hat{t}_m) = H(t_0).$$

Now

$$H(t_0) \cap \bar{V} = \overline{H(t_0) \cap V},$$

so, by Theorem I.1.10,

$$\varlimsup_{m \to \infty} \hat{H}(\hat{t}_m) = \varliminf_{m \to \infty} \left(H(\hat{t} \cap \bar{V}) \right) = H(t_0) \cap \bar{V} = \hat{H}(t_0).$$

For each m, the set $\hat{H}(t_m)$ is compact, so there is a point $x_m \in M(\varphi \mid \hat{H}(\hat{t}_m))$. By assumption, there is a point $y_m \in M(\varphi \mid H(t_m))$ which is not in U and hence not in V. Now $x_m \in \bar{V}$, so the line segment $[x_m, y_m]$ contains a point z_m in the boundary of V. We have $x_m, y_m \in H(t_m)$ which is convex, so $z_m \in H(t_m)$. Therefore , $z_m \in \hat{H}(t_m)$. Now $\varphi(y_m) \leq \varphi(x_m)$ and φ is quasi-convex so $\varphi(z_m) \leq \varphi(x_m)$. Hence, $z_m \in M(\varphi \mid \hat{H}(t_m))$. There is an infinite sequence $\{m_i\}$ such that $z_{m_i} \to z$ where z is in the boundary of V. By Theorem I.2.2,

$$z = \lim_{i \to \infty} z_{m_i} \in \varlimsup_{i \to \infty} M(\varphi \mid \hat{H}(t_{m_i})) \subset M(\varphi \mid \hat{H}(t_0)) \subset M(\varphi \mid H(t_0)).$$

But this contradicts the assumption that $M(\varphi \mid H(t_0)) \subset V$.

COROLLARY I.3.4. *Under the hypothesis of Theorem I.3.3, the function*

$$t \to M^*(\varphi \mid H(t))$$

is continuous at t_0 whenever t_0 is in its domain.

PROOF. Immediate.

II. LINEAR CONSTRAINTS

Section II.1

In Part II we study the continuity properties of $M(\varphi \mid H)$ and $M^*(\varphi \mid H)$, where φ is a real-valued function on E^n, and where H is defined by linear inequalities. In particular, we wish to obtain conditions for $M(\varphi \mid H)$ to be a closed function and $M^*(\varphi \mid H)$ to be a continuous function of the parameters in the linear inequalities defining H. According to the results of Part I, we need only look at the behavior of $\underline{\lim}_{i \to \infty} H_i$, and $\overline{\lim}_{i \to \infty} H_i$, where $\{H_i\}$ is a sequence of subsets of Euclidean space, the H_i being defined by linear inequalities whose parameters converge as $i \to \infty$.

Since every linear equality can be represented by two linear inequalities, results for constraint sets defined by systems of linear inequalities can be applied to constraint sets defined by systems of linear equalities and linear inequalities.

We first wish to establish some basic notions and results.

By an *affine function* $f : E^n \to E^m$ we mean a function definable by $f(x) = ax + b$, where a is an m by n matrix and b is an m-dimensional column vector. Note that f defines a and b uniquely. The functions $f(x)_1, \ldots, f(x)_m$ will be called the *coordinates* of f. The numbers $\{a_{ij} \mid 1 \leq i \leq m, 1 \leq j \leq n\}$ and $\{b_r \mid 1 \leq r \leq m\}$ will be called the *coefficients* of f. Every affine function f, from E^n to E^m, can be identified with the point in $E(n+1)m$ defined by its coefficients. Thus, the set of affine functions from E^n to E^m can be regarded as a metric space.

If x, $y \in E^n$, then the statement $x \leq y$ will mean that $x_i \leq y_i$ for each pair of corresponding components x_i, y_i. By $x < y$ we mean $x_i < y_i$ for each i.

PROPOSITION II.1.1. *Let $\{f^r\}$ and f be affine functions from E^n to E^m. The following statements are equivalent:*
(a) $f^r \to f$,
(b) $f^r(x) \to f(x)$ for each $x \in E^n$,
(c) $f^r(x) \to f(x)$ uniformly in x on every bounded subset of E^n.

PROOF. Immediate.   Q.E.D.

If f is an affine function from E^n to E^m, then $H(f)$ will denote the subset of E^n defined by

$$H(f) = \{x \in E^n \mid f(x) \leq 0\}.$$

We will also consider the set function

$$f \to H(f) \cap C,$$

where C is a fixed subset of E^n. This set function will be denoted $H \cap C$. We are thus interested in the behavior of such objects as

$$\varliminf_{r \to \infty} (H(f^r) \cap C) \quad \text{and} \quad \varlimsup_{r \to \infty} (H(f^r) \cap C)$$

for convergent sequences, $\{f^r\}$, of affine functions.

THEOREM. *Let C be a closed convex set with nonempty (topological) interior. Let f and $\{f^r\}$ be affine functions from E^n to E^m with $f^r \to f$. Then*

(II.1.2). $\varlimsup_{r \to \infty}(H(f^r) \cap C) \subset H(f) \cap C$.

(II.1.3). $\varlimsup_{r \to \infty}(H(f^r) \cap C)$ is a closed convex subset of $H(f) \cap C$.

(II.1.4).   *If $H(f) \cap C$ has nonempty interior and no component of f is identically zero, then* $\lim_{r \to \infty}(H(f^r) \cap C) = H(f) \cap C$, *and*

(II.1.5). *if $H(f) \cap C$ has a nonempty interior or some component of f is identically zero, then, for any closed subset Q of $H(f) \cap C$, the functions f^r may be chosen so that*

$$\lim_{r \to \infty} (H(f^r) \cap C) = Q.$$

PROOF OF (II.1.2). Let $x \in \varlimsup_{r \to \infty}(H(f^r) \cap C)$. Then $x = \lim x_i$, where $x_i \in H(f^{r_i} \cap C$ for some infinite sequence $\{r_i\}$. Now C is closed, so $x \in C$. The sequence $\{x_i\}$ is bounded because it is convergent and $f^{r_i} \to f$ as $i \to \infty$. Hence

$$f(x) = \lim_{i \to \infty} f^{r_i}(x_i) \le 0,$$

so $x \in H(f)$.   Q.E.D. (II.1.2).

(II.1.3) follows from (II.1.2) and properties (I.1.2), (I.1.4), and (I.1.7) of the inner limit.   Q.E.D. (II.1.3).

The proof of (II.1.4) and (II.1.5) depends on the following lemmas.

LEMMA II.1.6. *A closed convex subset Q of E^n is equal to the intersection of countably many closed half-spaces.*

PROOF. According to Berge ([1], p. 166)), Q is representable in the form $Q = \bigcap_{\alpha \in A} H_\alpha$ where $\alpha \in A$ indexes the supporting half-spaces of Q. Since E^n has a countable basis, A has a countable subset A' with

$$\bigcap_{\alpha \in A'} H_\alpha = \bigcap_{\alpha \in A} H_\alpha. \qquad \text{Q.E.D. (II.1.6)}.$$

LEMMA II.1.7. *The closure of the interior of a convex set Q with nonempty interior is the closure of Q.*

PROOF. Eggleston ([2], Corollary 3, p. 11).   Q.E.D. (II.1.7).

Now suppose that the hypotheses of (II.1.4) are satisfied. Let x be in the interior of $H(f) \cap C$. We claim $f(x) < 0$. If not, $f_i(x) = 0$ for some component f_i of f. Now f_i is nonconstant, for if it were constant it would be identically zero. Hence there are no points y arbitrarily close to x for which $f_i(y) > 0$. This contradicts the assumption that x is in the interior of $H(f) \cap C$.

Now,

$$\lim_{r \to \infty} f^r(x) = f(x) < 0,$$

so $f^r(x) < 0$ for r sufficiently large. Hence $x \in H(f^r) \cap C$ for r sufficiently large. Therefore,[d]

$$x = \lim_{r \to \infty} x_r \in \varliminf_{r \to \infty} (H(f^r) \cap C).$$

Since $\varliminf_{r \to \infty} (H(f^r) \cap C)$ is closed and contains the interior of $H(f) \cap C$, by Lemma II.1.7, $H(f) \cap C \subset \varliminf_{r \to \infty} H(f^r) \cap C$. Hence

$$\varliminf_{r \to \infty} (H(f^r) \cap C) \subset \varlimsup_{r \to \infty} (H(f^r) \cap C) \subset H(f) \cap C \subset \varliminf_{r \to \infty} H(f^r) \cap C,$$

and the conclusion follows.   Q.E.D. (II.1.4).

Finally, suppose that the hypotheses of (II.1.5) are satisfied. Suppose that $f(x) < 0$ for some $x \in C$. Then no component of f vanishes identically, so $H(f) \cap C$ must have empty interior. But there is an open neighborhood U of x such that $f(y) < 0$ for $y \in U$. By Lemma II.1.7, U intersects the interior of C so a nonempty open subset of U is contained in $H(f) \cap C$. This is a contradiction. Hence the system of inequalities $f(x) < 0$ has no solution $x \in C$. Therefore, according to Berge ([1], p. 200), there is a point $\theta \in E^m$ with $\theta \geq 0$ and $\theta \neq 0$ such that[e]

$$\theta \cdot f(x) = \sum_{i=1}^{m} \theta_i f_i(x) \geq 0 \qquad \text{for all} \qquad x \in C.$$

By Lemma II.1.6, there is a sequence of affine functions $\{g^1, g^2, \ldots\}$, $g^r : E^n \to R$, such that Q consists of exactly those points x for which $g^r(x) \leq 0$ for all r. Since $g^r(x) \leq 0$ if and only if $\lambda g^r(x) \leq 0$, where λ is any positive real number, we may assume that the coefficients of the g^r are uniformly bounded.

We define a sequence of affine functions $\{h^r\}$, $h^r : E^n \to R$ as follows:

$$h^1 = g^1$$
$$h^2 = \tfrac{1}{2}g^1, \quad h^3 = \tfrac{1}{3}g^2,$$
$$h^4 = \tfrac{1}{4}g^1, \quad h^5 = \tfrac{1}{5}g^2, \quad h^6 = \tfrac{1}{6}g^3,$$

$$\vdots$$

Let i_0, $1 \leq i_0 \leq m$, be such that $\theta_{i_0} > 0$. Let $f^r : E^n \to E^m$ be the affine function with components

$$f_j^r = \begin{cases} f_j & \text{if} & j \neq i_0, \\ f_{i_0} + h^r & \text{if} & j = i_0. \end{cases}$$

Then $f^r \to f$ because the coefficients of the g^r are uniformly bounded.

Let $x \in Q \subset H(f) \cap C$. Then $f(x) \leq 0$ and $g^r(x) \leq 0$ for all r. Hence, $f^r(x) \leq 0$ for all r, so

$$x = \lim_{r \to \infty} x_r \in \varliminf_{r \to \infty} (H(f^r) \cap C).$$

Therefore, $Q \subset \lim_{r \to \infty}(H(f^r) \cap C)$.

Now let $x \in \lim_{r \to \infty}(H(f^r) \cap C)$. Then $x = \lim_{r \to \infty} x_r$, where $x_r \in H(f^r) \cap C$ for r sufficiently large. If $x \notin Q$, then $g^k(x) > 0$ for some k. Hence $g^k(x_r) > 0$ for some r sufficiently large. Let $\{r_i\}$ be the infinite sequence of integers such that $h^{r_i} = (1/r_i)g^k$. For i sufficiently large

$$h^{r_i}(x_{r_i}) = \frac{g^k(x_{r_i})}{r_i} > 0.$$

Now $x_{r_i} \in H(f^{r_i}) \cap C \subset C$, so $\theta \cdot f(x_{r_i}) \geq 0$. Hence

$$0 < \theta_{i_0} h^{r_i}(x_{r_i}) \leq \theta_{i_0} h^{r_i}(x_{r_i}) + \theta \cdot f(x_{r_i}) = \theta \cdot f^{r_i}(x_{r_i}),$$

but this contradicts the fact that $f^{r_i}(x_{r_i}) \leq 0$. Therefore, $x \in Q$. Q.E.D. (II.1.5).

We will call an affine function f *nondegenerate with respect to the set* C if f satisfies the hypothesis of (II.1.4). Otherwise, f will be called *degenerate with respect to* C. Theorems II.1.2 through II.1.5, together with the preceding theorems, show that if φ is continuous and C is closed and convex, then the set function $M(\varphi \mid H(f) \cap C)$ of f is closed at every nondegenerate point f (see Theorem I.2.2). Furthermore, $M^*(\varphi \mid H(f) \cap C)$ is continuous at a nondegenerate point f in its domain, provided that either φ is quasi-convex or $H(f) \cap C$ is bounded (see Theorems I.3.2 and I.3.3).

On the other hand, if f is degenerate, then for some continuous φ, $M(\varphi \mid H \cap C)$ is not closed at f, and for some convex φ, f is in the domain of $M^*(\varphi \mid H \cap C)$ but this function is not continuous at f.

Section II.2

Even though the functions $M(\varphi \mid H \cap C)$ and $M^*(\varphi \mid H \cap C)$ need not be well behaved at a degenerate point when we consider them as functions on the entire space of affine functions, we can guarantee that the functions are respectively closed and continuous at a degenerate point f if we restrict their domains to a suitable subspace of the space of affine functions. To make our results as sensitive as possible, we will phrase them in terms of conditions on a sequence $\{f^r\}$ of affine functions converging to an affine function f which will insure that $\underline{\lim}_{r\to\infty}(H(f^r)\cap C)$ and $\lim_{r\to\infty}(H(f^r)\cap C)$ have suitable properties even though f is degenerate.

Our basic results are Theorems II.2.1 and II.2.2. These theorems are basic only in the logical sense. The most useful results are their corollaries, which are given in Section II.3. The corollaries have, generally, the same conclusions, but have hypotheses which are easier to verify in practice.

The proofs of II.2.1 and II.2.2 are long and complicated. We suggest that anyone planning to read them first arm himself with motivation by reading Section II.3.

Theorem II.2.2 asserts that under certain conditions either $\lim_{r\to\infty} H(f^r) = H(f)$ or $H(f^r)$ is empty for infinitely many r. This is equivalent to the condition on the limiting behavior of the $H(f^r)$ hypothesized by Theorems I.3.2 and I.3.3. Furthermore it implies that $\underline{\lim}_{r\to\infty} H(f^r)$ is either empty or equal to $H(f)$, which is the condition hypothesized by Theorem I.2.2.

We have included Theorem II.2.3 for completeness. It asserts that Theorem II.2.2 is in some sense a best possible result.

Let

$$P^m = \{\theta \in E^m \mid \theta \geq 0 \text{ and } \theta \neq 0\}.$$

If $\theta \in P^m$, we define the *carrier*[f] of θ by

$$\operatorname{carr}\theta = \{i \mid 1 \leq i \leq m,\ \theta_i > 0\}.$$

Let

$$\Delta^{m-1} = \{\theta \in P^m \mid \theta_1 + \cdots + \theta_m = 1\}.$$

Then Δ^{m-1} is a compact subset of P^m.

THEOREM II.2.1. *Let $\{f^r\}$ and f be affine functions from E^n to E^m with $f^r \to f$. Let C be a closed convex subset of E^n. Suppose that, for each $\theta \in \Delta^{m-1}$ such that $\theta \cdot f(x) \geq 0$ for all $x \in C$, there is a sequence $\{\theta^r\} \in \Delta^{m-1}$ such that $\operatorname{carr}\theta^r \subset \operatorname{carr}\theta$ and $\theta^r \cdot f^r(x) \leq 0$ for all $x \in C$ and all sufficiently large r. Then*

$$\lim_{r\to\infty} (H(f^r)\cap C) = H(f)\cap C.$$

PROOF. By Theorem II.1.2, it is sufficient to show that

$$H(f)\cap C \subset \lim_{r\to\infty} (H(f^r)\cap C).$$

Suppose that $x_0 \in H(f)\cap C$ and $x_0 \notin \underline{\lim}_{r\to\infty}(H(f^r)\cap C)$. Then there is an $\epsilon > 0$ and an infinite subset I of the positive integers such that

$d(x_0, H(f^r) \cap C) \geq \epsilon$ for each $r \in I$. Hence, if we let

$$N = \left\{ x \in C \mid d(x, x_0) \leq \frac{2}{\epsilon} \right\},$$

the system of inequalities

$$f^r(x) \leq 0$$

has no solution in N where $r \in I$. Now N is a compact convex subset of E^n so, according to Berge ([1], p. 202), for each $r \in I$ there is a point $\theta^r \in \Delta^{m-1}$ such that

$$\theta^r \cdot f^r(x) > 0, \quad \text{for} \quad x \in N.$$

We may assume that θ^r is chosen so that carr θ^r contains as few elements as possible.

Since each carr θ^r is a subset of a fixed finite set, there is an infinite subset I' of I such that carr $\theta^r =$ carr θ^s for every $r, s \in I'$. Since Δ^{m-1} is compact, there is an infinite subset $J \subset I'$ such that the sequence $\{\theta^r\}, r \in J$ converges to a point $\theta \in \Delta^{m-1}$.

The points $\{\theta^r\}, r \in J$ all have the same carrier, so carr $\theta \subset$ carr θ^r for $r \in J$. Furthermore, since $f^r \to f$,

$$\theta \cdot f(x) \geq 0 \quad \text{for} \quad x \in N.$$

Now

$$x_0 \in H(f) \cap C \subset H(f) \quad \text{and} \quad x_0 \in N,$$

so

$$0 \geq \theta \cdot f(x_0) \geq 0$$

so that $\theta \cdot f(x_0) = 0$. Let x be any point in C. For each real t let

$$g(t) = \theta \cdot f((1 - t)x_0 + tx).$$

We have $g(0) = \theta \cdot f(x_0) = 0$. Since x_0 and x are both in C, $(1-t)x_0 + tx \in C$ for $0 \leq t \leq 1$. Hence, by the definition of N, $(1 - t)x_0 + tx \in N$ for all sufficiently small positive t. Thus, for all positive t,

$$g(t) = \theta \cdot f((1 - t)x_0 + tx) \geq 0.$$

This, the linearity of g, and the fact that $g(0) = 0$ imply that $\theta \cdot f(x) = g(t) \geq 0$. We have thus shown that

$$\theta \cdot f(x) \geq 0 \quad \text{for all} \quad x \in C.$$

Let r be a sufficiently large element of J. Since $\theta \in \Delta^{m-1}$, by hypothesis there is a point $\varphi^r \in \Delta^{m-1}$ such that carr $\varphi^r \subset$ carr $\theta \subset$ carr θ^r and

$$\varphi^r \cdot f^r(x) \leq 0 \quad \text{for all} \quad x \in C.$$

Hence,

$$(\theta^r - t\varphi^r) \cdot f^r(x) > 0, \qquad \text{for} \qquad x \in N \qquad \text{and} \qquad t \geq 0.$$

Since $\operatorname{carr} \varphi^r \subset \operatorname{carr} \theta^r$, we can choose $t > 0$ so that $\theta^r - t\varphi^r \geq 0$ and $\operatorname{carr}(\theta^r - t\varphi^r) \subsetneqq \operatorname{carr} \theta^r$. Now $\theta^r - t\varphi^r \neq 0$ because $x_0 \in N$ and hence $(\theta^r - t\varphi^r) \cdot f^r(x_0) > 0$. Therefore, there is a $\lambda > 0$ such that $\lambda\theta^r - \lambda t\varphi^r \in \Delta^{m-1}$. But

$$(\lambda\theta^r - \lambda t\varphi^r) \cdot f^r(x) > 0 \qquad\qquad x \in N$$

and

$$\operatorname{carr}(\lambda\theta^r - \lambda t\varphi^r) = \operatorname{carr}(\theta^r - t\varphi^r) \subsetneqq \operatorname{carr} \theta^r.$$

which contradicts the minimality of the carrier of θ^r.   Q.E.D.

We will now use Theorem II.2.1 to prove a more general result. First, we need some additional notation.

Let f be an affine function from E^n to E^m. The (unique) matrix, a, such that $f(x) = ax + b$ will be called the *matrix of f* and the *rank of* this matrix will be called the *rank of f*. If

$$I = \{i_1, \ldots, i_r\}$$

is a subset of $\{1, \ldots, m\}$, then E^I will denote the space of r-tuples of real numbers $(x_{i_1}, \ldots, x_{i_r})$ indexed on the set I. f_I will denote the affine function from E^n to E^I with coordinates $(f_{i_1}, \ldots, f_{i_r})$. If c is a point in E^m, then $f + c$ will denote the affine function with coordinates

$$f_i + c_i, \qquad 1 \leq i \leq m.$$

THEOREM II.2.2 *Let $\{f^r\}$ and f be affine functions from E^n to E^m with $f^r \to f$. Let*

$$I = \{i \mid 1 \leq i \leq m \text{ and } f_i(x) = 0 \text{ for all } x \in H(f)\}.$$

Suppose that

$$\limsup_{r \to \infty}(\operatorname{rank} f_I^r) \leq \operatorname{rank} f_I.$$

Then either

$$\lim_{r \to \infty} H(f^r) = H(f)$$

or $H(f^r)$ is empty for infinitely many r in which case

$$\varliminf_{r \to \infty} H(f^r)$$

is empty.

PROOF. If $H(f)$ is empty, the conclusion follows from Theorem II.1.2, taking $C = E^n$, so we suppose that $H(f)$ is nonempty.

LEMMA II.2.3. *Let $J = \{1, \ldots, m\} - I$. There is an $x_0 \in H(f)$ such that $f_J(x_0) < 0$.*

PROOF. By definition, for each $j \in J$ there is an $x_j \in H(f)$ such that $f_j(x_j) < 0$. Let x_0 be the average of the x_j, $j \in J$.   Q.E.D. (II.2.3).

LEMMA II.2.4.. *There is a $\theta \in E^I$ such that $\theta > 0$ and $\theta \cdot f_I$ is identically zero.*

PROOF. For each $i \in I$ we will construct a $\theta \in E^I$ with $\theta \geq 0$, $\theta_i > 0$, and $\theta \cdot f_I = 0$. The sum of these θ's will be the point required.

Let $i_0 \in I$ and suppose that the system of inequalities

$$f_i(x) \leq 0, \qquad i \in I, \qquad i \neq i_0,$$
$$f_{i_0}(x) + 1 \leq 0$$

has a solution $x \in E^n$. Since $f_I(x_0) < 0$, for t sufficiently small and positive, $(1 - t)x_0 + tx \in H(f)$. But $x_0 \in H(f)$ so $f_{i_0}(x_0) \leq 0$. This and the fact that $f_{i_0}(x) \leq -1$ imply that

$$f_{i_0}((1 - t)x_0 + tx) < 0,$$

contradicting the fact that $i_0 \in I$. Hence the system of inequalities has no solution. By Motzkin's Theorem there exists a $\theta \in E^I$ with $\theta \geq 0$ such that

$$\theta \cdot f_I(x) + \theta_{i_0} > 0 \qquad \text{for all} \qquad x \in E^n.$$

Hence $\theta \cdot f_I(x)$ is constant. Now $\theta \cdot f_I(x) = 0$ (because $x_0 \in H(f)$) so $\theta \cdot f_I = 0$. Finally,

$$\theta_{i_0} = \theta_{i_0} + \theta \cdot f_I(x_0) > 0.$$

$$\text{Q.E.D. (II.2.4)}$$

If $H(f^r)$ is empty for infinitely many r, we are done. Hence we may assume that there is a sequence $\{x_r\} \subset E^n$ with $x_r \in H(f^r)$ for r sufficiently large.

Let $k = \operatorname{rank} f_I$ and let I' be a subset of I containing exactly k elements such that $\operatorname{rank} f_{I'} = k$. Since the rank of a matrix is a lower semicontinuous function of its coefficients,

$$k = \operatorname{rank} f_{I'} \leq \liminf_{r \to \infty} \operatorname{rank} f_{I'}^r.$$

By assumption,

$$\limsup_{r \to \infty} \operatorname{rank} f_{I'}^r \leq \operatorname{rank} f_I = k.$$

Hence, for r sufficiently large,

$$k \leq \operatorname{rank} f_{I'}^r \leq \operatorname{rank} f_I^r \leq k,$$

so that $\operatorname{rank} f_{I'}^r = \operatorname{rank} f_I^r = k$, for all large r.

Let $K = \{0\} \cup I' \cup J$. Define affine functions h and $\{h^r\}$ from E^n to E^K by

$$h_i(x) = \begin{cases} -\sum_{j \in I'} f_j(x) & \text{if} \quad i = 0, \\ f_i(x) & \text{if} \quad i \in I' \cup J, \end{cases}$$

$$h_i^r(x) = \begin{cases} -\sum_{j \in I'} (f_j^r(x) - f_j(x_r)) & \text{if} \quad i = 0, \\ f_i^r(x) - f_i^r(x_r) & \text{if} \quad i \in I', \\ f_i^r(x) & \text{if} \quad i \in J. \end{cases}$$

These functions have the following properties:

(1) $H(f) \subset H(h)$,
(2) $H(h^r) \subset H(f^r)$ for r sufficiently large, and
(3) $h^r \to h$.

Statement (1) is trivial since, if $x \in H(f)$, then $f_J(x) \leq 0$ and $f_I(x) = 0$. To see (2), let r be so large that $x_r \in H(f^r)$ and $\operatorname{rank} f_{I'}^r = \operatorname{rank} f_I^r = k$. Let $x \in H(h^r)$ and let $i \in I'$. Then

$$0 \geq h_i^r(x) \geq \sum_{i \in I'} h_i^r(x) = -h_0^r(x) \geq 0,$$

so $f_{I'}^r(x) = f_{I'}^r(x_r)$. If i is any element of I, then

$$f_i^r = \mu \cdot f_{I'}^r + C$$

for some $\mu \in E^{I'}$ and some constant C. Hence,

$$f_i^r(x) = \mu \cdot f_{I'}^r(x) + C = \mu \cdot f_{I'}^r(x_r) + C = f_i^r(x_r).$$

Therefore, $f_I^r(x) = f_I^r(x_r)$. But $x_r \in H(f^r)$, so $f_I^r(x_r) \leq 0$. Thus,

$$f_I^r(x) \leq 0.$$

Finally,

$$f_J^r(x) = h_J^r(x) \leq 0,$$

so $x \in H(f^r)$.

To prove (3) it suffices to show that

$$f_I^r(x_r) \to 0.$$

LEMMA II.2.5. For r sufficiently large, there is a $\theta^r \in E^I$ such that $\theta^r \cdot f_I^r$ is constant. The sequence $\{\theta^r\}$ may be chosen to that $\theta^r \to \theta$ (where θ is as in Lemma II.2.4), in which case $\theta^r > 0$ for r sufficiently large (because $\theta > 0$).

PROOF. Let r be so large that rank $f_I^r = $ rank $f_{I'}^r$. Then there is a $\mu^r \in E^{I'}$ and a constant c^r such that

$$\theta \cdot f_I^r = \mu^r \cdot f_{I'}^r + c^r.$$

Now μ^r is the unique solution of a system of linear equations whose coefficients depend continuously on f_I^r. In the limit,

$$\theta \cdot f_I = 0 = 0 \cdot f_{I'}^r + 0,$$

so $\mu^r \to 0$. Define θ^r by

$$\theta_i^r = \begin{cases} \theta_i - \mu_i^r & \text{if} \quad i \in I', \\ \theta_i & \text{if} \quad i \in I - I'. \end{cases}$$

Then $\theta^r \to \theta$ and

$$\theta^r \cdot f_I^r = \theta \cdot f_I^r - \mu^r \cdot f_{I'}^r = c^r.$$

$$\text{Q.E.D. (II.2.5).}$$

Now let r be so large that $x_r \in H(f^r)$ and $\theta^r > 0$. Let $i \in I$. Then

$$0 \geq \theta_i^r f_i^r(x_r) \geq \theta^r \cdot f_I^r(x_r) = \theta^r \cdot f_I^r(x_0).$$

Now

$$\theta^r \cdot f_I^r(x_0) \to \theta \cdot f_I(x_0) = 0 \quad \text{and} \quad \theta_i^r \to \theta_i \neq 0.$$

Therefore, $f_i^r(x_r) \to 0$, and (3) is established.

We claim that the functions h and $\{h^r\}$ satisfy the hypotheses of theorem II.2.1 with $C = E^n$. Let ℓ be the cardinality of K. Suppose that for some $\varphi \in \Delta^{\ell-1}$, $\varphi \cdot h(x) \geq 0$ for all $x \in E^n$. If $j \in J$, $h_j(x_0) = f_j(x_0) < 0$. But $x_0 \in H(f) \subset H(h)$, so

$$\varphi_j h_j(x_0) \geq \varphi \cdot h(x_0) \geq 0.$$

Therefore, $\varphi_j = 0$. Hence,

$$\varphi \cdot h = \varphi_0 h_0 + \sum_{i \in I'} \varphi_i h_i = \sum_{i \in I'} (\varphi_i - \varphi_0) f_i.$$

Now $\varphi \cdot h$ is constant and the rows of the matrix of $f_{I'}$ are linearly independent, so

$$\varphi_i - \varphi_0 = 0 \qquad \text{for each} \qquad i \in I'.$$

Consequently, for each r,

$$\varphi \cdot h^r = \varphi_0 h_0^r + \sum_{i \in I'} \varphi_i h_i^r = \sum_{i \in I'} (\varphi_i - \varphi_0) h_i^r = 0 \leq 0,$$

so we may take the sequence $\{\varphi^r\}$ required by the hypothesis of Theorem II.2.1 to be constantly equal to φ.

Now we have, by (1), (2), and Theorem II.2.1,

$$H(f) \subset H(h) = \lim_{r \to \infty} H(h^r) = \varinjlim_{r \to \infty} H(h^r) \subset \varinjlim_{r \to \infty} H(f^r),$$

so Theorem II.2.2 follows from Theorem II.1.2.   Q.E.D. (II.2.2).

In the above argument we have tacitly assumed that I and J are nonempty. If I is empty, the result reduces to Theorem II.1.4. If J is empty, we take x_0 to be any point in $H(f)$, and the above argument applies.

Observe that the hypotheses of Theorem II.2.2 place restrictions only on the matrices of the functions f_I^r, not their constant coefficients. We now show that Theorem II.2.2 is the best possible result in the sense that if the condition on the matrices of the f_I^r is not satisfied, then for suitable choices of the constant coefficients of the f^r, the conclusion of Theorem II.2.2 does not hold.

THEOREM II.2.6 *Let f, $\{f^r\}$, and I be as in Theorem II.2.2, with $f^r \to f$. Suppose that $H(f)$ is nonempty and that*

$$\limsup_{r \to \infty} \operatorname{rank} f_I^r > \operatorname{rank} f_I.$$

Then there is a sequence $\{c^r\}$ of points in E^m with $c_i^r = 0$ for $i \notin I$ and $c^r \to 0$ such that $\varliminf_{r \to \infty} H(f^r + c^r)$ is a proper, nonempty subset of $H(f)$.

PROOF. Let $J = \{1, 2, \ldots, m\} - I$. By Lemma II.2.3 there is a point $x_0 \in H(f)$ such that $f_J(x_0) < 0$. Define the sequence $\{c^r\}$ by

$$c_i^r = \begin{cases} -f_i^r(x_0) & \text{if} \quad i \in I, \\ 0 & \text{if} \quad i \in J. \end{cases}$$

Then $c^r \to 0$ (because $f_I^r(x_0) \to f_I(x_0) = 0$).

We have

$$f_I^r(x_0) + c_I^r = f_I^r(x_0) - f_I^r(x_0) = 0$$

and

$$\lim_{r \to \infty} f_J^r(x_0) = f_J(x_0) < 0,$$

so $x_0 \in H(f^r + c^r)$ for r sufficiently large. Hence, $x_0 \in \underline{\lim}_{r \to \infty} H(f^r + c^r)$.

It remains to show that there is a point in $H(f)$ which is not in $\underline{\lim}_{r \to \infty} H(f^r + c^r)$. Let A denote the matrix of f_I, and A^r denote the matrix of f_I^r. Then

$$\limsup_{r \to \infty} \operatorname{rank} A^r > \operatorname{rank} A,$$

so there is an infinite subset K of the positive integers such that

$$\operatorname{rank} A^r > \operatorname{rank} A \qquad \text{for all} \qquad r \in K.$$

In the following a point in E^k will be regarded as a $k \times 1$ matrix. If M is a matrix, $\tilde{M}$ will denote its transpose. For $v \in E^k$, $\|v\| = (\tilde{v}v)^{1/2}$ will denote the usual norm in E^k.

Let

$$V = \{v \in E^n \mid Av = 0\}.$$

For each $r \in K$ let

$$C_r = \{\tilde{A}^r \mid \theta \in E^I \text{ and } \theta > 0\}.$$

Now V and C_r are convex subsets of E^n. Suppose that for all sufficiently large $r \in K$, the sets V and C_r are disjoint. Then by Berge ([1], p. 163), for each such $r \in K$ there is a hyperplane separating V and C_r. Hence there is nonzero $u^r \in E^n$ and a real number a^r such that

$$u^r \cdot x \geq a^r \qquad \text{if} \qquad x \in V,$$

and

$$u^r \cdot x \leq \qquad \text{if} \qquad x \in C_r.$$

We may assume $\|u^r\| = 1$.

If $x \in V$, then $\lambda x \in V$ for any real λ. Therefore,

$$\lambda u^r \cdot x \geq a^r \qquad \text{for all real } \lambda \qquad \text{and} \qquad x \in V.$$

Hence,

$$u^r \cdot x = 0 \qquad \text{for any} \qquad x \in V,$$

and also

$$a^r \leq 0.$$

This implies that $\tilde{u}^r$ is a linear combination of the rows of A. That is,

$$\tilde{u}^r = \tilde{\theta}^r A \qquad \text{or} \qquad u^r = \tilde{A}\theta^r$$

for some $\theta^r \in E^I$. If I' is the set of indices of a maximal linearly independent subset of the rows of A, we may choose θ^r with $\operatorname{carr} \theta^r \subset I'$. With this additional restriction θ^r is unique, and it is a continuous function of u^r.

Let $\{r_i\} \subset K$ be an infinite subsequence such that $u^{r_i} \to u$. Then $\theta^{r_i} \to \theta$, where $u = \tilde{A}\theta$. The coordinates of the points θ^{r_i} are uniformly bounded since $\{\theta^{r_i}\}$ is a convergent subsequence. By Lemma II.2.4 there is a $\bar{\theta} \in E^I$ with $\bar{\theta} > 0$ and $\bar{\theta} \cdot f_I = 0$. For λ sufficiently large, $\theta^{r_i} + \lambda\bar{\theta} > 0$ for all i. Now $\tilde{A}\bar{\theta} = 0$, so

$$\tilde{A}(\theta^{r_i} + \lambda\bar{\theta}) = \tilde{A}\theta^{r_i} = u^{r_i}.$$

We have $\tilde{A}^{r_i}(\theta^{r_i} + \lambda\bar{\theta}) \in C_{r_i}$, so

$$\tilde{u}^{r_i}\tilde{A}^{r_i}(\theta^{r_i} + \lambda\bar{\theta}) \le a^{r_i} \le 0.$$

Therefore,

$$0 \ge \lim_{i\to\infty} \tilde{u}^{r_i}\tilde{A}^{r_i}(\theta^{r_i} + \lambda\bar{\theta}) = \tilde{u}\tilde{A}(\theta + \lambda\bar{\theta}) = \tilde{u}u = 1,$$

which is a contradiction. Consequently, $C_r \cap V$ is nonempty for infinitely many $r \in K$.

If $C_r \cap V = \{0\}$, then $\tilde{A}^r\theta = 0$ for some $\theta \in E^I$ with $\theta > 0$. Therefore,

$$\tilde{A}^r x = \tilde{A}^r(x + \lambda\theta) \in C_r \qquad \text{for} \qquad x \in E^I$$

if we take λ so large that $x + \lambda\theta > 0$. Hence, C_r is the subspace of E^n generated by the rows of A^r. Now

$$\dim V + \dim C_r = n - \operatorname{rank} A + \operatorname{rank} A^r > n.$$

This contradicts our assumption that $C_r \cap V = \{0\}$. Therefore, for infinitely many $r \in K$ there is a nonzero $v^r \in V \cap C_r$ which we may assume to have norm 1.

Let $\{r_i\} \subset K$ be an infinite sequence such that $v^{r_i} \to v$. Then $\|v\| = 1$, and $Av = 0$. Since $f_J(x_0) < 0$, we may choose $\sigma > 0$ so small that $f_J(x_0 + \sigma v) \le 0$. Now

$$f_I(x_0 + \sigma v) = f_I(x_0) + A(\sigma v) = f_I(x_0) \le 0,$$

so $x_0 + \sigma v \in H(f)$. Suppose that $x_0 + \sigma v \in \underline{\lim}_{r\to\infty} H(f^r + c^r)$. Then $x_0 + \sigma v = \lim_{r\to\infty} x_r$, where $x_r \in H(f^r + c^r)$ for r sufficiently large.

For each i, let $u^{r_i} = x_{r_i} - x_0$. Then $u^{r_i} \to \sigma v$. For i sufficiently large,

$$A^{r_i}u^{r_i} = A^{r_i}x_{r_i} - A^{r_i}x_0 = f_I^{r_i}(x_{r_i}) - f_I^{r_i}(x_0)$$

$$= f_I^{r_i}(x_{r_i}) + c_I^{r_i} \le 0.$$

Now $v^{r_i} \in C_{r_i}$, so $v^{r_i} = \tilde{A}^{r_i}\theta^{r_i}$ for some $\theta^{r_i} > 0$. Therefore,

$$\tilde{v}^{r_i}u^{r_i} = \bar{\theta}^{r_i}A^{r_i}u^{r_i} \le 0 \qquad \text{for} \qquad i \text{ large.}$$

Hence,

$$0 \geq \lim_{i \to \infty} \tilde{v}^{r_i} u^{r_i} = \tilde{v}\sigma v = \sigma > 0.$$

This contradiction shows that $x_0 + \sigma v \notin \underline{\lim}_{r \to \infty} H(f^r + c^r)$.

Q.E.D. (II.2.6).

Section II.3

In this section we obtain a number of results which follow quickly from the theorems of Section II.2. Some of these results have hypotheses which are considerably easier to verify than those of Section II.2.

COROLLARY II.3.1. *Let f be an affine function from E^n to E^m, and let $\{c^r\}$ be a sequence of points in E^m with $c^r \to 0$. Then either*

$$\lim_{r \to \infty} H(f + c^r) = H(f)$$

or $H(f + c^r)$ is empty for infinitely many r.

PROOF. Since the matrix of $f + c^r$ is the same as the matrix of f, this follows at once from Theorem II.2.2   Q.E.D.

COROLLARY II.3.2. *Let f and $\{f^r\}$ be affine functions from E^n to E^m with $f^r \to f$. Let*

$$I = \{i \mid 1 \leq i \leq m \text{ and } f_i(x) = 0 \text{ for all } x \in H(f)\}.$$

If the matrix of f_I has full rank, then either

$$\lim_{r \to \infty} H(f^r) = H(f)$$

or $H(f^r)$ is empty for infinitely many r.

PROOF. Theorem II.2.1.   Q.E.D.

If f and g are affine functions from E^n to E^m and $E^{m'}$, respectively, we define

$$H(f, g) = \{x \in E^n \mid f(x) \leq 0 \text{ and } g(x) = 0\}.$$

Thus $H(f, g)$ represents a constraint set defined by a mixed system of linear equalities and linear inequalities.

COROLLARY II.3.3. *Let f, $\{f^r\}$, g, $\{g^r\}$ be affine functions from E^n to E^m and $E^{m'}$ with $f^r \to f$ and $g^r \to g$. Let C be a convex subset of E^n. Suppose for every θ, φ with $\theta \in E^m$, $\varphi \in E^{m'}$, $\theta \geq 0$, for which not both θ and φ are zero and such that $\theta \cdot f(x) \geq 0$ and $\varphi \cdot g(x) = 0$ for all*

$x \in C$, there are sequences $\{\theta^r\}$ of E^m and $\{\varphi^r\}$ of $E^{m'}$ such that for all sufficiently large r we have $\theta^r \geq 0$, not both θ^r and φ^r are zero, $\theta^r \cdot f(x) \leq 0$ and $\varphi^r \cdot g(x) = 0$ for all $x \in C$, and carr $\theta^r \subset$ carr θ and carr $\varphi^r \subset$ carr φ. Then

$$\lim_{r \to \infty} (H(f^r, g^r) \cap C) = H(f, g) \cap C.$$

PROOF. Let $h = (f, g, -g)$ and $h^r = (f^r, g^r, -g^r)$. Then $h^r \to h$ and $H(h) = H(f, g)$. Apply Theorem II.2.1.   Q.E.D.

COROLLARY II.3.4. Let f, $\{f^r\}$, g, $\{g^r\}$ be affine functions from E^n to E^m and $E^{m'}$ with $f^r \to f$ and $g^r \to g$. Let

$$I = \{i \mid 1 \leq i \leq m,\ f_i(x) = 0 \text{ for all } x \in H(f, g)\}.$$

Suppose that

$$\limsup_{r \to \infty} \operatorname{rank}(f_I^r, g^r) \leq \operatorname{rank}(f_I, f).$$

Then either $\lim_{r \to \infty} H(f^r, g^r) = H(f, g)$ or $H(f^r, g^r)$ is empty for infinitely many r.

PROOF. Let $h = (f, g, -g)$ and $h^r = (f^r, g^r, -g^r)$. Then $h^r \to h$, $H(h) = H(f, g)$, and $H(h^r) = H(f^r, g^r)$. Let

$$I'\{i \mid h_i(x) = 0 \quad \text{for all} \quad x \in H(h)\}.$$

Then

$$h_{I'} = (f_I, g, -g) \quad \text{and} \quad h_{I'}^r = (f_I^r, g^r, -g^r).$$

Now

$$\operatorname{rank}(f_I, g, -g) = \operatorname{rank}(f_I, g) \quad \text{and} \quad \operatorname{rank}(f_I^r, g^r, -g^r) = \operatorname{rank}(f_I^r, g^r),$$

so the conclusion follows from Theorem II.2.2.   Q.E.D.

COROLLARY II.3.5. Let f, $\{f^r\}$ and g, $\{g^r\}$ be affine functions from E^n to E^m and $E^{m'}$, respectively, with $f^r \to f$ and $g^r \to g$. Let

$$I = \{i \mid 1 \leq i \leq m,\ f_i(x) = 0 \text{ for all } x \in H(f, g)\}.$$

Let A be the matrix of f_I and B be the matrix of g. If the matrix $\binom{A}{B}$ has full rank, then either

$$\lim_{r \to \infty} H(f^r, g^r) = H(f, g)$$

or $H(f^r, g^r)$ is empty for infinitely many r.

PROOF. Corollary II.3.4.   Q.E.D.

COROLLARY II.3.6.[1] *Let g and $\{g^r\}$ be affine functions from E^n to E^m with $g^r \to g$. Let*

$$H = \{x \in E^n \mid x \geq 0 \text{ and } g(x) = 0\}$$

Let

$$H^r = \{x \in E^n \mid x \geq 0 \text{ and } g^r(x) = 0\}$$

Let

$$I = \{i \mid 1 \leq i \leq n \text{ and } x_i = 0 \text{ for all } x \in H\}.$$

If the matrix obtained from the matrix of g by deleting those columns whose indices are in I has full rank, then either $\lim_{r\to\infty} H^r = H$ or H^r is empty for infinitely many r.

PROOF. Corollary II.3.5 and some simple matrix manipulations. Q.E.D.

REFERENCES

[1] C. BERGE. "Topological Spaces." Macmillan, New York, 1963.

[2] H. G. EGGLESTON. "Convexity." Cambridge University Press, Cambridge, England, 1958.

[3] G. DANTZIG. "Linear Programming and Extensions." Princeton University Press, Princeton, New Jersey, 1963.

---

[1]This result in the case where I is empty and the g^r all have the same matrix was obtained by Lloyd Shapley prior to the authors' proof.

Part IX: Complementarity Problems

The first of the two papers in this final part deals with what has come to be called the *linear complementarity problem* (or the *fundamental problem*, as it is identified there). Such a problem is actually an inequality system based on an affine transformation of real n-space into itself. With this transformation, one seeks a nonnegative vector whose image is also nonnegative and such that the vector and its image are perpendicular. (The orthogonality of the two nonnegative vectors is equivalent to their inner product being nonpositive.)

In a way, a linear complementarity problem is an abstraction that captures the essential features of various necessary (and often sufficient) conditions one wants to satisfy so as to solve some other type of problem. As the paper illustrates, the necessary and sufficient conditions for optimality in linear programming can be expressed as a linear complementarity problem. The same is true for convex quadratic programming. (For nonconvex quadratic programming, satisfaction of these conditions alone is not sufficient to guarantee optimality.) In addition to being applicable to these broad classes of optimization problems, linear complementarity problems of a particular sort are equivalent to the systems that define Nash equilibria for finite, two-person, nonzero-sum (or "bimatrix") games. These formulations are all given in this paper. The relevance of the linear complementarity problem to others—such as economic equilibrium problems, contact problems, and optimal stopping problems—came later.

Beyond calling attention to the linear complementarity problem as an important model, this paper reviews a few pivoting algorithms for the linear complementarity problem. These include versions of Lemke's algorithm, the Lemke-Howson algorithm for the bimatrix game problem, and a version of the principal pivoting algorithm of Cottle and Dantzig.

In the study of the linear complementarity problem, considerable attention has been devoted to investigating the *existence* of solutions to the problem as given, and to the ability of certain algorithm to compute a solution. In this regard, much depends on the coefficient matrix of the affine transformation. The authors of this paper discuss the interplay between algorithms and matrix classes, some familiar, some new (at the time). From this standpoint, Lemke's algorithm is more versatile than the principal pivoting method.

Over the years, the richness of the linear complementarity problem has been revealed in many ways. One striking illustration of this is the fact that there are significant matrix classes that can be characterized in terms of the linear complementarity problem. Another is the motivation it has given to extending and generalizing the model.

The linear complementarity problem has been generalized in many ways. Even before the problem was named and identified as a fruitful object of study, it appeared in a paper by Samelson, Thrall, and Wesler (1958) in a form that would now be called the *horizontal generalization*.

The model given in Chapter 24 is the earliest of its kind. This one is called the *vertical generalization*. Here the matrix of the affine transformation is partitioned vertically into blocks forming a "stack" of, say, k matrices each having k columns. This gives a one-to-one correspondence between each independent variable and a set of dependent variables. As before, all the variables are required to be nonnegative; however, the orthogonality condition becomes the requirement that the product of each independent variable and its corresponding set of dependent variables be zero.

In the paper, the authors generalize certain matrix classes in this "vertical" manner and show that a version of Lemke's algorithm is capable of solving the new problem. Another contribution of this paper is its interpretation of Lemke's almost-complementary pivoting scheme in graph-theoretic terms.

Chapter 23

Complementary Pivot Theory of Mathematical Programming

RICHARD W. COTTLE AND GEORGE B. DANTZIG
Stanford University
Stanford, California

1. FORMULATION

Linear programming, quadratic programming, and bimatrix (two-person, nonzero-sum) games lead to the consideration of the following *fundamental problem*[1]: Given a real p-vector q and a real $p \times p$ matrix M, find vectors w and z which satisfy the conditions[2]

$$(1) \qquad w = q + Mz, \qquad w \geq 0, \quad z \geq 0,$$

$$(2) \qquad zw = 0.$$

The remainder of this section is devoted to an explanation of why this is so. (There are other fields in which this fundamental problem[a] arises—see, for example, [6] and [13]—but we do not treat them here.) Sections 2 and 3 are concerned with constructive procedures for solving the fundamental problem under various assumptions on the data q and M.

Consider first linear probrams in the symmetric primal-dual form due to J. von Neumann [20].

---

[1] The fundamental problem can be extended from p sets each consisting of a pair of variables only one of which can be nonbasic to k set of several variables each, only one of which can be nonbasic. To be specific, consider a system $w = q + Nz$, $w \geq 0$, $z \geq 0$, where N is a $p \times k$ matrix ($k \leq p$) and the variables $w_1, \dots, w_p$ are partitioned into k nonempty sets S_l, $l = 1, \dots, k$. Let $T_l = S_l \cup \{z_l\}$, $l = 1, \dots, k$. We seek a solution of the system in which exactly one member of each set T_l is nonbasic. (The fundamental problem is of this form where $k = p$ and $T_l = \{w_l, z_l\}$.) The underlying idea of Lemke's approach (Section 2) applies here. For example, it can be shown that this problem has a solution when $N > 0$. A paper is currently being prepared for publication in which this extension is developed in detail.

[2] In general, capital italic letters denote matrices while vectors are denoted by lowercase italic letters. Whether a vector is a row or a column will always be clear from the context, and consequently we dispense with transpose signs on vectors. In (2), for example, zw represents the scalar product of z (row) and w (column). The superscript T indicates the transpose of the matrix to which it is affixed.

Primal linear program: Find a vector x and minimum $\bar{z}$ such that

(3) $$Ax \geq b, \qquad x \geq 0, \qquad \bar{z} = cx.$$

Dual linear program: Find a vector y and maximum $\underline{z}$ such that

(4) $$yA \leq c, \qquad y \geq 0, \qquad \underline{z} = yb.$$

The duality theorem of linear programming [3] states that $\min \bar{z} = \max \underline{z}$ when the primal and dual systems (3) and (4), respectively, are consistent or—in mathematical programming parlance—"feasible." Since

$$\underline{z} = yb \leq yAx \leq cx = \bar{x}$$

for all primal-feasible x and dual-feasible y, one seeks such solutions for which

(5) $$yb = cx.$$

The inequality constraints of the primal and dual problems can be converted to equivalent systems of equations in nonnegative variables through the introduction of nonnegative "slack" variables. Jointly, the systems (3) and (4) are equivalent to

(6)
$$Ax - v = b, \quad v \geq 0, \quad x \geq 0,$$
$$A^T y + u = c, \quad u \geq 0, \quad y \geq 0,$$

and the linear programming problem becomes one of finding vectors u, v, x, y such that

(7) $$\begin{bmatrix} u \\ v \end{bmatrix} = \begin{bmatrix} c \\ -b \end{bmatrix} + \begin{bmatrix} 0 & -A^T \\ A & 0 \end{bmatrix} \begin{bmatrix} x \\ y \end{bmatrix}, \qquad \begin{matrix} u \geq 0, & v \geq 0, \\ x \geq 0, & y \geq 0, \end{matrix}$$

and, by (5),

(8) $$xu + yv = 0.$$

The definitions

(9) $$w = \begin{bmatrix} u \\ v \end{bmatrix}, \quad q = \begin{bmatrix} c \\ -b \end{bmatrix}, \quad M = \begin{bmatrix} 0 & -A^T \\ A & 0 \end{bmatrix}, \quad z = \begin{bmatrix} x \\ y \end{bmatrix}$$

establish the correspondence between (1), (2) and (3), (4).

The *quadratic programming problem* is typically stated in the following manner: Find a vector x and minimum $\bar{z}$ such that

(10) $$Ax \geq b, \qquad x \geq 0, \qquad \bar{z} = cx + \tfrac{1}{2} xDx.$$

In this formulation, the matrix D may be assumed to be symmetric. The minimand $\bar{z}$ is a globally convex function of x if and only if the quadratic form xDx (or matrix D) is positive semidefinite, and when this is the case, (10) is called the *convex quadratic programming problem*. It is immediate that when D is the zero matrix, (10) reduces to the linear program (3). In this sense, the linear programming problem is a special case of the quadratic programming problem.

For any quadratic programming problem (10), define u and v by

$$(11) \qquad u = Dx - A^T y + c, \qquad v = Ax - b.$$

A vector x^0 yields minimum $\bar{z}$ only if there exists a vector y^0 and vectors u^0, v^0 given by (11) for $x = x^0$ satisfying

$$
\begin{aligned}
x^0 \geq 0, \qquad u^0 \geq 0, \qquad y^0 \geq 0, \qquad v^0 \geq 0, \\
(12) \\
x^0 u^0 = 0, \qquad y^0 v^0 = 0.
\end{aligned}
$$

The *necessary conditions* for a minimum in (10) are a direct consequence of a theorem of H. W. Kuhn and A. W. Tucker [14]. It is well known—and not difficult to prove from first principles—that (12), known as the Kuhn-Tucker conditions,[b] are also *sufficient* in the case of convex quadratic programming. By direct substitution, we have for any feasible vector x

$$
\begin{aligned}
\bar{z} - \bar{z}^0 &= c(x - x^0) + \tfrac{1}{2}xDx - \tfrac{1}{2}x^0 Dx^0 \\
&= u^0(x - x^0) + y^0(v - v^0) + \tfrac{1}{2}(x - x^0)D(x - x^0) \\
&= u^0 x + y^0 v + \tfrac{1}{2}(x - x^0)D(x - x^0) \geq 0,
\end{aligned}
$$

which proves the sufficiency of conditions (12) for a minimum in the convex case.

Thus, the problem of solving a quadratic program leads to a search for solution of the system

$$
\begin{aligned}
(13) \qquad
& u = Dx - A^T y + c, && x \geq 0, \quad y \geq 0, \\
& v = Ax - b, && u \geq 0, \quad v \geq 0,
\end{aligned}
$$

$$(14) \qquad\qquad\qquad xu + yv = 0.$$

The definitions

$$(15) \qquad w = \begin{bmatrix} u \\ v \end{bmatrix}, \qquad q = \begin{bmatrix} c \\ -b \end{bmatrix}, \qquad M = \begin{bmatrix} D & -A^T \\ A & 0 \end{bmatrix}, \qquad z = \begin{bmatrix} x \\ y \end{bmatrix}$$

establish (13), (14) as a problem of the form (1), (2).

Dual of a convex quadratic program. From (15) one is led naturally to a consideration of a matrix $M = \begin{bmatrix} D & -A^T \\ A & E \end{bmatrix}$ wherein E, like D is positive semidefinite. It is shown in [1] that the

Primal quadratic program: Find x and minimum $bar z$ such that

(16) $Ax + Ey \geq b,$ $x \geq 0,$ $\bar{z} = cx + \frac{1}{2}(xDx + yEy),$

has the associated

Dual quadratic program: Find y and maximum $\underline{z}$ such that

(17) $-Dx + A^T y \leq c,$ $y \geq 0,$ $\underline{z} = by - \frac{1}{2}(xDx - yEy).$

All the results of duality in linear programming extend to these problems, and indeed they are jointly solvable if either is solvable. When $E = 0$, the primal problem is just (10), for which W. S. Dorn [5] first established the duality theory later extended in [1]. When both D and E are zero matrices, the dual pair (16), (17) reduces to the dual pair of linear problem (3), (4).

Remarks. (a) The minimand in (10) is strictly convex if and only if the quadratic form xDx is positive definite. Any *feasible* strictly convex quadratic program has a unique minimizing solution x^0. (b) When D and E are positive semidefinite (the case of convex quadratic programming), so is

$$M = \begin{bmatrix} D & -A^T \\ A & E \end{bmatrix}.$$

A *bimatrix* (or two-person nonzero-sum) *game*, $\Gamma(A, B)$, is given by a pair of $m \times n$ matrices A and B. One party, called the *row player*, has m pure strategies which are identified with the rows of A. The other party, called the *column player*, has n pure strategies which correspond to the columns of B. If the row player uses his ith pure strategy and the column player uses his jth pure strategy, then their respective *losses* are defined as a_{ij} and b_{ij}, respectively. Using *mixed strategies*,

$$x = (x_1, \ldots, x_m) \geq 0, \qquad \sum_{i=1}^{m} x_i = 1,$$

$$y = (y_1, \ldots, y_n) \geq 0, \qquad \sum_{j=1}^{n} y_j = 1,$$

their expected losses are xAy and xBy, respectively. (A component in a mixed strategy is interpreted as the probability with which the player uses the corresponding pure strategy.)

A pair (x^0, y^0) of mixed strategies is a *Nash* [19] *equilibrium point* of $\Gamma(A, B)$ if

$$x^0 A y^0 \leq x A y^0, \quad \text{all mixed strategies } x,$$

$$x^0 B y^0 \leq x^0 B y, \quad \text{all mixed strategies } y.$$

It is evident (see, for example, [15]) that if (x^0, y^0) is an equilibrium point of $\Gamma(A, B)$, then it is also an equilibrium point for the game $\Gamma(A', B')$ in which

$$A' = [a_{ij} + K], \qquad B' = [b_{ij} + L],$$

where K and L are arbitrary scalars. Hence there is no loss of generality in assuming that $A > 0$ and $B > 0$, and we shall make this assumption hereafter.

Next, by letting e_k denote the k-vector all of whose components are unity, it is easily shown that (x^0, y^0) is an equilibrium point of $\Gamma(A, B)$ if and only if

(18) $$\qquad (x^0 A y^0) e_m \leq A y^0 \qquad (A > 0),$$

(19) $$\qquad (x^0 B y^0) e_n \leq B^T x^0 \qquad (B > 0).$$

This characterization of an equilibrium point leads to a theorem which relates the equilibrium-point problem to a system of the form (1), (2). For $A > 0$ and $B > 0$, if u^*, v^*, x^*, y^* is a solution to the system

(20) $$\begin{aligned} u &= Ay - e_m, \quad u \geq 0, \quad y \geq 0, \\ v &= B^T x - e_n, \quad v \geq 0, \quad x \geq 0, \end{aligned}$$

(21) $$\qquad\qquad xu + yv = 0,$$

then

$$(x^0, y^0) = \left(\frac{x^*}{x^* e_m}, \frac{y^*}{y^* e_n} \right)$$

is an equilibrium point of $\Gamma(A, B)$. Conversely, if (x^0, y^0) is an equilibrium point of $\Gamma(A, B)$, then

$$(x^*, y^*) = \left(\frac{x^0}{x^0 B y^0}, \frac{y^0}{x^0 A y^0} \right)$$

is a solution of (20), (21). The latter system is clearly of the form (1), (2), where

$$w = \begin{bmatrix} u \\ v \end{bmatrix}, \quad q = \begin{bmatrix} -e_m \\ -e_n \end{bmatrix}, \quad M = \begin{bmatrix} 0 & A \\ B^T & 0 \end{bmatrix}, \quad z = \begin{bmatrix} x \\ y \end{bmatrix}.$$

Notice that the assumption $A > 0$, $B > 0$ precludes the possibility of the matrix M above belonging to the positive semidefinite class.

The existence of an equilibrium point for $\Gamma(A, B)$ was established by J. Nash [19] whose proof employs the Brouwer fixed-point theorem.[c] Recently, an elementary constructive proof was discovered by C. E. Lemke and J. T. Howson, Jr. [15].

2. LEMKE'S ITERATIVE SOLUTION OF THE FUNDAMENTAL PROBLEM

This section is concerned with the iterative technique of Lemke and Howson for finding equilibrium points of bimatrix games which was later extended by Lemke to the fundamental problem (1), (2). We introduce first some terminology common to the subject of this section and the next. Consider the system of linear equations

$$(22) \qquad\qquad w = q + Mz,$$

where, for the moment, the p-vector q and the $p \times p$ matrix M are arbitrary. Both w and z are p-vectors.

For $i = 1, \ldots, p$ the corresponding variables z_i and w_i are called *complementary* and each is the *complement* of the other. A *complementary solution* of (22) is a pair of vectors satisfying

$$(23) \qquad\qquad z_i w_i = 0, \qquad i = 1, \ldots, p.$$

Notice that a solution $(w; z)$ of (1), (2) is a nonnegative complementary solution of (22). Finally, a solution of (22) will be called *almost complementary* if it satisfies (23) except for one value of i, say $i = \beta$. That is, $z_\beta \neq 0$, $w_\beta \neq 0$.

In general, the procedure assumes *as given* an extreme point of the convex set

$$Z = \{z \mid w = q + Mx \geq 0, \quad z \geq 0\},$$

which also happens to be the end point of an almost complementary ray (unbounded edge) of Z. Each point of this ray satisfies (3) but for one value of i, say β. It is not always easy to find such a starting point for an arbitrary M. Yet there are two important realizations of the fundamental problem which can be so initiated. The first is the bimatrix game case to be discussed soon; the second is the case where an entire column of M is positive. The latter property can always be *artificially* induced by augmenting M with an additional positive column; as we shall see, this turns out to be a useful device for initiating the procedure with a general M.

Each iteration corresponds to motion from an extreme point P_i along an edge of Z all points of which are almost complementary solutions of (22). If this edge is bounded, an adjacent extreme point P_{i+1} is reached which is either complementary or almost complementary. The process terminates if (i) the edge is unbounded (a ray), (ii) P_{i+1} is a previously generated extreme point, or (iii) P_{i+1} is a complementary extreme point.

Under the assumption of nondegeneracy, the extreme points of Z are in one–to–one correspondence with the *basic feasible solutions* of (22) (see [3]). Still under this assumption, a *complementary basic solution* is one in which the complement of each basic variable is nonbasic. The goal is to obtain a basic feasible solution with such a property. In an almost complementary basic feasible solution of (23), there will be exactly one index, say β, such that both w_β and z_β are basic variables. Likewise, there will be exactly one index, say ν, such that both w_ν and z_ν are nonbasic variables.[3]

An almost complementary edge is generated by holding all nonbasic variables at value zero and increasing either z_ν or w_ν of the nonbasic pair w_β, z_β. There are consequently *exactly two* almost complementary edges associated with an almost complementary associated with an almost complementary extreme point (corresponding to an almost complementary basic feasible solution).

Suppose that z_ν is the nonbasic variable to be increased. The values of the basic variables will all change linearly with the changes in z_ν. For sufficiently small positive values of z_ν, the almost complementary solution remains feasible. This is a consequence of the nondegeneracy assumption. But in order to retain feasibility, the values of the basic variables must be prevented from becoming negative.

If the value of z_ν can be made arbitrarily large without forcing any basic variable to become negative, then a *ray* is generated. In this event, the process terminates. However, if some basic variable *blocks* the increase of z_ν (i.e., vanishes for a positive value of z_ν), then a new basic solution is obtained which is either complementary or almost complementary. A complementary solution occurs only if a member of the basic pair blocks z_ν. A new almost complementary extreme point solution is obtained if the blocking occurs otherwise. In the complementary case, we have the desired result: a complementary basic feasible solution. In the almost complementary case, the nondegeneracy assumption guarantees the uniqueness of the blocking variable. It will become nonbasic in place of z_ν and its index becomes the new value of ν.

The complementary rule

The complement of the (now nonbasic) blocking variable—or equivalently put, the other member of the "new" nonbasic pair—is the next nonbasic variable to be increased. The procedure consists of the iteration of these steps. The generated sequence of almost complementary extreme points and edges is called an *almost complementary path*.

---

[3]C. van de Panne and A. Whinston [21] have used the appropriate terms *basic* and *nonbasic pair* for (w_β, z_β) and (w_ν, z_ν), respectively.

THEOREM 1. *Along an almost complementary path, the only almost complementary basic feasible solution which can reoccur is the initial one.*

Proof. We assume that all basic feasible solutions of (22) are nondegenerate. (This can be assured by any of the standard lexicographic techniques [3] for resolving the ambiguities of degeneracy.) Suppose,

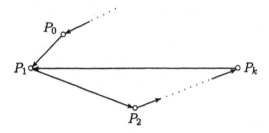

contrary to the assertion of the theorem, that the procedure generates a sequence of almost complementary basic feasible solutions in which a term other than the first one (P_0 in the accompanying figure) is repeated (say P_1). By the nondegeneracy assumption, the extreme points of Z are in one-to-one correspondence with the basic feasible solutions of (22). Let P_2 denote the successor of P_1 and let P_k denote the second predecessor to P_1, namely the one along the path just before the return to P_1. The extreme points P_0, P_2, P_k are distinct and each is adjacent to P_1 along an almost complementary edge. But there are only two such edges at P_1. This contradiction completes the proof.

We can immediately state the

COROLLARY. *If the almost complementary path is initiated at the end point of an almost complementary ray, the procedure must terminate either in a different ray or in a complementary basic feasible solution.*

It is easy to show by examples that starting from an almost complementary basic feasible solution which is *not* the end point of an almost complementary ray, the procedure *can* return to the initial point, regardless of the existence or nonexistence of a solution to (1), (2).

Example 1. The set Z associated with

$$q = \begin{bmatrix} 1 \\ -1 \\ 3 \end{bmatrix}, \qquad M = \begin{bmatrix} 0 & 0 & 0 \\ 1 & 0 & 0 \\ -1 & -1 & -1 \end{bmatrix}$$

is nonempty and bounded. It is clear that no solution of (1) can also satisfy (2) since $z_1 w_1 > 0$. Let the extreme point corresponding to the solution

$w = (1,0,0,)$, $z = (1,0,2)$ be the initial point of a path which begins by increasing z_2. This will return to the initial extreme point after 4 iterations.

Example 2. The set Z associated with

$$q = \begin{bmatrix} 1 \\ -1 \\ 3 \\ 1 \end{bmatrix}, \quad M = \begin{bmatrix} 0 & 0 & 0 & 0 \\ 1 & 0 & 0 & 1 \\ -1 & -1 & -1 & -1 \\ 0 & 0 & 0 & -1 \end{bmatrix}$$

is likewise nonempty and bounded. The corresponding fundamental problem (1), (2) has a complementary solution $w = (1, 0, 1, 0)$, $z = (0, 1, 0, 1)$. Yet by starting at $w = (1, 2, 0, 1)$, $z = (3, 0, 0, 0)$ and increasing z_3, the method generates a path which returns to its starting point after 4 iterations.

Furthermore, even if the procedure is initiated from an extreme point at the end of an almost complementary ray, termination in a ray is possible whether or not the fundamental problem has a solution.

Example 3. Given the data[d]

$$q = \begin{bmatrix} 1 \\ -1 \\ 3 \\ 1 \end{bmatrix}, \quad M = \begin{bmatrix} 0 & 0 & 0 & 1 \\ 1 & 0 & 0 & 1 \\ 1 & -1 & 1 & 1 \\ 0 & 0 & 0 & -1 \end{bmatrix},$$

the point Z which corresponds to $w = (1, 0, 4, 1)$, $z = (1, 0, 0, 0)$ is at the end of an almost complementary ray, $w = (1, w_2, 4 + w_2, 1)$, $z = (1 + w_2, 0, 0, 0)$. Moving along the edge generated by increasing z_2 leads to a new almost complementary extreme point at which the required increase of z_3 is unblocked, so that process terminates in a ray, and yet the fundamental problem is solved by

$$w = (2,0,3,0), \qquad z = (0,1,0,1).$$

Example 4. In the problem with

$$q = \begin{bmatrix} 1 \\ -1 \end{bmatrix}, \quad M = \begin{bmatrix} 0 & 0 \\ 1 & -1 \end{bmatrix}$$

the inequalities (1) have solutions, but none of them satisfies (2). The point corresponding to $(w; z) = (1, 0; 1, 0)$ is at the end of an almost complementary ray $w = (1, w_2)$, $z = (w_2, 0)$. When z_2 is increased, it is not blocked, and process terminates in a ray.

Consequences of termination in a ray

In this geometrical approach to the fundamental problem, it is useful to interpret algebraically the meaning of termination in an almost complementary ray. This can be achieved by use of a standard result in linear inequality theory [11, 3].

LEMMA. *If $(w^*; z^*)$ is an almost complementary basic feasible solution of (22), and $(w^*; z^*)$ is incident to an almost complementary ray, there exist p-vectors w^h, z^h such that*

$$(24) \qquad w^h = Mz^h, \qquad w^h \geq 0, \qquad z^h \geq 0, \qquad z^h \neq 0$$

and points along the almost complementary ray are of the form

$$(25) \qquad\qquad (w^* + \lambda w^h; z^* + \lambda z^h), \qquad \lambda \geq 0,$$

and satisfy

$$(26) \qquad (w_i^* + \lambda w_i^h)(z^* + \lambda z_i^h) = 0 \qquad \text{for all } \lambda \geq 0, \text{ and all } i \neq \beta.$$

THEOREM 2. *If $M > 0$, (22) has a complementary basic feasible solution for any vector q.*

Proof. Select $w_1, \ldots, w_p$ as the basic variables in (22). We may assume that $q \neq 0$ for otherwise $(w; z) = (q; 0)$ immediately solves the problem. A starting ray of feasible almost complementary solutions is generated by taking a sufficiently large value of any nonbasic variable, say z_1. Reduce z_1 toward zero until it reaches a value $z_1^0 \geq 0$ at which a unique basic variable (assuming nondegeneracy) becomes zero. An extreme point has been reached.

The procedure has been initiated in the manner described by the corollary above, and consequently the procedure must terminate either in a complementary basic feasible solution or in an almost complementary ray after some basic feasible solution $(w; z^*)$ is reached. We now show that the latter cannot happen. For if it does, conditions (24)–(26) of the lemma obtain with $\beta = 1$. Since $M > 0$ and $z^h \geq 0$, this implies $w^h > 0$. Hence by (26), $z_i^* = z_i^h = 0$ for all $i \neq 1$. Hence the only variables which change with λ are z_1 and the components of w. Therefore the final generated ray is the same as the initiating ray, which contradicts the corollary.

THEOREM 3. *A bimatrix game $\Gamma(A, B)$ has an extreme equilibrium point.*

Proof. Initiate the algorithm by choosing the smallest positive value of x_1, say x_1^0, such that

$$(27) \qquad\qquad v = -e_n + B_1^T x_1^0 \geq 0,$$

where B_1^T is the first column of B^T. With

$$v^0 = -e_n + B_1^T x_1^0$$

it follows (assuming nondegeneracy) that v^0 has exactly one zero component, say the rth. The ray is generated by choosing as basic variables x_1 and all the slack variables u, v except for v_r. The complement of v_r, namely y_r, is chosen as the nonbasic variable to increase indefinitely. For sufficiently large values of y_r, the basic variables are all nonnegative and the ray so generated is complementary except possibly $x_1 u_1$ might not equal 0. Letting y_r decrease toward zero, the initial extreme point is obtained for some positive value of y_r.

If the procedure does not terminate in an equilibrium point, then by the corollary, it terminates in an almost complementary ray. The latter implies the existence of a class of almost complementary solutions of the form[4]

$$(28) \qquad \begin{bmatrix} u^* + \lambda u^h \\ v^* + \lambda v^h \end{bmatrix} = \begin{bmatrix} -e_m \\ -e_n \end{bmatrix} + \begin{bmatrix} 0 & A \\ B^T & 0 \end{bmatrix} \begin{bmatrix} x^* + \lambda x^h \\ y^* + \lambda y^h \end{bmatrix}$$

$$\left. \begin{aligned} (29) \qquad & (u_i^* \lambda u_i^h)(x_i^* + \lambda x_i^h) = 0, & \text{all } i \neq 1 \\ (30) \qquad & (v_j^* \lambda v_j^h)(y_j^* + \lambda y_j^h) = 0, & \text{all } j \end{aligned} \right\} \text{all } \lambda \geq 0.$$

Assume first that $x^h \neq 0$. Then $v^h = B^T x^h > 0$. By (30), $y_j^* + \lambda y_j^h = 0$ for all j and all $\lambda \geq 0$. But then $u^* + \lambda u^h = -e_m < 0$, a contradiction. Assume next that $y^h \neq 0$ and $x^h = 0$. Then $u^h = A y^h > 0$. By (29), $x_i^* = 0$ for all $i \neq 1$; and $x_i^h = 0$ for all i. Hence $v^h = B^T x^h = 0$ and v^* is the same as v defined by (27) since x_1 must be at the smallest value in order that $(u^*, v^*, x^*, y*)$ be an extreme-point solution. By the nondegeneracy assumption, only $v_r^* = 0$, and $v_j^* > 0$ for all $j \neq r$. Hence (30) implies $y_j^* + \lambda y_j^h = 0$ for all $j \neq r$. It is now clear that the postulated terminating ray is the original ray. This furnishes the desired contradiction. The algorithm must terminate in an equilibrium point of the bimatrix game $\Gamma(A, B)$.

A modification of almost complementary basic sets
    Consider the system of equations

$$(31) \qquad w = q + e_p z_0 + M z,$$

where z_0 represents an "artificial variable" and e_p is a p-vector $(1, \ldots, 1)$. It is clear that (31) always has nonnegative solutions. A solution of (31)

---

[4]The notational analogy with the previously studied case $M > 0$ is obvious.

is called *almost complementary* if $z_i w_i = 0$ for $i = 1, \ldots, p$ and is *complementary* if, in addition, $z_0 = 0$. (See [16, p. 685] where a different but equivalent definition is given.) In this case, let

$$Z_0 = \{(z_0, z) \mid w = q + e_p z_0 + M z \geq 0, \quad z_0 \geq 0, \quad z \geq 0\}.$$

We consider the almost complementary ray generated by sufficiently lage z_0. The variables $w_1, \ldots, w_p$ are initially basic while $z_0, z_1, \ldots, z_p$ are nonbasic variables. For a sufficiently large value of z_0, say z_0^+,

$$w^+ = q + e_p z_0^+ > 0.$$

As z_0 decreases toward zero, the basic variables w_i decrease. An initial extreme point is reached when z_0 attains the minimum value z_0^0 for which $w = q + e_p z_0 \geq 0$. If $z_0^0 = 0$, then $q \geq 0$; this is the trivial case for which no algorithm is required. If $z_0^0 > 0$, some unique basic variable, say w_r, has reached its lower bound 0. Then z_0 becomes a basic variable in place of w_r and we have $\nu = r$. Next, z_r, the complement of w_r, is to be increased.

The remaining steps of the procedure are now identical to those in the preceding algorithm. After a blocking variable becomes basic, its complement is increased until either a basic variable blocks the increase (by attaining its lower bound 0) or else an almost complementary ray is generated. There are precisely two forms of termination. One is in a ray as just described; the other is in the reduction of z_0 to the value 0 and hence the attainment of a complementary basic feasible solution of (31), i.e., a solution of (1), (2).

Interest now centers on the meaning of termination in an almost complementary ray solution of (31). *For certain classes of matrices, the process described above terminates in an almost complementary ray if and only if the original system (1) has no solution.*[e] In the remainder of this section, we shall amplify the preceding statement.

If termination in an almost complementary ray occurs after the process reaches a basic feasible solution $(w^*; z_0^*, z^*)$ corresponding to an extreme point of Z_0, then there exists a nonzero vector $(w^h; z_0^h, z^h)$ such that

$$(32) \qquad w^h = e_p z_0^h + M z^h, \qquad (w^h; z_0^h, z^h) \geq 0.$$

Moreover for every $\lambda \geq 0$,

$$(33) \qquad (w^* + \lambda w^h) = q + e_p(z_0^* + \lambda z_0^h) + M(z^* + \lambda z^h)$$

and

$$(34) \qquad (w_i^* + \lambda w_i^h)(z_i^* + \lambda z_i^h) = 0, \qquad i = 1, \ldots, p.$$

The case $z^h = 0$ is ruled out, for otherwise $z_0^h > 0$ and then $w^h > 0$ because $(w^h; z_0^h, z^h) \neq 0$. Now if $w^h > 0$, (34) implies $z^* + \lambda z^h = z^* = 0$. This, in turn, implies that the ray is the original one, which is not possible.

Furthermore, it follows from the almost complementarity of solutions along the ray that

$$(35) \qquad z_i^* w_i^* = z_i^* w_i^h = z_i^h w_i^* = z_i^h w_i^h = 0, \qquad i = 1, \ldots, p.$$

The individual equations of the system (32) are of the form

$$(36) \qquad w_i^h = z_0^h + (Mz^h)_i, \qquad i = 1, \ldots, p.$$

Multiplication of (36) by z_i^h leads, via (35), to

$$(37) \qquad 0 = z_i^h z_0^h + z_i^h (Mz^h)_i, \qquad i = 1, \ldots, p,$$

from which we conclude that

THEOREM 4. *Termination in a ray implies there exists a nonzero nonnegative vector z^h such that*

$$(38) \qquad z_i^h (Mz^h)_i \leq 0, \qquad i = 1, \ldots, p.$$

At this juncture, two large classes of matrices M will be considered. For the first class, we show that termination in a ray implies the *inconsistency* of the system (1). For the second class, we will show that termination in a ray cannot occur, so that for this class of matrices, (1), (2) always has a solution regardless of what q is.

The first class mentioned above was introduced by Lemke [16]. These matrices, which we shall refer to as *copositive plus*, are required to satisfy two conditions:

$$(39) \qquad uMu \geq 0 \quad \text{for all} \quad u \geq 0,$$

$$(40) \qquad (M + M^T)u = 0 \quad \text{if} \quad uMu = 0 \quad \text{and} \quad u \geq 0.$$

Matrices satisfying conditions (39) alone are known in the literature as *copositive* (see [18, 12]). To our knowledge, there is no reference other than [16] on copositive matrices satisfying the condition (40). However, the class of such matrices is large and includes

(i) all *strictly copositive matrices*, i.e., those for which $uMu > 0$ when $0 \neq u \geq 0$;

(ii) all *positive semidefinite matrices*, i.e., those for which $uMu \geq 0$ for all u.

Positive matrices are obviously strictly copositive while positive definite matrices are both positive semidefinite and strictly copositive. Furthermore, it is possible to "build" matrices satisfying (39) and (40) out of smaller ones. For example, if M_1 and M_2 are matrices satisfying (39) and (40), then so is the block-diagonal matrix

$$M = \begin{bmatrix} M_1 & 0 \\ 0 & M_2 \end{bmatrix}.$$

Moreover, if M satisfies (39) and (40) and S is any skew-symmetric matrix (or its order), then $M + S$ satisfies (39) and (40). Consequently, block matrices such as

$$M = \begin{bmatrix} M_1 & -A^T \\ A & M_2 \end{bmatrix}$$

satisfy (39) and (40) if and only if M_1 and M_2 do too. However, as Lemke [16, 17] has pointed out, the matrices encountered in the bimatrix game problem with $A > 0$ and $B > 0$ need not satisfy (40). The Lemke-Howson iterative procedure for bimatrix games was given earlier in this section. If applied to bimatrix games, the modification just given always terminates in a ray after just one iteration, as can be verified by taking any example.

The second class, consisting of matrices having *positive principal minors*, has been studied by numerous investigators; see, for example, [2, 4, 8, 9, 10, 22, 24]. In the case of symmetric matrices, those with positive principal minors are positive definite. But the equivalence breaks down in the nonsymmetric situation. Nonsymmetric matrices with positive principal minors need not be positive definite. For example, the matrix

$$\begin{bmatrix} 2 & -7 \\ -1 & 4 \end{bmatrix}$$

has positive principal minors but is indefinite and not copositive. However, positive definite matrices are a subset of those with positive principal minors. (See, e.g., [2].)

We shall make use of the fact that $w = q + Mz$, $(w; z) \geq 0$, has no solution if there exists a vector v such that

$$(41) \qquad\qquad vM \leq 0, \qquad vq < 0, \qquad v \geq 0$$

for otherwise $0 \leq vw = vq + vMz < 0$, a contradiction. Indeed, it is a consequence of J. Farkas' theorem [7] that (1) has no solution if and only if there exists a solution of (41).

THEOREM 5. *Let M be copositive plus. If the iterative procedure terminates in a ray, then (1) has no solution.*

Proof. Termination in a ray means that a basic feasible solution $(w^*; z_0^*, z^*)$ will be reached at which conditions (32)–(34) hold and also

$$(42) \qquad\qquad 0 = z^h w^h = z^h e_p z_0^h + z^h M z^h.$$

Since M is copositive and $z^h \geq 0$, both terms on the right side of (42) are nonnegative, hence both are zero. The scalar $z_0^h = 0$ because $z^h e_p > 0$. The vanishing of the quadratic form $z^h M z^h$ means

$$M z^h + M^T z^h = 0.$$

But by (32), $z_0^h = 0$ implies that $w^h = M z^h \geq 0$, whence $M^T z^h \leq 0$ or, what is the same thing, $z^h M \leq 0$. Next, by (35),

$$0 = z^* w^h = z^* M z^h = z^*(-M^T z^h) = -z^h M z^*,$$

and we obtain again by (35)

$$0 = z^h w^* = z^h q + z^h e_p z_0^* + z^h M z^* = z^h q + z^h e_p z_0^*.$$

It follow that $z^q < 0$ because $z^h e_p z_0^* > 0$. The conditions (1) are therefore inconsistent because $v = z^h$ satisfies (41).

COROLLARY. *M is strictly copositive, the process terminates in a complementary basic feasible solution of* (31).

PROOF. If not, the proof of Theorem 5 would imply the existence of a vector z^h satisfying $z^h M z^h = 0$, $0 \neq z^h \geq 0$, which contradicts the strict copositivity of M.

This corollary clearly generalizes Theorem 2. We now turn to the matrices M having positive principal minors.

THEOREM 6. *If M has positive principal minors, the process terminates in a complementary basic solution of* (31) *for any q.*

Proof. We have seen that termination in a ray implies the existence of a nonzero vector z^h satisfying the inequalities (38). However, Gale and Nikaidô [10, Theorem 2] have shown that matrices with positive principal minors are characterized by the impossibility of this event. Hence termination in a ray is not a possible outcome for problems in which M has positive principal minors.

We can even improve upon this.[f]

THEOREM 7. *If M has the property that for each of its principal submatrices $\tilde{M}$, the system*

$$\tilde{M}\tilde{z} \leq 0, \qquad 0 \neq \tilde{z} \geq 0,$$

has no solution, then the process terminates in a complementary basic solution of (31) *for any q.*

Proof. Suppose the process terminates in a ray. From the solution $(w^h; z_0^h, z^h)$ of the homogeneous system (32), define the vector $\tilde{w}^h$ of components of w^h for which the corresponding component of $z^* + z^h$ is positive. Then by (34) $\tilde{w}^h = 0$. Let $\tilde{z}^h$ be the vector of corresponding components in z^h. Clearly $0 \neq \tilde{z}^h \geq 0$, since $0 \neq z^h \geq 0$ and any positive component of z^h is a positive component of $\tilde{z}^h$ by definition of $\tilde{w}^h$. Let $\tilde{M}$ be the corresponding principal submatrix of M. Since $\tilde{M}$ is a matrix of order $k \geq 1$ we may write

$$\tilde{w}^h = e_k z_0^h + \tilde{M}\tilde{z}^h.$$

Hence

$$\tilde{M}\tilde{z}^h \leq 0, \qquad 0 \neq \tilde{z}^h \geq 0,$$

which is a contradiction.

3. THE PRINCIPAL PIVOTING METHOD

We shall now describe an algorithm proposed by the authors [4] which predates that of Lemke. It evolved from a quadratic programming algorithm of P. Wolfe [26], who was the first to use a type of complementary rule for pivot choice. Our method is applicable to matrices M that have positive principal minors (in particular to positive definite matrices) and, after a minor modification, to positive semidefinite matrices.

In Lemke's procedure for general M, an artificial variable z_0 is introduced in order to obtain feasible almost complementary solutions for the augmented problem. In our approach, only variables of the original problem are used, but these can take initially negative as well as nonnegative values.

A *major cycle* of the algorithm is initiated with the complementary basic solution $(w; z) = (q; 0)$. If $q \geq 0$, the procedure is immediately terminated. If $q \not\geq 0$, we may assume (relabeling if necessary) that $w_1 = q_1 < 0$. An almost complementary path is generated by increasing z_1, the complement of the selected negative basic variable. For points along the path, $z_i w_i = 0$ for $i \neq 1$.

Step I: Increase z_1 until it is blocked by a positive basic variable decreasing to zero or by the negative w_1 increasing to zero.

Step II: Make the blocking variable nonbasic by pivoting its complement into the basic set. The major cycle is terminated if w_1 drops out of the basic set of variables. Otherwise, return to Step I.

It will be shown that during a major cycle w_1 increases to zero. At this point, a new complementary basic solution is obtained. However, the number of basic variables with negative values is at least one less than at the beginning of the major cycle. Since there are at most p negative basic variables, no more than p major cycles are required to obtain a complementary feasible solution of (22). The proof depends on certain properties of matrices invariant under principal pivoting.

Principal pivot transform of a matrix

Consider the homogeneous system $v = Mu$ where M is a square matrix. Here the variables $v_1, \ldots, v_p$ are basic and expressed in terms of the nonbasic variables $u_1, \ldots, u_p$. Let any subset of the v_i be made nonbasic and the corresponding u_i basic. Relabel the full set of basic variables $\tilde{v}$ and the corresponding nonbasic variables $\tilde{u}$. Let $\tilde{v} = \tilde{M}\tilde{u}$ express the new basic variables $\tilde{v}$ in terms of the nonbasic ones. The matrix $\tilde{M}$ is called a *principal pivot transform* of M. Of course, this transformation can be carried out only if the principal submatrix of M corresponding to the set of variables z_i and w_i interchanged is nonsingular, and this will be assumed whenever the term is used.

THEOREM 8 (Tucker [24]). *If a square matrix M has positive principal minors, so does every principal pivot transform of M.*

The proof of this theorem is easily obtained inductively by exchanging the roles of one complementary pair and evaluating the resulting principal minors in terms of those of M.

THEOREM 9. *If a matrix M is positive definite or positive semidefinite, so is every principal pivot transform of M.*

Proof. The original proof given by the authors was along the lines of that for the preceding theorem. P. Wolfe has suggested the following elegant proof. Consider $v = Mu$. After the principal pivot tranformation, let $\tilde{v} = \tilde{M}\tilde{u}$, where $\tilde{u}$ is the new set of nonbasic variables. We wish to show that $\tilde{u}\tilde{M}\tilde{u} = \tilde{u}\tilde{v} > 0$ if $uMu = uv > 0$. If M is positive definite, the latter is true if $u \neq 0$, and the former must hold because every pair $(\tilde{u}_i, \tilde{v}_i)$ is identical with (u_i, v_i) except possibly in reverse order. Hence $\sum_i \tilde{u}_i\tilde{v}_i = \sum_i u_i v_i > 0$. The proof in the semidefinite case replaces the inequality $>$ by $\geq$.

Validity of the algorithm

The proof given for $p = 3$ goes through for general p. Consider

$$w_1 \quad\quad = q_1 + m_{11}z_1 + m_{12}z_2 + m_{13}z_3$$
$$w_2 \quad = q_2 + m_{21}z_1 + m_{22}z_2 + m_{23}z_3$$
$$w_3 = q_3 + m_{31}z_1 + m_{32}z_2 + m_{33}z_3$$

Suppose that M has positive principal minors so that the diagonal coefficients are all positive:

$$m_{11} > 0, \quad\quad m_{22} > 0, \quad\quad m_{33} > 0.$$

Suppose furthermore that some q_i is negative, say $q_1 < 0$. Then the solution $(w; z) = (q_1, q_2, q_3; 0, 0, 0)$ is complementary, but not feasible because a particular variable, in this case w_1, which we refer to as *distinguished* is negative. We now initiate an almost complementary path by increasing the complement of the distinguished variable, in this case z_1, which call the driving variable. Adjusting the basic variables, we have

$$(w; z)^1 = (q_1 + m_{11}z_1, q_2 + m_{21}z_1, q_3 + m_{31}z_1; 0, 0, 0).$$

Note that the distinguished variable w_1 increases strictly with the increase of the driving variable z_1 because $m_{11} > 0$. Assuming nondegeneracy, we can increase z_1 by a positive amount before it is blocked either by w_1 reaching zero or by a basic variable that was positive and is not turning negative.

In the former case, for some positive value z_1^* of the driving variable z_1, we have $w_1 = q_1 + m_{11}z_1^* = 0$. The solution

$$(w; z)^2 = (0, q_2 + m_{21}z_1^*, q_3 + m_{31}z_1^*; 0, 0, 0)$$

is complementary and has one less negative component. Pivoting on m_{11} replaces w_1 by z_1 as a basic variable. By Theorem 8, the matrix $\tilde{M}$ in the new canonical system relabled $\tilde{w} = \tilde{q} + \tilde{M}\tilde{z}$ has positive principal minors, allowing the entire major cycle to be repeated.

In the latter case, we have some other basic variable, say $w_2 = q_2 + m_{21}z_1$ blocking when $z_1 = z_1^* > 0$. Then clearly $m_{21} < 0$ and $q_2 > 0$. In this case,

$$(w; z)^2 = (q_1 + m_{11}z_1^*, 0, q_3 + m_{31}z_1^*; z_1^*, 0, 0).$$

THEOREM 10. *If the driving variable is blocked by a basic variable other than its complement, a principal pivot exchanging the blocking variable with its complement will permit the further increase of the driving variable.*

Proof. Pivoting on m_{22} generates the canonical system

$$w_1 \qquad = \bar{q}_1 + \bar{m}_{11}z_1 + \bar{m}_{12}w_2 + \bar{m}_{13}z_3$$

$$z_2 \quad = \bar{q}_2 + \bar{m}_{21}z_1 + \bar{m}_{22}w_2 + \bar{m}_{23}z_3$$

$$w_3 = \bar{q}_3 + \bar{m}_{31}z_1 + \bar{m}_{32}w_2 + \bar{m}_{33}z_3$$

The solution $(w; z)^2$ must satify the above since it is an equivalent system. Therefore setting $z_1 = z_1^*$, $w_2 = 0$, $z_3 = 0$ yields

$$(w; z)^2 = (q_1 + m_{11}z_1^*, 0, q_3 + m_{31}z_1^*; z_1^*, 0, 0),$$

i.e., the same almost complementary solution. Increasing z_1 beyond z_1^* yields

$$(\bar{q}_1 + \bar{m}_{11}z_1, 0, \bar{q}_3 + \bar{m}_{31}z_1; z_1, 0, 0)$$

which is also almost complementary. The sign of $\bar{m}_{21}$ is the reverse of m_{21} since $\bar{m}_{21} = -m_{21}/m_{22} > 0$. *Hence z_2 increases with increasing $z_1 > z_1^*$*; i.e., the new bsic variable replacing w_2 is not blocking. Since $\bar{M}$ has positive principal minors, $\bar{m}_{11} > 0$. *Hence w_1 continues to increase with increasing $z_1 > z_1^*$.*

THEOREM 11. *The number of iterations within a major cycle is finite.*

Proof. There are only finitely many possible bases. No basis can be repeated with a larger value of z_1. To see this, suppose it did for $z_1^{**} > z_1^*$. This would imply that some component of the solution turns negative at $z_1 = z_1^*$ and yet is nonnegative when $z_1 = z_1^{**}$. Since the value of a component is linear in z_1 we have a contradiction.

Paraphrase of the principal pivoting method
    Along the almost complementary path there is only one degree of freedom. In the proof of the validity of the algoithm, z_1 was increasing and z_2 was shown to increase. The same class of solutions can be generated by regarding z_2 as the driving variable and the other variables as adjusting. Hence within a major cycle, the same almost complementary path can be generated as follows. The first edge is obtained by using the complement of the distinguished variable as the driving variable. As soon as the driving variable is blocked, the following steps are iterated:

(a) replace the blocking variable by the driving variable and terminate the major cycle if the blocking variable is distinguished; if the blocking variable is not distinguished

(b) let the complement of the blocking variable be the new driving variable and increase it until a new blocking variable is identified; return to (a).

The paraphrase form is used in practice.

THEOREM 12. *The principal pivoting method terminates in a solution of (1), (2) if M has positive principal minors (and, in particular, if M is positive definite).*

Proof. We have shown that the completion of a major cycle occurs in a finite number of steps, and each one reduces the total number of variables with negative values. Hence in a finite number of steps, this total is reduced to zero and a solution of the fundamental problem (1), (2) is obtained. Since a positive definite matrix has positive principal minors, the method applies to such matrices.

As indicated earlier, the positive semidefinite case can be handled by using the paraphrase form of the algorithm with a minor modification. The reader will find details in [4].[g]

ACKNOWLEDGMENTS

Richard W. Cottle's research was partially supported by National Science Foundation Grant GP-3739; George B. Dantzig's research was partially supported by U.S. Army Research Office Contract No. DAHC04–67–C–0028, Office of Naval Research Contract ONR–N–00014–67–A–0112–0011, U.S. Atomic Energy Commission Contract No. AT(04–3)–326 PA #18, and National Science Foundation Grant GP 6431.

REFERENCES

[1] R. W. Cottle, Symmetric dual quadratic programs, *Quart. Appl. Math.* **21** (1963), 237.243.

[2] R. W. Cottle, Nonlinear programs with positively bounded Jacobians, *SIAM J. Appl. Math.* **14** (1966), 147–158.

[3] G. B. Dantzig, *Linear Programming and Extensions*, Princeton Univ. Press, Princeton, New Jersey, 1963.

[4] G. B. Dantzig and R. W. Cottle, Positive (semi-) definite programming, ORC 63–18 (RR), May 1963, Operations Research Center, University of California, Berkeley. Revised in *Nonlinear Programming* (J. Abadie, ed.), North-Holland, Amsterdam, 1967, pp. 55-73.

[5] W. S. Dorn, Duality in quadratic programming, *Quart. Appl. Math.* **18** (1960), 155–162.

[6] P. Du Val, The unloading problem for plane curves, *Amer. J. Math.* **62** (1940), 307–311.

[7] J. Farkas, Theorie der einfachen Ungleichungen, *J. Reine Angew. Math.* **124** (1902), 1–27.

[8] M. Fiedler and V. Pták, On matrices with non-positive off-diagonal elements and positive principal minors, *Czech. Math. Journal* **12** (1962), 382–400.

[9] M. Fiedler and V. Pták, Some generalizations of positive definiteness and monotonicity, *Numerische Math.* **9** (1966), 163–172.

[10] D. Gale and H. Nikaidô, The Jacobian matrix and global univalence of mappings, *Math. Ann.* **159** (1965), 81–93.

[11] A. J. Goldman, Resolution and separation theorems for polyhedral convex sets, in *Linear Inequalities and Related Systems* (H. W. Kuhn and A. W. Tucker, eds.), Princeton Univ. Press, Princeton, New Jersey, 1956.

[12] M. Hall, Jr., *Combinatorial Theory*, Blaisdell, Waltham, Massachusetts, 1967, Chapter 16.

[13] C. W. Kilmister and J. E. Reeve, *Rational Mechanics* American Elsevier, New York, 1966, §5.4.

[14] H. W. Kuhn and A. W. Tucker, Nonlinear programming, in *Second Berkeley Symposium on Mathematical Statistics and Probability* (J. Neyman, ed.) Univ. of California Press, Berkeley, California, 1951.

[15] C. E. Lemke and J. T. Howson, Jr., Equilibrium points of bimatrix games, J. Soc. Indust. Appl. Math. **12** (1964), 413–423.

[16] C. E. Lemke, Bimatrix equilibrium points and mathematical programming, *Management Sci.* **11** (1965), 681–689.

[17] C. E. Lemke, Private communication.

[18] T. S. Motzkin, Copositive quadratic forms, *Nat. Bur. Standards Report* **1818** (1952), 11–12.

[19] J. F. Nash, Noncooperative games, *Ann. Math.* **54** (1951), 286–295.

[20] J. von Neumann, Discussion of a maximum problem, *Collected Works VI* (A. Taub, ed.), Pergamon, New York, 1963.

[21] C. van de Panne and A. Whinston, A comparison of two methods of quadratic programming, *Operations Res.* **14** (1966), 422–441.

[22] T. D. Parsons, A combinatorial approach to convex quadratic programming, Doctoral Dissertation, Department of Mathematics, Princeton University, May 1966.

[23] A. W. Tucker, A combinatorial equivalence of matrices, *Proceedings of Symposia in Applied Mathematics* **10** (R. Bellman and M. Hall, eds.), American Math. Soc., 1960.

[24] A. W. Tucker, Principal pivotal transforms of square matrices, *SIAM Review* **5** (1963), 305.

[25] A. W. Tucker, Pivotal Algebra, Lecture notes (by T. D. Parsons), Department of Mathematics, Princeton, Univ., 1965.

[26] P. Wolfe, The simplex method for quadratic programming, *Econometrica* **27** (1959), 382–398.

Chapter 24

A Generalization of the Linear Complementarity Problem[*]

RICHARD W. COTTLE[†] AND GEORGE B. DANTZIG[‡]

Department of Operations Research, Stanford University, Stanford, California 94305

ABSTRACT

The linear complementarity problem: find $z \in R^p$ satisfying

$$w = q + Mz$$
$$w \geq 0, \; z \geq 0 \qquad \text{(LCP)}$$
$$z^T w = 0$$

is generalized to a problem in which the matrix M is not square. A solution technique similar to C. E. Lemke's (1965) method for solving (LCP) is given. The method is discussed from a graph-theoretic viewpoint and closely parallels a proof of Sperner's lemma by D. I. A. Cohen (1967) and some work of H. Scarf (1967) on approximating fixed points of a continuous mapping of simplex into itself.

1. INTRODUCTION

For a given p-square matrix M and a (column) p-vector q, the *linear complementarity problem* is that of solving the system

(1) $$w = q + Mz,$$

(2) $$w \geq 0, \; z \geq 0, \qquad \text{(I)}$$

(3) $$z^T w = 0.$$

Under a rather wide range of assumptions regarding M (and q), it is known that such a system (I) has a solution whenever the system (1), (2) has a

---

[*] Presented at the Yale University Conference on Combinatorial Theory in honor of Professor Oystein Ore (May, 1968).

[†] Research partially supported by Office of Naval Research, Contract ONR-N-00014-67-A-0112-0011; U.S. Atomic Energy Commission, Contract AT[04-3] 326 PA#18; and National Science Foundation Grant GP 6431.

[‡] Research partially supported by Office of Naval Research, Contract ONR-N-00014-67-A-0112-0011 and ONR-N-00014-67-A-0116; U.S. Atomic Energy Commission, Contract AT[04-3] 326 PA#18; National Science Foundation Grant GP 6431; U.S. Army Research Office, Contract DACH04-67-C0028; and National Institutes of Health, Grant GM 14789-02.

solution. Reference [2] summarizes the significance of the linear complementarity problem and a portion of the related pivot theory. In this paper, we describe a particular generalization of (I). The new problem is formally stated in Section 2. The main results appear in Sections 3 and 4, where we give a graph-theoretic interpretation and slight extension of Lemke's ingenious iterative method [5] of solving (I). Section 5 is devoted to further discussion of a class of matrices mentioned in Section 2.

2. STATEMENT OF THE PROBLEM

The name "linear complementarity problem" stems from the linearity[a] of the mapping $W(z) = q + Mz$ and the *complementarity*[1] of the vectors w and z. We shall consider here a system $w = q + Nz$ where N is a $p \times k$ matrix with $k \leq p$. In accordance with the number, k, of columns in N, we partition the vector w into k subvectors, w^j. We will generalize the notion of complementarity by seeking solutions $w \geq 0$, $z \geq 0$ such that at least one component of w^j or else z_j is zero, $(j = 1, \ldots, k)$. See the footnote on page 103 of reference [2].

By a *vertical block matrix of type* $(p_1, \ldots, p_k)$ we shall mean a matrix

$$N = \begin{bmatrix} N^1 \\ \vdots \\ N^k \end{bmatrix}$$

where the j-th block N^j has order $p_j \times k$. Thus for

$$p = \sum_{j=1}^{k} p_j$$

the matrix N is of order $p \times k$. We assume that the constant p-vector q and the variable p-vector w are decomposed in conformity with N:

$$q = \begin{bmatrix} q^1 \\ \vdots \\ q^k \end{bmatrix}, \qquad w = \begin{bmatrix} w^1 \\ \vdots \\ w^k \end{bmatrix}.$$

Therefore $q^j = (q^j_i)$ and $w^j = (w^j_i)$ are p_j-vectors. For a k-vector $z = (z_l)$ the equation

$$w = q + Nz$$

---

[1] In a solution $(\bar{w}, \bar{z})$ of (I), the *indices* corresponding to positive components of $\bar{w}$ and $\bar{z}$ form disjoint subsets of $\{1, \ldots, p\}$ and, in the non-degenerate case, these subsets are complementary.

is equivalent to the system

$$w^j = q^j + N^j z \qquad (j = 1, \ldots, k).$$

The *generalized linear complementarity problem* is to solve

(4) $$w = q + Mz,$$

(5) $$w \geq 0, \ z \geq 0, \qquad\qquad\qquad (II)$$

(6) $$z_j \prod_{i=1}^{k} w_i^j = 0 \qquad (j = 1, \ldots, k)$$

This clearly agrees with (I) when $p_j = 1$, $p = k$, and N^j is the j-th row of M.

We shall establish here our claim [2, p. 103n] that Lemke's computational scheme [5] for solving (I) can be extended to (II) when N is a positive matrix. Naturally, one is prompted to ask about other types of matrices for which one can solve (II). To this end, we introduce a definition that makes it possible to apply our knowledge of (I) to the new problem at hand.

DEFINITION 1. *Let N be a vertical block matrix of type $(p_1, \ldots, p_k)$. A k-square submatrix M of N is called a "representative submatrix" if its j-th row is drawn from the j-th block, N^j, of N.*

Obviously, a vertical block matrix of type $(p_1, \ldots, p_k)$ has $\prod_{j=1}^{k}$ representative submatrices.

In much of the sequel, the properties of N will be based upon properties of its representative submatrices. Having this concept, we can talk about principal submatrices of the *rectangular* matrix N.

DEFINITION 2. *Let N be a vertical block matrix of type $(p_1, \ldots, p_k)$. A "principal submatrix" of N is a principal submatrix of a representative submatrix of N. The determinant of such a matrix is called a "principal minor" of N.*

It now makes sense to call a vertical block matrix with all positive principal minors—after Gale and Nikaido [4]—a "*P*-matrix." We shall show, via Lemke's method, that when N is a *P*-matrix the system (II) is always solvable.

3. LEMKE'S METHOD

In [5], Lemke has developed a method for solving the linear complementarity problem (I). Based on an earlier procedure (see Lemke and Howson [6]) for constructively solving the bimatrix game problem,

$$(7) \qquad \begin{bmatrix} w_0 \\ w \end{bmatrix} = \begin{bmatrix} q_0 \\ q \end{bmatrix} + \begin{bmatrix} 0 & -e_p^T \\ e_p & M \end{bmatrix} \begin{bmatrix} z_0 \\ z \end{bmatrix},$$

$$(8) \qquad \begin{bmatrix} w_0 \\ w \end{bmatrix} \begin{bmatrix} z_0 \\ z \end{bmatrix} \geq 0, \qquad \qquad (I')$$

$$(9) \qquad \begin{bmatrix} z_0 \\ z \end{bmatrix}^T \begin{bmatrix} w_0 \\ w \end{bmatrix} = 0,$$

where q_0 is a suitably large positive scalar and $e_p = (1, \ldots, 1)^T$ has p components. Problem (I') *always has a solution*, and a solution of (I') in which $z_0 = 0$ is a solution of (I). For certain classes of matrices M, it can be shown that $z_0 = 0$ is the only possible outcome in a solution of (I'). For other classes of matrices, it can be shown that, if the final solution of (I') has z_0 at a positive level, then (I) has no solution at all—indeed, (1) has no non-negative solution.

The proof that (I') has a solution is geometric, if not graph-theoretic, in spirit. The underlying idea has been employed quite successfully by H. Scarf [8] and D. I. A. Cohen [1] in papers[2] dealing with Sperner's lemma, a result from combinatorial topology often used for proving the Brouwer Fixed Point Theorem. The basic notion is captured by the following theorem (for terminology the reader is referred to Ore [7]):

THEOREM 1. *Let* $\mathcal{G} = (V, E)$ *be a finite graph with no loops or multiple edges. Suppose* $\mathcal{G}$ *has the following properties:*

(a) *the vertex set V is the disjoint union of three sets B, G, and R;*

(b) *B is non-empty;*

(c) *every vertex v in B has degree $\rho(v)$ equal to 1;*

(d) *every vertex in B is adjacent to a vertex in G;*

(e) *every vertex in G has even degree, $\rho(v)$.*

Then if $v_0 \in B$, there is a path in $\mathcal{G}$ of the form $v_0, v_1, \ldots, v_l$ where $l \geq 2$, $v_l \in B \cup R$ and $v_1, \ldots, v_{l-1} \in G$.

EXISTENCE PROOF: Clearly any path $v_0, v_1, \ldots, v_l$ of maximal length which begins at a vertex $v_0 \in B$ and repeats no edge must have $l \geq 2$ and $v_l \in B \cup R$, for otherwise $v_l \in G$ and has odd degree.

CONSTRUCTIVE PROOF: Choose an arbitrary vertex $v_0 \in B$. v_0 is adjacent to a unique vertex $v_1 \in G$. Mark edge (v_0, v_1). By (e) there is an unmarked edge (v_1, v_2) incident to v_1. (Note that $v_2 \neq v_0$ by (c).)

---

[2]See also the extension of Cohen's argument used by K. Fan [3].

If $v_2 \in B \cup R$, stop; v_0, v_1, v_2 is the desired path. If $v_2 \in G$, mark (v_1, v_2). There remains an odd number of unmarked edges incident to v_2. Let (v_2, v_3) be one of these. If $v_3 \in B \cup R$, stop. If $v_3 \in G$, mark (v_2, v_3). Notice that v_3 cannot equal any of its predecessors. There is an odd number of unmarked edges incident to v_3; let (v_3, v_4) be one of these. Again stop if $v_4 \in B \cup R$. If $v_4 \in G$, it might coincide with v_1 but no other vertex on the path. In any even, there is an unmarked edge (v_4, v_5) incident to v_4. In general, if v_i is the last vertex on the path developed so far there are two possibilities: either $v_i \in B \cup R$ and the process terminates, or (v_{i-1}, v_i) gets marked and there exists an unmarked edge (v_i, v_{i+1}) incident to v_i. By the finiteness of $\mathcal{G}$, the desired path will always be found.

We can state two immediate corollaries.

COROLLARY 1. *If $\rho(v) = 2$ for every $v \in G$, then any path of the theorem is simple.*

COROLLARY 2. *If B consists of one element, then $v_l \in R$.*

Only slightly more complicated is

COROLLARY 3. *If $\rho(v) = 1$ for every $v \in R$ and B contains an odd number of elements, then R contains an odd number of elements.*

PROOF: Suppose first $\rho(v) = 2$ for all $v \in G$. An even number (possibly zero) of elements in B are connected to each other by paths having intermediate vertices in G. This leaves an odd number of elements of B which are connected by paths to elements of R. Since $\rho(v) = 1$ for all $v \in B \cup R$ and $\rho(v) = 2$ for all $v \in G$, all of these paths are vertex disjoint. Suppose there is a non-empty subset $\bar{R} \subset R$ consisting of elements which have not yet been connected by paths to elements of B. Let $\bar{v}$ be any such element. By hypothesis, $\rho(\bar{v}) = 1$, so $\bar{v}$ is adjacent to an element of G or R. If $\bar{v}$ is adjacent to an element of G, there is a path from $\bar{v}$ to an element $\bar{\bar{v}} \in \bar{R}$. If $\bar{v}$ is adjacent to an element $\bar{\bar{v}}$ of R, then $\bar{\bar{v}} \in \bar{R}$. In either case, the elements of $\bar{R}$ are paired by paths. Hence R contains an odd number of elements.

Suppose more generally that $\rho(v)$ is even for each $v \in G$. By a slight modification of $\mathcal{G}$, a graph $\mathcal{G}'$ satisfying the previous hypotheses can be constructed. Let $\mathcal{G}' = (V', E')$ where $V' = B' \cup G' \cup R'$, $E' = E$, $B' = B$, and $R' = R$. It remains to define G' and the incidence relations. For each $v \in G$, we may pair off the $\rho(v)$ edges adjacent to v and then replace v by $\rho(v)/2$ vertices each one incident to both members of a pair of edges. G' is the set of all these new vertices each of which has degree 2. The proof given above applies to $\mathcal{G}'$ and shows that $R' = R$ has an odd number of elements.

DISCUSSION. Corollaries 1 and 2 describe the situation at hand in Lemke's solution to the linear complementarity problem (I').

The solutions of (7) and (8) form a set Z'. The construction of $\mathcal{G}$ begins with the almost complementary extreme points of Z'. These points correspond to the elements of G. The complementary extreme points of Z' are the elements of R. For each almost-complementary extreme point which happens to be the end point of an almost-complementary ray, we formally introduce a "point at infinity" as the other end of the ray. These points at infinity form the vertex set B in $\mathcal{G}$. As it happens, Z' contains only one almost-complementary ray (the one corresponding to indefinite increase of z_0) and hence B is a one-element set. This element is clearly of degree 1. In general, to guarantee that the elements of G be of degree 2 requires some care. Under non-degeneracy, this is the case for almost-complementary extreme points of Z'. The edges incident to these vertices are almost-complementary point sets generated by increasing one of the two non-basic variables having the same index (so-called *complementary variables*; see Section 4). A vertex in B, G, or R is the only possible endpoint of such an edge. If $q \not\geq 0$, the graph $\mathcal{G}$ is well defined and satisfies the conditions of the theorem and Corollaries 1 and 2. The essence of [5, Theorem 2] is captured in Corollary 3.

4. SOLUTION OF PROBLEM (II)

We shall now quickly review some terminology pertaining to the generalized linear complementarity problem, (II). Needless to say, the problem has the obvious solution $w = q$, $z = 0$, when $q \geq 0$ and so we assume that $q \not\geq 0$.

In the initial form of equation (4), that is

$$w = q + Nz,$$

we regard the variables w_i^j as *basic* and the variables z_l as *non-basic*. For each $j = 1, \ldots, k$ there is a j-th set of variables

$$z_j, w_1^j, \ldots, w_{p_j}^j$$

which are termed *related*. A solution of (4) is said to be *proper* if it also satisfies (6). Thus a solution of (II) is a non-negative proper solution of (6). A *proper basis* in $[I, -N]$ contains exactly p_j columns corresponding to variables in the j-th related set ($j = 1, \ldots, k$)). A feasible proper basis yields a non-negative proper solution of (4), i.e., a solution of (II).

On the other hand, a solution of (4) is *almost-proper* if it satisfies (6) for all but one value of j. An *almost-proper basis* contains all the columns corresponding to one related set of variables, all but two of the columns corresponding to another related set, and otherwise precisely p_j columns corresponding to the j-th related set. As an alternative, we can characterize such a basis in terms of the *non-basic* columns. The latter must include exactly two columns corresponding to one related set of variables, no columns corresponding to another related set, and just one column for each of the remaining related sets.

We shall say that a solution $(\bar{w}, \bar{z})$ of (4) is *non-degenerate* if it contains at most k zero components. As usual, we make the non-degeneracy assumption for all solutions of (4). There is no loss of generality in so doing, and we thereby gain assurance of a one-to-one correspondence between the basic feasible solutions of (4) and the extreme points of the set

$$Z = \{z \mid q + Nz \geq 0,\; z \geq 0\}.$$

An *extreme point* of Z may be called *proper* or *almost-proper* according as the corresponding basic feasible solution is *proper* or *almost-proper*.

For purposes of preliminary exposition, we embed problem (II) in a larger problem of the same general type, yet having two special properties. The technique is precisely analogous to Lemke's.

Let q_1^0 be a real number larger than the sum of the components of any extreme point of Z. (Such a number clearly exists, and fortunately one can ignore it in carrying out the computational scheme.) Let e_p denote the column vector of length p having all components equal to 1.[b] (e_k denotes a similar vector of length k.) Let z_0 denote a variable and define the complement of z_0 by[c]

$$(10) \qquad\qquad w_1^0 = q_1^0 + 0 \cdot z_0 - e_k^T z.$$

We are taking $p_0 = 1$. The new problem to be solved is

$$(11) \qquad \begin{bmatrix} w_1^0 \\ w \end{bmatrix} = \begin{bmatrix} q_1^0 \\ q \end{bmatrix} + \begin{bmatrix} 0 & -e_k^T \\ e_p & N \end{bmatrix} \begin{bmatrix} z_0 \\ z \end{bmatrix},$$

$$(12) \qquad \begin{bmatrix} w_1^0 \\ w \end{bmatrix} \begin{bmatrix} z_0 \\ z \end{bmatrix} \geq 0, \qquad\qquad (\text{II}')$$

$$(13) \qquad z_j \prod_{i=1}^{p_j} w_i^j = 0, \qquad j = 0, 1, \ldots, k.$$

Putting

$$Z' = \left\{ \begin{bmatrix} z_0 \\ z \end{bmatrix} \;\middle|\; \begin{bmatrix} q_1^0 \\ q \end{bmatrix} + \begin{bmatrix} 0 & -e_k^T \\ e_p & N \end{bmatrix} \begin{bmatrix} z_0 \\ z \end{bmatrix} \geq 0,\; \begin{bmatrix} z_0 \\ z \end{bmatrix} \geq 0 \right\}$$

we notice that Z' is non-empty and contains exactly one ray emanating from an almost-proper extreme point of Z'. Each such ray consists of points which correspond to almost-proper solutions of (9).

Thinking of "the point at infinity" as one end-point of this unique ray, we may begin to establish a correspondence between Z' and the graph $\mathcal{G}$ in Theorem 1. In particular, the set V of vertices will be composed of:

B = the point at infinity;

G = the set of almost-proper extreme points of Z';

R = the set of proper extreme points of Z'.

By definition, $\mathcal{G} = (V, E)$ where V is the (obviously disjoint) union of B, G, and R; the edges in E consist of the "almost-proper point sets" in Z' which lead out of almost-proper extreme points. Such point sets are line segments connecting almost-proper extreme points, line segments between almost-proper and proper extreme point, or—in a more general situation—rays from almost-proper extreme points to "points at infinity." As mentioned above, there is only one such ray in Z'.

The hypotheses of Theorem 1 all hold. That the vertices of G are of degree 2 is seen by observing that there are just two almost-proper point sets out of an almost proper extreme point. These are the points generated by increasing one of the two non-basic variables belonging to the same related set.

Thus from Theorem 1 we conclude

THEOREM 2. *Problem* (II') *always has a solution.*

This conclusion is not a satisfactory solution of (II), for a solution of (II') in which $z_0 \neq 0$ implies the existence of an almost-proper point set in Z' which would have been a ray if it were not for the enforcement of $x_1^0 \geq 0$. By dropping this constraint, we can initiate the algorithm in the same way and infer that the process will terminate in finitely many steps [either] in a solution of (II) or in the generation of an almost-proper ray.

It now seems necessary to resort to a more algebraic treatment of the consequences of termination in an almost-proper ray. Suppose the algorithm has reached an almost-proper basic feasible solution $(\hat{w}, \hat{z}_0, \hat{z})$ of (11) from which an almost-proper ray is generated.. It follows by a standard result of linear inequality theory that there exists a non-zero non-negative solution $(\bar{w}, \bar{z}_0, \bar{z})$ of the corresponding homogeneous system of equations:

$$(14) \qquad \bar{w} = e_p \bar{z}_0 + N\bar{z}, \qquad 0 \neq (\bar{w}, \bar{z}_0, \bar{z}) \geq 0.$$

For all $\lambda \geq 0$, we have

$$\hat{w} + \lambda \bar{w} = q + e_p(\hat{z}_0 + \lambda \bar{z}_0) + N(\hat{z} + \lambda \bar{z})$$

and

$$(15) \qquad (\hat{z}_j + \lambda \bar{z}_j) \prod_{i=1}^{p_j} (\hat{w}_i^j + \lambda \bar{w}_i^j) = 0 \qquad (j = 1, \ldots, k).$$

If $\bar{z} = 0$, then $\bar{z}_0 > 0$ (otherwise $\bar{z}_0 = 0$ and $\bar{w} = 0$, a contradiction) and then $\bar{w} > 0$. But $\bar{w} > 0$ implies $\hat{z} = 0$, and this means that the ray is the initial one, which is impossible. Thus we conclude that $0 \neq \bar{z} \geq 0$.

Now for $j = 1, \ldots, k$, we have from (15)

$$(16) \qquad \hat{z}_j \prod_{i=1}^{p_j} (\hat{w}_i^j + \lambda \bar{w}_i^j) = \bar{z}_j \prod_{i=1}^{p_j} (\hat{w}_i^j + \lambda \bar{w}_i^j) = 0,$$

In view of the non-negativity of all the variables, it even follows that for $j = 1, \ldots, k$

$$\hat{z}_j \prod_{i=1}^{p_j} \hat{w}_i^j = \hat{z}_j \prod_{i=1}^{p_j} \bar{w}_i^j = \bar{z}_j \prod_{i=1}^{p_j} \hat{w}_i^j = \bar{z}_j \prod_{i=1}^{p_j} \bar{w}_i^j = 0.$$

We utilize the last of these. Substituting for $\bar{w}_i^j$ from (14) we obtain for each $j = 1, \ldots, k$

$$(17) \qquad \bar{z}_j \prod_{i=1}^{p_j} [\bar{z}_0 + (N\bar{z})_i^j] = 0.$$

Hence, for every $j = 1, \ldots, k$, there exists an i_j such that

$$(18) \qquad \bar{z}_j [\bar{z}_0 + (N\bar{z})_i^j] = 0.$$

Consequently, there is a representative submatrix M of N such that

$$(19) \qquad \begin{aligned} \bar{z}_j (M\bar{z})_j &\le 0 \qquad (j = 1, \ldots, k), \\ 0 &\ne \bar{z} \ge 0. \end{aligned}$$

Next we notice that (17) cannot hold if $N > 0$. More generally, if the representative submatrices of N are strictly copositive [2], then (18) cannot hold. If N is a P-matrix, then (19) cannot hold. Thus for these cases termination in an almost-complementary ray is ruled out.

If the process terminates in an almost-complementary ray and the representative submatrices of N are copositive-plus [2], then (4) has no non-negative solution. Indeed, it follows from (18) that there is a k-vector $v = (v_1, \ldots, v_k)^T$ such that

$$v^T M \le 0, \qquad \sum_{j=1}^{k} v_j q_{i_j}^j < 0, \qquad v \ge 0.$$

But clearly we can extend v to a vector u such that

$$(20) \qquad u^T N \le 0, \qquad u^T q < 0, \qquad u \ge 0,$$

merely by defining $u_{i_j}^j = v_j$, $u_i^j = 0$ if $i \ne i_j$. The existence of a solution to (20) precludes the existence of a non-negative solution of (4).

In line with our terminology pertaining to P-matrices, we shall speak of N belonging to a particular class of matrices if all of its representative submatrices do. Accordingly, the extensions above can be summarized as follows:

THEOREM 3. *If the matrix N is either strictly copositive or a P-matrix, then* (II) *has a solution. If the matrix N is copositive-plus and the procedure fails to produce a solution of* (II)*, then* (4) *has no non-negative solution, i.e., Z is empty.*

5. SOME PROPERTIES OF P-MATRICES

In closing, we mention some properties of vertical block matrices N of type $(p_1, \ldots, p_k)$ having positive principal minors, that is, P-matrices.

Given the positive integers $p_1, \ldots, p_k$, let $u^1, \ldots, u^k$ be a collection of semipositive (i.e., non-zero, non-negative) *row vectors* such that u^j has p_j coordinates. If, as above, we let $p = \sum_{j=1}^{k} p_j$, then

$$(21) \qquad U = \begin{bmatrix} u^1 & & 0 \\ & \ddots & \\ 0 & & u^k \end{bmatrix}$$

is of order $k \times p$. The j-th row of the matrix

$$M = UN$$

is the u^j-weighted sum of the rows of N^j.

THEOREM 4. *If N is a P-matrix and U is given by* (21) *with semipositive rows, then $M = UN$ is a P-matrix.*

PROOF.: Let $(N^j)_i$ denote the i-th row of block N^j. Then

$$M = UN = \begin{bmatrix} \sum_{i=1}^{p_1} u_i^1 (N^1)_i \\ \vdots \\ \sum_{i=1}^{p_k} u_i^k (N^k)_i \end{bmatrix}.$$

The determinant of a matrix is a multilinear function of its rows. Hence

$$(22) \qquad \det M = \sum_{i_1}^{p_1} \cdots \sum_{i_k=1}^{p_k} \prod_{j=1}^{k} u_{i_j}^j \det \begin{bmatrix} (N^1)_{i_1} \\ \vdots \\ (N^k)_{i_k} \end{bmatrix}.$$

All the terms in (22) are non-negative and at least one is positive since for every $j = 1, \ldots, k$ there exists an index i_j such that $u_{i_j}^j > 0$.

This theorem paves the way for an extension of the linear inequality theory related to ordinary P-matrices (see [4]).

THEOREM 5. *If N is a P-matrix, then system of inequalities*

$$(23) \qquad\qquad Nz \leq 0, \qquad z \geq 0$$

has only the trivial solution, $z = 0$.

PROOF: Suppose on the contrary that there exists a non-trivial solution to (23). Let

$$U = \begin{bmatrix} u^1 & & 0 \\ & \ddots & \\ 0 & & u^k \end{bmatrix}$$

be any row-wise semipositive block diagonal matrix as in (21). then $M = UN$ is a P-matrix. Hence

$$Mz \leq 0, \qquad z \geq 0$$

has a non-trivial solution which is impossible [4].[d]

THEOREM 6. *If N is a P-matrix, the system of inequalities*

$$(24) \qquad\qquad Nz > 0, \qquad z > 0$$

has a solution.

PROOF: Suppose otherwise. Then the system

$$(25) \qquad\qquad uN \leq 0, \qquad 0 \neq u \geq 0$$

has a solution for some row vector u. We may think of u as a direct sum of k subvectors, $u^j = (u_1^j, \ldots, u_{p_j}^j)$. We may even assume that each u^j is semipositive. (For otherwise we can delete the block and columns corresponding to $u_i^j = 0$; the result of this refinement is a P-matrix and a solution of a system like (25) with semipositive vectors.) Forming the row-wise semipositive block diagonal matrix

$$U = \begin{bmatrix} u^1 & & 0 \\ & \ddots & \\ 0 & & u^k \end{bmatrix}$$

we may take a k-vector $e_k^T = (1, \ldots, 1)$ and write

$$(26) \qquad\qquad e_k^T UN = uN \leq 0.$$

Since UN is a k-square P-matrix, the inequalities (26) state a contradiction: $(UN)^T$ reverses the sign [4] of a non-zero vector.

REFERENCES

[1] D. I. A. COHEN, On the Sperner Lemma, *J. Combinatorial Theory* **2** (1967), 585–587.

[2] R. W. COTTLE AND G. B. DANTZIG, Complementary Pivot Theory of Mathematical Programming, *J. Linear Alg. Appl.* **1** (1968), 103–125.

[3] K. FAN, Simplicial Maps from an Orientable n-Pseudomanifold into S^m with the Octahedral Triangulation, *J. Combinatorial Theory* **2** (1967), 588-602.

[4] D. GALE AND H. NIKAIDO, The Jacobian Matrix and the Global Univalence of Mappings, *Math. Ann.* **159** (1965), 81–93.

[5] C. E. LEMKE, Bimatrix Equilibrium Points and Mathematical Programming, *Management Sci.* **11** (1965), 681–689.

[6] C. E. LEMKE AND J. T. HOWSON, JR., Equilibrium Points of Bimatrix Games, *J. Soc. Indust. Appl. Math.* **12** (1964), 413–423.

[7] O. ORE, *Theory of Graphs*, American Mathematical Society, Providence, R. I., 1962.

[8] H. SCARF, The Approximation of Fixed Points of a Continuous Mapping, *SIAM J. Appl. Math.* **15** (1967), 1328–1343.

Editor's Notes

Chapter 1

[a] The original has $\xi > \xi_0$ (or $\xi < 0$) rather than $\xi > \xi_0$ (or $\xi < \xi_0$).

[b] The $\sqrt{n}$ in (16) has been changed from $\sqrt{N}$ as in the original.

Chapter 2

[a] See footnote 3 on page 13.

[b] See footnote 3 on page 13.

[c] See footnote 3 on page 13.

Chapter 3

[a] The five individuals mentioned in this opening sentence are Wassily Leontief (1906–1999), Karl Schlesinger (1889–1938), Abraham Wald (1902–1950), John von Neumann (1903–1957), and Tjalling C. Koopmans (1910–1986). Schlesinger, Wald and von Neumann were participants in Karl Menger's Mathematical Colloquium during the mid-1930s. Schlesinger is noted for his book *Theorie der Geld- und Kreditwirtschaft* (München: Verlag von Duncker & Humblot, 1914), and more so for his paper "Uber die Produktionsgleichung der ökonomischen Wertlehre" ("On the Production Equations of Economic Value Theory"), which was published in Menger's journal *Ergebnisse eines mathematischen Kolloquiums* (1935). Schlesinger was a banker and an economist; he was tutored in mathematics by Wald between 1931 and 1937. See Karl Menger, *Reminiscences of the Vienna Circle and the Mathematical Colloquium* [posthumously edited by Louise Golland, Brian McGuiness and Abe Sklar] (Dordrecht: Kluwer Academic Publishers, 1994).

Chapter 4

[a] There is a typographical error in the stated inequality. It should read $ax + by + c \geq 0$.

[b] That is to say, Euclidean m-space, R_m.

[c] The notation here is intended to mean that z is a variable defined as the value of the linear form $\lambda_1 c_1 + \lambda_2 c_2 + \cdots + \lambda_n c_n$ and that its value is to be maximized.

ᵈ This is a rather strong form of the nondegeneracy assumption.

ᵉ The question of which point P_j to choose has been the subject of many studies. Selecting it according to the criterion of greatest increase in objective function value can turn out to be a myopic rule. The same is true of the rule whereby it is chosen as that which offers the greatest rate of increase of the objective function. At least the latter rule requires a bit less computation.

ᶠ In light of how this hypothesis is used in Theorem 3, (30) should hold for all $j = 1, 2, \cdots, n$.

Chapter 5

ᵃ Actually, it is a set of solutions of perturbed problems that converge to a solution of the original problem.

ᵇ Here, as in other places, we have evidence of the authors' preference for constructive proofs. This philosophy is a perfect match for the practical ends of the subject.

ᶜ This important paper subsequently appeared as G. B. Dantzig and W. Orchard-Hays, "The product form for the inverse in the Simplex Method," *Mathematical Tables and Aids to Computation* 8 (1954) 67–67.

ᵈ A version of this paper (including "minor stylistic changes and the correction of obvious typographical errors" as well as two supplementary footnotes all provided by H. W. Kuhn and A. W. Tucker) appears in *John von Neumann: Collected Works Volume VI*, A. H. Taub, ed. (Oxford: Pergamon Press, 1963, pp. 89–95).

Chapter 6

ᵃ From today's perspective, such a problem would be considered tiny.

ᵇ What this statement about "the negative of the usual simplex criterion" comes down to is $\text{Max}\,\beta(P_j) > 0$.

ᶜ The ratio of the number of nonzero entries in a matrix to the total number of entries is called the *density* of the matrix. The matrix is said to be *sparse* when the density is low. The matrix of a large-scale linear system tends to be quite sparse, generally less than a few percent. Much attention has been given to the numerical handling of such matrices.

ᵈ The paper alluded to here is probably G. B. Dantzig and S. Johnson, "A Production Smoothing Problem," *Proceedings of Second Symposium on Linear Programming*. National Bureau of Standards and Comptroller, U.S.A.F. Headquarters, January 1955, pp. 151–176.

ᵉ This article can be found in *Management Science* 1 (1954) 86–91.

Chapter 7

ᵃ That is, convex sets.

^{b} One may be inclined to ask, "what, exactly, is the principle here?" It can be said that it is a systematic procedure for decomposing a large, structured linear program into smaller, more manageable subproblems and for coordinating the solutions of the smaller subproblems to achieve an optimal solution of the given linear program.

^{c} The vector P_0 contains one nonzero element, which is a 1.

^{d} That is, an extreme solution to a homogeneous system.

^{e} Geometrically, such a homogeneous solution is a point that generates an extreme ray of a polyhedral cone. By a classical theorem, every polyhedral cone is finitely generated. See the Editor's Note e to Chapter 20.

Chapter 8

^{a} In [1], the size of the working basis is $2M \times 2M$.

^{b} In each of the last L equations, the coefficients are all nonnegative, and there is no variable having two or more positive coefficients among these last L.

^{c} That is, to determine what must leave.

^{d} In the discussion that follows columns are oten referred to as variables. There is, of course, a one-to-one correspondence between variables and (labeled) columns.

^{e} For the definition of y, refer to (4).

^{f} These running times, actual and estimated, provide an interesting contrast with what one would experience today.

Chapter 9

^{a} The "space" is a cell (i,j) containing a sequence of numbers. These numbers t_{ij}^k represent times (for example dates) when a tanker is to be fully loaded at i for delivery at j. These times reflect when the tanker will be ready to sail.

^{b} This array is referred to later as t.

^{c} The transportation problem with integral right-hand side is guaranteed to have an integral solution. The forcing of certain variables to equal zero does not alter this fact.

Chapter 10

^{a} At this stage in the development of nonlinear programming, there were essentially two options: convex quadratic programming and separable convex programming.

^{b} Actually $\alpha_j = x_j/\bar{x}$ and $\beta_j = \alpha_j \ln \alpha_j$.

^{c} That is, the first approximating linear program.

^{d} To see how this might be done, see (14).

Chapter 11

[a] First appearing in K. J. Arrow, *Social Choice and Individual Values* (New York: John Wiley & Sons, 1951), the famous Impossibility Theorem, as it is commonly known, has to do with social welfare functions. It asserts that if there are at least three distinct social states and the set of individuals is finite, then there is no social welfare function satisfying a certain set of conditions. Sen's review article (reference [10] in this chapter) covers the "content, context, and relevance of Arrow's theorem."

Whether this particular result is what the authors really had in mind is hard to say. One thing is clear: Sen's review (published in 1985) makes no reference to the Arrow-Debreu paper on the existence of an equilibrium for a competitive economy (published in 1954). Likewise, the Arrow-Debreu paper does not cite Arrow's social choice publication mentioned above.

[b] Perhaps this reference to "Arrow's Impossibility Theorem" is intended to signify a theorem from the Arrow-Debreu paper (reference [1]). In that paper there is no nonexistence theorem as such; there is, however, a one-paragraph comment—not identified as a theorem, and in small print—pointing out that if the last of seven assumptions fails to hold, then a competitive equilibrium might fail to exist. See [1, p. 281].

[c] For a discussion of integrability, see M. Carey, "Integrability and Mathematical Programming," *Econometrica* 45 (1977) 1957–1976.

[d] At this stage, reference to primal and dual constraints is a bit premature inasmuch as the requisite properties of the functions have not been stated.

[e] There is in fact a one-to-one correspondence between coordinates of the primal vector Y_t and those of the dual slack vector $\hat{Y}_t$.

[f] Accordingly, the function $U^i(X^i)$ is strictly concave.

[g] Here, I is supposed to indicate the income of an individual i in period t, but apparently this notation has been suppressed.

[h] This ratio is called the condition number of $\bar{H}^i$.

[i] As defined a little later, the symbol $\doteq$ means *approximately equal to* .

[j] If ρ_1 and ρ_2 are meant to be the condition numbers of the matrices H_1 and H_2 in the example of Theorem 10, then they are incorrect. They should be approximately 118.99.

[k] The standard reference for this result is H. W. Kuhn and A. W. Tucker, "Nonlinear programming," in J. Neyman, ed., *Proceedings of the Second Berkeley Symposium on Mathematical Statistics and Probability* (Berkeley: University of California Press, 1951, pp. 481–493).

Chapter 12

[a] This paper has no other major headings except the the reference list; it appears that the Summary ends at the bottom of the first page of the paper.

[b] The "separate joint paper" on this subject is A. R. Ferguson and G. B. Dantzig, "The allocation of aircraft to routes: An example of linear programming under uncertain demand," *Management Science* 3 (1956) 45–73. The Research Memorandum cited in [4] was published as A. R. Ferguson and G. B. Dantzig, "The problem of routing aircraft," *Aeronautical Engineering Review* 14 (1956) 51–55.

[c] The function is separable and convex.

[d] Note that in (31) the variables are suppressed in the notation ϕ.

[e] The number is in fact k. The vectors $b_2^{(1)}, b_2^{(2)}, \cdots, b_2^{(k)}$ are a set of possible outcomes.

Chapter 13

[a] This is not to say, however, that $b \geq Ax$ and $b < Ax$ are the only options.

[b] The existence theorem of linear programming states that when a linear program and its dual are both feasible, then both have optimal solutions and the objective function values of the two programs are equal. This theorem can be obtained by specializing the more general Theorem 4 in the paper D. Gale, H. W. Kuhn, and A. W. Tucker, "Linear programming and the theory of games," in T. C. Koopmans, ed., *Activity Analysis of Production and Allocation* (New York, John Wiley & Sons, 1951, pp. 317–329). The theorem in the form stated above appears on page 78 of D. Gale's book, *The Theory of Linear Economic Models* (New York, McGraw-Hill, 1960).

[c] Here "prices" means "dual variables."

[d] This RAND paper was published as G. B. Dantzig, "General convex objective forms," in K. J. Arrow, S. Karlin, and P. Suppes (eds.), *Mathematical Models in the Social Sciences* (Stanford, California, Stanford University Press, 1960, pp. 151-158).

[e] This paper appeared in the *Journal of the Society for Industrial and Applied Mathematics* 8 (1960) 703–712.

[f] This paper was published in the *Journal of the Society for Industrial and Applied Mathematics* 9 (1961) 481–488.

Chapter 14

[a] IIASA is an acronym for "International Institute for Applied Systems Analysis," which is located in Laxenburg, Austria.

[b] The original had "dimension p."

[c] D-W refers to Dantzig-Wolfe decomposition, as in Chapter 7 of this volume.

[d] Actually, the Technical University of Vienna. G. Infanger is now a Consulting Associate Professor at Stanford.

Chapter 15

[a] In addition to the literature cited in the text could now be added G. Infanger, *Planning Under Uncertainty* (Danvers, Mass.: Boyd and Fraser Publishing Company, 1994), and J. R. Birge, *Introduction to Stochastic Programming* (New York: Springer, 1997).

[b] The superscript j is a dummy index belonging to the set $\{1, \ldots, h_t\}$

Chapter 16

[a] Establishing optimality in integer linear programming is more challenging than in ordinary linear programming.

[b] By today's standards, a 49-city problem would not be considered large. For a concise up-to-date account of the literature reporting the solution of ever-larger traveling salesman problems, see p. 995 of the masterful three-volume work A. Schrijver, *Combinatorial Optimization* (Berlin: Springer, 2003). There one can pick out the following sequence of problem sizes (number of cities): 42, 48, 57, 64, 80, 100, 120, 318, 532, 666, 7,397, 13,509.

[c] Presumably the program would have to be feasible. Under these conditions (feasibility and boundedness) an optimal solution is certain to exist. The estimate can be based on comparison between the primal and dual objective function values.

[d] The editors of this book were H. W. Kuhn and A. W. Tucker.

Chapter 17

[a] This probably refers to L. R. Ford, Jr. and D. R. Fulkerson, "Maximal flow through a network," *Canadian Journal of Mathematics* 8 (1956), 399–404.

[b] The reference given by Dantzig and Fulkerson for Menger's Theorem is König's graph theory book [5]. The original source is K. Menger, "Zur allgemeinen Kurventheorie," *Fundamenta Mathematicae* 10 (1927), 96–115.

Chapter 18

[a] For a survey of early publications on the shortest paths, see S. E. Dreyfus, "An appraisal of some shortest-path algorithms," *Operations Research* 17 (1969) 395–412. See also Chapter 7 of R. E. Tarjan, *Data Structures and Network Algorithms* (Philadelphia: Society for Industrial and Applied Mathematics, 1983).

[b] A more complete citation is E. F. Moore, "The shortest path through a maze," *Proceedings of the International Symposium on the Theory of Switching, Part II, April 2–5, 1957,* The Annals of the Computation Laboratory of Harvard University, 30 (Cambridge: Harvard University Press, 1959).

Chapter 19

[a] Such a function is said to be *separable*.

[b] It appears that each function φ_j is assumed to be defined over a closed bounded interval of the nonnegative real line.

[c] The paper on which this chapter is based has no equation (27) per se.

[d] The conjecture was announced in L. Euler "Recherches sur une nouvelle espèce de carrés magiques," *Verhandelingen uitgegeven door he zeeuwsch Genootschap der Wetenschappen te Vlissingen* Middelburg (1782) 85–239. This paper was reproduced in *Commentationes Arithmeticæ Collectæ* II (1849) 302–361. A full citation for the work alluded to in Footnote 2 of Chapter 19 is R. C. Bose and S. S. Shrikhande, "On the construction of sets of mutually orthogonal latin squares and the falsity of a conjecture of Euler," *Transactions of the American Mathematical Society* 95 (1960) 191–209.

Another publication on this topic is R. C. Bose, E. T. Parker, and S. S. Shrikhande, "Further results on the construction of sets of mutually orthogonal latin squares and the falsity of Euler's conjecture," *Canadian Journal of Mathematics* 12 (1960) 189–203.

[e] The Four Color Problem has since been solved. See K. Appel and W. Haken "Every planar map is four colorable, Part I: Discharging," *Illinois Journal of Mathematics* 21 (1977) 429–490; K. Appel, W. Haken, and J. Koch, "Every planar map is four colorable, Part II: Reducibility," *Illinois Journal of Mathematics* 21 (1977) 491–567; and K. Appel and W. Haken. "Every planar map is four colorable," *Contemporary Mathematics* 98 (1989) 1–741.

This work has been criticized for its extensive use of computers to verify a very large number of cases. For new proof of the Four Color Theorem, see N. Robertson, D. P. Sanders, P. D. Seymour and R. Thomas "A new proof of the four colour theorem," *Electronic Research Announcements of the American Mathematical Society* 2 (1996) 17–25; and N. Robertson, D. P. Sanders, P. D. Seymour and R. Thomas, "The four colour theorem," *Journal of Combinatorial Theory, Series B* 70 (1997) 2–44.

Chapter 20

[a] T. S. Motzkin's carefully written and scholarly dissertation reveals his keen awareness of the literature on linear inequalities that predated his own investigation of the subject. Indeed, he cites no fewer than 46 separate names—and many more publications—including those of Fourier and Dines. He was as good a "grave-digger" as anyone and surely would not have objected to sharing credit for the elimination method with Fourier and Dines. As Motzkin himself wrote [*Beiträge*, p. 2]

> *Bei dem vielfachen Ineinandergreifen aller Tatsachen in dem*
> *behandelten Gebiet wird es oft schwer fallen zu entscheiden, wo*

ein neuer Satz aus schon bekannten durch Kombination und wo er durch Synthese hervorgeht.

[Because of the many interrelations between statements in the area under consideration it will often be difficult to decide when a new theorem emerges through combination of already known results and when through through synthesis.]

[b] In this paper, the authors often write expressions like $i = (1, \ldots, m)$. These have been converted to the style $i = 1, \ldots, m$ which is more standard.

[c] It is significant that Kuhn's proof of this result is constructive. In the early days of mathematical programming, this philosophical approach assumed great importance.

[d] This appears to be an interesting (Freudian?) slip. The theorem quoted is actually (a special case of) Motzkin's *Transposition* Theorem. (See [*Beiträge*, Satz D6, p. 51].) But the system of equations in nonnegative variables given in (25) is of the form found in the classical (Hitchcock) transportation problem.

[e] According to Alexander Schrijver (*Theory of Linear and Integer Programming*, p. 157), the dual of Fourier-Motzkin elimination was used by J. Farkas in a paper published in 1898 to prove that every polyhedral cone is finitely generated (a theorem often attributed to H. Minkowski). The original is in Hungarian, but is available in a German translation. These sources are given in detail by Schrijver who also notes that "this dual was studied by Abadie [1964]." Here he is referring to a talk given that year by Jean Abadie at the International Symposium on Mathematical Programming held in London. The talk was based on two internal research reports written by Abadie in 1963 and 1964. These papers (the first in English, the second in French) do not explore the connection with integer programming.

[f] Actually, the vectors D_i, E_j, F_k each have $n-1$ components as $\bar{x}$ does.

[g] The summation sign should read $\displaystyle\sum_{j=1}^{n}$.

[h] In equation (25), the positions of "$j = (1, 2, 3)$" and "$i = (1, 2, 3)$" should be interchanged. The second sum should be over i running from 1 to 3.

[i] In the original publication, this equation lacks the number, (33), even though it is cited in the text.

[j] Details in some of the references have been amended.

[k] Motzkin's thesis was published in Jerusalem in 1936 by Buchdruckerei Azriel. In 1952, an informal (and unpolished) English translation by D.R.

Fulkerson was issued by the RAND Corporation as technical report T-22. It is available in D. Cantor, B. Gordon, and B. Rothschild, eds., *Theodore S. Motzkin: Selected Papers* (Boston: Birkhäuser, 1983).

Chapter 21

[a] Unlike all the other chapters in this anthology, Chapter 19 is based on a section from George Dantzig's book *Linear Programming and Extensions.* Thus, the section numbers alluded to here are in reference to that publication. §24-1 is titled "General Theory" and begins with an analog of the (Karush) Kuhn-Tucker theorem on necessary conditions of optimality for the convex but *nondifferentiable* case. The restrictions imposed are fairly strong, however. The domain of variation is assumed to be compact as well as convex; the constraint functions are assumed to be continuous and convex and to satisfy the so-called Slater condition. Dantzig develops a column generation algorithm that converges to an optimal solution of the original problem. §24-3 is concerned with the case of separable convex objectives and gives an algorithm for solving such problems.

[b] At first glance, equations (5) and (7) look incorrect, specifically, off by a factor of 2 in front of C. As it happens, the absence of a linear term from the objective function makes (7) a homogeneous linear inequality, and this makes the condition correct, albeit unconventional.

[c] The original text has $x^T Q x$ rather than $x^T C x$, but this is a misprint.

[d] This clearly should read $\lambda C_4 \lambda^T \geq 0$.

[e] Actually, P_0 gives the values of the *basic* variables in the cited basic solution.

[f] The subscripts in the expression $\lambda_i = \lambda_i'$ should be j, not i.

Chapter 22

[a] The integer n which represents the dimension of a Euclidean space should not be confused with the index by which various general members of sequences (such as $\{A_n\}$) are tagged.

[b] Another commonly used term for set-valued function is *point-to-set mapping.*

[c] In contrast to a convex function on E^n, a quasi-convex function on E^n need not be continuous, hence the assumption that φ is a continuous quasi-convex function on E^n entails no redundancy.

[d] Presumably, x_r is an element of $H(f^r) \cap C$. This is confirmed by usage that comes somewhat later.

[e] Berge's *Topological Spaces* is a translation by E. M. Patterson of the French original *Espaces Topologiques.* Patterson notes in the preface that the English translation contains "various amendments and the addition of new material, mainly in Chapter VIII." This is precisely the chapter from

which the cited theorem comes. It does not appear in the French version. Neither edition contains a bibliography.

[f] Another term for "carrier" is *support*.

Chapter 23

[a] In the literature of the linear complementarity problem, the class of real square matrices M with the property that (2) has a solution whenever it is feasible, that is, $w = q + Mz$, $w \geq 0$, $z \geq 0$ is consistent is denoted by Q_0 and has been the subject of intensive study for many years.

[b] The same first-order optimality conditions were discovered by William Karush in his (then unpublished) master's thesis, "Minima of Functions of Several Variables with Inequalities as Side Conditions," Department of Mathematics, University of Chicago, December 1939. For decades now, the result has been called the Karush-Kuhn-Tucker Theorem. For a re-creation of a portion of Karush's thesis, see H. W. Kuhn, "Nonlinear programming: A historical review," *Nonlinear Programming*, Volume IX, SIAM-AMS Proceedings, R. W. Cottle and C. E. Lemke, eds. (Providence, R.I.: American Mathematical Society, 1976, pp. 1–26).

Another account of this development will be found in the essay H. W. Kuhn, "Nonlinear Programming: A Historical Note," in J. K. Lenstra, A. H. G. Rinnooy Kan, and A. Schrijver, eds., *History of Mathematical Programming* (Amsterdam: North-Holland, 1991, pp. 82–96).

[c] Since the early days of mathematical programming, there has been strong interest in establishing existence theorems constructively. This philosophy was articulated by L. R. Ford, Jr. and D. R. Fulkerson in the preface to their classic monograph *Flows in Networks*. They wrote:

> Throughout the book the emphasis is on constructive procedures, even more on computationally effective ones. Other things being nearly equal, we prefer a constructive proof of a theorem to a non-constructive one, and a constructive proof that leads to an efficient computational scheme is, to our way of thinking, just that much better.

[d] An error in the matrix M (as given in the original) has been corrected here.

[e] This relates to the study of the matrix class Q_0 mentioned in Editor's Note a above.

[f] Matrices satisfying the property described in Theorem 7 are now called *strictly semimonotone*.

[g] For another account of the principal pivoting method in the positive semi-definite case, see R. W. Cottle, "The principal pivoting method of quadratic programming," in G. B. Dantzig and A. F. Veinott, Jr., eds., *Mathematics*

of the Decision Sciences, Part 1 [Lectures in Applied Mathematics, Volume 11] (Providence, R.I.: American Mathematical Society, 1968).

Chapter 24

[a] Strictly speaking, if $q \neq 0$, the mapping $W(z) = q + Mz$ is affine, not linear.

[b] Here the term *length* refers to the number of coordinates.

[c] A flaw in the numbering system of the original paper has been corrected here. (Equation numbers (8) and (9) were each used twice.)

[d] In [4], Gale and Nikaido characterize P-matrices with a theorem to the effect that a real square matrix has positive principal minors if and only if it reverses the sign of no vector but zero, i.e.,

$$z_i(Mz)_i \leq 0 \quad \text{for all } i \quad \Longrightarrow \quad z = 0.$$

There are other interesting and useful characterizations of the class P. One of these comes from the article H. Samelson, R. M. Thrall, and O. Wesler, "A partition theorem for Euclidean n-space," *Proceedings of the American Mathematical Society* 9 (1958) 805–807. In effect, it says that an $n \times n$ matrix M belongs to P if and only if for every vector q in R^n, the linear complementarity problem formed with data q and M has one and only one solution.

Publications of George B. Dantzig

Adler, I., and Dantzig, G.B. (1974). "Maximum Diameter of Abstract Polytopes," *Mathematical Programming Study* 1, 20–40.

Adler, I., Dantzig, G.B., and Murty, K. (1974). "Existence of A-Avoiding Paths in Abstract Polytopes," *Mathematical Programming Study* 1, 41–42.

Avi-Itzhak, B., Dantzig, G.B., and Iusem, A.N (1983). "The Consumers Energy Services Model of the PILOT System," in B. Lev (ed.), *Energy Models and Studies*, Studies in Management Science and Systems 9, North-Holland Publishing Co., Amsterdam, 195–220.

Beale, E.M.L., Dantzig, G.B., and Watson, R.D. (1986). "A First Order Approach to a Class of Multi-Time-Period Stochastic Programming Problems," *Mathematical Programming Study* 27, 103–117.

Collen, M.F., Rubin, L., Neyman, J., Dantzig, G.B., Baer, R.M., and Siegelaub, A.B. (1964). "Automated Multiphasic Screening and Diagnosis," *American Journal of Public Health* 54, 741–750.

Connolly, T.J., Dantzig, G.B., and Parikh, S.C. (1978). "The Stanford PILOT Energy/Economic Model," *Policy Analysis and Information Systems* 2, 23–51. Also in R. El Mallakh and D.H. El Mallakh (eds.), Proceedings of the 4th International Conference on Energy Options and Conservation, October 17–19, 1977, The International Research Center for Energy and Economic Development, Boulder, Colorado, 1978, 87-119. Also in *Advances in the Economics of Energy and Resources, Volume 1 – The Structure of Energy Markets*, JAI Press, 1979, 77–103.

Cottle, R.W., and Dantzig, G.B. (1968). "Complementary Pivot Theory of Mathematical Programming," in G.B. Dantzig, and A.F. Veinott, Jr., (eds.), *Mathematics of the Decision Sciences, Part 1*, American Mathematical Society, Providence, R.I., 115–136. Also in *Linear Algebra and its Applications* 1, 103–125. Also in G.B. Dantzig and B.C. Eaves (eds.), *Studies in Optimization*, MAA Studies in Mathematics, Vol. 10, Mathematical Association of America, Washington, D.C., 27–51.

Cottle, R.W., and Dantzig, G.B. (1970). "A Generalization of the Linear Complementarity Problem," *Journal of Combinatorial Theory* 8, 79–90.

Dantzig, G.B. (1939). "On a Class of Distributions that Approach the Normal Distribution Function," *Annals of Mathematical Statistics* 10, 247–253.

Dantzig, G.B. (1940). "On the Non-Existence of Tests of Students' Hypothesis Involving Power Functions Independent of Sigma," *Annals of Mathematical Statistics* 11, 186–192.

Dantzig, G.B. (1949a). "Programming in a Linear Structure," Report of the September 9, 1948 meeting in Madison, *Econometrica* 17, 73–74.

Dantzig, G.B. (1949b). "Programming of Interdependent Activities, II: Mathematical Model," *Econometrica* 17, 200–211; also in T.C. Koopmans (ed.), *Activity Analysis of Production and Allocation*, John Wiley & Sons, New York, 1951, 19–32.

Dantzig, G.B. (1951a). "Maximization of a Linear Function of Variables Subject to Linear Inequalities," in T.C. Koopmans (ed.), *Activity Analysis of Production and Allocation*, John Wiley & Sons, New York, 339–347.

Dantzig, G.B. (1951b). "Application of the Simplex Method to the Transportation Problem," in T.C. Koopmans (ed.), *Activity Analysis of Production and Allocation*, John Wiley & Sons, New York, 359–373.

Dantzig, G.B. (1951c). "A Proof of the Equivalence of the Programming Problem and the Game Problem, in T.C. Koopmans (ed.), *Activity Analysis of Production and Allocation*, John Wiley & Sons, New York, 330–335.

Dantzig, G.B. (1951d). "Linear Programming," in *Problems for the Numerical Analysis of the Future*, Proceedings of Symposium on Modern Calculating Machinery and Numerical Methods, UCLA, July 29–31, 1948, Appl. Math. Series 15, Department of Commerce, National Bureau of Standards, June 1951, 18–21.

Dantzig, G.B. (1954). "A Comment on Eddie's 'Traffic Delays at Toll Booths'," *Journal of Operations Research Society of America* 2, 339–341.

Dantzig, G.B. (1955a). "Developments in Linear Programming," Proceedings Second Symposium on Linear Programming, National Bureau of Standards and Comptroller, U.S.A.F. Headquarters, January, 667–685.

Dantzig, G.B. (1955b). "Linear Programming Under Uncertainty," *Management Science* 1, 197–206. Also in A.F. Veinott, Jr. (ed.), *Mathematical Studies in Management Science*, The Macmillian Co., New York, 1965, 330-339.

Dantzig, G.B. (1955c). "Upper Bounds, Secondary Constraints, and Block Triangularity in Linear Programming," *Econometrica* 23, 174–183.

Dantzig, G.B. (1955d). "Optimal Solution of a Dynamic Leontief Model with Substitution," *Econometrica* 23, 295–302.

Dantzig, G.B. (1956a). "Constructive Proof of the Min-Max Theorem," *Pacific Journal of Mathematics* 6, 25–33.

Dantzig, G.B. (1956b). "Recent Advances in Linear Programming," *Management Science* 2, 131–144.

Dantzig, G.B. (1956c). "Note on Klein's 'Direct Use of Extremal Principles in Solving Certain Problems Involving Inequalities'," *Operations Research* 4, 247–249.

Dantzig, G.B. (1957a). "Thoughts on Linear Programming and Automation," *Management Science* 3, 131–139.

Dantzig, G.B. (1957b). "Concepts, Origins and Use of Linear Programming," in M. Davies, R.T. Eddison, and T. Page (eds.), *Proceedings of First International Conference on Operations Research*, Operations Research Society of America, Baltimore, December, 100–108.

Dantzig, G.B. (1957c). "Discrete Variable Extremum Problems," *Operations Research* 5, 226-277.

Dantzig, G.B. (1959a). "On The Status of Multi-Stage Linear Programming Problems," *Management Science* 6, 1959, 53–72. Also in A.F. Veinott, Jr. (ed.), *Mathematical Studies in Management Science*, The Macmillian Co., New York, 1965, 303–320.

Dantzig, G.B. (1959b). "Note on Solving Linear Programs in Integers," *Naval Research Logistics Quarterly* 6, 75–76.

Dantzig, G.B. (1960a). "Inductive Proof of the Simplex Method," *IBM Journal of Research and Development* 4, 505–506.

Dantzig, G.B. (1960b). "On the Shortest Route Through a Network," *Management Science* 6, 187–190. Also in Fulkerson, D. R. (eds.), *Some Topics in Graph Theory*, MAA Studies, No. 11, 1975, 89–93.

Dantzig, G.B. (1960c). "On the Significance of Solving Linear Programming Problems with Some Integer Variables," *Econometrica* 28, 30–44.

Dantzig, G.B. (1960d). "General Convex Objective Forms," in K.J. Arrow, S. Karlin, and P. Suppes (eds.), *Mathematical Methods in the Social Sciences*, Stanford University Press, Stanford, California, 151–158.

Dantzig, G.B. (1960e). "A Machine-Job Scheduling Model," *Management Science* 6, 191–196.

Dantzig, G.B. (1963a). "Compact Basis Triangularization for the Simplex Method," in R.L. Graves and P. Wolfe (eds.), *Recent Advances in Mathematical Programming*, McGraw-Hill, New York, 125–132.

Dantzig, G.B. (1963b). *Linear Programming and Extensions*, Princeton University Press, Princeton, New Jersey. Revised edition 1966; fourth printing, 1968, 621 pages. [Japanese translation, Tutte-Mori, Inc., Tokyo, 1983.]

Dantzig, G.B. (1964a). "New Mathematical Methods in the Life Sciences," *The American Mathematical Monthly* 71, 4–15. Also in R.W. Stacy and B.D. Waxman (eds.), *Computers and Biomedical Research 1*, Academic Press, New York, March 1965.

Dantzig, G.B. (1964b). "Research Problems," *Bulletin of the American Mathematical Society* 70, 499–501.

Dantzig, G.B. (1965a). "Operations Research in the World of Today and Tomorrow," *Operations Research Verfahren* 3, 113–118; presidential address, TIMS 1966, entitled "Management Science in the World of Today and Tomorrow" in *Management Science* 13 1967, C-107–C-111.

Dantzig, G.B. (1965b). "Optimization in Operations Research," in W.A. Kalenich (ed.), *Information Processing 1965*, Proceedings, International Federation for Information Processing Congress 65, Spartan Books, Washington, D.C., 173–176.

Dantzig, G.B. (1965c). "The Simplex Method," in Machol, R. (ed.), *System Engineering Handbook*, McGraw-Hill, New York, Chapter 25, 10 pages.

Dantzig, G.B. (1966a). "Linear Programming and its Progeny," *Naval Research Reviews* XIX (6), 1; also in E.M.L. Beale (ed.), *Applications of Mathematical Programming Techniques*, English Universities Press, Ltd., London, 1970, 3–16.

Dantzig, G.B. (1966b). "Linear Control Processes and Mathematical Programming," *SIAM Journal on Control and Optimization* 4, 1966, 56–60. Also in in J. Abadie (ed.), *Nonlinear Programming*, North-Holland, Amsterdam, 1967, 281–286. Also in in G.B. Dantzig and A.F. Veinott, Jr. (eds.), *Mathematics of the Decision Sciences Part 2*, American Mathematical Society, Providence, R.I., 1968, 31–36. Also in A.K. Aziz (ed.), *Lecture Series in Differential Equations 1*, Van Nostrand Reinhold Co., New York, 1969, 1–7.

Dantzig, G.B. (1966c). "All Shortest Routes in a Graph," in P. Rosenstiehl (ed.), *Theorie Des Graphes*, Dunod, Paris, 91–92.

Dantzig, G.B. (1968). "Large-Scale Linear Programming," in G.B. Dantzig and A.F. Veinott, Jr. (eds.), *Mathematics of the Decision Sciences*, the American Mathematical Society Summer Seminar, Providence, R.I., 1968, 77–92; also "Large-Scale Systems and the Computer Revolution," H.W. Kuhn (ed.), *Proceedings of the Princeton Symposium on Mathematical Programming* Princeton University Press, Princeton, New Jersey, 1970, 51–72.

Dantzig, G.B. (1970). "Complementary Spanning Trees," in J. Abadie (ed.), *Integer and Nonlinear Programming*, North-Holland, Amsterdam, 499–505.

Dantzig, G.B. (1971). "A Control Problem of Bellman," *Management Science* 16, 542–546.

Dantzig, G.B. (1973). "The ORSA New Orleans Address on Compact City," *Management Science* 19, 1151-1161.

Dantzig, G.B. (1974). "On a Convex Programming Problem of Rozanov," *Applied Mathematics and Optimization* 1, 189-192. Also entitled "A Generalized Programming Solution to a Convex Programming Problem with a Homogeneous Objective," *Symposia Mathematica*, Vol. XIX, Monograf, Bologna, Italy, Academic Press, 1976, 209–214.

Dantzig, G.B. (1975). "Drews' Institutionalized Divvy Economy," *Journal of Economic Theory* 11, 372–384.

Dantzig, G.B. (1976a). "On the Reduction of an Integrated Energy and Interindustry Model to a Smaller Linear Program," *Review of Economics and Statistics* 58, 248–250.

Dantzig, G.B. (1976b). "Linear Programming, Past and Future," in E.I. Salkovitz (ed.), *Science Technology, and the Modern Navy, Thirtieth Anniversary*, ONR-37, Office of Naval Research, 85–95.

Dantzig, G.B. (1979). "The Role of Models in Determining Policy for Transition to a More Resilient Technological Society," IIASA Distinguished Lecture Series /1, Vienna, June 12, International Institute for Applied Systems Analysis, Laxenburg, Austria.

Dantzig, G.B. (1980a). "Note on the Objective Function for the PILOT Model," in A. Prekopa (ed.), *Survey of Mathematical Programming*, Proceedings, IXth International Symposium on Mathematical Programming, Publishing House of the Hungarian Academy of Sciences, Budapest, 325–328.

Dantzig, G.B. (1980b). "Comments on Khachian's Algorithms for Linear Programming," *SIAMNews* 13, October.

Dantzig, G.B. (1981a). "Are Dual Variables Prices? If Not, How to Make them More So," in G. Castellani and P. Mazzoleni (eds.), Mathematical Programming and its Economic Applications, Proceedings of the international symposium held in Venice, June 1978, F. Angeli, Milano, Italy, 135–148.

Dantzig, G.B. (1981b). "Time-Staged Methods in Linear Programming; Comments and Early History, in G.B. Dantzig, M.A.H. Dempster, and M.J. Kallio (eds.), *Large-Scale Linear Programming*, Vol. 1, CP-81-51,

IIASA Collaborative Proceedings Series, Laxenberg, Austria, 1981, 3–16. Also in Y.Y. Haimes (ed.), *Large Scale Systems*, Studies in Management Science and Systems, Vol. 7, North-Holland Publishing Company, Amsterdam, 1982, 19–30.

Dantzig, G.B. (1981c). "Contributions of Mathematics to Planning During and Immediately After World War II," *History of American Mathematics in World War II*, Mathematical Association of America, Committee Records.

Dantzig, G.B. (1982a). "Reminiscences About the Origins of Linear Programming," *Operations Research Letters* 1, 43–48. Also in A. Bachem, M. Grotschel, and B. Korte (eds.), *Mathematical Programming: The State of the Art, Bonn 1982*, Springer-Verlag, Berlin, 1983, 78–86; also in *Memoirs of the American Mathematical Society* 48, 1984, 1–11. Also in R.W. Cottle, M.L. Kelmanson, and B. Korte (eds.), *Mathematical Programming*, Proceedings of the International Congress on Mathematical Programming, Rio de Janeiro, Brazil, April 6–8, 1981, North-Holland Publishing Co., Amsterdam, 1984, 105–112.

Dantzig, G.B. (1982b). "The PILOT Energy-Economic Model for Policy Planning," in T.N. Veziroglu (ed.), Alternative Energy Sources IV, Proceedings of the 4th Miami International Conference on Alternative Energy Sources, Volume 8, Ann Arbor Science Publishers, Ann Arbor Michigan, 409–415.

Dantzig, G.B. (1982c). "Time-staged Methods in Linear Programs," in Y.Y. Haimes (ed.), *Large-Scale Systems*, Studies in Management Science, Vol. 7, North-Holland, Amsterdam, 19–30.

Dantzig, G.B. (1983a). "Concerns About Large-Scale Models," in R.M. Thrall, R.G. Thompson, and M.L. Holloway (eds.), *Large-Scale Energy Models*, AAAS Selected Symposia Series 73, Westview Press, Inc. Boulder, CO, for the Amer. Assoc. for the Adv. of Sc., Washington, D.C., 15–20, 1983.

Dantzig, G.B. (1983b). "Mathematical Programming and Decision Making," *Joho-Shori (Transactions of the Information Processing Society of Japan)* 24, 604–609. [In Japanese.]

Dantzig, G.B. (1987a). "Linear Programming," in J. Eatwell, M. Milgate, and P. Newman (eds.), *The New Palgrave: A Dictionary of Economic Theory and Doctrine*, Vol. 3, The Macmillian Press, Ltd., London, 203–206.

Dantzig, G.B. (1987b). "Simplex Method for Solving Linear Programs," in J. Eatwell, M. Milgate, and P. Newman (eds.), *The New Palgrave: A Dictionary of Economic Theory and Doctrine*, Vol. 4, The Macmillian Press, Ltd., London, 337–340.

Dantzig, G.B. (1987c). "Origins of the Simplex Method," in S.G Nash (ed.), *Proceedings of the ACM Conference on a History of Scientific Computing*, ACM Press, Addison-Wesley Publishing Company, 1990, 141–151.

Dantzig, G.B. (1988a). "Planning Under Uncertainty Using Parallel Computing," *Annals of Operations Research* 14, 1–16.

Dantzig, G.B. (1988b). "Impact of Linear Programming on Computer Development," *ORMS Today* 14, August, 12–17. Also in D.V. Chudnovsky and R.D. Jenks (eds.), Computers in Mathematics, Lecture Notes in Pure and Applied Mathematics, v. 125, New York, Marcel Dekker, Inc., 1990, 233–240.

Dantzig, G.B. (1989a). "Making Progress During a Stall in the Simplex Algorithm," *Linear Algebra and its Applications* 114/115, 251–259.

Dantzig, G.B. (1989b). "Decomposition Techniques for Large-Scale Electric Power Systems Planning Under Uncertainty," in R. Sharda, *et al.* (eds.), *Impact on Recent Computer Advances on Operations Research*, North Holland, Amsterdam, 3–20.

Dantzig, G.B. (1990). "The Diet Problem," *Interfaces* 20:4, July/Aug, 430–47.

Dantzig, G.B., Blattner, W.O., and Rao, M.R. (1967a). "Finding a Cycle in a Graph with Minimum Cost to Time Ratio with Application to a Ship Routing Problem," in P. Rosenstiehl (ed.), *Theorie Des Graphes*, Dunod, Paris, 77–83.

Dantzig, G.B., Blattner, W.O., and Rao, M.R. (1967b). "All Shortest Routes from a Fixed Origin in a Graph," in P. Rosenstiehl (ed.), *Theorie Des Graphes*, Dunod, Paris, 85–90.

Dantzig, G.B., and Cottle, R.W. (1967). "Positive (Semi-) Definite Matrices and Mathematical Programming," in J. Abadie (ed.), *Nonlinear Programming*, North-Holland, Amsterdam, 55–73.

Dantzig, G.B., and Cottle, R.W. (1974). "Optimization, Mathematical Theory of (Linear and Nonlinear Programming)," *Encyclopaedia Britannica*, Vol. 13, 628–632.

Dantzig, G.B., Cottle, R.W., Eaves, B.C., Hillier, F.S., Manne, A.S., Golub, G.H., Wilde, D.J., and Wilson, R.B. (1973). "On the Need for a System Optimization Laboratory," in T.C. Hu and S.M. Robinson (eds.), *Mathematical Programming*, Academic Press, New York, 1–32.

Dantzig, G.B., and DeHaven, J. (1962). "On The Reduction of Certain Multiplicative Chemical Equilibrium Systems to Mathematically Equivalent Additive Systems," *Journal of Chemical Physics* 36, 2620–2627.

Dantzig, G.B., DeHaven, J., Cooper, I., Johnson, S.M., DeLand, E., Kanter, H.E., and Sams, C.F. (1961). "A Mathematical Model of the Human External Respiratory System," Perspectives in Biology and Medicine 4, 324–376.

Dantzig, G.B., DeHaven, J., and Sams, C.F. (1960). "A Mathematical Model of the Respiratory System," in Proceedings, Fourth Air Pollution Medical Research Conference, San Francisco, December, 72–95.

Dantzig, G.B., DeHaven, J., and Sams, C.F. (1961). "A Mathematical Model of the Chemistry of the External Respiratory System," in J. Neyman (ed.), *Proceedings 4th Berkeley Symposium on Mathematical Statistics and Probability*, University of California Press, Berkeley, California, 181–196.

Dantzig, G.B., Dempster, M.A.H., and Kallio, M.J. (eds.), (1981). *Large-Scale Linear Programming*, 2 Vols., CP-81-51, IIASA Collaborative Proceedings Series, Laxenberg, Austria.

Dantzig, G.B., and Eaves, B.C. (1973). "Fourier-Motzkin Elimination and Its Dual," *Journal of Combinatorial Theory* 14, May 1973, 288–297. Also in in B. Roy (ed.), *Combinatorial Programming: Methods and Applications*, D. Reidel Publishing Co., Boston, 1975, 93–102.

Dantzig, G.B., and Eaves, B.C., (eds.) (1974). *Studies in Optimization, MAA Studies in Mathematics*, Vol. 10, Mathematical Association of America, Washington, D.C.

Dantzig, G.B., Eaves, B.C., and Gale, D. (1979). "An Algorithm for a Piecewise Linear Model of Trade and Production with Negative Prices and Bankruptcy," *Mathematical Programming* 16, 190–209.

Dantzig, G.B., Eaves, B.C., and Rothblum, U. (1985). "A Decomposition and Scaling-inequality for Line-sum-symmetric Nonnegative Matrices," *SIAM Journal on Algebraic and Discrete Methods* 6, 237–241. April 1985.

Dantzig, G.B., Eisenberg, E., and Cottle, R.W. (1965). "Symmetric Dual Nonlinear Programs," *Pacific Journal of Mathematics* 15, 809–812.

Dantzig, G.B., Ullman, R.J., and Kawaratani, T.K. (1960). "Computing Tetraethyl-Lead Requirements in a Linear-Programming Format," *Operations Research* 8, 24–29.

Dantzig, G.B., Folkman, J., and Shapiro, N. (1967). "On the Continuity of the Minimum Set of a Continuous Function," *Journal of Mathematical Analysis and Applications* 17, 519–548.

Dantzig, G.B., Ford, L.R., and, Fulkerson, D.R. (1956). "A Primal-Dual Algorithm for Linear Programs," in H.W. Kuhn and A.W. Tucker (eds.), *Linear Inequalities and Related Systems*, Annals of Mathematics Study No. 38, Princeton University Press, Princeton, New Jersey, 171–181.

Dantzig, G.B., and Fulkerson, D.R. (1954). "Minimizing the Number of Tankers to Meet a Fixed Schedule," *Naval Research Logistics Quarterly* 1, 217–222.

Dantzig, G.B., and Fulkerson, D.R. (1955). "Computation of Maximal Flows in Networks," *Naval Research Logistics Quarterly* 2, 277–283.

Dantzig, G.B., and Fulkerson, D.R. (1956). "On the Max-Flow Min-Cut Theorems of Networks," in H.W. Kuhn and A.W. Tucker (eds.), *Linear Inequalities and Related Systems*, Annals of Mathematics Study No. 38, Princeton University Press, Princeton, New Jersey, 215–221.

Dantzig, G.B., Fulkerson, D.R., and Johnson, S.M. (1954). "Solution for a Large-Scale Traveling Salesman Problem," *Journal of Operations Research Society of America* 2, 393–410.

Dantzig, G.B., Fulkerson, D.R., and Johnson, S.M. (1959). "On a Linear Programming Combinatorial Approach to the Traveling Salesman Problem," *Operations Research* 7, 58–66.

Dantzig, G.B., and Glynn, P.W. (1990). "Parallel Processors for Planning Under Uncertainty," *Annals of Operations Research* 22, 1–21.

Dantzig, G.B., and Harvey, R.P., McKnight, R.D., and Smith, S.S. (1969). "Sparse Matrix Techniques in Two Mathematical Programming Codes," in R.A. Willoughby (ed.), *Proceedings of the Symposium on Sparse Matrices and Their Applications*, September 9–10, 1968, RA-1, IBM Watson Research Center, Yorktown Heights, New York, 85–99.

Dantzig, G.B., Harvey, R.P., Lansdowne, Z.F., Maier, S.F., and Robinson, D.W. (1979). "Formulating and Solving the Network Design Problem by Decomposition," *Transportation Research* B, 13B, 5–17.

Dantzig, G.B., Harvey, R.P., and McKnight, R. (1965). "Updating the Product Form of the Inverse for the Revised Simplex Method," *A.C.M. Proceedings* 20, 288–295; also Summary in *Journal of the A.C.M.* 12, 603.

Dantzig, G.B., and Hoffman, A.J. (1956). "Dilworth's Theorem on Partially Ordered Sets," in H.W. Kuhn and A.W. Tucker (eds.), *Linear Inequalities and Related Systems*, Annals of Mathematics Study No. 38, Princeton University Press, Princeton, New Jersey, 207–213.

Dantzig, G.B., Hoffman, A.J., and Hu, T.C. (1983). "Triangulations (Tilings) and Certain Block Triangular Matrices," *Mathematical Programming* 31, 1985, 1–14.

Dantzig, G.B., Holling, C.S., Baskerville, C., Jones, D.D., and Clark, W. C. (1975). "A Case Study of Forest Ecosystem/Pest Management," Prepared for Proceedings International Canadian Conference on Applied Systems Analysis, 1975, WP-75-60, International Institute for Applied Systems Analysis, Laxenburg, Austria, June 1975.

Dantzig, G.B., Holling, C.S., Clark, W.C., Jones, D.D., Baskerville, G., and Peterman, R.M. (1976). "Quantitative Evaluation of Pest Management Options: The Spruce Budworm Case Study," in D.L. Wood (ed.), *Proceedings of the XVth International Congress of Entomology*, August. Also in W.E. Waters (ed.), *Current Topics in Forest Entomology*, U.S. Government Printing Office, Washington, D.C., February 1979, 82–102.

Dantzig, G.B., Holling, C.S., and Winkler, C. (1986). "Determining Optimal Policies for Ecosystems," *TIMS Studies in the Management Sciences*, 21, 1986, 453-473.

Dantzig, G.B., and Infanger, G. (1991). "Multi-Stage Stochastic Linear Programs for Portfolio Optimization," *Proceedings of the Third RAMP Symposium* (Tokyo, November 1991), 63–83. [RAMP = Research Association on Mathematical Programming.] Also in *Annals of Operations Research* 45 1993, 59–76.

Dantzig, G.B., and Infanger, G. (1992a). "Large-Scale Stochastic Linear Programs: Importance Sampling and Benders Decomposition," in C. Brezinski and U. Kulsich (eds.), *Computation and Applied Mathematics—Algorithms and Theory*, Proceedings of the 13th IMACS World Congress on Computation and Applied Mathematics, Dublin, Ireland, July 22–26, 1991, 111–120.

Dantzig, G.B., and Infanger, G. (1992b). "Approaches to Stochastic Programming with Applications to Electric Power Systems," *Proceedings of tutorial on Optimization in Planning and Operation of Electric Power Systems*, October 15-16, 1992, Thun, Switzerland, 141–157.

Dantzig, G.B., and Iusem, A. (1983). "Analyzing Labor Productivity Growth with the PILOT Model," in S. Schurr, S. Soneblum, and D. Wood (eds.), *Energy, Productivity and Economic Growth*, A Workshop sponsored by the Electric Power Research Institute, Oelgeschlager, Gunn & Hain, Cambridge, Mass., 1983, 347–366.

Dantzig, G.B., and Jackson, P. (1980). "Pricing Underemployed Capacity in a Linear Economic Model," in R.W. Cottle, F. Giannessi, and J.L. Lions (eds.), *Variational Inequalities and Complementarity Problems: Theory and Applications*, John Wiley & Sons, Ltd., London, 127–134.

Dantzig, G.B., and Johnson, D.L. (1963). "Maximum Payloads per Unit Time Delivered Through an Air Network," *Operations Research* 12, 230–236.

Dantzig, G.B., and Johnson, S. (1955). "A Production Smoothing Problem," Proceedings, Second Symposium on Linear Programming, National Bureau of Standards and Comptroller, U.S.A.F. Headquarters, January, 151–176.

Dantzig, G.B., Johnson, S., and Wayne, W. (1958). "A Linear Programming Approach to the Chemical Equilibrium Problem," *Management Science* 5, 38–43.

Dantzig, G.B., Levin, S., and Bigelow, J. (1967). "On Steady-State Intercompartmental Flows," *Journal of Colloid and Interface Science* 23, 572–576.

Dantzig, G.B., and Madansky, A. (1961). "On the Solution of Two-Staged Linear Programs Under Uncertainty," in J. Neyman (ed.), *Proceedings 4th Berkeley Symposium on Mathematical Statistics and Probability*, University of California Press, Berkeley, California, 165–176.

Dantzig, G.B., and Manne, A.S. (1974). "A Complementarity Algorithm for an Optimal Capital Path with Invariant Proportions," *Journal of Economic Theory* 9, 312–323.

Dantzig, G.B., McAllister, P.H., and Stone, J.C. (1988). "Formulating an Objective for an Economy," *Mathematical Programming* 42, (Series B), 11–32.

Dantzig, G.B., McAllister, P.H., and Stone, J.C. (1989a). "Deriving a Utility Function for the U.S. Economy, Part I," *Journal for Policy Modeling* 11, 1989, 391–424.

Dantzig, G.B., McAllister, P.H., and Stone, J.C. (1989b). "Deriving a Utility Function for the U.S. Economy, Part II," *Journal for Policy Modeling* 11, 569–592.

Dantzig, G.B., and Orchard-Hays, W. (1954). "The Product Form for the Inverse in the Simplex Method," *Mathematical Tables and Other Aids to Computation* 8, 64–67.

Dantzig, G.B., and Orden, A. (1952). "A Duality Theorem Based on the Simplex Method," *Symposium on Linear Inequalities and Programming*, Report 10, Project SCOOP, Planning Research Division, Director of Management Analysis Service, Comptroller, U.S.A.F. Headquarters, April, 51–55.

Dantzig, G.B., Orden, A., and, Wolfe, P. (1955). "The Generalized Simplex Method for Minimizing a Linear Form Under Linear Inequality Constraints" *Pacific Journal of Mathematics* 5, 183–195.

Dantzig, G.B., and Parikh, S.C. (1976). "On a PILOT Linear Programming Model for Assessing Physical Impact on the Economy of a Changing Energy Picture," in F.S. Roberts (ed.), *Energy: Mathematics and Models*, Proceedings of a SIMS Conference on Energy, held at Alta, Utah, July 7–11, 1975, SIAM, 1–23. Also in IIASA Conference '76, May 10–13, 1976, 183–200. Also in P. Lax (ed.), *Mathematical Aspects of Production and Distribution of Energy*, Proceedings of the Symposium in Applied Mathematics, January 20–21, 1976, San Antonio, Texas; Vol. 21, American Mathematical Society, Providence, R.I., 1977, 93–106.

Dantzig, G.B., and Parikh, S.C. (1978a). "Energy Models and Large-Scale Systems Optimization," in W.W. White (ed.), *Computers and Mathematical Programming*, Proceedings of the Bicentennial Conference on Mathematical Programming, held at the National Bureau of Standards, Gaithersburg, Maryland, November 29 – December 1, 1976. Also in NBS Special Publication 502, February 1978, 4–10.

Dantzig, G.B., and Parikh, S.C. (1978b). "At the Interface of Modeling and Algorithms Research" in O.L. Mangasarian, R.R. Meyer, and S.M. Robinson, (eds.), *Nonlinear Programming 3*, Academic Press, New York, 283–302.

Dantzig, G.B., and Parikh, S.C. (1978c). "PILOT Model for Assessing Energy-Economic Options," in T. Bagiotti and G. Franco (eds.), *Pioneering Economics*, Edizioni Cedam, Padova, Italy, 271–276.

Dantzig, G.B., and Ramser, J.H. (1959a). "Optimum Routing of Gasoline Delivery Trucks," Proceedings, World Petroleum Congress, Session VIII, Paper 19, 1959, 1–10.

Dantzig, G.B., and Ramser, J.H. (1959b). "The Truck Dispatching Problem," *Management Science* 6, 80–91.

Dantzig, G.B., and Saaty, T.L. (1973). *Compact City*, Freeman, San Francisco.

Dantzig, G.B., and Sethi, S.P. (1981). "Linear Optimal Control Problems and Generalized Linear Programming," *Journal of the Operational Research Society* 32, 467–476.

Dantzig, G.B., and Tomlin, J.A. (1987). "E.M.L. Beale, FRS: Friend and Colleague," *Mathematical Programming* 38, 117–131.

Dantzig, G.B., and Van Slyke, R.M. (1966). "A Generalized Upper Bounded Technique for Linear Programming," in *Proceedings of the IBM Scientific Computing Symposium on Combinatorial Problems*, March 16–18, 1964, Yorktown Heights, New York, 249–261.

Dantzig, G.B., and Van Slyke, R.M. (1967). "Generalized Upper Bounding Techniques," *Journal of Computer and System Science* 1, 213–226.

Dantzig, G.B., and Van Slyke, R.M. (1971). "Generalized Linear Programming," in David Wismer (ed.), *Optimization Methods and Applications for Large Systems*, McGraw-Hill, New York, 75–120.

Dantzig, G.B., and Veinott, A.F., Jr. (eds.), (1968a). *Mathematics of the Decision Sciences*, American Mathematical Society, Providence, R.I.

Dantzig, G.B., and Veinott, A.F., Jr. (1968b). "Integral Extreme Points," *SIAM Review*, 10, 371–372.

Dantzig, G.B., and Veinott, A.F., Jr. (1978). "Discovering Hidden Totally Leontief Substitution Systems," *Mathematics of Operations Research* 3, 102–103.

Dantzig, G.B., and Wald, A. (1951). "On the Fundamental Lemma of Neyman and Pearson," *Annals of Mathematical Statistics* 22, 87–93.

Dantzig, G.B., and Wolfe, P., (1960). "Decomposition Principle for Linear Programs," *Operations Research* 8, 101–111. Also in P. Wolfe (ed.), *RAND Symposium on Mathematical Programming*, March 1959, RAND R-351, page 5.

Dantzig, G.B., and Wolfe, P. (1961). "The Decomposition Algorithm for Linear Programming," *Econometrica* 29, 767–778. Also in G.B. Dantzig and B.C. Eaves (eds.), *Studies in Optimization*, MAA Studies in Mathematics, Vol. 10, Mathematical Association of America, 1974, 160–174.

Dantzig, G.B., and Wolfe, P. (1962). "Linear Programming in a Markov Chain," *Operations Research* 10, 702–710.

Ferguson, A.R., and Dantzig, G.B., (1956). The Allocation of Aircraft to Routes—An Example of Linear Programming under Uncertain Demand," *Management Science* 3 1, 45–73. Also in E.H. Bowman and R.B. Fetter (eds.), *Analysis of Industrial Operations*, Richard D. Irwin, Inc., Homewood, Illinois, 1959, 85–114.

Fulkerson, D.R., and Dantzig, G.B. (1955). "Computations of Maximal Flows in Networks," *Naval Research Logistics Quarterly* 2, 277–283.

Hirsch, W.M., and Dantzig, G.B. (1968). "The Fixed Charge Problem," *Naval Research Logistics Quarterly* 15, 413–424. [This first appeared in 1954 as RAND P-648.]

Leichner, S.A., Dantzig, G.B., and Davis, J.W. (1993). "A Strictly Improving Linear Programming Phase I Algorithm," *Annals of Operations Research* 46/47, 409–430.

Levin, S.A., Dantzig, G.B., and Bigelow, J. (1967). "On Steady-State Intercompartmental Flows," *Journal of Colloid and Interface Science* 23, 572–576.

Perold, A.F., and Dantzig, G.B. (1979). "A Basic Factorization Method for Block Triangular Linear Programs," in I.S. Duff and G.W. Stewart (eds.), *Sparse Matrix Proceedings*, SIAM, Philadelphia, 283–312.

Stone, J.C., McAllister, P.H., and Dantzig, G.B. (1987). "Using the PILOT Model to Study the Effects of Technological Change," in B. Lev, J. Bloom, A. Gleit, F. Murphy, and C. Shoemaker (eds.), *Strategic Planning in Energy and Natural Resources*, Proceedings of the 2nd Symposium on Analytic Techniques for Energy, Natural Resources and Environmental Planning April 1986. Studies in Management Science and Systems, Vol. 15, North-Holland, Amsterdam, 31–42.

White, W., Johnson, S., and Dantzig, G.B. (1958). "Chemical Equilibrium in Complex Mixtures," *Journal of Chemical Physics* 28, 751–755.

Wood, M.K., and Dantzig, G.B. (1949). "Programming of Interdependent Activities, I: General Discussion," *Econometrica* 17, 193–199; also in T.C. Koopmans (ed.), *Activity Analysis of Production and Allocation*, John Wiley & Sons, New York, 1951, 15–18.

Index

Lightning Source UK Ltd.
Milton Keynes UK
UKHW041843150123
415253UK00010B/338/J